Carolina ROOTS

From Whence I Came

Tom Shytle

ISBN: 1-4196-9519-3
ISBN-13: 9781419695193

Visit www.booksurge.com to order additional copies.

Table of Contents

To Mil

Preface

To be born in 1932 and live until sometime in the first quarter of the 21st century meant living and witnessing the greatest advancements in the history of man. Unless you were an Aborigine living in the remote jungles of New Guinea your life was grossly affected by the profound changes that took place during that period. It's hard to grasp how fast everything has changed in such a short amount of time.

Aviation was still in its infancy in 1932, but less than forty years after I was born Neil Armstrong stepped out of the lunar landing module, made "one giant step for mankind," and left his footprints on the surface of the moon. He was followed shortly by his travelling companion Edwin "Buzz" Aldrin while the third man, Michael Collins continued to orbit the moon in the command module. Not only did the crew of Apollo Eleven complete that extraordinary event, but they were safely returned home. And the feat was successfully repeated five more times. Another ten American astronauts walked on the moon before the Apollo missions were concluded in late 1972.

It would be hard to compare the amazing procedures that medical people routinely perform on the human body in 2008 to the ancient methods used by doctors in 1932. Vital organ transplants, pacemakers, and micro surgery were inconceivable back then; yet today there are thousands of people walking around with someone else's heart keeping them alive. On a regular basis the evening news will report that a new miracle drug has been developed that will wipe out a dreaded disease or will help us to live longer.

Some people, after they die, are having their bodies frozen and kept at an ultra low temperature so that they can be thawed out and resurrected when science finds a cure for the one that got them. Cryonics, the science of using cold temperatures to preserve human life with the intent of restoring good health when technology becomes available would have been considered "voodoo" medicine in 1932; but Alcor Life Extension Foundation located near Scottsdale, Arizona has applied breakthroughs in organ banking research to the much more difficult problem of preserving whole people. They already have a bunch, mostly just severed heads, waiting to be brought back.

If you could bring back an individual who had lived and died prior to 1932 and show them the place where they had lived, and try to explain the advancements in transportation, communications, aviation and space exploration, and medicine, they would be astounded, disbelieving to say the least.

Satellite communications and television were in the distant future when my family moved into a log cabin in the mountains near Bryson City, NC in the mid 30's. World news made its way around mostly by word of mouth, from cove to cove, and family to family. In the mountains of western North Carolina there were a few battery powered radios scattered around that were owned by the more affluent families. "Affluent" used to describe the economic status of a mountain family simply means that their annual earnings were slightly above the regional average, and, as a result, their children had enough to eat. It is very doubtful that anyone who lived in Bryson City or surrounding areas in the early 1930s could be considered "affluent" by any criterion.

For most of the population in Western North Carolina, they were already behind the economic curve in more ways than one. They were trapped in a cycle of poverty; poor sanitary conditions resulted in high rates of tuberculosis, typhoid, and infant mortality among other health concerns. That, coupled with a school system that produced a lower quality of education almost guaranteed a decreasing standard of living that would have been way below a line defining poverty.

In 1932 the national average income was close to $1900.00. In some areas of Appalachia, and more especially in the North Carolina counties west of Asheville, a good percentage of families, mostly farmers who lived there, survived on an annual income as low as $100.00.

The great depression was at its peak in 1932.

It must have been awfully upsetting to my parents in the early fall of 1931 to learn that Mama was pregnant again. My oldest sister, who was less than three years old, had been a problem for Mama to carry. She almost died giving birth and had been advised not to have any more children.

The mills where they worked weren't running, people were going hungry, no one had any money, and the banks were closing.

It's hard to imagine how Daddy must have felt. People were jumping out of buildings in New York City for lesser problems than he must have had. He wasn't alone. The whole country was in a big mess. Depression was gnawing at the soul of the country and the soup lines were getting longer.

Then a glimmer of hope! My Grandpa Shytle was still living in the mountains near Bryson City. He wrote and offered Daddy a small piece of land on which to build a house if he would bring his family back to the mountains. It must have been an offer that was hard to refuse. He was being given an opportunity to go back to living off the land from whence he came; and he probably considered the offer a gift from God and an answer to prayer.

What I intend to write about is a chronicle of the experiences I can recall coupled with a lot of what I remember being told starting with my earliest recollection in the mountains, followed by ten years at the Park Yarn cotton mill village near Kings Mountain. That was followed by twenty-five years in the United States Air Force. After leaving the military we moved to where we now live, just south of Kings Mountain near the National Military Park. It is a wonderful little corner of paradise.

There is no way I can know what will be written in the pages to follow. There is no other reason to write except to leave something for my children, their children, and their children, so that they may know something of the world in which I lived because it was so much different than the world in which they now live.

It would be a tragedy for that to be lost completely. It may be that everything has already been written that could mean anything to anyone else. Maybe not! My thoughts are that what I write may mean something to those that I love. I hope that will be the case.

Nothing to be written in this journal has been planned or even thought of, except to try and follow the sequence of events in the order that they occurred. Some socio-economic-political details, and how they affected our folks, will have to be included in order for the reader to understand why we, and those who preceded us, reacted the way we did to the conditions forced upon us by world and local issues.

We were required to live on the low end of the economic scale by conditions over which we had little or no control. Management in the cotton mills had dictatorial power over the employees, and as a group they were driven by greed, and could freely conspire to keep the workload of their employees heavy and wages low; and the majority of workers had no option but to accept what was offered.

Promotions into supervisory or management positions were rare. If an individual learned to be a "spinner" in a cotton mill as a youngster, in all likelihood, that person would still be a spinner when old age or bad health forced him or her out. But it was a job and there were those who didn't even have that during the great depression.

Local farmers didn't have to put up with greedy overseers, but life for them was a gamble and they were always at the mercy of unreliable weather conditions coupled with a shaky market every growing season. Even now a late spring freeze will wipe out an entire year of work by a peach or apple grower, and a drought will create monstrous problems for a soy bean or cotton farmer.

It seems that there has been, and will probably forever be, something to keep wage earners in a definitive social or economic class. There are exceptions to be sure, but for the most, blue collar workers will stay where they are. They know "where they belong" on the scale that measures class. Try talking to a stranger and within a few short minutes you'll know where he belongs compared to your own economic status.

Someone might tell you that you can make it from the cotton mill to the country club by working hard, but that isn't true. Hard, back-breaking work and a cotton mill go hand in hand.

My parents probably thought that when I became old enough I would be working at the Park Yarn cotton mill just as they had done for most of their adult lives. A lot of my friends did just that, and even married each other, without ever realizing that a big part of their lives had been laid out by a class system that wouldn't allow them to move up the ladder.

At the same time the "uptown" crowd was being programmed to go to college after high school with a promise of taking over Dad's business when the time came; or a job in management with automatic promotions and opportunities to move up. With few exceptions everybody was locked in place.

Following World War II the GI Bill offered returning servicemen a chance to break out of the mold; and a lot of them took advantage of the opportunity that allowed them to learn a different trade or earn a college degree. My Dad was one of the returning veterans who took advantage of the educational assistance being offered by the Veterans

Administration. He enrolled in a technical school near Blacksburg learning the various jobs needed for the construction industry. He was already a good carpenter but still learned a lot from the formal schooling.

A song that became popular during the war asked the question "How you gonna keep em down on the farm, after they've seen Paree"? Many of them didn't stay down on the farm, and I didn't stay in a cotton mill; not that the work was beneath me, or anyone else, because a lot of outstanding people including my Mom and Dad, spent most of their lives working in a cotton mill. It was an honorable way to make a living, and it is a well known fact that the economy of our country depends on the working class.

I didn't place myself in front of or behind anyone. What bothered me more than anything was the hard work and low pay.

When I left the Park yarn I vowed never to work in a cotton mill again, and was fortunate enough not to break that vow.

Mama knew the importance of education, but on the other hand Daddy held to a different persuasion. His mindset was focused on earning a living and education was secondary to that belief. The status quo was good enough for him and "if it wasn't broke, it didn't need fixing." The basics of life were all that anyone needed and progress wasn't always a good thing.

After he passed away we learned that he had been giving his Church and a radio minister over half of his monthly income. A long time after his death we were still getting letters from the radio preacher telling him he was behind in his obligations.

He was a humble, hard working Christian who followed his faith everyday and maintained that there was dignity in honesty. He was the man of the house and his opinions usually won. Mama seldom argued with him about anything. He was convinced that as soon as a youngster was old enough, he or she should be out there making a living.

Consequently, I found myself following his advice on the subject and when I turned seventeen in July 1949 was already working at the mill. Most of the young boys fell into the same rut after growing up at the Park Yarn, and a lot of the girls were right there with the boys. If it was good enough for their Mom and Dad, it was good enough for them. And it was- for them.

There were few options for me and a career in the spinning room laying up roping was at the bottom of that list. An enlistment in the military services was right at the top and going back to school was somewhere in between. Earning a living had to be a factor in my decision and going back to school with little or no income just wouldn't cover that consideration.

A hitch in the military would not only provide an income but also the opportunity to continue my education; and it would take me out of the cotton mill.

The incentives were all there. In addition to all the other positives, the foreign ports and exotic girls in far off places were too much to stop thinking about. It didn't take me long to look for a recruiter.

I must have been born to be a career soldier because I even loved basic training. Being in the military put me in a different world and nothing I was told to do gave me reason enough to rebel against those who had authority over me.

The regimentation, forced marches, and physical training were minor challenges. Some of the guys in my flight complained about the food, and anything else they didn't like to do, or considered an inconvenience. Some thought the food was lousy; I thought it was very good most of the time. The die was cast long before I re-enlisted.

Life is more than a career, and my role as a husband and father has been far and away the most important responsibility given to me.

Mil was, and will forever be, the most important individual in my life. Our children and grandchildren are a close second. That's the way it should be and that's the way it is for me.

The details of my life that follow will hopefully reflect my love of God, family and country. I will try to be honest and factual and write about events that had an impact on me or my family; I will include the bad with the good. Whatever follows will be my thoughts and mine alone.

CHAPTER 1

The Park Yarn and the Great Depression 1932-1933

It had to be a tough time in their young married lives. Mama and Daddy had been married less than a year when my oldest sister Christina Juanita, "Coot", as we always knew her, was born in Oct 1929. I have no idea where the nickname "Coot" came from. More than likely Daddy gave it to her because he had a reputation for "nick-naming" his children and grandchildren.

She was less than two weeks old when the stock market crashed on Tuesday Oct 24th. That marked the beginning of the "great depression".

But the events leading up to "black Tuesday" were already playing out for them. Cotton mills located throughout the Piedmont and foothills of North Carolina were curtailing their hours of operation because of a shortage of orders. The Park Yarn was running three days a week and threatening to lay off most of the work force. Rumors were flying that all of the Park Yarn employees would be out of work before Christmas. There was no good reason to doubt the rumors were true. Mills all over the Piedmont were shutting their doors almost daily; and unemployed textile workers were everywhere looking for jobs that no longer existed.

Things didn't look good anywhere in the country, especially in the Southern Appalachian region.

Daddy's family were mountain people. Grandpa Shytle was married to Dovie Green, who was half Cherokee Indian, on June 28th 1903. Grandpa was descended from German immigrants that had left the Bavarian region of Germany and settled in Pennsylvania sometime in the early 1700s. They migrated south and settled near Chimney Rock where they worked the land and found the long growing season and fertile new ground just what they were looking for to grow their crops.

Most of the people who settled in the mountains of western North Carolina were independent to a fault. They were clannish; they didn't trust outsiders, and didn't have anything to do with strangers. They settled way back in the coves and didn't want any visitors coming around. They especially didn't want the federal government messing in their affairs; they didn't trust the government to do right by them. It wasn't that they had anything to hide from anyone, except for the people involved in making and selling illegal whisky; being fiercely independent but loyal to each other was an integral expression of their character. The code of the hills was not there to be broken.

In the early 1900s most families in the mountain counties still had living relatives who had fought for the Confederacy. Grandpa was born in April 1871, the son of Jeremiah and Melissa Shytle. According to Rutherford County records, during the Civil War, Jeremiah Shytle was captured at Falling Waters, Maryland on July 14th, 1863 by

Union forces. He was confined as a POW at the Old Capitol Prison, Washington, DC until released on March 2nd 1865 in a prisoner exchange at Aiken's landing, James River, Virginia.

His brother, Martin died after being wounded at Chancellorsville, Virginia on May 2nd, 1863. He was taken from the field of battle to Richmond so that his wounds could be treated but died on or about May 21st.

Grandpa named his youngest son Martin in honor of his uncle that died fighting for the south. His full name was Martin Asbury Shytle. Where my Grandpa got the name "Asbury", no one will probably ever know.

When the United States was forced into World War II following the Japanese attack on Pearl Harbor, Martin Asbury volunteered to enlist in the army and was wounded in France during that conflict. He survived his wounds and following a few weeks in a hospital was returned to duty until the end of the war. On the day he returned home he gave me an insignia from a German uniform that he carried all the way from Germany.

Stories from family members indicated that Grandpa Tom Shytle had quite a reputation as a young man. They say he could teach a good Sunday School lesson, lead the choir, then get out following church services on Sunday afternoon and get in a fight.

Court records in Rutherford County mention his name quite a few times. One newspaper article reads "Tom Shytle is the man who shot a Negro, Cabe Doggett, at Duncan's store about three miles east of town. He was considered a desperate character, but showed no disposition to resist the officers. As the officers approached the house of

Taylor Bennett, Shytle ran out of the door, and, as one of the officers expressed it, "commenced to ride saplings". Deputy Sheriff Rollins ran him about three hundred yards, when Shytle fell from exhaustion. Rollins says he "got up laughing", and saluted him with a very pleasant "good morning sir". Shytle is the son of Jeremiah Shytle of Chimney Rock Township, a peaceable, law abiding man and a good citizen."

There's no doubt that another Uncle was in fact a real desperado. We had always been told that my great uncle Pink Shytle was involved in a shootout with a local law enforcement officer on the banks of the river that runs through Chimney Rock. According to Grandpa the lawman confronted Uncle Pink and accused him of possessing a bottle of illegal moonshine whisky, and in the exchange of words that followed issued a challenge to Uncle Pink. Both men drew their pistols; Uncle Pink beat him to the draw and shot the lawman dead.

After he was caught and tried the results were published in "The Highlander and Shelby News" dated November 15, 1923. The story was headlined "Shytle Draws 8 Years in Pen." and reads as follows, "Pink Shytle, white man, of Rutherford County, was last week given eight years in the state penitentiary for killing Officer Reuben Lee at Chimney Rock, August 26. Shytle was acquitted of first and second degree murder charges and found guilty of manslaughter for which he received the sentence of eight years. Able counsel was employed on both sides; five lawyers were engaged in the prosecution. Honorable Clyde R. Hoey assisted other counsel in the defense."

The story above is exactly as it appeared in the Highlander newspaper. I have a copy of the paper that was published on November 15, 1923 and related the story verbatim as it was printed. Clyde R. Hoey later went on to become Governor of North Carolina from 1937 until 1941, and was elected to the US Senate from 1945 until May 1954 where he died in office to be replaced by Sam Irvin.

When my Great Grandpa and his clan settled in the Chimney Rock – Lake Lure community another brother, John, settled in Lincoln County. Records for Lincoln County note that brother John Shytle's clan lost several members in the Civil War also. One account states that one was killed at Antietum, another at Gettysburg; and another was wounded at Gettysburg and in spite of his wounds was the last Confederate soldier to retreat from the field of battle there.

Daddy was one of eight children born to Grandpa and Grandma Shytle. He was born on November 12th, 1907 in Sylva.

Mama's family background is not nearly as clear as Daddy's. They were originally from Cleveland County. Her Daddy was James Johnson and her Mother was Rachel B. Wright. That is the only record we have of her ancestors. No one knows anything further back than that.

My Grandpa Johnson passed away a young man. He died after suffering a cerebral hemorrhage and Grandma remarried Charlie Stinson. He was the person I remember as "Grandpa" on my Mother's side of the family. Mama had a brother and a sister; they both lived in and around Kings Mountain.

Her sister, Aunt Mary Morgan, was a wonderful person. She was a Godly woman who lived and practiced Christian principles every day. She was never very far away from her Bible which she read daily. She was a friend to everyone she met and shared whatever she had with them. Her needs came second to everyone else. She worked hard all her adult life, and died of complications from diabetes while still relatively young.

The same thing can't be said of Mama's younger brother, J.L. Johnson (Uncle Jay as we called him). In my opinion he was a scoundrel. He married Ethel Owens and they had two little girls, Rebecca and Judy. Aunt Ethel had a seizure or a stroke, and after being examined, the doctors discovered a tumor on her brain.

They had to operate to remove the tumor that would have killed her had they not been able to operate. The operation was partially successful. Partially successful because they didn't kill her on the operating table; but she was completely paralyzed on her left side for the rest of her life. Not long afterwards Uncle Jay disappeared.

Absolutely no one knew of his whereabouts. Aunt Ethel was left to raise those two little girls even though the paralysis prevented her from being able to use her left arm or leg. She had no means of support other than her family and whatever handouts the local relief organizations would do for her. I'm sure the local churches also helped her a lot.

I remember Grandma Stinson talking a lot about Uncle Jay, crying and wondering if he was all right. I don't remember how long he was gone, but eventually he showed up. He had gone out west to Montana when he disappeared but came back to South Carolina, had re-married there and had a son with his second wife.

He re-established a relationship with his two daughters and Grandma Stinson. I know they all forgave him. But Aunt Ethel and Grandma Stinson both passed away younger than they should have. His uncaring ways may have been a factor, maybe not.

Mama and Daddy were married on January 26th 1927 in York, SC.

Daddy's family were basically farmers, that is to say they lived off the land either by tilling and growing crops or working in the timber industry. Mama's family were textile workers.

Growing up in the mountains, Daddy was a farmer and woodsman. He used to tell how, as a young man, he would split oak logs to make shingles for houses. He also searched the mountain woods for "gen seng". I remember him telling me that a kitchen matchbox full of the gen seng root would sell for $5.00 way back then. That must have been an awfully lot of money for a young mountain man who later in life, during the depression, would work all day in a gravel pit, swinging a ten pound hammer for the WPA and make only one dollar.

Trying to make a living on a few acres of farmland that was supplemented by what he could make as a logger was probably the reason he migrated to the flatlands of the Piedmont around Cleveland and Gaston counties looking for work. Quite a few of the labor force in cotton mills were relocated farmers from the Appalachian Mountains of western North Carolina.

Following their marriage they set up housekeeping in a mill house on the Park Yarn mill hill a few miles South of Kings Mountain.

Storm clouds were already gathering for the cotton mills all over the south. Just as the mountain people were independent, the cotton mill people were individualistic also. They were mostly Baptists and linked organized labor to Communism. They had been told that communists turned people against God. They resisted the organized labor movement as a general rule.

Still the union organizers had their "foot in the door", so to speak. A lot of cotton mills had closed down in New England and moved south because northern mill owners had been told about the cheap unorganized white labor force in the south. They had lots of waterpower and very lenient labor laws. They could employ women and children; they were given tax exemptions to make the move and the raw materials used in cotton mills were locally grown, ginned, and baled.

By the mid to late 20s, there were more spindles in Gaston County than in any other county in the nation.

Lots of books have been written by experts about the causes of the great depression and the misery it caused the people in the cotton mill industry. Many believe the stock market crash was the beginning of the depression but most historians point out that it wasn't the sole cause. Most agree that there were several factors that influenced the economic collapse in the US, and it wasn't limited to a regional or even national problem. Europe, South America, and parts of Asia were also caught up in the mess.

One event that did hurt the cotton belt but had little or no effect on the rest of the world was the drought that hit the southern and southwestern US in the spring of 1930. The cotton farmers were so stretched out financially that one long dry season bankrupted many cotton plantations.

But no matter who you were or where you lived, every life was changed by the great depression. Even before the stock market crash, a lot of cotton mill workers were on short hours and feeling the economic squeeze. Farmers across the country were already in a crisis. Corn was selling for 3 cents a bushel and some farmers were burning corn in their homes for heat in winter.

Mill workers lived hard. In 1929 Mama and Daddy both worked at the Park Yarn and were probably making less than $25.00 weekly between them when they could get a full week in. The average pay for a forty hour work week in a cotton mill was $12. That equates to thirty cents per hour, and because of cutbacks in production and the fact that there was a surplus of people ready and willing to work they actually made much less. The Park Yarn was running only three days a week. If they got in 24 hours per week, they earned $7.20 each. They lived in a three-room mill house that they rented from the mill owners for 25 cents per room per week.

Most mills had a company store where food, mostly staples, and coal could be “charged” against future pay. Some mill owners even produced their own currency in the form of tokens that their workers could buy and use at the company store.

The houses had no underpinning and were heated only by a fireplace. Somebody once said “a mill house couldn’t be heated with a pipeline direct from hell.”

The cracks in the outside planking were sealed up using newspaper glued to the inside walls with glue made from a mixture of flour and water. Indoor plumbing was unheard of at the Park Yarn in 1929, and electricity was available only during the hours of darkness.

There were two separate and different thoughts about life on a mill village in the late twenties. One was that the families lived in a tight knit community and enjoyed a rich cultural experience; they were always there for each other in times of distress.

The reality was that mill workers didn’t have anything to look forward to but hard work, a low class existence, ill health and death. They were in fact a tight knit group; and when a death occurred in a family every other family was there to lend support. They helped each other as best they could, and faced uncertain futures together.

Many tragedies occurred when children were left unattended by a working mother who had to leave her child unsupervised because of her shift hours at the mill.

It hadn’t always been that way. Prior to World War I the mills in Piedmont North Carolina were booming; and with the US coming closer and closer to being committed to the war that was raging in Europe the mills were running full throttle to produce khaki material and tenting fabrics.

As more and more mills were built in the south, more and more people were recruited from western North Carolina. But by the early twenties the boom was over and there was an over abundance of a labor force available to the owners.

Additionally, production methods became more efficient. An individual who had been required to run half a dozen frames or three or four looms in the past now was required to run ten frames or half a dozen looms. Workloads were being increased in all sections of the mills. Wages were being cut in an effort to improve profit. The same amount of labor that required 300 workers in the past now required only 250. The raised workloads were commonly called "stretch-outs" and put a lot of the work, especially the work that was performed by women, on a "piece-work" basis. That is, they had to make what was referred to as "production". If they failed to make production, they didn't make as much per hour as they used to.

There was a surplus of laborers in the cotton mill industry. The result was a bunch of bitter people; many of them already out of work.

They had long resisted organized labor, but now many of them were receptive to at least talking with representatives of the National Textile Workers Union, a branch of the Communist Party that had been trying to make headway in the south for some time. Their objective was to start a strike at one mill and then to other mills as their resources would allow.

One of the biggest mills in the south was located in neighboring Gastonia.

The Loray mill supposedly had more "spindles" under one roof than any other cotton mill in the world and was the opening target for the National Textile Workers Union.

Workers walked off the job on April 1st, 1929. They were demanding and end to "piece-work" and "stretch-out" and a list of other demands that involved housing and pay. The superintendent rejected all their demands.

Almost everyone and everything sympathized with management from the local newspaper to the state government in Raleigh. The majority of people saw the strike as a communist effort and agreed with the mill owners that all unionists were communists.

Gastonia's police chief was killed in a fight with strikers and a woman employee of the union was shot and killed while riding with some strikers to a union rally. The strike failed, but a connection in mill workers minds between communism and organized labor was solidly rooted.

After the strike failed at the Loray mill, the owners could do just about anything they cared to with their labor force. Cotton mill workers were at the mercy of management.

These were the conditions in which Mama and Daddy found themselves along with a new baby daughter at the Park Yarn in October 1929, less than three years before I was born.

That leads us to the stock market crash that in turn led to terrible conditions for almost everyone in America for the next decade.

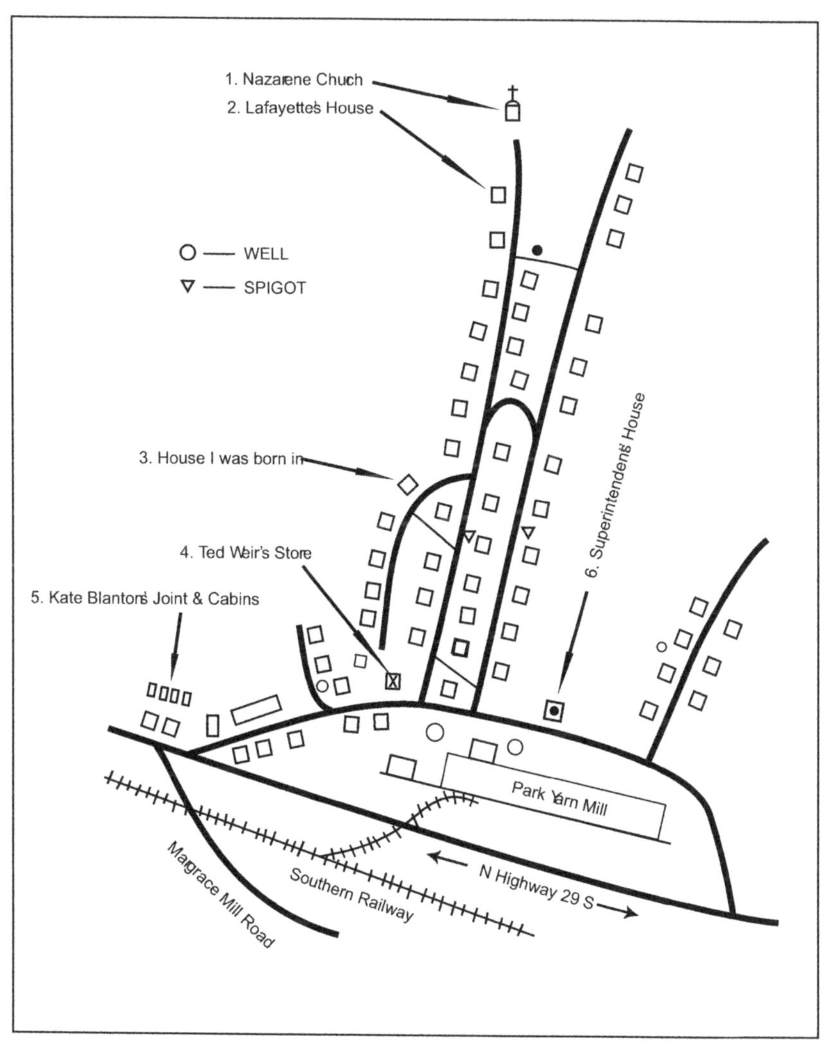

Layout of the Park Yarn mill village drawn from memory coupled with an aerial photograph taken by R.C. Pearson sometime during the late 1940s.

CHAPTER 2

Bryson City and Hard Times 1933-1939

The stock market crash didn't matter to Mama and Daddy. They probably didn't think much about it since they didn't have anything in the stock market; most of the people who lived at the Park Yarn had never even heard of Wall Street. It would have been absurd for them to think about investments.

No one in their world had money for anything other than bare essentials such as food, clothing, or medicine for a sick child; and that medicine, which was for most childhood ailments, a concoction of home grown herbal remedies. There were very few doctors in Kings Mountain and the towns in Cleveland and Gaston Counties, there were no telephones to call one in an emergency, and no money to pay for a doctor's house call anyway. Except for emergencies that absolutely required a medical doctor, most cuts, bruises, or ailments were treated at home using the herbal remedies. And for most injuries and sickness the herbal remedies worked. Babies were born at home, and if a doctor couldn't be found in time a midwife helped with the delivery.

The people at the Park Yarn were making barely enough wages to survive after paying for the simple necessities of life. A typical breakfast consisted of "Hoover gravy and biscuits." Hoover gravy was made by frying out a piece of fat-back, adding a little flour to the grease until it was brown and then water until it thickened. If they didn't have any fat-back, a little lard would be used instead. In times of plenty, evaporated milk from a can was used instead of water to make "milk gravy." Livermush was also a local breakfast staple especially during hog killing season. At other times of the year a one pound block could be bought at Ted Weir's store for a dime. Livermush was then and is now an important part of the local diet. Actually livermush is more than a staple; some consider it an institution.

Supper would simply be cornbread and milk; or more often than not, pinto beans and cornbread. During certain times of the year maybe an onion that had been quartered would be added to the meal. There were variations, of course. Sometimes it was butter beans or little white beans in place of the pintos; and, when they were available, fried potatoes might be added to the supper plate.

On rare occasions, if the preacher had been invited to be there for Sunday dinner, a chicken would be bought (or traded for) from a neighbor who kept chickens. Its neck would be wrung, it would be plucked and cleaned, and then fried up for a Sunday dinner that was a real treat.

Everything in our house was cooked on a wood-burning second hand kitchen stove that had been given to Mama by Aunt Mary Morgan after she bought a kerosene cook stove to replace the wood burner.

There are at least two distinct smells that immediately remind me of a long time ago at the Park Yarn. One of those is the smell of a kerosene heater, another is the smell of coal burning. It's been a very long time since I have experienced either of those two.

There is a third, and that is the smell of livermush frying, but, as I touched on the subject above, livermush has always been a staple for most of the people in Cleveland County and most folks in the neighborhood still eat livermush today. It's strictly a local item on the grocery shelf because you can drive a hundred miles in any direction away from Cleveland County and not find livermush for sale anywhere. Shelby, the county seat for Cleveland County hosts an annual livermush festival every October. The mayor of Shelby was quoted as saying that "livermush is the one perfect food" and whenever he writes about it he uses a capitol "L" out of respect.

Conditions worsened. Mills were not just running short hours; they were closing all over the south. Men left their families behind and were riding the rails trying to find a job. Hobo jungles sprang up outside towns all across the country. Cheap hotels called "flop houses" could be found in every large city. Soup lines formed and relief efforts by civic organizations and churches were everywhere.

Hungry men, beggars, came knocking on doors asking for a little something to eat. I remember these men after we came back to the Park Yarn when I was seven. They all looked the same, they were all desperate and they were all hungry. They were never turned away from Mama's door without something.

They never came in the house though. Whatever Mama gave them, they would always have to sit on the front porch to eat. Someone once said that "a hungry man is a desperate man, but a man with hungry children is a dangerous man". There were dangerous men riding the rails and walking through the towns and villages during the great depression.

Farmers across the country were hurting as much, if not more, than anyone. They couldn't sell their crops or livestock to anyone. No one had any money. Banks were closing without warning, leaving those who had saved a few dollars with nothing. It is very doubtful if anyone at the Park Yarn had a bank account at the time the stock market crashed. Saving money just wasn't a part of the cotton mill economy.

A lot of people blamed the President, Herbert Hoover. He had been elected in November 1928, but as the Secretary of Commerce for Calvin Coolidge a few years earlier, he had warned Coolidge, who was President at the time, as early as 1925 that the stock market was way over valued. He was inaugurated in March 1929, just a little over seven months before the crash. By March 1929 the crash was unavoidable; and, under the circumstances Hoover found himself, the best either he or congress could do was to do nothing that would make a bad thing worse.

Historians look back at what he did, or didn't do, after the crash, and don't know whether the blame was his or not. Even now, economists can't agree on what caused a temporary economic downturn to become a ten-year nightmare.

By the time President Roosevelt took office in March 1933, it is almost certain that Mama and Daddy had, by then, decided to move back to the mountains. It's unclear exactly when they did leave the Park Yarn mill village to relocate near Bryson City; but it seems reasonable enough to assume that it was during the summer of that year. I remember being told that I was a year old when the move took place.

Grandpa Shytle had offered Daddy a small piece of land on which to build if he would return to the mountains. His motive is unclear; but to make another assumption, his reasons could have been that he was aware of the economic conditions relating to the cotton mill industry, and wanted to help. Somehow, that doesn't seem to float with what I remember about the gruff old man I called Grandpa. But any other reason just simply doesn't make any sense.

My earliest memory is that of living in a log cabin with a dirt floor. It may not even be a real memory, but a recollection of something I heard someone talk about years ago. Still the picture of that hard packed dirt floor is impressed in my memory. However, I absolutely remember a big apple tree in the back yard of the log cabin we lived in, and I couldn't have been much over three.

Some may say that for an old man to remember something that occurred when he was only three years of age is an impossibility, but the apple tree is real in my memory; very foggy, but there nonetheless.

Roosevelt was in office and had already brought about a lot of changes in the way government did business. He started several "relief, recovery, and reform" programs using initials such as CCC, TVA, and WPA. People called them "alphabet soup." The CCC stood for Civil Conservation Corps.

When Daddy returned to the mountains he found out that two of his younger brothers had enlisted to work for the CCC. Martin and Walter (Bud) both were off somewhere in a CCC camp. He had an older brother, Taylor, who was a nomad. He moved around so much no one ever knew where he was.

Taylor was a self-taught artist, and he was good. His oil paintings were in high demand throughout the Carolinas. Apparently he made a good living selling his artwork. We have one of his paintings hanging in our living room to this day. At one time in later years he taught art in a local college, but the wonder-lust got the best of him and he moved on; to a destination no one, probably not even Taylor himself, knew. He just couldn't live in the same place very long.

The Civilian Conservation Corps was a work relief program originated by President Roosevelt shortly after he was inaugurated in March 1933.

Later on the Presidential inaugural would be moved to January following elections in November. Since then the incoming or re-elected President takes the oath of office in January.

The CCC was a part of his "New Deal," and was designed to help relieve some of the unemployment and poverty caused by the depression. Young men aged seventeen to twenty-three and veterans of any age could sign up for a six-month enrollment period and could extend another six months for up to two years. They made a minimum of $30.00 monthly and had to send $25.00 home each month. Their food, clothing, housing, and medical care were provided. They were required to work eight hours a day, five days a week. There was serious concern by the American Federation of Labor that the program would introduce unwelcome competition for an already crowded labor market; but Roosevelt convinced the union that the limited talents needed by the CCC wouldn't interfere with any industrial skills. Their work was confined to conservation projects in rural areas of the country.

They worked in forestry and flood prevention, and constructed trails in state and national parks that are still in use today. They planted billions of trees in national forests and created fire suppression and logging roads in federal and state lands scattered throughout the country. The program was a "new deal" success story.

The Works Progress Administration (WPA), later called the Work Projects Administration was created in May of 1935 by a presidential order and was the largest of all the "alphabet soup" programs. Several million Americans went off the unemployment rolls while working with the WPA. They built thousands of miles of roads; they built bridges, airport runways, small dams and many other projects for the federal government. When congress closed down the WPA in 1943, it was the largest employer in the country.

When he moved back to the mountains Daddy went to work for the WPA; his wages were a dollar a day. He worked in a rock quarry (gravel pit) that made gravel for the road construction crews and his equipment was a ten-pound hammer.

The land Grandpa gave Daddy and Mama was south of Bryson City alongside a logging road. The road led off a wider dirt road paralleling the Tuckaseigee River that ran through the city.

Bryson City was the county seat for Swain County, and the county courthouse was built in the center of town; it was the dominant building there. During the period of 1933–1939, I doubt if the population was more than a couple hundred people. The population in 2003, seventy years later, was only 1,392.

There was no industry to speak of. Almost everyone, excepting the few businessmen, school teachers, and city or county administrators were farmers or loggers. The gravel pit where Daddy worked was there only because of the WPA. Bryson City was way back in the mountains, but no one was starving to death in that part of the world. The land was fertile and the climate was good for growing almost anything.

Daddy started building the house where we lived (until 1939) on the land Grandpa gave him. It was on the side of a hill. It seemed to me everything was on a hill in that part of the state. As he made enough money to buy lumber he bought it, and not before. Nothing that went into construction of the house was bought on credit. The pillars were built with rocks brought up from the creek that ran on the other side of the logging road.

Lumber was cheap, but even so, a dollar a day couldn't buy much after living expenses. I remember later in life that he told me a board foot of lumber cost two cents. That meant he could buy a 1 by 6 inch plank 10 feet long for about fifteen cents.

We must have moved out of the log cabin and into the house around the time my youngest sister Faye was born in June 1935. The house had a plank floor with a full-length front porch. As well as I can recall there were three good sized rooms and a small back porch. The hillside had been dug out enough for a small back yard. Daddy had an oil drum sitting on a slab of concrete in the front room that was used to heat the house.

He had cut a square piece out of the side and hinged it back in place to form a door that was big enough to allow him to take out the ashes. A round hole had been cut in the top to mount a stovepipe. The stovepipe made a 90-degree turn and ran through a hole cut in the side of the house.

I can only assume the stovepipe hole was big enough to allow room for insulation between the pipe and wood planks to keep from setting the house afire. It never burned down, so it must have been safe enough.

Mama planted a garden near the house and raised a lot of the vegetables we had to eat. She dug a hole in the bank behind the house, lined it with straw and stored cabbage there. She covered it with dirt and when she wanted cabbage for supper, she dug out a place, reached in and retrieved what she needed; then closed the hole back in. Potatoes were stored the same way.

Even though Daddy was working we were still dirt poor and relied a lot on the good will of our neighbor on the other side of the hill. Mr. & Mrs. Breedlove had a milk cow and she churned butter and made buttermilk; and still had enough milk to share with our family. They also raised a hog to kill every fall.

A small creek ran alongside their house; Mr Breedlove built a small springhouse with a concrete cistern inside where they kept the round cakes of butter, cold milk and buttermilk. The cold spring water running through the cistern kept the milk and butter cold. I remember clearly how good her hot cornbread was with a cold glass of milk poured out of a jar floating in the cistern.

The Breedloves had a son named Farris. He was, or seemed to already be a grown man at the time, but more than likely he was in his late teens. Farris roamed the woods and did a lot of hunting in the mountains. Once he gave us part of a wild turkey he brought home from a hunting trip.

They realized our plot and were very generous to us. We weren't the only ones in Bryson City that needed help. There were for certain other families that were in need while some families that had chickens, pigs, milk cows, and raised vegetables in the summer. No doubt they shared their food with needy families also. Mountain people were independent, but charitable. No one starved to death.

There was also a government subsidy program that passed out staples to the families that qualified for assistance. There's no way for me to know if it was a county, state, or a federal relief program; we got the food regardless. They passed out flour, corn meal, evaporated milk, salad dressing, beans, rice, and no doubt a few other commodities.

I remember the salad dressing because when I started to school I carried a brown bag for lunch. My lunch at school was two biscuits with salad dressing. It never changed; that was my lunch, five days a week.

Sometime during the first grade a kitchen was opened in the elementary school and they prepared vegetable soup every day for the students that could afford three cents for a bowl of soup and crackers. To this day I can recall how good that soup smelled cooking. It seemed that I was starving by the time the bell rang for lunch, but the whole time I was there I never even tasted that soup. That was how poor we were. Mama did her best for us with what she had. I asked her to make the biscuits thin; I never liked big thick biscuits. She always made Daddy's breakfast with big fat biscuits, but made two real thin ones for my school lunch.

The local men that lived in and around Bryson City would sit around on park benches in front of the courthouse on Saturday. I don't know what they did other than talk about the depression and politics. Most of them would have a pocketknife in their hand whittling on a piece of wood.

One Saturday, Daddy took me to town with him. It seemed like a long, long, walk; but it wasn't more than a half or maybe three quarters of a mile. He traded at Thomas's store for all that we needed at home; and we stopped at the store where he bought a cantaloupe and we headed for the courthouse. We sat down on one of the park benches and he cut into the cantaloupe. I had never tasted anything so good. We ate the whole thing because I didn't want to take anything that good home with me and have to share it with my big sister.

Our front porch was high off the ground and one day we were playing around and I fell off the porch and slammed my head on a rock. It knocked me out cold; I woke up with my head on Mama's lap. There was a cut near my left eye. She had a cold wet rag on my forehead and another rag soaked in blood was lying beside me. Coot was crying.

Someone had to go get Daddy out of the gravel pit and help me. In all probability Mama thought I may have a skull fracture or concussion. I don't know who went after him, the nearest neighbor lived way up the cove; but someone eventually did go get him. But, by the time he got home I had recovered enough for them to disregard the possibility of a concussion. I think he was mad because he had to leave work for such a trivial thing.

Another time I smashed my right thumb with a hammer. I must have busted it pretty good, because after about a week the end of my thumb started rotting and my thumbnail fell off. They took me to Mrs. Breedlove to fix it up with one of her mountain remedies. It worked because the thumb started healing. When it grew back in, my thumbnail grew crooked; and to this day it is still growing crooked.

Daddy was the third child in a string of eight babies that were born to my Grandparents between 1905 and 1922. He was born in November 1907 in Sylva, another small mountain town not far from Bryson City. Although we don't have records to show the location of their birthplace Daddy stated several times that they were all born within a short radius of Bryson City.

When we moved back to the mountains in 1933 Bonnie was the only one left in the area. Bud and Martin were off in a CCC camp somewhere. No one knew the whereabouts of Taylor. Catherine and Ruby were married and raising families in Gaston County. Ruth had married a Nazarene preacher and lived in Kings Mountain.

Bonnie was married to a mean old recluse of a mountain man named Dan Shuler. I remember that he only had one hand and was told that he was baiting a bear trap with dynamite when an explosion blew one of his hands off. It's a mystery to me how someone baits a bear trap with dynamite. He had no visible means of support and was suspected to be a moonshiner. He had a small farm up one of the coves around deep creek where he grew corn.

Aunt Bonnie and Dan Shuler had a son, Denver, who was born in 1935 in Gastonia, NC. Therein we find a mystery. To the best of my knowledge and information provided by both Mama and Daddy; Dan Shuler never left the mountains to live in Gastonia. Aunt Bonnie did move around some, even though she was married, and it may be that she was in Gastonia when Denver was born. I do remember that some years later, after we were back in Kings Mountain, she would dress real sharp with bright colors and high heels. She was the first woman I ever saw wearing a fur coat.

She would ride the Greyhound or Trailways bus to Charlotte and be gone for days at a time. She lived a fancy lifestyle in an uptown apartment in Kings Mountain, so the gossip that she was a hooker was probably true. Sometime around the mid 1940s she left Dan Shuler and was living the high life in Kings Mountain. Denver was with his father back in Bryson City.

The story goes that Dan was drinking and threatening to drive to Kings Mountain and shoot Bonnie. Denver asked him several times not to hurt his Mother, but the threats continued. Denver went to his bedroom, picked up his hunting rifle, and walked back to the room where Dan was sitting. Standing behind his father, he asked him one last time if he still planned on going to Kings Mountain and shoot his mother. His last words were "you're dam right", or something to the affirmative. Ka-pow! Denver put a bullet in the back of his head. He then dragged the body out to the barn, dug a shallow grave and buried him.

Several days later Denver was seen driving Dan's old truck around Bryson City. He wasn't old enough to be driving and was stopped by a deputy sheriff. It wasn't long before the truth was out. He was convicted on charges that he killed his father, but because he was a juvenile, he was sent to a training school for boys until he was twenty-one years old.

Following his release he married and settled near Bessemer City and had a successful career working for a local industry. To the best of my knowledge he was never charged with anything again and passed away several years ago following a heart attack.

Aunt Bonnie seldom came around while we were living near Bryson City. One day, however, she was visiting and the two of us went across the hill to the Breedlove's. We were probably going to pick up some milk.

There was a long pasture on the other side of the hill and a mean mule was kept in the pasture. We were about half way across when the mule spotted us. He was grazing near the far end, and just as soon as he saw us, he broke into a gallop, heading in our direction.

Aunt Bonnie saw the mule moving toward us as fast as he could; she let out a whoop and broke into a run for the fence at the bottom of the hill. I reached the fence about the same time she did, but the mule was upon us; snorting and threatening. I dived under the lower strand of barbed wire; Aunt Bonnie went over the top like an Olympic athlete with the mule snipping at her dress-tail. She tumbled over the other side, barely making it. Needless to say, on the way back home, we went around the pasture.

I started the first grade in 1938 at Bryson City elementary. Faye was just three, so I walked to the bottom of the hill with Coot, who was now in the third grade. It was there that we caught the school bus.

I remember very little about the first grade; and don't remember the names of any teachers or schoolmates other than a boy named Max Shook. Max lived up the same cove where we lived, but had much further to walk to the bus stop than we did. Even after starting the second grade, I remember very little; but I can smell a crayon now, and will be reminded of early days in school.

President Roosevelt's "new deal" programs were starting to pay off and war clouds were gathering in Europe with Hitler threatening smaller countries around Germany. It was 1939, I was in the second grade, and the cotton mills were starting to run full time.

A letter from Aunt Mary Morgan brought news that the Park Yarn had enough orders to keep it running full time for a long time; and they were hiring more employees. Pay was up to eighty cents an hour for skilled workers. Mama and Daddy must have talked about it, and after several letters back and forth to Aunt Mary, a letter came with the promise of a job for them both along with a mill house ready to be moved into if they could make the move soon. They accepted and a reply was in the mail back to Aunt Mary the next day.

Plans were made; a few things were either sold or given away. Someone with a pick-up truck was hired to take us to Kings Mountain. The house and land was offered for sale. Then a buyer stopped by. The deal was made and the house and land went for $250.00. That was enough to make the move and get set up at the Park Yarn.

We said goodbye to the Breedloves, signed out of school, picked up report cards and loaded up everything on the back of the pick-up. We rolled down the old logging road late that evening. The truck had a canvas covering on the back like a prairie schooner, and everyone except Daddy and the driver was riding in the back under the canvas. There was a bench along one side to sit on. It was loaded with the remainder of mama's home furnishing and a few boxes of dishes and clothing.We probably looked like a Carolina version of "The Grapes of Wrath."

It was dark soon. My head was lying on Mama's lap. Coot was quiet; Faye was asleep on a quilt, and it wasn't long before I was asleep also. It was a long ride with a few stops along side the road to go to the bathroom and get a drink of water. A new school and new friends awaited me; and I was a little afraid of the unknown world that we were moving to.

Aunt Mary and Uncle Bill Morgan were glad to see us and it didn't take long to move the few things Mama brought with us into the mill house that was the same three room house I had been born in seven years earlier. Along with the stuff Aunt Mary gave us we had enough furnishings to get started.

Within a few weeks the weekly paychecks started coming in; I was attending the second grade at Park Grace elementary school and had a bunch of new friends to play with after school. A new world had opened up for me, one that included bananas, Pepsi Colas, Nehi grape and orange sodas, and the opportunity to earn a nickel or dime running errands for one of the neighbors. There were lots more people nearby and other kids my age to play with.

Everything was looking good at the Park Yarn, but not so good in Europe and Asia. The Germans were bullying their way through the little countries of Europe and Japan's military were rolling through China and Manchuria.

All those happenings were on the other side of the world however, and didn't matter to us. But in just two short years our country would be forced into that conflict in a big way.

CHAPTER 3

Pre War Years at the Park Yarn

None of the roads at the Park Yarn were paved. They were barely wide enough to provide room for passing cars. There was no need because very few cars were there anyway. Delivery trucks came and went occasionally such as Keebler in his ice truck; and insurance salesmen who came through on their weekly route to collect policy premiums on the policies that were written on Park Yarn residents.

When Mama passed away in 1982 she still had a policy that she bought in 1940 with a face value of one hundred and sixty dollars. The premium was paid weekly, cost ten cents per week, and was paid up after twenty years.

Ted Weir had an old pick up truck that he drove around delivering groceries to the people who had earlier dropped off their order at his store. Ted's store was situated just off the half-moon circle that led off highway 29, the main north-south highway that went through Charlotte to the north and Atlanta to the south.

He sold mostly staples; canned goods, a few seasonal vegetables like cabbage and potatoes, a small meat market and some clothing. None of the fresh vegetables that are stocked year round in the super markets now were available then except during the growing season.

The selection of clothing was limited to overalls, work pants and shirts, long johns, socks, and not much else. To supplement his meat market that was also very limited, he had live chickens for sale that were caged out back. About the only meat he sold was fat back, bologna, wieners, hoop cheese, and butter that was sold one stick at a time; most of the time he had stew meat and hamburger. Margarine hadn't been invented yet.

He had a coal bin outside and sold coal in burlap sacks. A set of scales outside by the coal bin was used to weigh the coal. Out front was a gasoline pump and along one side of the store a drum of kerosene. For the kids he sold candy and ice cream. There was also a "dope" box filled with ice water and stocked with Double Colas, Pepsi, and Coca-Colas. There was also Nehi grape and orange.

The gasoline pump wasn't electric powered; it had a glass tank on the top section with numbers that indicated the number of gallons it contained. A hand crank brought the gas up into the glass section and it was gravity fed down through the hose into the car's gas tank. The kerosene was simply hand pumped from a 55 gallon drum into the customer's container.

The women on the mill hill usually cooked on a kerosene cook stove. Some of the housewives, like Mama, still used wood burning stoves. Ted Weir had a monopoly on just about everything of necessity anyone might need that could be bought in a store. There were several grocery stores in Kings Mountain that sold a wider variety of most food items, but almost everyone who needed to go to

Kings Mountain got there by walking. Ted had a village full of captive customers.

The little house we moved into had a front room, a bedroom, and kitchen that wasn't really a kitchen, just another empty room with no cabinets or furnishings; and a small front and back porch. An outhouse stocked with old newspapers was thirty or forty yards out in the field behind the house. Toilet tissue may have been available to some of the people "uptown," but no one at the Park Yarn could afford such a luxury. A well was located near the junction of two roads near our house. Wells were positioned in half a dozen places so that none of the houses were very far from their only source of water.

There were two spigots centrally located, one on the lower road and the other between the first and second row of houses. Water was pumped from a springhouse inside the edge of a wooded area below the village.

Most cotton mill houses were the same. Some had an additional bedroom, but the rent was more. Families that had more than two or three kids needed the extra bedroom. Boys slept in one bedroom and girls in the other. The houses were owned by the people that owned the mill. To the best of my knowledge no one that worked in the mill owned their own homes. To rent one of the mill houses you had to be employed at the mill. Rent was twenty-five cents per room per week.

There was no such thing as a warm cotton mill house in the wintertime. Those families that could afford them bought 9' by 12' linoleum rugs to put down on the floors to not only make the floor look better and make it easier to keep clean, but also to help keep the room warmer.

It must have been late in the fall, or maybe even winter when we got settled in after leaving the mountains, because one of the first memories I have of that first house was the cold bedroom.

In the front room where Mama and Daddy had their bed there was a grate that would burn either coal or wood, but to get a fire started in the grate required kindling wood and newspaper. That front room grate was the only heater in the house except for the wood burning cook stove in the kitchen. That meant the bedroom where we slept there was no heat at all except for the residual heat from the living room.

Everybody, even the smallest kid, had their assigned chores and one of mine was to bring in the kindling before going to bed, so that when Daddy got up the next morning, he could get a fire started in the grate. I also had to make sure the coal bucket was full.

Once in a while I'd forget to bring in the fire starting stuff, or would just hope that Daddy would go get the kindling himself. That wouldn't happen. If he got up and found that there wasn't any kindling by the grate, or the coal bucket was empty, he'd wake me up and make me go out in the cold and bring some in.

At the time I thought he was being mean; but in reality he was teaching me the value of taking my responsibilities seriously. That kind of lesson would pay off in a big way more than once later in life.

We didn't have warm days in the wintertime back then. Every day was cold; or so it seemed. And springtime was a long time coming.

The entire electrical system in the house amounted to nothing more than an overhead fixture in the middle of each room. The on/off switch was a string dangling down from the fixture. There were no other outlets. The power line came into the back of the house straight into a fuse box that was screwed to the kitchen wall. The exposed wires ran up the wall and across the ceiling to the fixture. They were held out from the wall about two inches by stand-off insulators. There were no ground wires.

In the front room Daddy had a long string tied to the on/off string with the other end tied to the head of his bed; with that string he could turn the light on or off while still in bed. The power was controlled somewhere in the mill and was turned on at dark and off again at daylight. None of the houses had electrical power during the day.

Some of the more fortunate families had a radio that could be plugged in, using an extension cord, to one of the overhead light fixture outlets by attaching an adapter plug between the fixture and light bulb. Early on, the only radios around were battery powered. A few families had an electrical powered phonograph that played 78 RPM records. Most of the phonographs in 1939 were wound by hand to operate the turntable. No one called them phonographs, they were "Victrolas".

Sometime later, probably about the time World War II started, the power was left on full time, and folks could listen to their radio anytime, day or night. President Roosevelt talked to his "fellow Americans" regularly on the radio.

A family who wanted real luxury and had enough money, bought a fan to help circulate the air on muggy summer nights. That was about the extent of electrical appliances during the pre-war years. Eventually electric irons could be bought and then washing machines and refrigerators; but those things were unheard of at the Park Yarn in 1939.

Clothes were washed in the back yard in boiling water in an old iron wash-pot. While living in Bryson City, Mama used home-made lye soap that she got from Mrs. Breedlove; but at the Park Yarn she used "Octagon Soap" A big chunk of Octagon soap cost a nickel at Ted's store and was enough to last four or five wash days. When she boiled the overalls she would add bluing to the water to help slow down fading in the denim material. The dirty clothes would have to be scrubbed on a scrub board, rinsed and hung out to dry on a clothesline.

Water was the problem. Not the problem itself, but getting it out of the well and to the house was. Every drop of water, from the water we drank to that used to cook with, bathe with, or wash clothes had to be drawn out of the well and carried in water buckets to the house.

The busiest place anywhere near the Park Yarn on Saturday night was the boiler room at the mill. The boiler room generated steam that operated the belts for the machinery in the mill; steam meant hot water and a shower was installed in the boiler room by one of the more ambitious men. Even in the winter it was real warm in the boiler room. Timing was important because if you got to the boiler room at the wrong time you'd have to wait in line to get a shower.

In summer none of the boys needed a shower because we generally went swimming in the WPA hole almost daily. The WPA hole was an old rock quarry that had been dug, it was assumed, by the people working for the WPA, to make gravel for the roads. It was a dangerous place in more ways than one. After they abandoned the hole it wasn't filled in with dirt, but filled with water. That may have been the reason work was discontinued in the first place.

They may have opened up a spring in the bottom; and when it filled with water, they just left it. There was no way to know the water depth at any place. Some areas were shallow enough to stand up and walk around, and some were probably twenty or more feet deep.

None of the boys at the Park Yarn were allowed to swim in the WPA hole, but the truth is, most of the boys learned to swim there. No one obeyed the rule "do not go swimming in the WPA hole."

I was caught there one day by Daddy and remember the "whipping" to this day. Not only did I swim, but lied to him about it. He stayed in the woods watching us swim and when we were walking home through the woods he intercepted me and asked if I had been in the WPA hole. "No, we were not swimming, just walking around." My hair was still wet. He said "boy, I've been watching you for the past hour." Immediately, I knew I had made a big mistake. All he said after that was "git yonder"! That meant, get your tail home and don't stop anywhere on the way. There was no way to avoid what was coming, no amount of pleading would prevent or even stall the inevitable. My offense was serious; he was behind me somewhere, and sooner or later would be home. There was no place to hide; I thought about running away from home. The waiting was bad.

Then, without making any noise, he was standing in the door with a fresh cut dogwood limb. It probably looked bigger than it really was, but from my viewpoint it looked like it could bring blood.

After it was over he took me by the shoulder and we talked for a while about the dangers of going in the WPA hole. Of course, he did the talking, and I did the listening.

Then one day a young boy was drowned in the WPA hole and not long afterwards it was filled in and the city of Kings Mountain started a land-fill there. None of my gang ever wore swim suits or anything else while swimming in the hole, we always went naked; but for some reason the guy that drowned had swimming trunks on when they pulled him from the bottom. They used some kind of a rig with big hooks to snag him; it didn't take long to get him hooked and brought to the surface. But before the drowning happened another incident occurred at the WPA hole that could have been a matter of life or death, but in the end was more humorous than urgent.

During cold weather we used to throw bottles out in the water and shoot them with slingshots; never giving a thought about the broken glass sinking to the bottom to be stepped on in the summer while swimming there.

Sure enough, Buddy Dover stepped on a piece of glass one summer day and the bottom of his foot was bleeding badly. We tried to get the bleeding stopped with what we had, but it kept bleeding. We started home to get help and on the way he grew weak and nearly fainted. We had to carry him and found some old bed springs that someone had taken out to the woods to throw away. We put him on the springs, using them like a litter; he was getting heavy and we were getting tired. Lafayette hadn't helped carry him at all, and when we asked him to help, he said: "No, I didn't cut his foot and I won't help carry him, but I will pray for him!" There are enough stories about the WPA hole to write a book.

One strory involves Coot Camp the day Tooney Maddox dared him to swim across to the other side. It was winter time and was cold enough to form a thin skim of ice on the water, but Coot wasn't one to take a dare. Off came his clothes and he jumped right in. He not only swam to the other side, but jumped right back in and swam back across. He put his overalls, shoes and jacket back on before threatening to throw Tooney in the water.

The one good thing about the WPA hole was that we never needed a bath in the summer. Very few days passed while we were on summer vacation from school that we didn't go swimming. After the city started dumping garbage over what used to be the WPA hole we used our sling shots to shoot big wood rats that set up housekeeping in the piles of garbage.

Recently one of the girls that grew up at the Park Yarn was relating to me some of her childhood experiences while growing up there. Her parents were devout Christians and while they lived at the Park Yarn they attended the little one room Nazarene Church as did most of the population at the Park Yarn. All her brothers and sisters as well as most of the kids who lived there had to attend services whenever they were held including revivals, mid week, and Sunday night services.

The little one room Nazarene Church was small, it had no heating or any other utilities that I can recall, but the faithful kept coming; it was an important part of life at the Park Yarn.

That Church and the Pastor, John Gregory, along with the other church leaders had a strong influence on the kids at the Park Yarn. I know, and have stated many times, that besides our parents, John Gregory was more influential in planting the seeds of morality and integrity into the young kids at the Park Yarn than anyone else.

Of all the youngsters that grew up at the Park Yarn, I know of no one that ever went to jail, or used illegal drugs. Most turned out to be successful and honest citizens. A lot of the credit for that can honestly be given to the spiritual leaders of the little Nazarene Church.

During our discussion, the lady recalled her days at Park Grace school, and the admiration and respect we all had for the teachers. She remembered a fight between two boys that had to be broken up by Mrs. Nichols, the school Principal. After she had the two separated she told them "I came here to teach, not to referee a fight."

The mill was running full time just as Aunt Mary Morgan had written in her letters to Mama, and it wasn't just the Park Yarn. The textile industry in the south was going full throttle. The wages still weren't going to make wealthy people out of the workers, but they had a job and making enough to live a lot better than we did in the mountains.

For Mama and Daddy it was far better than the dollar a day he was making while working for the WPA in Bryson City. Both of them had jobs at the Park Yarn and were bringing home over $50.00 a week after taxes. In 1939 that was more money than they had seen in a long time, if ever.

Mama bought some furniture at Sterchi's furniture store in Kings Mountain and was making weekly payments out of her paychecks, but the furniture was in our house and was being put to good use. Daddy never was one to spend too much on groceries or anything else that wasn't absolutely necessary; the basics were good enough. As long as he had cornbread and buttermilk, that was a good supper for him, but with Mama doing the cooking, we were having good stew meat or chicken every Sunday.

Aunt Mary and Uncle Bill Morgan always had good food at their house; she was one of the best cooks anywhere. The first time I ever tasted a banana Aunt Mary gave it to me. The first time I ever smelled livermush frying, it was at her house, and the first time I ever tasted a Pepsi Cola she let me try it from one she was drinking. I had never seen anything like that in the mountains.

Our neighbor, Ben Page, had a hog lot in the field behind his house and every summer he kept a hog to be killed in the fall. We saved all the left over biscuits and other food scraps for him. Daddy kept a "slop" bucket hanging out on a nail and all the left over food went into the bucket for Ben to pick up and feed to his hog.

When it got cool enough in the fall to keep the curing hog meat from spoiling, Ben would dress out the hog and we'd have a "mess of backbones and ribs" in the pot. That was the best smelling stuff, ever; and it tasted just as good as it smelled cooking. They would make livermush and sausage; salt down the fat back and cure the hams and side meat. Daddy loved cornbread made with the rendered out fat they cooked to make lard. Ben would always give him some of the "cracklins."

Life was good not long after we moved back to the Park Yarn in 1939. In Europe and Asia life wasn't so good for a lot of people.

The world situation was beginning to worsen. Hitler was moving on neighboring countries in Europe. He had taken Austria and the Sudetenland. He and Mussolini had created the Berlin-Rome military alliance, and Japan entered the pact in 1939. In September of that year Hitler invaded Poland and before the month was over, England and France declared war on Germany.

Hitler continued to expand taking Denmark and Norway, then Belgium; and in June 1940 France fell to Germany. People in the US were getting nervous. Most of them remembered World War I and didn't want their country involved in another European war. That war brewing over in Europe was none of our affair and we needed to stay away from it.

This attitude was reflected in passage of the Neutrality Acts that dictated a hands off approach to the events in Europe. President Roosevelt explained and reinforced the Neutrality Acts in his 3rd inaugural speech in January 1941. But the Congress made concessions to that attitude by allowing the sale of arms to Britain and France on a "cash and carry" basis.

In July 1939 Roosevelt announced that the US would no longer trade any strategic materials including gasoline and iron to Japan because of their aggression in China. The Japanese started occupying Indonesia and in December 1941 launched their attack on Pearl Harbor.

World War II had started and our country was unavoidably forced to fight a war on two fronts because within four days after the Pearl Harbor attack, Hitler declared war on the US.

Our military would have their hands full in both Europe and the Pacific. All the young men at the Park Yarn were soon lining up to volunteer for active duty with the various military services.

In December 1941 I was only nine years old, and after listening to the President's "day of infamy" speech, thought about how long it would be before I would be old enough to enlist. I was secretly hoping the war wouldn't end before my time would come.

Most of the boys my age felt the same way. We didn't think about the pain and misery caused by war, but it wouldn't have mattered anyway because we wanted to be a part of the exciting events that were to come.

CHAPTER 4

The War Years

President Roosevelt's famous "day of infamy" speech was made following Pearl Harbor and the US was at war. Lines of volunteers formed at armed forces recruiting stations across the country and the "greatest generation" were all ready to show the world that they had the right stuff.

I had just turned nine in July but recall the way people at the Park Yarn were reacting and talking. All the eligible men volunteered and were gone in no time. There's no way, without a great deal of research that I could name them all, but as far as I know, every man that lived at the Park Yarn was ready and willing to serve. There were a few who were classified 4-F, or disqualified for military service for one reason or another, but not very many. Within days word concerning the whereabouts of the men kept filtering through. Some were at Camp LeJeune training with the Marine Corps; later to be a part of the island hopping campaigns in the Pacific, or at Randolph Air Base learning to become a gunner on a B-17 that would take part in the air war over Germany. Some were at Fort Jackson, South Carolina or in San Diego with the Navy.

Every man between eighteen and thirty-eight had to register with selective service. Daddy celebrated his thirty-fifth birthday in November 1941 just a few weeks before Pearl Harbor. He was thirty-six when his draft board notified him to report for induction.

Some would survive the war without a scratch, some would come home with missing parts or scars and disabilities; some wouldn't survive. At least two were killed on D-day, another one in France after the invasion, and another in Germany. Another would be captured by the Japanese and spend several years as a POW. Before the war, Pete Lynn used to pay me a nickel to go to Ted's store for him; Pete was one of the first to volunteer and was killed in Europe.

When Bob Gantt left to go overseas he left his dog with the young boys at the Park Yarn; we all enjoyed playing with him, a big collie. We promised to care for him and make sure he had everything he needed while Bob was gone . He didn't have a home, he belonged to all the boys. He really enjoyed playing hide and seek with us; we would go hide; he would wait a minute until someone gave him the signal and then run and find us. The day Bob was killed in France, his dog ran in front of a delivery truck and was killed. Maybe that was a coincidence, maybe not.

Of course, school was a big part of life for all the school age kids at the Park Yarn. We walked to the Park Grace elementary that taught grades one through seven. At the time it seemed a lot further than it really was. Most students walked home for lunch because the school didn't have a cafeteria until I was in the fourth or fifth grade.

A few of the students brought a bag lunch; particularly those who didn't live at one of the mill villages.

When we left the mountains I was in the second grade and as soon as we got back to the Park Yarn my older sister and I were enrolled in the school. Most of the years I spent there were war years. The principal, Mrs. Gladys Nichols had a son who was a naval aviator on an aircraft carrier somewhere in the Pacific. She was very proud of him and was one of the most patriotic ladies I ever knew.

Every day two students were given the honor of raising and lowering the flag that flew in front of the school building. They would raise it when the bell rang at eight thirty a.m. and lower it following the last class of the day at three p.m. Each morning every student was required to recite the pledge of allegiance. We also had a devotional following the flag raising ceremony and pledge of allegiance. Not having prayer in school would have been unthinkable at the time.

One Halloween night we raised some old junk up the flag pole and left it there until the next morning. Mrs. Nichols was the first to spot the old worn out pots and pans hanging where the flag would soon be flying. Every student was called in to assembly. She gave all of us a lecture about respect for our flag, and was brought to tears talking about it. She loved our country and never missed an opportunity to honor the flag. She was a wonderful person and teacher.

We placed school teachers a level or two above "ordinary" people. They were special, and we respected them, every one of them. In our eyes, they could do no wrong. A rumor started making its way through the class that Mrs. Clay, the second grade teacher, had been seen smoking a cigarette. We didn't believe she could do such a thing and the rumor soon died out.

At the beginning of the school year in September, Mama would look through the Sears & Roebuck catalog and order two new pair of bib overalls, two new checkered outing shirts, and a pair of brogans (high top shoes) for me to wear to school. That was my school clothes for the entire year. Usually the winter coat I wore last year would be let out in the sleeves and made to do another year. If it couldn't be done, she would place another order later in the year for a new winter coat.

Growing up on a cotton mill village was a unique experience, probably unlike any other anywhere in the country. I read somewhere that "you can take a boy out of the cotton mill village, but you can't keep lint from returning to his navel." Growing up in that environment teaches you early on that the world owes you nothing.

We learned how to improvise and invent ways to find our own entertainment. Hank Williams Jr. wrote a song a few years back that said "a country boy can survive" For us he could have said "a cotton mill boy WILL survive" and wouldn't be far from the truth.

We could take a ball of twine and a little friction tape and make a baseball out of it; we could take a broom handle and a sharpened piece of dogwood and have all the equipment needed to play a game called "peg" with all the complicated rules of a sophisticated sport. Or take a June bug and a piece of sewing thread and make a toy helicopter or airplane that would fly all day without refueling, or until his leg fell off and he flew off without one of his hind legs. We knew how to catch lightening bugs, put em in a jar and make a lantern that you could see a long way off at night.

We had a night game called “fox and dog.” It had to be a summer game because during the school year we were in bed early. We drew straws or named a “head” fox or dog who then took turns naming their team. If you were a fox, you were given a few minutes head start before the dogs were turned loose. They had a certain amount of time to find you and once you were discovered, you had to make it back to the light post that was home base before any of the dogs made it back. If you did, you were the winner, if not you were the loser. No self-respecting cotton mill boy could stand to be a loser- not at anything. Even so, as it is with most sports someone has to be the loser.

We could take a metal ring that came on a mill yarn can and a piece of heavy wire that we usually found around the edge of a set of bed springs someone had discarded in the woods, and make a “hoop and slide”. The wire would be bent into a “U” shape on one end, folded back to make a handle on the other, and would be used to push the metal ring in front of you. If a boy had one of these home built “toys”, it went wherever he went. You just didn’t leave home without the hoop and slide rolling out in front. With experience the ring could be made to do all kinds of tricks using the wire (the slide) to control it. It could be made to dip and turn and all sorts of maneuvers.

Buddy Dover was one of my very good friends who lived with his Grandmother a few houses below where we lived. Buddy had some grand ideas about how to make a lot of money. His step-grandfather had ordered a fur buyers catalog that indicated the fur buyers gave a lot of money for any kind of animal hide; everything from beaver to mink, muskrat, raccoon, and all the rest. Prices were given for the various grades of tanned hides. They even paid something like fifty cents for a rabbit hide that had been "cured" and stretched; but it couldn't have any shotgun pellet holes.

Rabbits were fairly common in the fields and woods that were almost in every direction around the village, so we made plans to trap every rabbit within miles around the Park Yarn, and started building rabbit boxes. A hollow sourwood tree cut to length could easily be made into a good rabbit box and we built a couple of those. I don't know why they were called "boxes" because the real term should have been "rabbit trap" Old lumber wasn't hard to find, and soon enough we had half a dozen boxes ready to set that were baited with apple peelings or pieces of cabbage leaves..The rabbits didn't cooperate and that about ended our fur trade business.

Later, we did catch quite a few rabbits, but that was after the fur trade died out. This time the boxes were stolen from the watchman at an old mine. He built the best rabbit boxes anywhere. He'd build them, and when we found one we would move it to our location and re-set it.

We weren't catching them to sell the hides, but to train our champion beagle. We'd half starve the rabbit after he was caught and brought to a cage in Buddy's back yard; after he was weakened somewhat, we'd turn him loose and give him a few minutes head start before we turned "Duke" our champion beagle loose on him.

After Duke's schooling was complete, we were going to sell him for a "thousand dollars."

Before the fur trade was discontinued, we found a dead muskrat that had fallen over the dam at the old city water lake. He hadn't been dead too long and his fur was in "prime " condition. We brought the carcass home, skinned him out and stretched the hide over a board to "cure" out. The catalog was offering $4.50 for a prime muskrat fur. All we had to do was cure it, mail it off and wait for the money. We didn't get all the meat off the hide when we scraped it, because the first time it was checked, maggots were moving around inside and it smelled like a long time dead possum. That was absolutely the end of the fur trade business.

Although Buddy wasn't much of a trapper he could catch knotty heads better than any other boy on the mill hill. The creek that ran below the city water lake dam had some pretty good pools and the knotty heads were there in all of them. They didn't get very big; a six inch knotty head was a monster sized fish.

I don't know what we did with them, but I don't remember ever taking them home to eat. Once we built a fire near the creek and stuck some on the end of a stick , roasted them and ate them for lunch. Buddy could catch a knotty head when no one else could.

One night Buddy and I were being ornery and went to an old guy's house, knocked on the door and ran. He came to the door, looked around and went back inside. We were foolish enough to try it again. This time when we knocked he jumped out at us with a .22 caliber rifle in his hand.

We really ran this time, Buddy ran towards the road and hit the ditch, I ran towards the next house. All of a sudden the rifle cracked. I kept running. The man walked towards where Buddy was hiding in the ditch. He couldn't see Buddy because it was pretty dark. Standing over the ditch he worked the bolt of the rifle and put another bullet in the chamber, then turned and walked back to his house. He was standing right over the ditch where Buddy was hiding, but never did see him.

Later in life we were laughing about the incident and Buddy told me: "when he shot, I thought he must have got you, because he didn't get me, and when he was standing over me as I lay in the ditch, and put another bullet in the gun, I was thinking to myself "if I had only known that was a single shot rifle, I sure wouldn't have stopped to hide in this ditch."

No cotton mill cowboy ever went anywhere, except maybe Church and school, without his sling shot and a pocket full of ammunition that had been picked up off the road. Sling shots were carried for several reasons. Self protection was one, because we might be attacked by a wild dog or some other critter anytime. Another was to make sure no birds came into our neighborhood. If they did they were taking an awful chance because they were sure to be shot at. Even in the woods they weren't safe. In the spring, Robins were easy targets for a Park Yarn sharpshooter.

Then, when the right time of year arrived, slingshots were used in acorn fights. In late fall when the big acorns started falling from oak trees we'd choose sides and walk off about fifty yards apart, armed with a sling shot and a pocket bulging with acorns.

At the signal, a war whoop from one of the boys, it was on. Using trees as a shield we'd sneak around waiting for one of the "enemy" to expose himself. Acorns were flying until a truce was called or somebody's daddy started whistling. Everyone knew the distinct sound of the whistle calling them home for supper. Whatever the reason, that boy had to go home.

I don't recall anyone ever being hit in the eye with an acorn, they were like a flying missile and could have caused some real damage, but it never happened. Our "Guardian Angel" was always there with us.

He was especially with us when we'd dive off the cross-tie that we formed into a raft floating in the WPA hole. Down we'd go trying to reach bottom through the cold dark water. We didn't know how deep it was, but we had to come back with a handful of mud to prove we reached the bottom. It was a dangerous game.

I believe God always gave special consideration to cotton mill boys. But at the same time we were always plagued with more mosquitoes and flies in the summer than most folks. Cotton mill boys attracted flies and gnats.

You, the reader, may think from the way "cotton mill boys" are referenced so much, there were no "cotton mill girls." Definitely not so! There were as many girls as boys; boys had their own games and the girls had "jack rocks" "jump ropes", and "doodle bugs." Mill houses were normally built on brick pillars and the girls "played house" under the house.

Cotton mill "boys" were 100% male. Of course we went to Church and school with the girls, but unlike a girl, known as a "tomboy," who was tough enough to beat up some of the boys, or liked to play baseball; the boys stayed away from the "sissy" stuff. I knew one girl who could beat most of the boys playing checkers, and that was generally considered a game the boys played. Checkers was one of the easiest games to play and could be made from a piece of cardboard and "dope" stoppers that had been converted to checkers.

A definition of "dope" and "stopper" is probably in order for those who might be wondering. "Dope" was any kind of cola drink that was sold; and it didn't have to be cola. A Nehi grape, or Orange Crush, was still a "dope." A cart that was pushed around the mill with cold drinks for sale was called a "dope wagon." A "stopper was nothing more than a bottle cap that came on top of a "dope."

To get rid of garbage most families had an old oil drum out back and they usually burned their garbage, but the drum would fill up, or there would be some junk that wouldn't burn. All that stuff was simply hauled off to the dump that was located down in the woods behind the Nazarene Church. A black guy, Will Burse, came around with his mule and wagon every month or so and dumped the trash into his wagon and took it to the trash dump. The trash dump was a good place to find a "dope" bottle to sell to Ted Weir. They were worth three cents, and two dope bottles would be enough for an ice cream cone and a penny's worth of candy.

Bert Blanton, who worked at Ted's store, would pile on the ice cream for us. Whenever you had enough money for a candy bar or ice cream cone you had to keep a sharp eye out for one of your "friends." Don't let anyone see you go into the store, and before leaving the store look out in all directions; and, if any of your chums are in sight, turn around and go out the other door. If anyone saw you eating a candy bar, all they had to do was say "tobey", and you would be obligated to save the last of the candy bar for them. There was only one way out of that; if you could say "no tobey's" before they could speak, you were home free, and the whole candy bar was yours. That was unwritten law. It was a cotton mill code that no one broke.

"Pup" Sanders didn't live at the Park Yarn, but across the tracks at the Margrace mill, and even though we generally fought with the guys across the tracks, we did intermingle some. The kids at the Margrace went to the Park Grace school with us and we had to get along with everyone at school; even the Margrace boys. Pup (his real name was Arthur) had a sadistic streak and invented ways to torment stray cats.

One time he tied a string of firecrackers to a cat's tail, lit the fuse and turned the cat loose. The firecrackers were exploding, the cat was screeching, cutting flips, climbing trees, and running under houses. He finally disappeared, still screeching. Pup lived in a house with a high porch. He had a big cannonball that had been dis-armed, and weighed ten or fifteen pounds. He tied a cat to one of the pillars, got up on the porch with the cannonball and waited for the cat to walk out from under the porch; then like a bombardier, he took careful aim and dropped the heavy cannonball on the unlucky cat. Another time he stripped the ends of an extension cord, wrapped the exposed wires around a cat's legs, and plugged it in.

The connection immediately popped a fuse, but not before the cat's hair was singed and stood straight out. That cat was making some screeching noise too before it left the neighborhood.

It was told around the Park Yarn that Pup tied Joe Plumley to the railroad track once and sat there waiting for a train. Joe either got loose, or someone came by and cut him loose, because he survived Pup's experiment.

Pup was too young to enlist in the Army during World War II, but in 1950 was sent to Korea. He was one of Cleveland Counties highest decorated soldiers during the Korean War. I don't think it was "valor" in its strictest terms, although I would never question his bravery under fire; he just liked to shoot at Chinese soldiers.

Joe Plumley survived being tied to the railroad tracks, but got burned in another incident earlier. Joe used to carry a pile of kitchen matches in his overall pocket as did some of the other "cotton mill cowboys." He was wrestling around on the ground with another boy when all at once smoke boiled up from between them, and Joe was on his feet like a shot, wiggling, hollering and smoking.

His overalls were on fire because the matches had ignited in his pocket. He started running, still hollering and grabbing at the overalls like he wanted to get rid of them but didn't know how to do it. Somebody tackled him and tried to pull the overalls off. When we finally got them off him, his leg was burned some, but he recovered.

Joe and I were both the same age; he had an older brother named Bryan. Bryan and I got a job at S.S. Weir's dairy farm that was on highway 29 just a little way from the Park Yarn. It was a small dairy operation with twenty-one cows. S.S. was Ted's father and was a tight-wad of the first order.

We worked for twenty cents an hour cleaning cow manure from the stalls, milking the cows, bottling and capping the milk, and we helped deliver the milk to customers. There couldn't have been a state or county health department back then, because that dairy would've been shut down as soon as an inspector could write it up. The cows were milked by hand and the bottling machine had swarms of flies buzzing around, and always smelled like old clabbered milk. It was a nasty place, but S.S. didn't care. Profit was his motive and he didn't waste anything that could be converted to cash. We didn't work there very long because it was a summer job between school years.

Just up the highway where the road leading up to Ted Weir's store broke to the left off highway 29, Kate and Carl Blanton had a beer joint. Behind Kate's place were four or five cabins they rented out by the hour or overnight. Just behind the cabins was the edge of a wooded area. Kate's place had a bad reputation with the good people that lived on the mill hill; and rightly so because a lot of drunks and bar flies hung out there. Men would take women back to the cabins, so the joint was more than just a place to have a few beers.

Once in a while we would find ourselves in the woods behind the cabins watching the activities. All the talk about "Kate Blanton's Place" intrigued us.

Late one evening we watched as a guy and girl went into one of the cabins; he was carrying a whole case of beer. Of course we couldn't see what was going on in the cabin, but they weren't there very long before they left and went back to the beer joint. He wasn't carrying the beer.

None of us had ever tasted beer and someone suggested that one of us should sneak in the cabin and get the beer. Red Morrison had the gumption to do it; so across the fence he went and into the cabin. He was out of the cabin and running towards us in less than a minute, he threw the beer across the fence; someone grabbed it and back through the woods we all ran. We stopped to see what we had and everyone grabbed a bottle. We started drinking. I had heard about that awful beer in Sunday school and really thought it tasted bad, but I forced down a few gulps. We had seen a tough cowboy break the top off a bottle of rye whisky on the edge of the saloon bar in one of the Saturday double features at the Dixie Theater; then turn it up for a big drink. Sure enough one of our guys did the same thing on a rock. He turned it up to take a drink and almost swallowed some glass splinters in the process. Luckily he spit it all out and no harm was done.

We sat around a while, and had another good sip or two. It wasn't very long before most of us started feeling the effects. Then someone mentioned the fact that "we were going to hell for what we were doing." One thought led to another and the "hell fire" talk continued. Pretty soon someone suggested that we needed to go to the Church and pray about the evil thing we had done. My uncle Bill was a deacon or board member in the Church and I suggested we go get him to go with us. He knew how to pray real good and we would be sure to be forgiven if he did the praying.

Off we went to find Uncle Bill. He was at home and when we told him what we had done, one of the guys asked him to go to the Church with us and he agreed to go. He prayed with us and we were convinced of our forgiveness. Uncle Bill promised to keep our secret; we split up and went home. Later I wondered what the guy thought when he went back to the cabin for his beer and found it gone. We never heard of the incident again.

The Nazarene church was set back in the edge of the woods and was further away from the highway than any other building or house on the village. As I mentioned earlier, John Gregory was the Pastor. I don't know if he was actually paid to preach or not, but regardless he was always available when a family needed spiritual guidance or comfort following the loss of a family member. His younger brother, Jennings was one of the first from the Park Yarn to be killed in action during the war.

Pastor John had a medical problem with some kind of a heart ailment that no one could do anything about and died while still relatively young. He was badly missed by everyone.

My Uncle Blanchard Horne was also a Nazarene preacher, but he was a full time pastor with a big church in Kings Mountain and was building a bigger church in town at the time. We used to help him with donations to help build the new Church. We would ask people for a dime to buy a brick, and I guess we helped quite a bit because the church was built and is still there today.

Later he would move up in the Church organization and ministered to a big Church congregation in Charlotte, and eventually on to Florida. After moving to Florida he was involved in a scandal with his church secretary. He lost his job as a preacher and my Aunt Ruth wound up a mental case because of that one affair.

Sometime before the outbreak of war in December 1941 we moved from the little three room house to a bigger four room house. There was also room to have a chicken lot behind the house. Daddy ordered a bunch of little chickens and we raised most of them till they were mature enough to be laying eggs. We ate some of the chickens but still had enough to produce lots more eggs than we could eat; Mama either gave them away or sold some, I can't remember.

We also had a big white rooster that you couldn't turn your back on. He'd jump you as soon as your back was turned to him.

One afternoon I was swinging on the front porch and a man came by asking if my Mom or Dad used snuff. I told him Mama did but she was working and wouldn't be home until after 3 p.m. He was passing out samples of "Top" brand snuff, and gave me a box to give her when she got home.

As soon as he was gone, I threw a pile of the dusty snuff under my lower lip, the same way Mama did. I kept swinging, but before long, I must have turned a pale green and was gagging and throwing up. That was a bad sick. To this day, I have never put any tobacco of any kind in my mouth again.

No one on the mill hill had any kind of refrigeration. Refrigerators most likely had already been in use elsewhere in the country, but no one at the Park Yarn had one. Just about everyone had a big ice box that kept food relatively cool. Between the Park Yarn and Kings Mountain there was an ice plant that produced ice in big three hundred pound blocks. The ice man, a husky black man named Keebler delivered ice to everyone on the village.

Each house had a square card with 25-50-75-and 100 on one of the corners. If you needed 25 pounds of ice the 25 would be turned up and Keebler would chop 25 pounds off the big block and put it in your ice box. That much would last three or four days, providing there weren't too many kids in the house.

As Keebler would chop the smaller chunks from the big block with an ice pick, he'd leave pieces of ice on the big green canvas that was used to cover the ice so it wouldn't melt too fast. He had some big tongs that he used to grab the ice with; then sling the tongs across his back and head for the back porch where the ice box usually was kept.

When he went around the corner, we made our move to the truck to get the little chunks of ice laying around. Then he'd come running back towards the truck, yelling and snapping those big tongs at us, trying to scare us. The truth was that he would leave ice laying around the wagon just for us. It was a game he played with us every time he came to make ice deliveries

When Daddy's draft board inducted him in 1943, we moved again. This time closer to the mill and close to a spigot that was our water supply. The spigot was not more than three, maybe four hundred feet from the house. At the other houses we had lived in, all the water had to be drawn out of a well.

It was my responsibility to carry all the water needed in the house. On wash day it was a big chore to fill all those wash tubs. It took a bunch of trips carrying two water buckets at a time.

Between this house and the Park Grace school was a big field that Marion Jackson kept under cultivation. He usually grew cotton, and had a team of mules used for plowing and when they turned the dirt we could find arrow heads in the field. But Marion Jackson didn't like anyone walking in his plowed fields. If he saw us looking for arrow heads he'd threaten us with those long leather straps he used to harness the mules.

Daddy had to leave for the army and hadn't been gone but a few days when a letter came telling Mama that he had been assigned to the air corps and would be taking basic training at Keesler Field in Mississippi.

Mama was left with the responsibility of taking care of all three kids, while still working eight hours a day in the mill. I have to admit that I did my part to give her problems. I must have, because when Daddy left there was a peach tree in our back yard that had lots of limbs. During the time he was gone she stripped the tree nearly bare of limbs that were used on my back side. She was more than fair, however, because I always deserved the whippings.

One day I played hooky from school with two other boys, Roy Morrison and Johnny Connor. We played around in the woods all morning long. At lunch time some of the other kids were walking from school to their house for lunch and told us that we had been caught already; Johnny's parents were already looking for him.

We knew that a good whipping was waiting for us when we went home, so rather than face our punishment, we decided to leave home. We had about twenty cents between us, and started walking. By late evening we had walked nearly all the way to Gastonia, which was about nine miles from Kings Mountain.

We had stopped at a service station to get some water on the way and while we were there Johnny used the phone to call his sister. He told her where we were and the direction we were going.

Roy and I didn't know about the phone call. We kept walking and thumbing. We hadn't had a single ride from anyone all afternoon; it was getting dark and drizzling rain. We were getting a little rattled and were cold and wet. We hadn't thought this thing out very well. We had no plan. Where were we going? We didn't know. Where would we spend the night? No one knew.

Then a car stopped to pick us up. In the car were Johnny's Mom and Dad, and my Mama. Johnny's Dad asked him, "where you going son?" Johnny looked at him and said, "I'm going home"! I crawled in the back seat with Mama and Roy jumped in too. Mama said "are you ready to go home too"; "I reckon so" I told her. Of course I got my whipping when we got home, but it wasn't as bad as I deserved.

While growing up on the mill village it seemed that every game was seasonal. We'd play marbles and the marble season would end and another season would begin. The dates probably rotated around the school year. Sometimes an adventure would come and go never to be repeated. An example of this involved a pile of old truck inner tubes we found at a pile of junked equipment at the Foot Mineral quarry.

We patched them up to where they would hold air and, at the top of the hill a rider would crawl inside the "donut hole", grab the stem and hold on. Some one would start rolling the tube and down the hill it would go. It would pick up speed as it rolled down the hill, roll across the relatively flat field at the bottom and eventually stop; the dizzy rider would get out and wobble back up the hill with the tube so that another rider could take his turn.

No one ever got hurt until we stacked the tubes on top of each other and Vester Page crawled on top of the pile, fell off and broke his collar bone. The tube rides didn't develop in to an annual happening.

Another one time adventure involved a flying squirrel. Someone saw the squirrel run into a hollow tree. We ran to the tree and stopped up the hole. We had him captured but had to chop the tree down and bring a piece of it home with us.

We got a wash tub and a window screen and dumped the squirrel out into the tub. We watched him run around the tub, trying to find a way out. We cut some grass and threw it in the tub, and tried to feed him a soda cracker.

Bobby Page said "I believe he's tame already and reached under the screen to pet him. All of a sudden the squirrel latched onto his hand between his thumb and forefinger. Bobby let out a scream and started flinging his hand around, but the squirrel wouldn't let go. Suddenly the squirrel did turn loose and went flying straight into Harold Hutto's face, Harold hollered and wet his pants; the squirrel ran off never to be seen again.

We never really got along with the boys who lived at the Margrace mill village which was located across highway 29 and the railroad tracks even though we all went to the same school. We had to coexist there because Mrs. Nichols wouldn't allow any arguments or fighting going on at school. A bow and arrow or sling shot fight would break out regularly after school with the railroad tracks serving as no man's land.

We would all gather with our home made bows and arrows and shoot at each other across the tracks. Recon patrols would be mounted by the more daring boys and forays across the tracks would be made. Then the enemy would rush the brave guys and they'd have to retreat back across the tracks.

There was a hay field between the tracks and the road leading to the Margrace mill houses. Johnny Conner had an exceptional episode of courage one afternoon; he went home and came back with his father's shotgun. He charged across the track and I fell in behind him.

All I had was my slingshot and a pocket full of rocks, but with the shotgun I knew we'd rout the Margrace boys. With me backing him up Johnny was even more courageous. We were a good hundred yards inside their territory and had a haystack for cover; Johnny stood up, stepped out in the open, raised the shotgun that was on full cock and "click"! The hammer fell on an empty chamber. No ammunition! The Margrace boys saw the same thing I was seeing and broke out in the open headed in our direction. I let a rock fly from my slingshot and did a fast retreat.

Johnny was behind me, but he had always been a little chubby and I was skinny as a fence post. I made it back across the tracks, but he didn't. They caught him and took the shotgun. Later the gun was returned to Johnny's Dad, but he didn't fare as well and got knocked around some before they turned him loose.

One of the families that lived near us took in a brother-in-law that worked in Roses Five and Dime located on main Street in Kings Mountain. He brought home several cardboard boxes of old outdated and condemned chocolate candy and dumped it in the pasture behind the house just to get rid of it.

He didn't think about the cow that belonged to Charlie Camp. Who would've thought that a cow would eat chocolate candy anyhow? But she did, and bloated up and couldn't even stand on her feet without falling over. Charlie got several of the men to help him get her to the barn and rig a sling under her belly that was tied to a rope slung over a rafter.

We were watching through the cracks when Charlie "unstopped" her. Her rear was pointed in our direction when a stream of stinking green stuff shot clear to the barn wall where we were peeking in. We survived and so did the cow, but there was a short time when that was doubtful.

After Daddy was drafted into the air corps, I was a handful for Mama. She had never been as strict as he was, and I probably thought that I could get away with more reckless activity. Lafayette's Daddy had been drafted too, but he seemed to show a little more "good judgement," and more restraint than I did. His Mom didn't have the problems with him that my Mom had with me.

Throughout our life he's always had an insight that allowed him to make good calls on what to do in a given situation. Several times in our lives he and I came out of a bad situation with our hides intact because of his instinctive reaction. That is not to say that along the way we didn't have our share of hard knocks, because we did, and most of the time it was something that I said or did that led to a confrontation. He normally wouldn't take chances that I would, but we were always pals no matter what.

In the summer we could make enough money cutting grass or running errands to make the Saturday double features at both the Dixie and Imperial theaters in Kings Mountain. And in the fall, we could pick cotton for Pierce Gray. He paid three cents a pound and the theater tickets only cost twelve cents; a big bag of popcorn was only a nickel. Every Saturday we would walk the railroad tracks to town and spend the whole day watching double features.

We could never get enough of "The Durango Kid, Lash LaRue, or Billy the Kid" or a host of other Western good guys. The "singing cowboys" like Gene Autry or Roy Rogers weren't my favorites. If they were playing, I'd watch them; but the fast action guys like Bob Steele were my kind of shooters.

Cotton picking time always came around after school started in September, and several schools around the county always allowed their students enough time away from classes to help their folks with that chore because they were farmers and the leading agriculture in Cleveland County was cotton farming.

Park Grace elementary was not one of those schools because our parents worked in the mills. We picked cotton for the money. By picking regularly after school and on

Saturday we could make two or three dollars a week. But the season for picking cotton only lasted a couple of weeks and the opportunity for big money was gone until next year.

By watching our cash flow real close we'd have enough to make the westerns at the Dixie and Imperial theaters on Saturday and still have enough to order some firecrackers for Christmas.

Looking back, I've often wondered why we set off fireworks during the Christmas season and the rest of the country had their fireworks on July 4th. Fireworks couldn't be ordered through the postal service, but had to be shipped by the railway express agency. I remember one particular December when I ordered an assortment of fireworks and waited three or four days before walking the railroad tracks all the way to the depot to pick up my order, but my fireworks didn't make it. We must have been out of school for Christmas break because I walked those tracks every day for about a week; and every day I walked back to the Park Yarn very disappointed; then finally they arrived. I was the envy of the whole mill hill walking around with a pocket full of firecrackers, and on Christmas Eve I even had some Roman candles and sky rockets to shoot.

Buddy Dover and I had more rabbit boxes than ever; none that we had built ourselves; the watchman at the mine was still making them and we were still finding and moving them around. John Richardson was paying us a quarter for a dressed out rabbit. There was always something we could find to do, that would give us a little spending money.

Summers between school terms were busy times. There were projects going on constantly. We couldn't wait until May 1st so we could go barefoot. For a few days after we were allowed to go barefoot the bottoms of our feet would be tender and bruise easily; but after several weeks of walking on the rocky roads they would toughen up like leather. After coming home at night Mama would always say "don't forget to wash your feet before you go to bed."

Summertime adventures were always time consuming and after school was out we'd always have something going in no time. We'd be damming up a creek to make a swimming hole or building a fort down in the woods. We'd plan camping trips to slick rock or an expedition to climb Kings Mountain.

It must have been the summer of 1944 that Lafayette and I saved and begged from our Moms enough money to go to Boy Scout camp. It was a week long trip but required $5.00 that had to be paid in advance. The whole troop we belonged to planned on going to the camp located in the foothills near Tryon. We came up with the money and got to go to the camp.

It was a week I'll never forget. We had a wonderful time doing everything you can imagine, and the food was so good and smelled good too. We ate like a pack of wolves and still got hungry before the next meal was ready.

The competition between troops was fierce, every event was made into a contest to see which troop was the best. Our troop was always right up there in everything. And we would have won the canoe race, which was one of the most important events, but we cut too close to the Judge's boat that was anchored at the turn and Lafayette hit the Judge in the head with his paddle. That disqualified us.

Every Scout had to earn at least one merit badge at the camp. Everyone in our troop earned two. I earned one in swimming and the other in leathercraft. That was the only summer that our troop went to the Boy Scout camp, but we never forgot that week.

The Park Yarn Mill property extended past the houses into the woods that covered the area all the way to Kings Creek road. Just inside the tree line a spring bubbled to the surface, and just below the spring someone had built a pump house. It must have been a good one because the pump brought water up to three or four spigots through an underground pipe to the mill village. Overflow from the pump house created a small creek that emptied into Kings Creek about a mile below the spring.

Some of the men had connected a water pipe running from the pump house down through the woods for about a hundred yards or so with a shower head attached to the end of the pipe. This one was in addition to the shower in the boiler room at the mill, but the water was cold, even in summer. That could be a plus, because it was a good way to cool off on a hot summer day.

One summer we tried to build a swimming hole in the creek by building a dam across a narrow point four or five hundred yards below the pump house. We had little trouble finding a bunch of burlap bags to fill with dirt; and we borrowed some shovels, hoes, and diggers and started filling the bags. We got a reasonable looking dam made and the water started backing up behind our dam.

The next night a storm came through with heavy rain and the dam washed away. That took care of about ten days of hard labor. Further down that same creek the people at the mine built a solid dam and a nice little lake formed behind their dam. It wasn't long before catfish could be caught in the lake.

I used to catch catfish with a single ended "trot line" made by tying hooks to a stout fishing line and tying one end to a bush on the bank, to the other I'd tie a rock. After baiting the hooks, I'd throw the rock out in the water.

The first thing I caught was a "cooter" (snapping turtle) about the size of a basketball. It took two of us to carry it back to the house. We gave it to Jim Bishop who cleaned it and had cooter for supper.

It wasn't long before bluegill perch could be caught in the lake. Between the catfish and perch, Mama had fish to fry for supper just about anytime she wanted.

Several times a year we would mount an expedition to climb to the top of Kings Mountain. It was several miles from the Park Yarn village to the top and a long hot march, but there were two creeks to cross on the way; so we didn't get thirsty. There was no water at the top, however, except rainwater that had pooled up in a rock. By the time we got to the top we were usually thirsty enough to drink the pooled up rainwater.

There was no explanation why, but one time Joe Plumley set off a big firecracker in the only pool of water we found. What little water was left was undrinkable. Someone threatened to throw him off the rock. Between the matches and Pup Sanders Joe lived through some hard times.

Baseball was one of our seasonable games; we cleaned off an area behind the rows of mill houses for a baseball diamond and outfield and used rocks for bases. The only piece of real baseball equipment we had was a bat. No one had gloves until one of the men at the mill gave us a catcher's mitt and two old baseballs; then someone gave us a couple of old fielder's gloves.

I was left-handed and no one had a baseball glove for a lefty, but I made out without one. Being left-handed I could throw a good side arm curve ball and after some practice could throw a sinker that was good enough to produce a few strikes. My problem was control; when the ball was released, I never knew for sure if it would go across home plate or not; and I never was a good hitter. Consequently, baseball wasn't one of my summertime favorites.

Building model airplanes held my interest, and the kits that were made of mostly balsa wood were relatively cheap; and when they were put together according to the instructions they looked a lot like the real thing. By the time any of us got into building model airplanes we were approaching our teen-age years and had matured enough to patiently work with the small delicate pieces of balsa wood.

We must have had a local aviator in the air force during the war because on several occasions a P-47 would appear overhead and do some buzzing around and perform aerial acrobatics for the spectators on the ground. That really excited me. I tried to imagine what it would be like rolling around in the sky; that guy must have been having a lot of fun.

Once in a while a formation of bombers would fly over. I loved the sound of those big engines; they always got my attention until they were out of sight. Where were they going? I thought, "soon they'll be dropping bombs on a target somewhere in Europe."

Christmas for most kids at the Park Yarn was a completely different kind of holiday in the early and mid 1940s. The real reason for Christmas was what it was all about. Churches were crowded and services were held more often. Christmas and Santa were for little kids; gifts were under the tree, but nothing like the gifts now.

The very first Christmas I can remember getting any kind of a present was a whistle and a bag of marbles. That was it; but that was good. I treasured those things. Most of the folks at the Park Yarn were good Christians who believed the Bible and that Christmas was a celebration of the birth of Jesus Christ. Santa and a decorated tree were part of it, but not as important as Church services. The only goodies we got were our treat bags at Church.

I was eleven years old in July 1943 and started the fifth grade in September. Mrs. Hughes was my fifth grade teacher at Park Grace elementary. All the teachers at Park Grace were good. Mrs. Hughes was great.

I was always blessed with the ability to listen to something being taught, or read something, and pass a test on what had been said or read just one time. Homework was never a problem for me.

Mrs. Hughes deserves credit for a lot of my capacity for learning. She knew how to teach. She was as strict as anyone; no foolishness went on in her classroom and everyone learned from her.

Even after growing up and having children of my own I would always go back and visit Mrs. Hughes; she would hug me like I was still an eleven year old boy. I liked all my teachers, but I loved Mrs. Hughes. She's gone now, but not forgotten, not by me and not by many other students who cared for her. Hopefully, I'll see her again.

It was in Mrs. Hughes fifth grade that I came to believe everything revolved around a girl. Betty Weaver lived at the Margrace mill village, and up to that time, girls were just there. I knew they were different, but there was no particular feeling.

Then all of a sudden something was different; suddenly I couldn't stop thinking about her and started following her around on the playground or just sitting around during recess talking to her.

She sat right in front of me in class and smelled so good; she must have had some kind of perfume in her hair. Marbles and rabbit boxes weren't important anymore. Even though it was at the Margrace, and I might run into a gang of those guys, I used to ride my bicycle past her house very slowly; maybe she would be on her front porch and I would have an excuse to stop and talk to her.

Then a girl, Doris Riddle, came to visit her Aunt at the Park Yarn. All of a sudden, Betty Weaver wasn't as important as before. Doris was very friendly and smiled at me. She was prettier and had prettier legs. She was the one! There could never be anyone else for me.

I could lay in bed at night, and just thinking about her would cause all the blood in my brain to head south.

Then Polly Singleton moved to the Park Yarn and overnight I really fell in love and forgot about Doris Riddle. This new girl was absolutely the one. That lasted a few weeks before Jack Rhea started hanging around. She didn't care for me anymore and I gave up on her too.

The little boy stuff was over; all the activities that used to be so important didn't mean a thing to me now. I had changed and thought about different things; my priorities were altogether different.

About a mile south of the Park Yarn Doc. Morrison built a short landing strip and a hanger big enough to hold two, maybe three, light aircraft. After school I used to ride my bike down to the strip and watch them take off and land. Mama knew what I was doing and she knew about my interest in airplanes.

One Saturday morning she asked a neighbor that had a car to take us to Gastonia to the Gaston County airport and paid $2.00 for me to take a ride in a J-3 cub. What a thrill! The flight didn't last more than fifteen or twenty minutes but it was the most exciting thing I had ever experienced. I couldn't quit talking about it for weeks.

I couldn't stop thinking about airplanes, but neither could I stop thinking about pretty girls and my blood was continually hanging out around the equator.

Buddy Dover had graduated from rabbit boxes to a twenty gauge shotgun. Duke was still with us, and even though we thought he was the best rabbit dog anywhere, no one had offered us a thousand dollars for him.

Buddy and Duke were going rabbit hunting almost daily. I needed a shotgun bad, but in the spring of 1945 I wasn't even thirteen yet and Mama thought that was a little young for me to be carrying a shotgun, so I had to wait. However, I was already thinking about ways to raise the $14.95 it would take to buy the one I wanted.

Phifer hardware had a twenty gauge Iver Johnson that would be perfect for me.

I started delivering The Gastonia Gazette. That worked out pretty good, but the money wasn't as good as expected. Although the amount of money I made was a disappointment I realized it was better than nothing and stayed with the Gazette over summer vacation, but had to give it up when school started in September.

It seemed that some customers wanted their paper every day, but when collection time came they were hard to find, or just wouldn't come to the door. The Gazette people had a rule for subscribers who failed to pay. After two weeks they were cut off, but once that happened there was no way to get the past due money.

If they aren't dead there are still some people out there that owe me for two weeks newspaper delivery. The Gazette had their backs covered; I was the one that had to absorb the loss, but even with a few deadbeats I managed to sock away a few bucks.

Boys raised on a cotton mill village usually grew up to be good people. They made a lot out of a little, and as adults could stand up with the best and be proud. After leaving home to make my way in the world, when asked about my heritage I was always proud to reply "I grew up on a cotton mill hill".

World War II had its impact on all of us. Of course, we at home didn't endure the misery and dying the guys in the military did. Almost everything was in short supply and rationed, but again, that was a small sacrifice compared to the guys who were a long way from home and doing the fighting and dying.

Everyone was solidly behind the war effort and supportive of anything President Roosevelt asked of them.

Early in the war bad news from the Pacific came almost daily. The Philippines fell to the Japanese and General Wainwright surrendered all the American forces on Bataan and Corregidor. That was followed by the infamous "death march." where eighteen thousand American and Filipino captives either died or escaped into the jungle. Most of them died at the hands of brutal guards.

Guam and Wake Island were taken; Singapore and the British garrison in New Guinea surrendered. The way was open for the Japanese to try and take Australia. Earlier, in Europe, Hitler's Air Force was constantly flying against England; bombing London and other targets, but the Royal Air Force was inflicting heavy losses on the Luftwaffe; and in the end prevented Hitler from carrying out a planned invasion of the British Isles.

When it was clear the German Air Force had been defeated, Prime Minister Churchill delivered his famous speech in which he stated "never in the field of human conflict has so much been owed by so many to so few." Of course he was making reference to the Royal Air Force and the "Battle of Britain."

Then in April 1942 everyone got some good news that made headlines in all the papers and was broadcast over the airways. Eighty airmen flying sixteen B-25 bombers had struck Tokyo. The Japanese sacred homeland had actually been bombed. It was a psychological victory; but came at a high price. Fifteen of the bombers made it to China where they all crashed, after the crew bailed out, or made a forced landing. One B-25 made it to Russia where the airplane was taken and the crew interred. They later escaped from the Russians and made their way to Iran and eventually back to the US. Not a single B-25 was lost to hostile fire, but some of the crewmen were captured in China by Japanese forces and were executed as war criminals. One airman was killed during his bailout attempt.

Most survived, however, and have held an annual reunion every year where they raise a toast to their comrades who have passed on. Their leader, Brigadier General Doolittle, recently died leaving only fourteen that are still with us.

In the fall of 1942 the Marines made an amphibious landing on Guadalcanal when it was discovered the Japanese were constructing an airfield there. Guadalcanal was located in the Solomon Islands not too far from Northeast Australia; and the war planners didn't want them to have an active air base that close to mainland Australia.

That was the first amphibious invasion in the Pacific and when the Japanese were beaten off the island it would become the turning point of the war because it stopped Japanese expansion in the South Pacific. The Marines began "island hopping" and didn't stop until the war's end. One of my cousins, a Lieutenant in the Marine Corps, was killed after landing on Tarawa.

In May 1943 the Germans surrendered their "Afrika Corps" and in August General Patton's troops took Sicily. By September Italy had surrendered.

On June 6th 1944 the allies invaded France conducting the largest amphibious operation in history. That same month the Marines took Saipan Island and in August liberated Guam. The battle of the bulge was fought in Northern Europe in December. That was Hitler's last offensive assault of the war and by March 1945 the Americans had crossed the Rhine River and were on German soil.

In April 1945 President Roosevelt died. He didn't live long enough to see the end of World War II, but he came close; because later that month Hitler shot himself as the Russians were closing in on his bunker in Berlin. And on May 7th Germany surrendered.

On August 6th the first atomic bomb was dropped on Hiroshima and the second was dropped on Nagasaki August 9th. And on August 15th, the Emperor of Japan surrendered his country to the allies.

In September of that year French forces occupied Indo China, laying claim to all the areas known as "French Indo-China" before the war. That action led to a long conflict and the ouster of the French from what we now know as Vietnam and the eventual involvement of American forces there.

World War II was the most widespread war in history with the US and Russia emerging as the world's leading super powers; setting the stage for the cold war that would last for the next forty-five years.

The war was over, the survivors were coming home and by the end of summer all the men from the Park Yarn were back home. None that I know of stayed in the military. Daddy was discharged at Seymour-Johnson Air Force Base and returned home. He was back on the job in the twister room at the Park Yarn mill by the middle of September.

Not long after he came home we moved into another house that was bigger and closer to Ted Weir's store. I had my own bedroom, my sisters had their bedroom and Mama and Daddy also had one.

Still, what we would call "primitive" today, existed. There was no indoor plumbing, the outhouse was still there in the field behind the house, and we were back to drawing water from a well.

Then Daddy and Rob Pearson bought adjoining properties out on the Shelby road and plans were made to build on the site.

World War II was over and a new chapter in my life was beginning.

CHAPTER 5

The Park Yarn and The Post War Years 1945–1949

With elementary school behind us the group of students that had finished the seventh grade at Park Grace started riding the bus to Central High School in September. Lafayette's older brother R.C., already a senior at Kings Mountain High School, drove our bus. We had an assistant driver that drove the bus whenever R.C. was sick or for any reason couldn't drive. The assistant was Jack Bobbit a wild and reckless son of the pastor of Macedonia Baptist Church. At night the bus was parked beside R.C.'s house; it didn't take long to make the three or four miles from the Park Yarn to Central High School. Once the bus was past Ted's store there were no other student pick-ups made.

Junior High School wasn't even thought of then; just elementary and high school. Grades eight through twelve were taught at central and kids from all the elementary schools around Kings Mountain went there. Incoming students from half a dozen cotton mills scattered all around the town were starting the eighth grade.

I met a lot of new people that year. There were some new and prettier girls; most of them uptown types, however the "lintheads" didn't meet the criteria to belong to the inner circle that was exclusive to the uptown students. But even with the differences most of the students were sincerely friendly and eager to socialize during school hours. We had to ride the bus and couldn't participate in any after class activities and that added to the disadvantages for us. To try out for any sport or take an active part in any of the clubs or student government required the student to be available for practice or meetings after class.

In the natural order of things you might think that the "bus riders" or the cotton mill kids who lived within walking distance of the school would feel somewhat inferior. That wasn't the case because we were in the majority. Lintheads were all over, in every class. Maybe some of them felt subdued or intimidated by the flashy clothes or cynical attitudes that were clearly demonstrated by a few of the upper crust, but the Park Grace kids imposed their own resolve. So did a lot of the students who were growing up on other mill hills. It was the "cotton mill cowboys" who dictated the terms in spite of the class differences; they weren't unfair, so everyone got along. Some of them made good football players and were active in after class activities and class government. However, most of the transplants from the Park Yarn and Margrace villages couldn't participate in anything that required us to be available in the evenings.

Class procedures were different at central. We changed classes every 45 minutes and marched around the hall to our next class; and we had study hall and physical education. It was altogether different from sitting in the same classroom all day every day with one teacher. The whole atmosphere was different; the teachers were good but their methods were more impersonal. They didn't appear to encourage student questioning about the subject they were teaching and presented the lesson one time; if you missed something you had to read it to learn it. They seemed to distance themselves from the students.

That may be a somewhat harsh judgment; because even though they rarely issued an invitation to ask about a particular point they would answer student questions and no matter the method of teaching their technique worked and we all learned.

School was always easy for me, and I never had to study much to make good grades. End of course examinations were passed without effort. Credit for that should go to the elementary teachers at Park Grace; teachers like Mrs. Hughes and Nichols, they were the ones who laid the foundation for any successes and "A" grades I made in high school.

The ride to and from school wasn't very long but it was noisy. R.C. Pearson was very tolerant and never called anyone down, even though he had the authority to do so. We had one girl, who rode the bus that tried to entertain the rest of us from time to time. She lived somewhere at the Margrace and was very well endowed up front by Mother Nature; she was proud of that (or them). She liked to sing and sometimes dance around on the bus. Several times she lifted her sweater to prove they were all hers, she never wore a bra. Things like that aren't easily forgotten.

Life away from the mill hill was changing at a fast pace for me. Life at home was in a rut.

The after school routine never changed. Get the home work done; draw water from the well and make sure all the water buckets were full; get away from home and mess around with the other guys until time to eat supper. After supper go see one of the girls and sit with her on the front porch swing or sit on the bank at Harold Hutto's house and watch the cars go by on highway 29.

Sometimes we could catch a glimpse of a leg inside a car; that always created a little excitement. When it was time to go to bed; heat some water in the foot tub, take it to the bedroom and wash off all over. Turn the radio on to WCKY in Cincinnati and listen to country music for a while and wonder what Polly Singleton would do if I tried to feel her leg or unbutton her blouse. That was about as exciting as it got for me over the course of the school year.

Bob Gantt had been killed in France, but he had two brothers who survived. One of the brothers, Jack, had been hit in the wrist with a German sub-machinegun bullet; he had to hold his hand all curled up and it was nearly useless, but he could still hold a rod and reel ok. The other brother, Issac, everyone called him "Ike" drove a half-track all the way from Normandy to Berlin, and came through the war without a scratch. Both he and his wife had a brother who was killed in the war, and she had a sister that lost her husband on D-Day. The people at the Park Yarn paid dearly for the war.

I used to stay with Ike's two small sons when he and his wife needed a baby-sitter. In turn Ike and his brother Jack would take me fishing with them on weekends when they went to Lake Wylie to catch crappie. Sometime we'd use a lantern and fish off a bridge at an inlet called "seven oaks". We would bring crappie home in buckets; there were so many it would take hours to clean them all.

One night we went to one of the coves backed up by Lake Wylie with Charlie Millen, Ike's brother-in-law, Shorty Fields, Bad-Eye Morgan, Wesley Moore, the Gantt brothers, and there was Harold Hutto and me. They were going to seine for fish, and that was against the game and fish laws; they took Harold and me along to be look-outs for them in case the game wardens came too close.

Our observation post was on one side of a small hill that overlooked one of the coves they would be operating in. They left Shorty on the other side of the hill. We had a flashlight with us to use as a signal in the event we saw someone coming.

They made a mistake with Shorty, however, because they also left a jug of moonshine with him. They were close to the far bank with the seine in the water when a boat approached them from Shorty's side of the hill. He didn't warn them, but when they heard the boat they scattered and made for the closest shore.

Ike made the bank near a trail where Shorty was supposed to be, but he was passed out in the trail from drinking too much moonshine. Ike hit the bank running and didn't see Shorty laying in the trail. He tripped over Shorty who let out a groan; Ike went tumbling down the trail thinking he had run into an alligator or something. When Ike realized that Shorty wasn't an alligator, he brought him back to the truck, still passed out. Except for Bad-Eye Morgan all the others made it back to the truck; someone even recovered the seine.

Bad-Eye made the shore on the other side and while running through a briar patch lost his overalls. We were waiting for him, sitting in the dark, when we saw a big white object coming up out of the water. We didn't know it was Bad-Eye, because he looked like a sea monster. He was a big fat guy anyway, and naked, in the dark, he didn't even look like a person. Harold probably wet his pants again. We all made it back home, but didn't have any fish to bring home that night.

Other than the time we stole the beer from one of Kate Blanton's cabins, I had never come close to drinking anything alcoholic until one day Ike asked me to go on a mission with him.

Ike had another brother who lived out in the country; his brother always raised several hogs, and had a young pig that needed to be castrated. All young male pigs that are raised for meat have to be cut while they are young. He needed someone to help hold the pig while he took care of the chore and Ike asked me to ride to the country with him to help hold the pig.

We took care of that easy enough and afterwards walked down to a creek. Out in the middle of the creek the water ran over a big flat rock that had a round hole about six inches across and about eight inches deep. A half-gallon fruit jar was sitting in the hole with three or four inches sticking above the water. It was full of home brew. The jar was passed around, and when it got to me, I took a big drink. It was a hot day and we had worked up a sweat holding the pig; the home brew tasted very good. It was passed around until it was empty.

Then another one was lifted out of the water that had been completely submerged. Soon it was empty. By that time I was feeling the effects of the home brew. You could say that I was tipsy. Ike figured it was time we got out of there; we left, but it was a while before I went home. If Mama had smelled that home brew on me, there's no telling how she would've reacted. It wouldn't have been pretty.

Years later that same creek runs through the property we bought after retirement from the air force. One of the first places I looked for after buying the place was that creek and the rock with the hole. It was, and is still there today, more than sixty years later; and it'll be there long after Mil and I are no longer here.

During the summer of 1947 I earned enough money cutting grass and delivering papers to buy the Iver Johnson 20 gauge shotgun at the hardware store. Cutting grass wasn't done like it is today. In the first place a lot of yards didn't even have grass and those that did were mostly made up of crabgrass. Cutting grass meant that I took a sling blade and whacked down the high weeds that grew between the houses and outhouses.

It was a happy day for me to come home with the brand new shotgun and a handful of shells. Twenty gauge shells cost a nickel each. I had graduated from the rabbit boxes. That shotgun is still one of my prized possessions today and it is still as good as new. I couldn't count the rabbits and squirrels that have been killed throughout the years with that shotgun.

My oldest sister Coot had graduated from high school and was now working for Southern Bell as a telephone operator in Charlotte. The folks were making enough so that they could afford for Faye and me to eat in the school cafeteria. The price of lunch was twenty cents a day. Faye was still at Park Grace.

There was a pool room in Kings Mountain that was popular with the guys at Central High School; Jack Rhea and I used to go there during our lunch period and shoot a couple games. Instead of eating lunch we'd drink a Pepsi and eat a pack of crackers.

It was about this time that I saw the girl that up to that time was the best looking I had ever seen. Her name was

Phyllis. I was a tenth grader and she was in her first year at Central, probably in the eighth grade, having finished elementary at one of the city schools. I wanted to get to know her better, but never had much of a chance because we never had a class together, and the only meeting we ever had was just passing in the hall between classes.

It was during this school year that my class had a picnic at Lake Montonio; We were all swimming around and I was fooling with some of the "uptown" girls; swimming underwater and grabbing their legs. I didn't know they were conspiring against me, but they were, and as I grabbed a leg, one of them grabbed me and held me till a couple others could help her. Together they tried to drown me. I finally broke loose from them and swam away.

Not long after the war ended someone started a city bus service that provided public transportation all around the City of Kings Mountain. One route came through the Park Yarn and Margrace. There were routes toward Gastonia, Bessemer City, Cherryville, and York. It only cost a dime to ride and with free transfers you could get on a bus for a dime and ride all day.

Not long after Daddy came home after the war someone gave me a puppy. It took some doing (because it was a female), and that could mean more puppies later, but I finally talked Daddy and Mama into letting me keep the puppy. We named her Trixie. She grew into a pretty little dog and never got very much bigger than a cat. She wasn't allowed in the house and slept out on the back porch. She was a lot of company for Faye and me; but one day her hair started falling out and she was scratching a lot. Daddy said she had the mange; and rather than try and cure her, he took her off somewhere way out in the country and dropped her off.

It seems cruel and probably wouldn't be handled like that now. He didn't tell me what his plans were until after she was gone, and he wouldn't tell me where he took her, but I got on one of the city busses and rode every route they had, looking everywhere for Trixie. I felt so bad for her and missed her a lot, but never saw her again.

The school year in 1948 was over in June and in July I turned sixteen. I never returned to Central High School. It was probably one of the worst decisions I ever made. In late summer I talked my folks into letting me go to work in the mill. Mama was very reluctant, but Daddy had no objections. An education wasn't important; making a living was. He was a good man but was living on a farm back in the 20's.

In September Jack Gantt gave me a job in the mill. I would start as a trainee, working forty hours a week, but while a trainee, I would only make forty cents an hour. Once my "on the job training" was over, I would advance to eighty cents per hour and hold down a full time position.

Jack was a supervisor over a section of the mill and they were in the process of overhauling all the spinning frames. I was given a bucket full of benzene (a cleaning fluid that smelled a lot like kerosene) and a brush. The rollers taken off the frames had to be cleaned from years of cotton dust accumulation. It was a tough job, but I could at least sit down most of the time.

The benzene turned my hands and lower arms, that had been exposed to the chemicals, red as an Indian.

They stayed irritated the whole time we were working on the frames, which took about two months.

My pay for forty hours came to $16.00 before taxes. Since I wasn't a student anymore and was making it on my own, Daddy figured that my room and board would cost $10.00 per week. After taxes, that left me with less than $4.00 for forty hours work.

Finally after about two months, I went to Jack to state my case; and that was, "my training days should be over, and I should be ready to handle a regular position." He agreed, and my pay went up to eighty cents an hour; $32.00 per week. Now, after rent and taxes I was clearing a little over $18.00 a week.

The work was hard. After eight hours, most of the time I went home and relaxed until bedtime. Weekends were free; I had spending money, and a friend with an old car. Tom Strickland lived in Blacksburg, South Carolina, but his sister lived at the Park Yarn with her husband. Either he owned the car or had access to it every weekend; and we burned a lot of gas between Friday afternoon and Monday morning. We cruised the skating rink looking for girls; we parked at every drive-in we knew about, but had no luck with the girls. It seemed every good looking girl in the country already had a boy wrapped around her neck.

Summer was almost over. I had been talking to Uncle Bill about the Navy and a good friend Ebb Oliver was thinking about it too. The rut I was in kept getting deeper and deeper. One day my buddy, Lafayette announced that he had enlisted in the air force and was leaving shortly for San Antonio, Texas. The more I thought about it, the harder the cotton mill job seemed; and the more exciting life in the US Navy (with a girl in every port) sounded to me. Some major changes in my life were straight ahead.

The Shytle family at the Park Yarn mill village. Photo was taken in 1941. Back row left to right: Daddy and Mama. Front row left to right: The author, Christina Juanita, (Coot) and Faye.

CHAPTER 6

The Wild Blue Yonder September 1949

Work in a cotton mill was hard and the wages low. Throughout the various sections of the mill from the bales of cotton that were opened and sent to the carding and picker rooms, to the finished product which was combed cotton threads, everyone employed there was overloaded.

My responsibilities included taking the big spools of roping that had been doffed from the slubber frames up an elevator and lay them up on top of the spinning frames to be spinned into smaller but more compact threads.

For a seventeen-year-old boy it was boring. Girls didn't think much of a lint-head; even lint-head girls. It was time to move on.

Every time an airplane flew over I would watch until it disappeared. Uncle Bill Morgan had spent the war years in the navy, and he convinced me that the navy not only had ships that took the sailors to ports around the world, but that military flying was a part of the navy too; flying wasn't limited to the air force.

Uncle Bill had to walk with a cane because of an injury aboard ship during the war. I don't think his injuries were directly caused by hostile action although his ship was involved in operations against the enemy when he was hurt. He was all navy and had an influence on my decision to talk to the navy recruiter. Since daddy had been assigned to the US Army Air Corps after he was drafted in 1943, I was pulled between the two, but decided to talk with the navy recruiter first. The difference between the two services didn't mean anything; if the army recruiter would have promised me flying duty I would have signed up with him without any other questions.

Elbert T. Oliver (everyone called him "Ebb") was one of the buddies I talked to about getting out of the mill and the two of us made it to Gastonia on a Trailways bus to talk with the navy guy. None of my friends had a car, in fact very few families that lived at the Park Yarn, even after the war, had any kind of transportation other than their two legs. Both the Trailways and Greyhound buses ran through Kings Mountain regularly.

We took the screening test and filled out a few application papers only to find out we would have to wait several weeks, maybe longer, as there was a waiting list for the navy. On top of that, I had a couple of cavities that would have to be filled before I could pass the physical examination.

We went down the street to a corner café to talk about our options and have a coke. Ebb wasn't too receptive to talking with the air force, but as far as I was concerned that was my only option left. We went back to the court house and Ebb walked down the hall straight to the army recruiter's office. He was on his way to Ft. Jackson in no time. The air force recruiting office was just down the hall;

that was my next stop. My long time buddy Lafayette had enlisted in the air force several weeks earlier but I hadn't heard a word from him or about him since he left. It was like he fell into a black hole.

The recruiter's name was Strickland: his screening test was simple and easy to pass; a few more papers were filled out and all the preliminary paperwork prior to the actual physical examination, aptitude testing and oath of enlistment were completed. I must have scored pretty high on the screening test because Strickland came as close as he could to guaranteeing me flying duty. But then, recruiters had a reputation for promising a young man anything.

There was one other very important requirement; parents of a seventeen year old were required to give their approval and sign an agreement before their son (or daughter) could enlist in the military. Daddy was easy, but Mama was a little reluctant at first. Before long she was convinced that this was a good thing; and much was to be said in favor of a hitch in the military for a young man on a cotton mill hill in 1949. So they both signed the enlistment release form.

All the preliminary paperwork was completed and everything was on go except for a physical exam and final testing to be done in Charlotte.

The date was Friday the 2nd of September. Labor Day weekend was at hand and everything would be closed down on Monday, September 5th. The recruiter made arrangements to pick me up on Tuesday morning, take me to town, and put me on the bus to Charlotte. There I would take the armed forces qualifying test, be given a physical examination and take the oath of enlistment.

Everything went as planned and by noon on Tuesday, September 6th the obligation was made to spend the next three years as a member of the USAF.

There were four new airmen in the group scheduled to board a train in Charlotte bound for San Antonio, Texas. The group consisted of myself, Joe Costner, (a friend from Kings Mountain High School) and another recruit from somewhere near Albemarle. His last name was Morgan (I don't remember his first name.) The fourth man was a prior serviceman who had re-enlisted and since he had previous military service he was given the responsibility of carrying all the enlistment paperwork for the entire group.

The train wasn't scheduled to leave Charlotte until late that evening and we didn't have anything to do until departure time. We were given a bunch of meal tickets that were good for lunch at a local diner. They were also good for meals aboard the train to San Antonio.

The enlistment station was located in the basement of the Federal Building on W. Trade St. and the four of us walked up the street to a contract café and had lunch.

My oldest sister "Coot" was working for Southern Bell in Charlotte along with a high school girlfriend Billie Hutto. She knew that I was in Charlotte to be enlisted, so she and Billie met me at the diner and took me back to their apartment to spend the afternoon. While there she let me call Mama to let her know everything had gone as planned, and of my scheduled departure from Charlotte.

I was back at the train depot an hour or so prior to departure time and re-joined the three other guys. The train was on time and that evening we boarded and were off to a new chapter in my young life.

The apprehension set in as the train started rolling west. At the same time the unknown future created a feeling of excitement. I was still a "boy" who would do a lot of growing up in a very short period of time. There was no way for me to know that I'd do more growing up in the next thirteen weeks than all the growing that I had done over the past several years. At seventeen I was a lot more "boy" than "man." That was about to change.

CHAPTER 7

Initiation to Basic Training September 1949

The train left Charlotte close to sundown moving west toward Asheville. It wasn't long before the clickety-clack noise made by the wheels almost put me to sleep. I had never been on a passenger train before, and had been through a long and busy day.

One time several years ago I had been given a ride with a friendly engineer on a freight train travelling between Kings Mountain and the Park Yarn; we probably didn't go any faster than five or ten miles per hour. This train was really moving down the track.

It was getting dark by the time we reached Asheville which was our first stop since leaving Charlotte. Shortly after the train left Asheville we went to the diner car and used some of the meal tickets the enlistment examining station in Charlotte had given us. I couldn't believe how elegant the diner car was set up with what appeared to be real silver and soft linen tablecloths and napkins; the servers were graceful and polite, and the food was very good. The guy that carried our records had travelled with medal tickets on a train before and said something to our waiter before we ordered. We used two meal tickets each, but we had more food than we could eat. It didn't matter, we had a stack of the meal tickets and it was only two days travel time to San Antonio.

By the time we were rolling through Tennessee some of the train crew came through and converted our seats to sleepers. I had heard of a Pullman car before but had never seen one.

Sleep must have come easy to me because I don't remember anything about Tennessee except stopping in Memphis for a delay. I woke up long enough to hear someone on the other side of my sleeper say something about Memphis. They must have known we were going all the way to Texas because no one bothered us throughout the night. We had another long stop sometime well after midnight but must have been on a siding waiting for another train to pass us going in the opposite direction.

Soon after daybreak someone came through the Pullman ringing a bell and announcing that breakfast was being served in the diner. We had a men's room and lounge at the front of our car and after getting dressed we had time to freshen up before going to the diner. Breakfast was served with as much formality as supper had been; and again the food was great, and again we gave the server extra meal tickets. While we were at breakfast our sleepers were converted back to seats.

We had picked up some young guys in Memphis who were heading for Lackland Air Force Base with us. Most of them were from St. Louis, Chicago, and around the State of Illinois. They talked some different than the North Carolina accent we were accustomed to. We probably sounded different to them too.

As we rolled to the southwest we continued to pick up other recruits on their way to Lackland. They were easy to spot; everyone of them were simply dressed and carried a small overnight bag. The train made stops in almost every town we came to; some for just a short few minutes and longer in others. We traveled through Little Rock, Dallas, and Austin before reaching our destination in San Antonio. The stops in most towns were short; just long enough to load and offload passengers. I don't remember ever having an opportunity to get off the train and walk around. We stopped in so many towns, large and small, the train we were on couldn't have been considered an "express."

Late in the afternoon of the second day we arrived at the station in San Antonio and a reception by two big guys in uniform who were waiting for us. After everyone was accounted for we loaded into an olive drab (OD) bus with OD seats, it even had an OD steering wheel, and rode out to the Air Force Base.

It didn't take long. The world changed for all of us the instant we unloaded in front of a great big green building. The yelling started immediately. Nothing anyone did was right.

"Fall in, four abreast; if you're taller than the man in front of you move up. Left face;" then again, "if you're taller than the man in front of you, move up." We were instructed to remember our position in the formation. "Look at the man in front of you, behind you, and beside you. Every time you fall in, remember your position!" We had been told by the recruiter not to bring anything with us but a small overnight bag with extra drawers, socks, shaving gear and toothbrush. Shaving gear I didn't need to use more than once a week; or so I thought up to that point. That changed overnight. Everyone in the air force shaves everyday; in basic training anyway.

Then! "Alright you dummies, single file, left column first and follow the yellow line into the building you see in front of you. If you don't know yellow from blue, just follow the man in front of you." "Pick up your bags, didn't your Mama teach you anything?" Constant harassment. No one was safe from these guys.

To make you understand they would get right in your face and yell to the point that it was hard to understand everything they were trying to say. Once inside the big green building, that we later learned was called "The Green Monster," we were assembled in a room and given a welcome to air force basic training lecture by a guy with a bunch of stripes on his sleeve.

Those first two loud guys only had two and three stripes. The Sergeant that delivered the welcome lecture must have been very important because he had five stripes. But he almost sounded human; he was even friendly and made us feel at ease. Even though the newly created United States Air Force was barely two years old he told us of the glorious history of the "Air Corps" from Eddie Rickenbacker in World War I to Jimmie Dolittle in World War II. And he reminded us of the feats of Chuck Yeager who, just recently, was the first man to break the sound barrier. His last words to us before releasing us to the two mean guys were "If you leave here after thirteen weeks of basic training with a PFC stripe, you will have the world by the ass."

We were herded into a room and told to strip. After striping naked we were issued a duffel bag and two towels (OD of course). We were told to place our civilian clothes and one towel in the duffel bag, and wrap the other towel around our waist. The next stop was the barbershop.

By then everyone knew that to open your mouth was to invite the wrath of the drill sergeant. We knew who they were because the nice guy with five stripes told us. A drill sergeant is no one to speak to without being asked. You don't even scratch an itch or shoo a fly from your face in his presence.

We were then given our first GI haircut. Then down the yellow stripe to the shower room where we showered; fifteen or twenty men in the shower room at a time. "Dry off with the towel, put your drawers, socks, and shoes back on and follow the yellow line to the supply room." We didn't go into a room, just to a window where a supply guy issued us a pair of flight fatigues and a fatigue cap.

We were then told to walk down a narrow hallway. "Follow the yellow line and when you come to a set of footprints in the floor, stop!" At the footprints there were openings on both sides of the narrow hallway. A medic was standing inside the window-like openings with a needle. As soon as I stopped on the footprints I got popped in both arms. A little further on was another set of footprints, two more windows and two more medics. Pop! Another needle to both arms!

There was another room at the end of the narrow hall with the two loud guys waiting for us. Before going outside we were told to put on the flight fatigues and cap.

"Fall out!" Information came at a fast pace. Quickly we learned how to stand at attention. "Hands cupped along the seam of your trousers, heels together, feet at a forty-five degree angle, shoulders erect, eyes forward." You don't move a muscle, no matter what. You don't even move an eyeball or blink. To do so would immediately bring the drill sergeant screaming in your face, threatening you with latrine duty or maybe something worse. There were those of us at that point that didn't even know what a "latrine" was; but "latrine duty" must be something bad. Nothing these guys threatened us with could be good.

The one with two stripes carried a walking cane, which I figured would be used to trip anyone who failed to stay in cadence with everyone else. Once we were issued helmet liners I learned it was used to whack us in the head when we failed to do something the right way. While marching in formation we never knew exactly where this guy was until it was too late. If the three striper, who always called out the "hut, two, three, four" yelled out "flight halt" we knew someone was about to get whacked and chewed out.

We had been assigned to the 3702nd Basic Training Squadron, flight number 4422. From the green monster we were marched in a ragged formation with our multi-colored shoes and socks to the squadron area and to our pre-assigned barracks. We halted in front of the squadron supply room and we were issued bedding consisting of two blankets, sheets, a pillowcase, pillow, and mattress cover.

GI cots with mattresses were already in the barracks. The barracks were standard open bay enlisted quarters for the time with two levels. At one end of the ground level "open bay" was a shower room with a dozen or so showerheads. On the same side was a latrine with a long trough for a urinal and eight or ten commodes. Now everyone knew what a latrine was. But none of us knew the latrine floor was supposed to be scrubbed inch by inch with a toothbrush. Pretty soon we would all know "latrine duty" involved a toothbrush.

Across from the shower and latrine were two rooms and a small room with a desk. This was the holy of holies where the drill sergeant and his assistant lived. No one entered this sanctuary without first knocking and getting permission to enter; and you better be absolutely certain you had a good reason to knock on that door.

The "open bay" area had alternating single and double bunks. My initiation to the military was just beginning. I had no hair, my arms were full of medication and hurt like the dickens. I looked around for Joe Costner, the only person I knew; if he was there I didn't recognize him and his bald head. We were standing around waiting for the drill sergeant to tell us what to do. We didn't have to wait very long.

Without warning the yelling started; someone was in trouble at the other end of the barracks. What in the world could he have done to be yelled at so loud and for so long. Then I realized; don't make eye contact with anyone with a stripe on his sleeve and don't move or make a sound whenever he is near. Whenever we were marching in formation I always imagined the guy with the cane was just out of sight behind me ready to whack my helmet liner; I tried to stay in step with the cadence caller all the time. Even so it didn't take much, sometimes nothing to stir up the displeasure of the two drill sergeants.

My mind was on ways to keep these guys away from me, even if it meant someone else would be whacked and chewed out. If the rest of these recruits could put up with the insults and nasty dispositions, so could I. My mind was made up then and there that when I left Lackland Air Base in thirteen weeks, I would have the world by the ass. Nothing these nasty sergeants could do to me would change that. I mentally prepared myself for the worst they could do to me.

There were fifty-eight recruits in our flight and in all probability the majority of them were wondering "whatever possessed me to sign those enlistment papers and leave a loving and caring family for this mess I've gotten myself into." There was no doubt that we were a sorry looking bunch of rookies at that point.

Just when we had a few minutes to start thinking the worst was behind us, everything changed – it got worse. Our first day of basic training was just beginning.

I had been told that drill instructors would always pick out the biggest and toughest looking guy in a new bunch of recruits and get in his face with their insults and loud mouths. That didn't hold true with these two guys, it didn't take them long to single me out, or so it seemed, and I was probably one of the smallest guys in the whole flight. I barely weighed 120 pounds. One of them even wrote my name on his note pad with the warning; "Shytle!! I'll remember that name." And he did; he was on my tail for the next several weeks and wouldn't let go.

By the time we were in our barracks it was getting late, probably around ten PM, we were getting hungry since we hadn't eaten since lunch, but no one dared mention food to the sergeant.

It had already been a long day but there were still lots to be done before we would get any sleep this night.

CHAPTER 8

Basic Training Part 2 September–December 1949

It was getting late when we finally got to our barracks with the bedding we had just been issued. I had been somewhat surprised to see that the sheets were white and not OD. We were instructed on how to put the mattress cover on and make a GI bunk.

There was an art to making a bunk with the hospital corners and a dust cover over the pillow with the second blanket. One little wrinkle, one little thing not quite right and everything would wind up on the floor including the mattress; and a mad drill sergeant would be all over you. I was assigned a top bunk and made my bed for the night. Apparently everything was tight enough because my bedding didn't get torn apart and thrown on the floor.

The sergeant with the note pad where he had written my name really gave my bunk a long look, and before moving on, gave me a long ugly look also. It was as if he was saying "you're at the top of my list, Shytle, before this is over you're hide will be mine."

We still hadn't eaten anything since getting off the train. Stomachs were beginning to growl; we were all young and healthy, accustomed to eating a lot and burning a lot of calories daily. Still no one dared mention food; to do so might result in having to clean the latrine floor. We were ordered out into the street with: "fall out and into formation." We had no idea where we might be going that late at night. No one would tell us anything about what the plan might be. We were marched to a nearby "mess hall" and lined up for our first meal at Lackland.

It was awful! It had probably been planned this way and the food was cold leftovers from supper. The entire meal was cold liver and whole boiled potatoes with nothing but water to drink. And when we were ready to carry our trays to the clipper we found out in a hurry that no one wasted food in basic training. Anyone with food left on their tray was very quickly and sternly told to return to the table and finish it off.

Everyone else fell out in the street and waited on these "idiots who tried to waste government money." I was one of the idiots and the sergeant with the note pad stopped right in front of me and wrote something else in the note pad while looking me straight in the eye. Trying to be quiet and inconspicuous didn't work all the time. There was no place to hide from the drill sergeant if you were less than perfect at anything.

We marched back to the barracks and before long were in bed. It had been a long day. I was in a strange place and somewhat scared of those who had been given authority over my every move; I didn't know anyone except Joe Costner and hardly recognized him without his hair.

I didn't have any hair left, and both my arms hurt like blazes from the shots I had been given. Even though I was young, healthy and full of pep and energy, I was completely and physically drained.

Lights out; time to relax and get some needed sleep, and then!!! Ding, Ding, Wham Bam, whistles started blowing, men were hollering “Fire Alarm” “fall out in the street” (with nothing on but drawers).

We milled about for a minute or two and were then ordered into formation for a head count. After a while we were allowed to go back in the barracks and back into bed.

Ten minutes later, another fire drill. This went on for the rest of the night. As soon as we fell asleep we'd have another fire drill.

Reveille was at 6am followed by a half-hour of physical training before breakfast. Other recruits in various phases of training used the squadron mess hall; some were nearing completion of training and some already had their PFC stripe. We were easily recognized as “rainbows” because of our civilian shoes and socks. We could hear the snickering and laughing going on amongst the “veterans”.

As well as I remember, breakfast that first day was very good, and I was starving; so I didn't let the jeering get to me. Besides, I had to be aware of where the drill sergeants were all the time. That was more important than those guys who were trying to make fun of us.

There's no such thing as leisure time at Lackland. Every waking minute is programmed into some activity. We were never out of sight of the watchful eyes of the drill sergeants.

Accordingly, our first day was filled with “in processing”. We filled out forms, answered a thousand questions, and were fitted for and given our "basic issue" of uniforms from head to toe. We had a dental examination, filled out a personal history statement, and completed everything needed for our personal "201" file.And they still found time for close order drill on the parade field teaching us the basics of marching. "Open ranks inspection, about face, left oblique, right oblique, parade rest; and on and on." We were given a serial number and told to memorize it well.

It's amazing how much information we were given: how much we had to learn those first few days. Through it all we were never away from the drill sergeants; from being awakened early in the morning until lights out and "taps" at night, we marched in formation everywhere we went.

They never let up. The constant "get your head out of your ass, Shytle" to "don't you dummies get it" never stopped. We were allowed to go to the PX for necessities, but were told exactly what to buy and nothing else.

We went to the tailor shop for measurements so that the new "class A" uniforms would fit well. Everything we were issued had to be stamped with the initial of our last name followed by the last four digits of our serial number. And, for some reason that I never understood, even though we still didn't have much hair, we got a haircut every seven days. The haircuts cost us forty-five cents out of our once-a-month pay.

I had my first dental appointment to have a tooth filled sometime during the second week. We marched to the dental clinic and I was told to "fall out" and "report to the clerk in the clinic". The sergeant then told me to go back to our barracks when my dental work was complete.

By now he was on someone else and their name was at the top of his list. Maybe my name had been taken off his list completely because he didn't chew on me like he did the first few days.

The rest of the troops had a first aid class to go to and they would meet me back at the barracks following my appointment with the dentist. After the dentist released me I walked out of the dental clinic with an odd feeling. What was I to do? There was no one there to tell me "fall in" or anything. The drill sergeant was not there. Was I actually free to walk by myself, alone, back to the barracks? It was a strange feeling. I started walking back to the barracks and suddenly felt free as a bird that has just been released from being caged up.

The fast pace suited me just fine and I was enjoying everything going on around me. Most of the guys in my flight were fast becoming buddies. There were a few exceptions however. One fellow had been given the important position of "acting squad leader". He was a recruit just like the rest of us but he let that awesome responsibility of acting squad leader get to him.

One morning we were waiting for the order to "fall out"; he came up to me and pointed out that my shoes weren't lined up straight enough under my bunk and proceeded to chew me out about it. I told him where to go and walked outside to where a group of guys were standing around waiting for the order to "fall into formation." I was smoking at the time; trying to learn how to smoke, I guess. A lot of the guys smoked then because it seemed the macho thing to do. He walked up to me, and with his fatigue cap knocked the cigarette out of my mouth.

There was a ring of little rocks that we had painted white and arranged in a circle near the steps of the barracks; I turned and picked up one of the little rocks with the end sticking out from my cupped hand. I made a wide haymaker swing from the left. (I don't think he expected a left-handed response.) I caught him on his right side just about the middle of his rib cage. I hit him hard enough to hear his rib crack, and enough to raise a blood blister on one of my fingers wrapped around the rock.

He didn't go down but he groaned a little while trying to catch his breath. Someone took him back inside and I don't remember him coming back out. I think they took him to sick call where they dressed his busted rib. I was never called in about it, so apparently he called it an accident to the medics; and he never approached me about my shoes or anything else after that incident. It may seem odd that I don't remember his name, but I do remember he was from Alton, Illinois.

As the days and weeks went by the pace never slackened. We spent two weeks on the rifle range firing the M-1 carbine and Colt 45 pistol. We fired the 45 caliber grease gun for familiarization.

There were three levels of qualifying for all weapons. The lowest being "marksman", then "sharpshooter", and the highest was "expert". I qualified as marksman with the pistol and made expert with the carbine. Since the machine gun was for familiarization, we didn't fire it to qualify.

Every Friday, after training was complete, we were all invited to a G.I party. The barracks had to be emptied of everything that could be removed. Everything went outside. The floor would be scrubbed and bleached inch by inch with a GI brush; then it would be rinsed, mopped and allowed to dry before the bunks, footlockers and clothing could be moved back inside. Because of so much cleaning and bleaching the wooden floors were almost white. The GI party, as it was called, was a weekly event.

After about the fourth or fifth week we were given some freedom to move about the base after finishing the day of training. We could go to the PX, spend some time in the day room lounging around, or even go to a refreshment stand, that was located near the squadron orderly room, and have a coke. We could even go to the base theater and see a movie, providing we were back at the barracks in time for bed check.

Still, there was no relaxation on the part of the drill instructors. By now we could sing "it's a long way to Tipperary," or "a rambling wreck from Georgia Tech" while marching with the best of them. The hot weather had cooled somewhat as we went through October.

We had a few forced marches, one in particular that lasted from just after supper till nearly daybreak. We pulled our share of KP duty and guard duty in four-hour tours that lasted throughout the night. We had to guard such things as an empty swimming pool with an empty rifle, or a parade field with nothing to guard but grass. That didn't matter because everything we did was a learning experience.

Every morning, before we marched away for the daily routine of training, someone was scheduled for duty as "barracks guard"; and everyday one of the squadron officers inspected the barracks after the flight had left.

My time for barracks guard duty eventually came and I was left alone to do that duty. While waiting for the inspecting officer to make his way to our barracks I was sitting on the steps looking down the line of buildings.

I finally spotted him walking towards me. My only thoughts were that I had to look sharp and do my flight proud. Competition was keen for “flight of the week” in the 3702nd squadron. The closer he came the shakier I felt. A 2nd Lieutenant was no one to be trifled with.

Then he was upon me. I sat there on the steps and presented him with a salute. Why I didn’t snap to attention on my feet could never be explained. Good Heavens!!! You’d have thought I had spit on the flag. He chewed on me for what seemed to be a long, long time, and threatened me with a court martial and a few other nasty judgements.

Finally he let up and I followed him through the inspection process. As he was about to depart for the next barracks on his list I popped to and snapped the best salute I could muster. He looked at me sort of sternly, returned my salute, and smiled a little before he turned away. He never reported the incident and I presume we passed inspection because I never heard of it again and we were the top rated flight in the squadron for the week.

After six weeks the normal routine for air force recruits at Lackland included a fifteen-hour pass to San Antonio. Our pass would last from Saturday morning at nine AM until midnight. We would have to be back in the barracks for bed check at the end of fifteen hours.

As we were nearing completion of our sixth week all the barracks talk was about the Mexican beauties that walked the streets near the Travelers Hotel in down town San Antonio.

We couldn't wait. This was really big!! The anticipation was electric. And then someone screwed up. The drill sergeant canceled our pass. We spent Saturday on the drill field. This was a letdown of major proportions. We were all sitting around the barracks on Saturday night feeling dejected and grumbling aloud about how we felt.

Before continuing with this little story it needs to be stated that in September 1949 the US Air Force was just barely two years old. In September 1947 President Harry Truman had signed the National Security Act of 1947 creating the Air Force as a separate and equal branch of service with the Army and Navy. Part of that act included integrating all the military services. We were still in what was called "the brown shoe days." Air Force recruits were still being issued OD uniforms. The blue suits would come later.

And, because of the act of 1947 we had two black fellow recruits in our flight. They were both from Chicago. One was called "Jeno", the other I don't remember. When we did our first open rank formation Jeno was the tallest and went to the front of his column. Because he was the tallest, he was our "guide on" bearer whenever we were in formation.

Anyway, back to the story. As we sat around the barracks that Saturday night, dejected, with nothing to do, everyone was thinking about the pass to San Antonio that we didn't get. Those Mexican beauties at the Travelers Hotel were mentioned more than once.

Then to break the monotony, someone suggested that everyone put a quarter in a hat, turn the lights out and everyone would "take matters into their own hand" for the manly relief we all needed. The first to "get it off" would win all the quarters. The plan was agreed to and off went the lights. In what seemed no more time than it took me to think about what I needed to do; someone let out a yell "Ooowee"!! Turn on the lights. There stood Jeno with the evidence in hand that he was the winner.

Our fifteen-hour pass was given to us following our eighth week. The air force shuttle bus picked us up and away we went. Free for fifteen hours. More importantly those Mexican beauties and cold beer were waiting for us at the Travelers Hotel. There were about twenty in our group that checked in to one room at the Travelers.

We all donated a few bucks and someone went for the beer. I remembered something that Mama said to me just before leaving for Charlotte with the recruiter. I still remember the words to this day and they mean more to me now than they did then. She said; "If I ever get word that you have been drinking (alcohol), I'll come to wherever you are and give you a whipping"!! I couldn't resist the cold beer, Mama would never know, so we sat around and had a couple. That's all it took to get the "buzz" on. Get ready for the beauties!

One of the guys brought her up and the line formed outside the room. We were all "overripe" and the line moved at a good pace. We found time to tour the Alamo, and when the time came, caught the bus back to Lackland, We were in the barracks well before bed check.

In early December our thirteen weeks of basic were finished. I had done well enough to make the promotion to PFC and "had the world by the ass". Sometime during the first few weeks we were given a battery of aptitude tests. Results of the tests, coupled with a list of career preferences we had indicated on one of the questionnaires, determined which career field we would be assigned.

I had indicated that I wanted any career field that would lead to a flying job. I was very pleased when orders came through for me to attend the radio operator course at Fort Monmouth, New Jersey. Every aircraft in the Air Force inventory carried a radio operator with the exception of fighter planes.

I said goodbye to all the chums in my flight and caught the bus out of San Antonio with a delay-en-route to Kings Mountain on my way to New Jersey. I had done a lot of growing up in a short period of time. The young boy that had left the Park Yarn cotton mill village was a completely different person. I was hard enough to stand up with the best of them and hold my ground. The 120 pound kid that left the Park Yarn three months earlier was now a 140 pound man. I felt that the world was mine for the taking and I intended to make the best of it.

The two drill sergeants that seemed so tough were human after all and during the last week or so were actually approachable on the same level. They had taught us well and following our graduation parade they were presented an award for having the top rated flight.

Basic training had been an unforgettable experience, but now a new and different adventure was waiting for me in New Jersey. I could hardly wait to get started.

CHAPTER 9

Radio School-Ft Monmouth NJ Dec. 1949–Sept. 1950

The bus ride home from basic training was uneventful. A change of buses in New Orleans resulted in two hours delay, but that didn't allow me enough time to do any touring so I didn't leave the bus terminal except to take a short walk outside and down the street for a coke. The same for Atlanta and before long we were in Spartanburg, then Gaffney, and Kings Mountain.

Daddy picked me up at the bus terminal and within minutes we were home with a big hug and welcome home from Mama. When I left for basic training in September we were living at the Park Yarn. Daddy had been building a new house west of town on Shelby road; it was completed sometime during my absence and they moved into the new place in October, Faye was still at home and in school, but because they now lived on the west side of town she was transferred from Kings Mountain to Beth Ware High School when they moved.

He had started the house over a year earlier when he and Rob Pearson bought side by side building lots. Daddy's lot faced highway 74 on Elam Road.

I had a little over a week to spend at home before leaving for New Jersey, and don't remember very much about where the time went. I went back to the Park Yarn several times to see some of the boys I grew up with, and spent some time with Steve and Dale Gantt. There was at least one visit to Park Grace elementary to see some of the teachers. Nothing seemed the same; except for my family the whole week was a big bore. It was a strange experience; like I was somewhere I didn't belong. I was constantly fidgety and restless; sleep didn't come easy. Until the day I left I could never figure it out.

Coot came home from Charlotte over the weekend, and Mama had a big Sunday dinner for the whole family. It would be a long time before we would all be together again.

I had only been home a day or two when Mama introduced me to a young girl who attended her church and we went out a couple times. Nothing remarkable; I don't even remember her name, and never saw her again after leaving for radio school at Fort Monmouth.

Things didn't seem the same in Kings Mountain; and I had only been gone a little over three months. I was anxious to be out of there and on my way again. Apparently some of the wanderlust that afflicted Uncle Taylor ran in my veins too. There never was even a twinge of homesickness during basic training. I loved my family, but didn't miss anyone or anything after leaving.

New places and what was beyond the next curve was what excited me. I was looking forward to finishing radio school, and with some luck, being assigned to a B-29 outfit.

When I left, it was just me, my duffel bag and a ticket that read: Kings Mountain, NC to New York City. Another ticket read: New York City to Red Bank, New Jersey. Mama looked a little sad and maybe a little tearful, but she was happy for me. Faye was ok, and Daddy just said "son, you be careful." He took me to the bus station and I was on my way again. I felt good. The strange feeling that had plagued me all week was completely gone.

The trip to New York didn't take as long as I expected. There were stops with delays in Washington and Philadelphia. But again, I didn't venture far from the bus station.

I had a strange experience in the station after arriving in New York. We had been warned about guys like him; but a guy started talking to me while I was waiting for the transfer bus to take me back into New Jersey. He wasn't in uniform; but told me he was in the army stationed at Fort Dix, which was in New Jersey also. He had brought a friend to the bus station and was on his way back to Fort Dix. He offered me a ride and told me he would take me right to the main gate at Fort Monmouth. To drop me off there wouldn't be very much out of his way. I hesitated, but after talking with him a while, I accepted his offer. He seemed nice enough.

Looking back, it could have been a dangerous thing to do, but if he was "not of my orientation" he never made a move in the wrong direction. He may have sensed that I might be the wrong target. He did as he said he would; I thanked him and bade him goodbye at the Ft. Monmouth front gate. Several weeks later he came by to see me. He had a lady with him, a real beauty that he introduced simply as a friend. This time he was in an Army uniform and had 1st Lieutenant bars on his shoulders. He said he just wanted to see how I was doing in radio school, he wished me luck, I saluted him, and he drove off. I never saw him again; and don't remember who he was or even where he was from.

After reporting in, I was assigned to I Company, Signal Training Regiment. The barracks were old World War II single level, open bay type. Everything was contained at company level; that is, the company had its own mess hall, supply room, and company Headquarters with a commander and first sergeant.

It was a good organization. Anything I needed was handled locally. Bedding was issued by the company supply sergeant; Everything we needed to know was posted on the bulletin board, the first sergeant was always available if needed, and we had our own company cooks. The mess hall was small and the food was good.

Training started right away. Classes were six hours a day, Monday through Friday. We had weeknights and weekends free. Basic training was over; things were a lot looser at Fort Monmouth than they had been at Lackland.

A typical day of training would begin with reveille at six am. We had half an hour to shave, shower, and take care of any other toiletries; we dressed in fatigues and fell out for roll call, inspection and a half-hour of physical training. We then went to breakfast. After breakfast, we went back to the barracks to make our beds and get our area ready for inspection. We were in formation at eight ready to march to the school. After three hours in class we marched back to the company area for lunch. After lunch we again marched to class; and after another three hours we marched back to the company area and stayed in formation for retreat ceremonies.

Every time we marched to and from class an army band played marching tunes for us. Not just over a loudspeaker, but a live band. At retreat the National Anthem would be played, again by the live band; and our flag would be lowered.

Retreat always moved me emotionally. Our flag has always made me swell with pride; I'm probably overly sentimental where our flag is concerned, but that is the way it is. After retreat we were dismissed. We would normally go directly to the chow hall for supper. Some of the best GI food I ever ate was in that small company mess at Fort Monmouth. Following supper we were free to do as we pleased.

One of the most popular places on the base was a beer garden behind the Post Exchange. The state of New Jersey didn't allow alcoholic beverages to be served to anyone under twenty-one; but if that law applied to the students at Fort Monmouth, it wasn't enforced. A large pitcher of draft Reingold was cheap, so we took advantage of that.

The course I had been assigned to was to last about thirty-six weeks. First we started learning the Morse alphabet and after that it was practice and more practice. We sat at a "position" with a machine called a "mill." The machine looked like a typewriter, but didn't have an lower case. Every letter and number was in caps.

We had a set of earphones and a sending key. The sending key was positioned on the right; I was left-handed and had to improvise by attaching a key to a board and extend the lines over to the key mounted on the right side; then connect the lines to the contact points. This worked out ok and I didn't have any problems learning to send the di-di-dum-dum-di-di.

To receive Morse signals, a tape constantly fed five letter groups into the earphones at speeds ranging from five words (or five letter groups) per minute to twenty-eight groups per minute.

After learning the alphabet we started at the slow speed of five groups per minute until proficient at that speed. After classes were over for the day we turned in the papers that had been typed from the tapes. Once a student proved himself to be proficient at five groups per minute he advanced to seven, then to nine, and on and on until graduation at twenty-five receiving and twenty sending with the hand key.

My progression was normal until I got stuck at sixteen groups per minute. Getting past sixteen was a tough nut to crack. Then an odd thing happened. Suddenly one day, a strange phenomenon occurred. I stopped thinking about what I was hearing over the earphones. My fingers were typing about three or four characters behind the signals that were coming out of the phones; it was like the information was being by-passed around my brain. I could actually carry on a conversation and receive messages simultaneously. The code went straight from the earphones to my fingers.

From that point on, it wasn't long before I passed on eighteen, then twenty and faster. Sending was just a matter of rhythm with a wrist action rather than tapping with fingers; and it wasn't long before my sending speed was up to the required twenty groups per minute.

Classes weren't limited to Morse code. We had field trips using communications equipment; learning how to tune and operate the various sets. We had classes on radio procedure, international signals, joint Army,Navy, and Allied procedures, we learned about antennas, wave propagation, fundamentals of radio maintenance, Q signals and Z signals; three letter groups that meant specific texts, or asked a specific question. We learned military radio networking procedures and lots more.

Having arrived at Fort Monmouth around the middle of December, I spent my first Christmas away from home in New Jersey. It was wintertime and cold but we marched to classes no matter what the weather. We had snow, but it wasn't as severe as I had been led to believe. The worst was the cold and rainy days.

On Christmas day the mess hall was decorated real pretty with Christmas music piped in over the "bitch box." Christmas dinner was special. The cooks worked hard to make us feel good about being there over the holidays. The meal included everything traditional for Christmas.

The term "bitch box" probably needs to be defined for anyone reading this that may not know. A two-way sound system was set up between the orderly room, supply room, mess hall, barracks, and day room so that the first sergeant or company clerk could talk to anyone he needed without leaving the orderly room. To reply, all you had to do was press a little lever and speak into the box, commonly known to all GIs as a "bitch box."

Fort Monmouth was located near the Jersey shore. The resort town of Long Branch, just a few miles from Fort Monmouth, was right on the beach, and girls from all over the area including Philadelphia, North Jersey, even the boroughs of New York would flock to the beaches of Long Branch and Asbury Park as soon as the weather turned warm. Atlantic City was seventy miles south; but we never went there because of the distance. Besides, there was plenty to see and do at Long Branch. The beaches were closed in winter, but there were other activities off post that kept our interest during off duty hours.

On occasion we would catch the commuter train from Red Bank to New York City. It didn't take long to get to Manhattan. The Soldier and Sailor's club was located on Lexington Avenue, not too far from 42nd Street and Broadway.We would go as a group of five or six and check in the club for the night. The Soldier and Sailor's club was managed by the USO; they had all kinds of programs. There was an Army port nearby, and the Brooklyn Navy yard wasn't too far away, so the club had plenty of customers.

Although I didn't drink anything stronger than a few beers, some of the guys would drink the hard stuff. That's what they were there for, and, of course, to try and meet a girl. The legal drinking age in New York was eighteen as opposed to twenty-one in New Jersey.

We would hit the bars or maybe ride the subway, or just walk up 42nd Street taking in the sights. There were girls at the club; but I don't ever remember being invited to go home with one of them. Neither did any of my buddies. After spending the night, we would catch the commuter back to Red Bank.

Once the cold of winter was passed, Mama and my older sister "Coot" made plans to come to New Jersey. It was sometime in April that I met them at the bus terminal in New York.

They checked in to the New Dixie hotel, right in the heart of Manhattan; we took in the sights and went to the top of the Empire State Building. We walked around Times Square and they did a little shopping. The three of us caught the commuter train back to Red Bank and Fort Monmouth; they stayed overnight in the guest house and caught the bus to go back home the next afternoon. Neither of them had ever been to New York and they enjoyed the trip a great deal.

There was one restaurant/bar in Long Branch that would serve us beer; it was an Italian place that had big brick ovens. Using a long handled spatula or shovel they would cook something they called "tomato pie". It was their specialty. We know it today as "pizza." I had never seen anything like it, or even heard of it; but we never grew tired of it from plain to all dressed up; and loved it. Tomato pie was especially good with a cold bottle of Hamm's beer.

Springtime arrived and the weather turned warmer. Radio school was progressing at a normal pace for me. Everything about the course was interesting and I was learning a lot about military communications.

It must have been in May; I was strolling along the boardwalk on Long Branch Beach with a few friends. We had a hot dog and coke and they gave us all a raffle ticket that put our names in the hat for a chance to win an Emerson console television set.

We didn't even have a television at home when I left Kings Mountain. There was only one station in piedmont North Carolina anyway. That was WBTV in Charlotte, and they hadn't been on the air very long. Programming was very limited; most of the time all you could see was a test pattern. Very few people had television sets in Kings Mountain during that time.

We all had raffle tickets, and after walking the beach for a while we went back to the hot dog stand for the drawing. They had been giving away the tickets for several weeks, and a big crowd of people were there, some with a handful of raffle tickets they had collected. I had one ticket and just happened by chance to be there on the beach the day of the drawing.

They drew my number!! I walked to the platform, and showed the man the winning ticket. They rolled out a huge box on a dolly and gave it to me. I didn't know what to do with it but luckily the man that had promoted the give-away offered to take the box to the Railway Express Agency in Red Bank for me. I thanked him very much and took him up on his offer. We drove to the train depot, addressed the box to Mama and Daddy, and sent it home. Television sets didn't last very long back then, but four years later they were still watching it; and it was still operational.

Soon after I got to Fort Monmouth one of the first students I met was an Italian guy from one of the New York boroughs. His name was DeSantis and we grew to be good friends. I don't know why, but I never went home with him on weekends. He invited me several times, but I always came up with an excuse not to go. He talked with me about the Italian lifestyle in New York.

As spring wore on and the weather became warmer we spent more time girl watching on Long Branch Beach. I met a pretty young lady, and before the weekend was over I had her home address and made plans to go see her in Hasbrouck Heights, a town across the river from Manhattan in New Jersey. Her name was Gloria Iovine, and she was Italian. When I mentioned her to DeSantis he warned me against trying anything with her. He said, "don't even try to kiss her unless you know she wants to kiss you. You could be in big trouble with her parents if you get out of line with her at all."

I went to see her several times. We walked from her home to the movies and afterwards walked straight back to her home. She came back to Long Branch Beach a time or two, and we would meet; but I never did get out of line with her. I played the polite "southern gentleman" always. Still, I enjoyed being with her and we had some good times.

After leaving Fort Monmouth we wrote for a while and she sent me some cookies while I was in Korea. And then it ended. I never heard from her again.

One day in June the company commander called the whole company into the orderly room for a briefing. He informed us that the North Koreans had invaded the South and that the US would be committed to help them. We were expected to be at war shortly.

Summer came and went; and in September my classes were over. I had passed all the proficiency tests and was receiving Morse code at a speed of twenty-eight and sending twenty on the hand key. I knew in detail every HF, VHF, and UHF radio set used by the army and air force. I knew radio procedures used by every allied nation and knew all about antennas and the effects of sun spot activity.

I was ready to leave the Army Signal School, get back on duty with the Air Force and do some flying.

When orders came I was re-assigned to the 81st Fighter Interceptor Wing at Larson Air Force Base, Moses Lake, Washington. Then I realized that fighter planes don't carry a radio operator as a crewman. There was nothing I could do but accept the orders and make the best of the assignment.

A good friend, Billy Martin, from Louisiana had orders to go to George Air Force Base in California. He would later be assigned to the 3rd Bomb Wing in Korea. The 3rd flew B-26 medium bombers. Billy and his crew were lost on a night mission shooting up trains. I would later be based with a fellow who served with the 3rd while Billy was there. His name was Thomas. It was reported that Thomas made the statement that "he would rather shoot up trains than to date Marilyn Monroe."

The story was told that she wrote to him and offered to go with him on a date when he returned home. He made it home safely. Another fellow student was assigned to a B-29 heavy bomb wing on Okinawa flying missions over Korea. On a mission over the north he jumped from his damaged aircraft, and was reported to have been captured. He was never heard from again.

Another friend who finished school with me at Fort Monmouth was also assigned to the 81st at Moses Lake. He was from Owensboro, Kentucky and we made plans to meet at the train station in Cincinnati and travel to Washington State together.

One of the guys bought a 1947 Plymouth at a used car lot in Red Bank, and after graduation he planned to drive home to Georgia. He offered me a ride home if I would share expenses with him and I gladly accepted. We had a third guy with us that we would drop off somewhere in Virginia.

I had a delay-en-route and my reporting date to Larson Air Force Base was about three weeks away. That gave me about two weeks to spend at home.

Before clearing the post, I was given my travel orders, a train ticket to Moses Lake, and a stack of government meal tickets that would cover three meals a day for three weeks with lots to spare.

There were no interstate highways and our route took us through many small towns. We probably didn't average much over 35 or 40 miles per hour. We cleared the base in mid afternoon; and had to cross the Delaware River on a ferryboat; that delayed us for a while. We traveled all night before reaching Kings Mountain. I slept some, but not much.

In order not to delay my friend, he dropped me off at a service station near the overhead bridge in Kings Mountain and Daddy picked me up there.

The next two weeks are a foggy mystery. I remember very little about the time spent at home. I have searched my memory and can't come up with anything much. Ebb Oliver was at home part of the time and we went out double dating once or twice. He either had a car or borrowed one from his brother, so we had some transportation.

I can't remember anything about the girl I went with or anything that happened. Did I make any time with her? I don't know. She must not have been very impressive. Thomas Wolfe said, "you can't go back home", and he was right. Kings Mountain wasn't my home anymore. My old friends weren't friendly; and nothing held my interest. I was bored and anxious to be on my way. The old restless feeling was there once again, but this time I knew what it was all about.

Not soon enough it was time to go. I called my friend in Owensboro, Kentucky and told him when I would be arriving in Cincinnati and the train I would be on. In order to go through Cincinnati, I had to go to Spartanburg to catch the train that would go through Asheville, Knoxville, Louisville, and then to Cincinnati. Daddy took me to Spartanburg. Mama and Faye went along, and before the train departed, I used some of my meal tickets and treated them all to lunch on the government. Then I was on my way again.

For some reason, I can't remember my friend's name. We rode across the country together; and spent time running around together after we got to Moses Lake; we even bought a car together; but I just can't remember who he was. I'll detail some the times we had together in Washington State later.

Anyway, he met me in Cincinnati as planned, and we were off to Chicago. We changed trains in Chicago; and changed stations as well. After catching a cab to the other station and a long delay we were off again; heading west across Minnesota, North Dakota, Montana, the panhandle of Idaho, and into Washington State.

We had stops with enough time to get off the train several times. We had a particularly long delay in Billings, Montana; and we went to a café' near the depot and had a meal. I remember thinking about how beautiful Montana was. We had crossed some mountains already, but I was to find out later that the highest mountains were in front of us.

We had another short stop in Butte, where we started talking with a young lady and the train almost left us. We traveled on towards central Washington. The train stopped at the small town of Othello; we were told that we were to get off there and check in with the station manager.

We did so and were told that another train would take us from Othello to Moses Lake. However, it would be several, maybe three or four hours before our train would be leaving.

Othello was a typical old western cowboy town with one wide street. Most of the buildings had a false front. The town might have had a population of forty or fifty people. It reminded me of main street in a Tex Ritter movie. The depot was on the edge of town up a small incline.

We had some time on our hands, so we walked down to check out the town. It had a movie theater, a few stores and saloons and a café'. That was it. There was a small café' in the depot, so we decided to have lunch there. They didn't have any knowledge of what government meal tickets were and seemed reluctant to take them as payment for the meal; but after we explained the details they agreed to accept them. I must have been hungry because I recall that I ate the best roast beef, potatoes and gravy that I ever tasted.

Our train finally arrived. It wasn't a train for passengers, but a freight train. They loaded us and our duffel in the caboose and away we went, bouncing across the central Washington desert.

There was absolutely nothing to be seen but small scrub brush, probably sage. There were no roads, no houses or even any livestock to be seen. It was like that for about twenty miles; the train was moving slow causing the distance to seem more like fifty miles.

The caboose had an observation port in its center with windows all around, so we climbed onto the elevated bench to see where we were headed. The first thing we spotted in the distance was a tall grain elevator and eventually we could see the buildings of another small town.

Soon we rolled into Moses Lake. Although we couldn't see anything indicating it was there, nearby was the Air Force Base that would be home for the next thirteen months.

CHAPTER 10

Larson Air Force Base
September 1950–November 1951

When we arrived at the railway express agency in Moses Lake we had to make a call out to the air base so they could send someone to pick us up. The railway leading into Moses Lake from the main east-west route of the Great Northern Railway was nothing more than a spur from Othello to Moses Lake. The town had no regular passenger service. Moses Lake was another small town in central Washington with a population of around 400, maybe a few more. There were no military representatives anywhere in town.

Eventually a weapons carrier came to get us. We threw our gear in the back and the driver gave us the scenic tour which was through the center of town and straight out the other side and out to the base. Other than the grain elevator there were no other buildings above ground level, no housing developments or anything else. We were either downtown or out in the countryside. Moses Lake and the surrounding region were a part of the Columbia River basin. The mighty Columbia had its headwaters somewhere in the northern Cascade Mountains and snaked its way south through central Washington approximately thirty five miles west of the Town of Moses Lake. A huge diversion canal to bring water to the basin was currently under construction. The planners were going to convert the high plains to rich agricultural country.

The countryside was rolling prairie; some sagebrush flats, but most was already under cultivation, probably wheat or some other grain. The farmers, in all likelihood, already had some kind of irrigation in service but the extra water the diversion canal would bring to the region would be a welcome supplement to any existing irrigation systems. Off to the west, in the distance, we could see a big snow capped mountain; just outside town we could see parts of the lake for which the town was named.

It wasn't long before we turned off the highway and approached the main gate to the air base; and after checking our orders, the main gate security guy directed us to the 81st Communications Squadron. Our driver dropped us by a security checkpoint at the entrance to the squadron orderly room. The orderly room was located inside a fenced area that looked like a maximum-security prison. The fence surrounding the building was at least ten feet tall with barbed concertino wire rolled on top and a well armed and alert security guard was on duty at the only entrance.

It immediately became obvious that something highly classified was kept within the secured compound. It wasn't long before we learned the reason for the added security was because a crypto room was in back of the orderly room along with the base switchboard and teletype room.

Crypto is a process whereby messages with a security classification are coded before being sent out over the airways or unsecured land-lines; upon arrival at their destination the messages are then decoded by the receiving addressee. The crypto machines and processes were highly classified and very well protected wherever they were used.

While learning to set up field communications equipment at the signal school, we were required to encode and decode messages on a small crypto machine; and even that process was classified. Because the authenticator tables changed daily and even hourly it was hard to understand how anyone could break our code. The truth is they probably didn't. Although I never came close to entering the crypto room because of the security surrounding that area I knew the coding procedures for that machine were much more complicated than the little field set we used at Fort Monmouth. Consequently the security was much tighter with a shoot to kill order for anyone trying to breach the protected area.

We were checked through security without any problems, but our ID and orders were thoroughly screened before we were cleared, and even then we had to have an armed escort take us to the orderly room

A clerk greeted us with the sign in book and then took us directly to the First Sergeant; and after checking our orders again the first sergeant took us to report to the commander. We followed military customs. After being asked to enter, we walked stiffly at attention into the commander's office. I saluted: "PFC Shytle reporting for duty, sir!", then the other guy reported in. We were placed at ease and went from attention to parade rest.

The commander Lieutenant Thomas J. Cavanaugh, a young Errol Flynn look-a-like with a little mustache welcomed us to the squadron. He was sharp! And he wore a pair of navigator wings with several rows of ribbons indicating he had flown combat missions in the European theater.

I never knew if he was one of the reserve officers who had left the air force and had been recalled to active duty because of Korea, or if he had stayed in the air force following the war. He gave the impression that he held a regular commission rather than a reserve officer that had been recalled. He was the only commissioned officer assigned to the communications squadron.

Following the introductions he gave us a short lecture about our responsibilities and the mission of the 81st Fighter Interceptor Wing, and the role of the communications squadron.

After we were dismissed and released back to the first sergeant we were given an additional lecture relating to squadron duties. A clerk took us to our barracks and supply room to get our bedding. In addition to the bedding we were issued a parka with a furry hood. September was half gone and severe winter weather could be expected any time according to the clerk who was escorting us. The flat to rolling landscape was an invitation for the wind, snow, and cold to come howling out of the Cascades that were to our northwest.

After being assigned a bunk we went back to the orderly room and processed in. The first sergeant gave us another lecture relating to squadron standards of conduct and dress. By the time the latest remarks were passed on to us we knew exactly what was expected of us; our indoctrination into the squadron was over. Following his speech were given a meal pass and class "A" pass that allowed us to leave the base anytime we were off duty. We were also issued a security ID that would allow us to come and go freely through the security check point without having to wait on a clearance from the first sergeant and an armed escort.

The meal pass was used to get into the mess hall. Other units of the "Air Base Group" also ate at the mess hall we were to use. The organizational structure of the wing, in addition to the Fighter Group, included the "Air Base Group" which included our squadron, along with base security, air installations, and food service squadrons.

There was also a WAF (Women's Air Force) unit. The WAFs performed duty for the medics as trained medical technicians, nurse assistances and dental technicians, and administrative duties for other units around the base. The communications squadron had a few WAF working as switchboard operators.

The other groups were the aircraft maintenance, supply, and medical group. Other supporting people included weather, special services and Chaplains. Aircraft control operations (control tower) was the responsibility of the Air and Airways Communications Service. They took care of all flight line operations relating to air traffic control and instrument landing systems including ground control approach.

Our mess hall fed everyone assigned to the air base group and in addition to the regular daytime meals they also served what we called "midnight chow" for those people on duty at night. The medics and base security had people on duty twenty-four hours a day. So did the communications squadron that had teletype, telephone switchboard, radio shack, and crypto people on duty around the clock. Every squadron on base had a CQ on duty at night manning the orderly room after the commander, first sergeant, and administrative clerks left for the day. CQ stands for "charge of quarters."

The barracks were tarpaper shacks shaped like an H. Three legs were open bay living quarters, the fourth a supply room. The middle was a latrine and shower room. For heating, each bay had a large pot-belly stove and there was a coal bin located behind the barracks. It was up to the guys that lived there to see that a fire was burning in the stoves. I woke up lots of mornings in a freezing cold barracks; but, because I lived there too, it was as much my responsibility to see that the stoves were fed as anyone else. It was a little primitive for the "modern day" newly created air force, but Larson hadn't been operational very long.

The 81st was in the Northwest US as part of the western air defense force. Its mission was to defend that part of the country in the event it became necessary. The first thing I noticed was the slick F-86 fighter jets lined up on the runway. Next to the propeller driven World War II vintage P-51 Mustang (later designated the F-51) the F-86 was the sharpest fighter we had. In 1950 it was the most outstanding fighter plane in the USAF inventory. The MIG 15 was the only fighter in the world that could compare with its flight characteristics. The Russian Mig-15 could out maneuver the F-86 at certain altitudes, and it may have had a faster climb ratio, but USAF pilots flying the

F-86 in Korea were shooting down the Migs at a ratio of better than 10 to 1 even though they were strapped with limited time for actual air to air combat because of fuel limitations. All the MIGs had to do were take off from their sanctuary just inside China and climb to altitude. The F-86s on the other hand had to burn a lot of their fuel just getting to "MIG Alley".

Special Services at Larson opened a theater; there was an NCO club and a hobby shop of sorts, but not much more. I think a bowling alley opened up sometime after I arrived. That was about it for off duty entertainment on base.

There wasn't much locally off base either. I don't think there were any available young ladies living in Moses Lake. The town of Ephrata, twenty miles northwest of the base had a few bars, but not much else. Soap Lake, five miles from Ephrata had an elk's club (or was it a moose club?- I don't remember) that had a dance on Saturday night. There were a few ranch girls at the dance, but competition was fierce. The local cowboys already had a rope on most of the available girls.

Not long after arriving at Larson my friend from Kentucky and I bought an old 1932 Chevrolet for $20.00. It wasn't much, but it was dependable and would get us to the Ephrata bars and Soap Lake dances. We had to park it off base (across the main road to Moses Lake) because we didn't have insurance. Liability insurance was required to get a base sticker. Besides, we didn't even have a driver's license.

We didn't have anti-freeze, so when we went to Ephrata we would fill up some water jugs we kept in the back.

We crossed a creek between Ephrata and the base; and would stop at the creek to fill up the water jugs on our way back to the base at night. When we parked the car, we would open the pet-cock under the engine and drain all the water to keep the motor from freezing. The next time we drove to town we would close the pet-cock, fill the radiator from the jugs, and take off. On the way back we would repeat the process.

That old car had a heater that used gas from the car's fuel tank. I don't know how it ignited, but it would heat up and blow hot air as soon as it was turned on. We let someone borrow it one day to drive to town. He came back without it because he blew the engine. He said that when the engine blew up it: "layed one of the cylinders out on the fender." That was the end of the 32' Chevvy.

Soon afterwards we bought a 1936 Ford for $50.00. It didn't last very long either. Again, we let someone borrow it. He was on the way back from Ephrata and a band of wild horses ran across the road in front of him. He rolled the car, not just once, but two times up a hill and two times back down landing upright on its wheels, but it was a total loss. The Ford had been with us less than a month.

At least, just once before the guy crashed it, I remember going to Soap Lake one Saturday night and took a ranch girl home following the dance.

My duties as a radio operator were carried out in the radio shack that was just a small building behind the orderly room; but still within the secured area. For security purposes, the radio operator on duty had to wear a .45 Colt automatic pistol, and there was a loaded grease gun hanging on the wall. We had standard high frequency equipment and were part of a radio network of stations all over the west. We didn't have UHF or VHF capability. Those frequencies were used in the control tower and radar site.

We had six or seven radiomen assigned to the squadron. A real nice guy, SSgt Peterson, was the NCO in charge of radio operations. He reminded me of the movie star Jeff Chandler. He wasn't an old vet from World War II, but was probably in his mid twenties and had a tour in Alaska behind him. He made our duty schedule and we were directly responsible to him.

The town of Moses Lake had a bell telephone switchboard that relayed all commercial phone calls to Larson through our switchboard.

Although I never met her, there was a switchboard operator in Moses Lake that used to call while we both were on duty late at night; I in the radio shack and she at her switchboard in Moses Lake. She sounded so beautiful, and used to sing to me over the phone; "I can't give you anything but love,,,baby" I was young and easily excitable over anything like that. It isn't very hard to remember that kind of stuff. She eventually hooked up with Sgt. Peterson and they were married. I have no idea what happened to either of them. His enlistment ended and he left the air force.

Although President Harry Truman had integrated all the military services in 1947 we had very few black troops at Larson. We only had one black guy who was from California assigned to the communications squadron. He worked in the teletype room located directly behind the switchboard.

The base switchboard was located between the orderly room and teletype room; rumors started flying that this guy had been seen close to a white female WAF switchboard operator. News reached the first sergeant about the liaison between the two. They were both pulling night duty when they were seen together, and he was called in for a talk with the first sergeant. He was ordered to terminate the association immediately. Their duty schedules were changed to different hours, but apparently the relationship continued and he was called in to talk with the squadron commander.

For a while that seemed to have ended it; however the black guy put in for a furlough and went home to California. The WAF, from somewhere back east, had also gone on leave.

At the time, an enlisted person had to ask for, and receive, permission from his commander to get married. This was done to allow the Chaplain an opportunity to council the lovers before they made the big step. While the guy was on leave, he sent the commander a telegram requesting permission to be married. He was refused, and we never saw him again. Word circulated that he was transferred to a base in California even before reporting back to Larson; and the WAF was transferred to a base unknown to anyone as soon as she returned to Larson. Nothing was heard from either of them again.

In the fall of 1950 World War II hadn't been over too many years, the Korean War was heating up, and a lot of World War II guys were being recalled to active duty. Following the war the air force had an excess number of good pilots and RIF'd a lot of them. RIF is a military abbreviation meaning "Reduction in Force." Some of these people were given the opportunity to revert to enlisted status if they wanted to stay active. A lot did. They were given the rank of Master Sergeant with a date of rank being the date they were commissioned, or completed flight training.

Later, during my career in the USAF I served with a Master Sergeant. who had flown a glider into Normany on D-day; and another, a Technical Sergeant. (he had been busted down one stripe) was a P-38 fighter pilot. Both were decorated combat pilots.

And, several years later, when we were stationed in France Master Sergeant Ray Reed; a RIF'd bombardier on a B-17 during the war, was our neighbor at the housing project where we lived; he told me about one of his missions over Germany. On this particular mission he was flying in the middle element when a German fighter collided with one of the lead planes above and in front of his airplane. One of the waist gunners tumbled out of the crippled plane, and was reaching for his parachute that was trailing behind him as he sailed past Ray's window. He was falling too fast to reach the chute. On another mission he saw a crewman falling past him with his parachute on fire.

One guy at Larson, a Corporal, who had also been busted from MSgt. wore command pilot wings. To wear wings with a star and wreath meant he had thousands of flying hours behind him. He had survived the war as a B-24 bomber pilot and had commanded one of the lead groups on the famous Ploesti, Romania oil field raids. Another Corporal, that had been a POW for several years in Germany, had been hurt during his bailout; his injuries were worsened by the harsh treatment he received while imprisoned, and as a result he couldn't eat anything solid. He lived on fruit juice, tomato soup and baby food. Had the medics known the seriousness of his condition they would have recommended a medical discharge, but he kept it from them so that he could continue to serve. Although he would never be able to fly again he loved the air force.

These people were my heroes. They still are. Having known such men I find it very offensive to hear someone refer to a football player who scored the winning touchdown as "hero."

After arriving at Larson I fell in with a buck sergeant, Robert K. Monion, who had been recalled to active duty. He had left the military and returned to his home in Santa Monica, California following the war. He was one of the radio operators that had been recalled to serve a specific amount of time so that someone else with the same air force specialty code could be sent to Korea.

The day I was promoted to Corporal Monion said, "let's go; you and I have somewhere we need to go." It wasn't far from our barracks to the NCO club, an old building that had been converted into a club with a bar on one end, a few tables and chairs, a place to dance, and a stage on the other end.

Off we went to the club. A Corporal was considered an NCO at the time, so I could now "join the club" so to speak. After I got my club card we walked up to the bar and Mnion ordered two shots of vodka. "Down the hatch" they went. That was the beginning of my first affair with vodka and with very few exceptions, the last.

This was on Friday, and every Friday we had "sheet change day." We folded our mattresses and took the sheets and pillowcase that we had been using the past week to the supply room for clean ones. When Monion and I left for the club my bunk hadn't been re-made after changing the sheets. That was a mistake.

I don't remember leaving the NCO club and don't remember walking back to the barracks; but I woke up the next morning looking down at the floor through the wire mesh springs on my bunk. There was a big pile of puke on the floor directly under my face and there were wire mesh marks on my face all day, not to mention a bad hangover that plagued me until the next day. My mattress, blankets, pillow, and clean linen had been flung to the floor near my bunk. That was my initiation to the NCO ranks.

September 30th rolled around and it was payday! This was my first payday at Larson and it was snowing like crazy. This would be a good time to try the parka that had been issued to me during in-processing. I put the parka on, headed to the orderly room and took my place at the end of the pay line.

There was a strict procedure to follow at pay call. First, when you reached the front of the line, you had to sign the pay roster. You had to sign within the block opposite your name and the amount of pay you were to receive. If, when signing, you touched a line with any part of your signature, you would be red-lined and have to wait until a new roster arrived. It would be several days before you could be paid. After signing you walked up to the pay table, reported to the officer with the money. A salute and "PFC Shytle reporting for pay, Sir!" If all went well, the Sergeant sitting beside the officer would state the amount of money that was due; the officer counted out the money, and laid it down. You picked it up, stepped back one pace, saluted, did a left face, and walked away; temporarily a rich man!

On this payday I wasn't red-lined, but rejected by the paymaster, who happened to be Lt. Cavanaugh. When I reported for pay he looked up at me and said; "What the hell are you wearing that parka for?" I replied "Sir, it's snowing like the dickens out there." He said; "Get your ass out of here and pull the dam thing off, winter isn't here yet." He was right. Winter hadn't arrived yet. But it did, and it was as he said it would be. That first snowstorm in September was mild compared to what was yet to come. It was snowy and cold all winter long. I later got back in the pay line with just my fatigues on and didn't have any problem getting my $72.00 that would have to last me a whole month. Next payday I would get a few extra bucks because of the Corporal stripes.

After being paid we would generally go to the PX to get toiletries, shoeshine gear, and other items we would need over the next thirty days. Those who smoked bought enough cigarettes to last until next payday.

Sherman Dillon was another fellow at Larson that was a good friend. He was originally from Ohio, but his father was diagnosed with tuberculosis and his folks moved to Prescott, Arizona on recommendation of his doctor. The high and dry Arizona climate was supposed to be a tonic for those with tuberculosis. Sherman was a big man whose people originally came from Norway. We called him "Oley."

When Oley enlisted in the air force he left behind a 1936 Ford "hot rod" he had worked on, and when his folks moved to Arizona, one of his parents drove the car to Prescott. He asked if I would go with him to Arizona, there we would pick up his car and drive it back to Washington State. It sounded like another adventure, so I gladly agreed to go with him.

We both had some leave time coming and applied for a ten day furlough. We packed an AWOL bag and caught a flight over to McChord Air Force Base in Tacoma, and from there got a hop in an Oregon Air National Guard C-47 to Hamilton Air Force Base that was just a short drive north of San Francisco. We were stuck there; prospects didn't look good for a hop to Tucson or Phoenix, so we started hitch-hiking south.

We had little trouble getting rides; we were in uniform and in 1950 men in uniform hitch-hiked all over the country. Soon we made our way to Los Angeles and from there over to Wickenburg, Arizona.

We got stuck again in Wickenburg, and rode a bus from there to Prescott. His folks set us up in a camper-trailer because we had planned to stay in Prescott for four days and leave there in time to make the trip north to Moses Lake before our leave was over. By using the trailer we could come and go without disturbing Oley's folks.

His old "hot rod" was in good condition and we were running around Prescott in no time. On our very first night there we met a couple of cuties and spent the rest of our time with them. I teamed up with the best looking of the two although they were both real beauties, and we spent a lot of back seat time in Oleys car over the next four days. She was the daughter of the county sheriff and was as wild as anything I had ever seen. She taught me a few things about girls. We really had some good times. The girls would even sneak into the camper-trailer with us and Oley's folks never knew they were there.

All too soon it was time to go; we said goodbye to the girls, and to Oley's folks. One of Oley's Mother's friends; a lady who lived in Las Vegas was spending some time with her in Prescott and needed a ride home, so she and her little boy rode with us to Las Vegas. It was evening when we got there and we spent the night at her home. Las Vegas in 1950 wasn't much of a big city. It was more a western cowboy town; there were casinos and slot machines everywhere, but nothing at all like it is now.

I spent the night on the lady's back porch. Then we were off to Reno. Reno was also a shadow of what it is today. It was, even then, called "the biggest little city in the world."

We drove through Oregon all night and were running low on gas. We had a state map to look at and didn't see anything encouraging for our route that lay ahead. No towns were indicated. Surely there would be a break in the endless fir tree lined highway ahead with a village or an isolated service station. But that wasn't to be. We went for miles without seeing anything other than tall fir trees. No towns or people; not even other cars. Finally around daybreak we spotted a place that looked like it had a gas pump. We pulled in but couldn't find anyone until finally an old man opened an upstairs window, peeked out, and told us he couldn't pump any gas until the electricity came on at seven o'clock.

We had about an hour to wait, but didn't have a choice because by then we didn't have very much fuel left in the tank. Finally at seven the pump came on. The old man came out and filled our tank. Before long we crossed the Columbia at Pasco and we were back in Moses Lake before dark.

Near the entrance to the orderly room the first sergeant kept a bulletin board that posted information for the squadron. For example the KP roster would be posted, so it was necessary for everyone to read the information daily. If you failed to report for KP, you could be given an article 104. It was called a summary court, but it didn't go on record and only amounted to two weeks extra duty policing up the squadron area. Still, no one ever failed to report for KP.

If your name appeared on the KP roster, you tied a towel on the bottom of your bunk and the CQ would wake you up at 4:30. The earlier you reported to the mess hall the better, because the best jobs like dining room orderly went to the early birds. Pots and pans were the worst, followed by the clipper. All nasty work that nobody liked. Of all the duties on KP, cleaning the grease pit was the absolute worst. But that didn't have to be done very often.

The group had an education officer and there was a notice on the bulletin board about college courses being available to us, which were taught by the University of Maryland extension. Nighttime classes were held.

Since I had left high school before graduating, I went by the education office one day and checked into the availability of high school courses. Soon I was enrolled and started attending classes at night to get my diploma. Additionally they had courses offered by mail through an outfit called USAFI; short for US Armed Forces Institute. Through the education office I received some study material to help me pass a general education development test.

Once all the GED equivalency tests were successfully passed an individual would receive the equivalent high school diploma. I took and passed the GED, but continued with the actual high school courses until I was given a high school diploma by the state of North Carolina.

Meeting all the requirements for a state issued diploma didn't all occur at Larson. It was 1952 before I successfully passed all the requirements for the NC diploma.

During one of my visits to the education office I learned that a college degree wasn't required to apply for the "Aviation Cadet" program. That was one avenue that would lead to pilot training.

The "hot shots" that flew the slick F-86's could be spotted a long way off. It didn't matter if they were wearing flying gear, a class "A" uniform, or were in civvies. They had a certain air, a fighter pilot swagger, an attitude of confidence; something about them that identified them as different. I couldn't imagine anyone not wanting to be a fighter pilot.

Someone wrote that; "You can tell a bomber pilot by the crush in his cap, and you can tell a fighter pilot, but you can't tell him much!"

Since I met the basic qualification requirements, I completed an application and submitted it. Part of the process involved a written test and physical requirements such as 20/20 vision, no color blindness, and good depth perception. None of the prerequisites gave me a problem.

It wasn't long after the application went forward, with the favorable endorsement of Lt. Cavanaugh, that the 81st Fighter Wing was alerted for deployment to England. I returned from a short furlough to find the education office closed down, and not long afterward I had orders to Korea; my application for Aviation Cadet had been lost in the instability that followed.

When my orders to Korea were issued they overrode and negated anything else that was pending, including my hopes for the Aviation Cadet program.

Prior to the news about the overseas deployment someone told a friend and I that a rodeo was scheduled in the town of Cle Elum, about a hundred miles west of Moses Lake; Cowboys and rodeos attracted pretty girls, so the two of us headed to Cle Elum with a three-day pass.

We were there a day before the rodeo was scheduled to start, and it was to be a week-long affair. We checked into a hotel and waited for the girls to arrive. We went to a local bar, and sure enough, some of the girls were already there. Then our plans were almost upset. After a couple beers we went back to our hotel. We hadn't done very well at the bar but when we walked into the hotel lobby we met two good looking sweeties. They were very friendly and even invited us to their room for a beer.

We were there when one of the girls' Father came in. He didn't act too mad, but wanted to know who we were. We were introduced and he went away without questioning us further. When we went back through the lobby we were told by the hotel clerk that we had to check out because the entire hotel had been rented by the guy who ran the rodeo. We protested, but were losing when one of the girls we had met came by and rescued us. It was then we learned that her Father, the fellow we met in the room, was running the whole rodeo.

We were allowed to keep our room, paid for by her father, and even helped him unload a truckload of liquor and other stuff to set up a hospitality room. We got free rodeo tickets to the best seats in the arena, and had our run of the hospitality room until we had to leave for Moses Lake. We didn't spend another dime on food or anything to drink. The longer we stayed, the friendlier the girls were. We weren't happy about having to go, but we had no choice when our three day pass was up.

Another town that was within range for a weekend of cruising and bar hopping was Coeur d' Alene, Idaho, just across the state line from Spokane. It was a fun town located in one of the prettiest settings in the country, and it was a wide open town. One saloon always gave change with silver dollars; the bar in that saloon was covered with hundreds of silver dollars. They may not have been legal, but it wasn't hard to find slot machines in Coeur d' Alene.

During football season we watched Washington State play a football game in the stadium at Spokane that was just a short distance to the Idaho state line and Coeur d' Alene just a few miles further. There were always lots of pretty girls at the games.

In 1950 the air force simply didn't condone anything remotely associated with the gay lifestyle. They didn't call them gay; homosexuals were "queers" And everyone referred to them as such. The only reason I would even mention anything about that subject is because of the following:

We had an airman from New Orleans assigned to the communications squadron whose name was Butterworth. He never approached anyone in our unit to the best of my knowledge, and was a likeable fellow, but there seemed to be something about the fancy way he talked, or some of his mannerisms that were a bit out of the ordinary. He lived in our barracks, ate with us, drank with us at the NCO club and worked in the communications center with the other teletype guys.

One night we were having a few beers at the club; he had one too many and almost passed out. We had to carry him back to the barracks and on the way the cold night air sort of revived him; he broke free and ran like a booger was after him. We finally corralled him, got him to the barracks, stripped him and threw him in the shower. He escaped again, this time completely naked. We had a dozen or so people out after him; they finally caught him and punched him out cold. They dragged him back to the barracks and threw him on his bunk. I actually felt sorry for him because he just didn't fit the mold of a military man. He complained a lot about the regimentation.

He must have been under some kind of investigation because one day he packed up his gear and reported to the orderly room. According to the administrative clerk, someone in uniform drove him away in a GI vehicle, and he was never heard from again. Word was that he was queer and had been given a bad discharge.

Sometime not long after the guy wrecked the 1936 Ford the Kentuckian and I bought together, I went to

Wenatchee for an overnight stay and spotted a 1938 Ford in a dealership showroom. It was a used vehicle, but sharp enough to be placed in the showroom with the new vehicles. I asked about it and was told the price was $250.00.

Of course I didn't have that much cash; that was a lot of money. It was sometime in April; I had made Sergeant and was making enough to afford it, so I asked the man to hold on to it for a little while. I wrote to daddy and asked to borrow $100.00. I had some cash rat-holed away and the money from him made up the difference. In a few days the $100.00 was wired to me by Western Union and I returned to Wenatchee with $250.00. I offered the man $200.00 for the car; we talked a little and the deal was made for $225.00. I drove the car back to Moses Lake.

This was the third car I had owned and still didn't have a driver's license. I had to leave the car outside the base until I could get to town and buy Insurance. Right away the insurance salesman let me know that I couldn't buy insurance without a driver's license. The department of motor vehicles wasn't more than a block away, so I took the test, passed with no problems and got the license. The insurance agency had a policy that was good only on the air base for $10.00. That was what I bought and was all set. The car was mine and I had the right to bring it on base and park it right behind the barracks.

A short time before the 81st was alerted to move to England, Monion and I were going to Ellensburg, another small resort town that had possibilities to make a score. I hadn't owned the 38 Ford very long and didn't pay much attention to the gauges other than the fuel gauge. We were about half way between Moses Lake and Ellensburg when Monion looked over at the gauges and saw that the oil pressure was low.

I didn't know anything about "oil pressure." He did, and told me to stop and pull off the road. We checked the oil level, and the dip stick just showed a little thick sludge. We hailed a passing car and caught a ride to the nearest service station; we bought four or five quarts of oil and hitch-hiked back to the Ford. We had to add most of the oil we had just bought to bring the dip stick reading to "full." Monion told me that I should sell the car as soon as I could find a buyer because I could expect major engine problems if I continued to drive it. Besides, if the rumors were true that we would all be leaving for England in the near future the car would have to be sold anyway.

When the Wing went on alert, I knew it wouldn't be long before reassignment orders would be issued and the car was sold.

Wenatchee, the apple capitol of the country, was about seventy miles to the northwest of the base on the eastern edge of the Cascade Mountains. It was beautiful country; apple trees were in every direction around the town. It wasn't very big, but had more people than the towns near the base. We went there frequently. Before anyone in my circle of friends had a car we used to hitch-hike there. We never seemed to have any problems catching a ride, because the locals knew who we were and knew we wouldn't be a problem. The farmers and cowboys were always driving around the countryside and they would never pass us without stopping with a friendly "Hi fellows, get in, you guys going to Wenatchee?"

The small town of Quincy was about twenty miles west of Ephrata; the road forked there with one fork going south towards Yakima, the other west to Wenatchee. Not far out of Quincy the road ran parallel to the Columbia River the rest of the way to Wenatchee.

There was a small café' in Quincy that served some of the best chili in the country. A sign behind the counter advertised the chili that read; "A Bullfight In Every Bowl." The sign did not lie, and the chili was delicious. Not long after the 38 Ford was bought, Bob Shields suggested that we go to Wenatchee to try our luck with the girls. Off we went, and less than two hours later we were in downtown Wenatchee.

Bob didn't tell me he had previously set up a rendezvous with a girl he knew in Wenatchee, and near sundown he suggested we drive out to her place; when we got there she jumped in the back seat and so did Bob. "Let's go for a drive out in the country," he said. By then there was no option left for me, so off we went driving past the apple orchards.

We stopped in an out of the way place, and he and she proceeded to "take care of business." There we were in my car, I had no partner, and Bob was doing his thing. I had been tricked into the situation. We were there for what seemed an hour, and I was getting somewhat restless! I cranked the car and headed back to town after telling him: "I ain't running no taxi cab."

We were moving down a country road, apple trees lined both sides and suddenly a stop sign appeared. I slammed the brakes, and nothing happened! The road dead-ended about fifty yards ahead; I kept pumping the brakes and reached for the parking brake about the time we intersected with the "T". I steered to the right but didn't make it; the car hit a ditch while turning and nearly flipped. Luckily we stayed upright but were running under a sluice box that carried water through the apple trees. We tore through several supports and were back on the road, still on our wheels.

During the wild ride the front seat supports broke and I ended up on my back, on top of Bob and his girl. The car stopped, and we got out to make a survey of the damage. The car was all right; the bumper had caught the sluice supports and didn't have a dent. The sluice was tilted and pouring water out into the ditch. We repaired the seat support by placing a screwdriver in the place where the broken seat bolt had been and got out of there before someone came by. The brake problem turned out to be something minor, like a loose cable that had to be tightened.

We dropped his girl friend at home and drove back to the base. For some time after that, Shields would look at me, laugh, and say, "I ain't running no taxi."

Not long after that incident, James Fields, Bob Shields and myself were cruising the streets of Wenatchee and passed the hotel (Wenatchee only had one). Fields looked in the lobby and spotted a young lady. He said "stop, go on around the block; I'll have her on the street with me when you get back." It was already getting late at night, so we didn't think his plan would work; but it did. By the time we made the circle there they were, waiting for us.

The four of us went to the local café' for a drink. Fields didn't return to the base with us; however, by the time we left I had set up a rendezvous with her at the hotel the next evening. We were both scheduled for duty the next day, but I arranged for early relief, and drove back to Wenatchee late in the afternoon. She was waiting in the lobby and I was soon checked in with a room on the second floor at the end of the hallway.

I had no way of knowing it but her mother and brother were at the hotel with her. After I checked in the room the door was left open. Her brother stepped out in the hall by their room and said, "go on, he's waiting for you." It was a little awkward but a short time later she walked through the door to my room.

They were from Portland, Oregon, and my guess was that they were there to pick apples. Fields had given me a detailed report on her when he got back to base and his description of the time he spent with her must have been right on. There were thoughts that she may have been a "professional", but that wasn't the case. She was pretty and very friendly.

We had a wonderful time. The next morning it was nearing the time for me to leave; we went to the café' for breakfast and when we finished I dropped her off at the hotel and was on my way back to the base. I never heard from her or saw her again, but the experience stayed with me for a long time.

Based on what was written about the thirteen months spent at Moses Lake, you could assume all that happened there was "let the good times roll" with nothing but girl chasing; nothing is further from the truth. We had an important job to do.

The squadron commander was very much concerned about national security, and threatened to bust me back to PFC once when I sent a message to an officer at McChord Air Force Base in the clear instead of routing it through the crypto room to be encoded.

He made it official by writing a letter telling me it was his intention to take one of my stripes. He afforded me the opportunity to talk to the group commander about the matter. My reply letter told him that I did want to see the group commander. After explaining my position to him and showing him that no breach of security had been made, he disagreed with the squadron commander and stated in his reply that he "did not concur" with the recommendation. So my corporal stripe was secure. Not long afterward Lieutenant Cavanaugh promoted me to Sgt.

Part of the lake that the town of "Moses Lake" was named for ran alongside the highway between Moses Lake and Ephrata. There were some monster carp in the lake that we caught by snagging. Special Services had fishing gear that we could check out, so we took treble hooks that were weighted with lead sinkers and with a spotter on the hill above the lake shore directing us when to throw and start reeling in we could snag them on the treble hook. As the line ran over top of the fish, the hook would snag them in the side. When that happened, the fight was on. Some of the carp were nearly three feet long.

We didn't keep them. If they weren't hurt by the snagging we threw them back in. If it appeared they were going to die we just left them on the bank for the scavengers.

We had a chapel on base and a Protestant, Jewish, and Catholic Chaplain was assigned to care for our spiritual needs. A lot of guys didn't go to services regularly, but we were required to listen to a "Character Guidance" lecture once monthly. One of the Chaplains conducted the lecture, and a Chaplain was on duty twenty-four hours a day, seven days a week in case of a personal emergency. Special Services scheduled entertainment at the service club with appearances by well known groups of singers and entertainers. Special events at the NCO club also brought in entertainers.

Bob Wills and His Texas Playboys were there one night and we listened to him play his "San Antonio Rose", and "Faded Love." A fight broke out and the show didn't get to finish.

In late spring someone in the communications center intercepted a message addressed to the squadron commander and rumors started flying. The message indicated that the entire 81st Wing would be moving overseas to England before summer. It wasn't long before a meeting was held in the base theater that was mandatory for everyone in the squadron to attend. There it was announced that the rumors were true. The 81st would be leaving Larson real soon.

I still had about two weeks of leave time accrued and put in the papers for a furlough home because when the unit left for England everyone had been scheduled to fly directly from Larson to the east coast and from there to Bentwaters, England.

I caught a hop over to McChord Air Force Base near Tacoma and from there hitched a ride on a

C-54 navigational training flight to Philadelphia. The student navigators were “shooting the stars” with their sextants to plot our position, so it was an overnight flight with stops in Great Falls, Montana, and Truax Field in Madison, Wisconsin, then on to Philadelphia. It was morning when we landed in Philadelphia. The airplane was scheduled for a round-robin training flight down to Macon, Georgia, but didn’t have permission to land, and the co-pilot offered to drop me and my parachute near Kings Mountain if I wanted, however the airplane commander stepped in and wouldn’t allow it. I wasn’t planning on taking him up on the offer anyway, although when he proposed it to me I gave it some serious thought.

I hitch-hiked the rest of the way home from Philadelphia with very little trouble. Again, there’s not much to remember about being home. Very few of the boys I grew up with were there anymore. I only had about a week before I rode a bus to Washington, DC and checked in to base operations at Bolling Air Force Base to catch a hop to the west coast.

I lounged around the operations building for the best part of a whole morning without getting a flight when word came that an airplane was leaving Andrews Air Force Base, Maryland that afternoon and had room for some passengers. It wasn’t far to Andrews and someone gave me a ride over to that base and I was in the air by mid afternoon going back to McChord.

After arriving back at Larson the activity was surprising. People were moving around everywhere packing up everything. Upon reporting in I learned that a few people would be staying at Larson for reassignment after the Wing had left for England.

I was one of the few in communications that would be left behind. The day arrived for their departure and a bunch of C-46 airplanes landed and loaded everyone up for the flight to the east coast and on to Bentwaters.

I felt sort of sad. Maybe I was experiencing a touch of homesickness for all the guys that I had worked and lived with the past year. Shields didn't go but was nearing the end of his enlistment, and was going home. Monion had already completed his recall to active duty time and had gone back to Santa Monica. Oley boarded the plane and I waved goodbye to him. There were others, including the Kentuckian; and some that I don't remember today. They all left, never to be seen or heard from again. I felt alone.

After the 81st left I received orders transferring me to the 101st Air Base Group until a permanent reassignment could be worked out. The few people that were left didn't have very much to do duty wise.

All the communications equipment had been packed up for shipment to England and we had a temporary officer that we were responsible to. About all we could do was keep the area clean and wait.

Finally my orders came through. I was being sent to the 136th Fighter-Bomber Wing in Korea. Good news! That was where everything was happening anyway. I was glad now that orders to England didn't include me. I would get another delay-en-route to Camp Stoneman, California for overseas deployment. That gave me another ten days at home to see everyone again.

This time I was happy to be able to get back to Kings Mountain. Little did I know that the most important earthly event in my life would take place within the next several weeks.

Christmas wasn't far off and on December 21st I would meet the beautiful young lady, my soul mate, with whom I would spend the rest of eternity.

CHAPTER 11

Meeting the Light of my Life December 1951

After clearing Larson Air Force Base during the early part of December 1951, I made my way to Spokane to catch the Great Northern to Chicago and home to spend Christmas with the folks.

My reporting date to the overseas replacement depot at Camp Stoneman, California would allow me to be home Christmas day, but to make it all the way across the country I'd have to leave the day after Christmas. I could stay one additional day, but that would require me to make every connection to get to the west coast by my reporting date. To get there late might bring me more problems than I would care to face. And to miss an overseas shipment date would definitely mean serious trouble; my schedule was almost carved in stone. I could always leave early but that would mean leaving on or before Christmas day.

The train carried me across the Idaho panhandle into Montana. We stopped in Missoula for an hour or so, and a group of college students who were attending the University in Missoula boarded the train. They were going home on Christmas break, and it wasn't long before I got close to a pretty student going home to Wisconsin.

It was a long ride across the wide states of Montana and North Dakota and we had time to really get acquainted. There was an empty passenger car behind the one where we were seated; the lights were out in the empty car, and before long we were snuggled up in the darkened car. The cowgirls of the west were easier to get close to than the girls back home and it seemed there was no limit with them. Some, like the student from Wisconsin and the Sheriff's daughter in Prescott, Arizona were friendly to the point of being the aggressor. And there was another one in Wenatchee that was the runner-up to the "Apple Blossom Queen;" she was a real beauty and loved to hear me talk – among other things. She couldn't get enough of my Carolina drawl and promised to send me a picture if she won the contest next year. But when I left, that was the end of it. I lost her address somewhere in the move and couldn't write, so I never heard from her.

One of the train crewmen came by, probably a conductor, and told us to get out of that car and return to our seats. We did so; however, when the conductor left we sneaked back into the dark car. We didn't expect him back, but come back he did. This time he warned me "get back to your car, and if you can't stay there, I'll have you put off this train at our next stop." He didn't threaten the girl with eviction.

The next stop was Bismarck, North Dakota. His warning was heeded and he wasn't given any more reasons to put me off the train. I did sit with the girl, but we stayed in the lighted car we were assigned to.

When the train arrived at the station in Bismarck and pulled to a stop by the loading ramp, I looked out the window and saw a man standing there wearing a big buffalo or bear coat that covered him from head to toe. He had on glasses that looked like he had two ice cubes over is eyes. He hardly moved.

I walked to the end of the car and opened the door to step outside. When the door opened, a blast of air hit me that was so cold I could hardly breathe. Wow! I thought about what the conductor had threatened me with. No one could have lived very long in that cold. I shut the door, and was awfully glad that I was still on the warm train.

The next afternoon we arrived in Chicago. I don't remember having to change stations that time, but usually when travelling through Chicago that was the case. As always, there was a delay in the windy city. The college student from Missoula had left the train somewhere behind us; I don't even remember when or where she got off. It was a cold dreary day; the "windy city" lived up to its name and I was happy when the train that would carry me south started rolling.

Indianapolis wasn't far in front of us, then on to Cincinnati, Knoxville and home. There were other stops along the way, but the trip that brought me clear across the country was more or less routine except for the time spent with Miss Missoula. Again, there were plenty of meal tickets to turn in to the dining car crew, and as before, the food was very good.

Travelling by train was an enjoyable experience. Strangers liked to start a conversation and ask a lot of questions. Almost without exception when I started talking to anyone they would follow up with " where are you from?" or "you must be from the south," or maybe "boy, you sure got a southern accent." It was all really interesting, and I was always proud to tell them I was from North Carolina. Even though we now have Amtrak, it isn't the same. The Pullman cars, dining cars, and club cars were very different. The club car waiters could even be slipped a meal ticket in exchange for a couple beers.

I never knew why the people who issued the meal tickets weren't held accountable for the number of tickets they gave me. There were always several left over at the end of a trip, even after using some of them for something other than food.

The first few days at home went by with nothing of any consequence happening. Mama knew that I would be leaving shortly after Christmas and showed me how good she really could cook. They were working at the mill and Faye was away at school all day.

I used daddy's car a lot, especially after they got home from the mill in the afternoon. It worried Daddy that I would be off and gone in his car until late at night. He knew they would have to leave for work early the next morning, and to be late for work just didn't happen.

They would normally be asleep when I came home, but I knew, when he went to sleep, he was concerned about me and his car. Thank goodness nothing like an accident happened and I always made it back without incident.

One of the neighbors received word that their son had been killed in Korea and that caused them to be more concerned about me. We had gone to Kings Mountain High School together, but his folks lived out on the Shelby road and I really didn't remember too much about him.

Apparently nothing happened that was worth remembering the first five or six days I was home; in fact I don't remember much about how I spent my time, but must have driven down to the Park Yarn to visit with friends there.

Some of my old Park Grace elementary and Kings Mountain High School buddies had enlisted and were scattered in far away places. Curtiss Wright was in the navy but was serving with the marine corps in Korea; Jack Wells had enlisted in the navy also and was with the 7th fleet off the Korean coast. Lafayette was in the far north, above the Arctic Circle somewhere taking care of the radios, and no doubt freezing his tail off.

There were others scattered around the world. Some were still in school and others were still there and working in the mill. They were already in a mundane existence and didn't know it. Who knows, maybe that was exactly what they wanted to be doing. They all seemed to be happy enough.

I have thought many times since about the events that occurred on Wednesday evening, December 21st 1951. There is absolutely no doubt that it was predetermined by the hand of Providence that directed me to be at a given place, at a given time that evening. It is beyond "chance" that brought everything together as they evolved. I believe, as much as I believe anything, that statement to be true.

On the evening on December 21st I was driving around, going nowhere in particular with nothing special in mind when I spotted two young ladies walking on the sidewalk up ahead. It was Wednesday; and later I learned they were on their way home from services at Second Baptist Church.

I stopped and asked them for directions to a friend's house. Although it was dark, the street light was burning nearby and I looked at one of the girls and saw "without question," the prettiest girl I had ever seen, anywhere in my entire life. Her hair was black and put up with little curls all over, everything about her was amazing. Even though the other girl, her sister, was also very pretty, there was no doubt that I had to do something that would lead to my knowing this girl.

It was hard for me to believe that a hundred young men weren't following right behind her, begging to be given a chance with her. There is no exaggeration in my description of her, or my thoughts. This girl had to be something very special.

We had a conversation and before driving off I had her name and telephone number. It was tough driving off and leaving them; "something may happen, maybe she gave me the wrong telephone number." Bad thoughts went through my mind. Did I actually have a chance to really meet her? She was too beautiful not to have a string of boyfriends. Was she really accessible? What was wrong with the guys that lived near her? There was no way I could forget her. The beauty was etched in my mind. I could still smell the perfume she wore even though she was never closer than a few feet from the car window.

That was the end of my night of cruising around. I was so fidgety I couldn't think straight. I went directly home and couldn't wait to call her. I had to know if the meeting really happened. Maybe it was a dream. I called the number she had given me. She answered the phone! Thank You! Thank You!, My Guardian Angel was on duty!

We talked; she asked a lot of questions about me. We had gone to Kings Mountain High School at the same time, but she was a grade below me and I didn't remember her. When asked if I could see her the next night, she told me she already had a date, but her sister was free. OK! That was good enough. We would double date. Even though I would be with her sister, it would be close enough – for now.

Our date was set at seven o'clock. It was a long time before I drifted off to sleep. The next day dragged on forever; then it was time for the date. I picked them both up and we drove off to pick up the other guy. It was a cool introduction. I didn't like him, and I sensed that she didn't care an awfully lot about the situation either. Her sister, Mary, was nice; we got a little close, but nothing really; there was no way I could think about anything else but her sister Mil being in the back seat with the other guy. I couldn't have been a very good date for Mary. It just wasn't working out.

It wasn't long before we dumped the other guy. I took them home, said good night to Mary and asked Mil to stay with me for a while. Then it was the two of us. That was it! The impossible dream had come true. I had never felt so good in my entire life. She was wonderful! Life was wonderful! I didn't want to leave her and go home. From the very first kiss, I knew that was it. She was so special, it was unbelievable. That was how it was then, and how it has been until this very moment.

It would be time to leave in a very few days; but we were together as much as possible. Those were some of the most memorable days of my life. I was in heaven when we were together. We were inseparable. We grew very close in a short period of time, but not intimately so. Things were going too well to try and push too far, too fast. It was still incredible just to spend time with her.

Then it was time to go; this time leaving was different. This time there was someone I was leaving behind other than family. And I knew that sometime in the future, if everything went right for me, she would be mine. The fact that I would be gone for a long time concerned me because a girl that beautiful wouldn't be left alone by the neighborhood young men. That was a disturbing fact I'd have to live with for the next year or possibly longer.

My soul mate and light of my life

CHAPTER 12

Camp Stoneman and the USS Randall Dec. 1951–Jan. 1952

Christmas 1951 was spent at home with the family. I was so stricken with Mildred Roper that very little can be recalled about time spent at home. I remember very little about the holidays except for the time spent with her. Some of my time was spent with Steve and Dale, my two little buddies at the Park Yarn.

We had a traditional Christmas dinner and exchanged gifts at home. Coot had married Bill Tallon in the summer of 1950 while I was still attending signal school in New Jersey; they had set up housekeeping in Pineville and she was due to deliver a baby in January. She was having some problems with her pregnancy and didn't spend much time with us in Kings Mountain over the Christmas season. Shortly before leaving I drove over to Fairview Street to say goodbye to Mil. We promised to write and even though I felt that we both knew we had a long future together, we didn't make any permanent commitments. I was free to pursue any eventuality and so was she. It was a good arrangement for us both, but I still had disturbing thoughts about leaving her.

The 27th was my planned departure date and that was a day later than I should be leaving.The schedule that required me to leave on the 26th was changed to allow me one more evening with her. I needed to see Mil just once more. It was just four days before my reporting date at Camp Stoneman, California. My scheduled arrival at Camp Stoneman was early enough, but I couldn't be delayed or miss a connection for any reason and still make it in time.

The base there was used as an overseas processing depot and was located near Pittsburg, about thirty-five miles up the bay from San Francisco. It would take me a little over three days by train to get there. The route would again take me through Chicago.

When I arrived in Chicago I had less than an hour to get to Union Station to catch a Southern Pacific train to the west coast. Again, the weather was dreary; the snowplows had dumped deep piles of snow between the street and sidewalks. Everything I had was carried in my duffel. It had been checked through to Chicago, but I had to pick it up and carry it to Union Station.

Cabs were scarce, the wind was blowing, it was freezing cold and I started walking up the street away from the station in order to hail a cab. I had already wasted about twenty minutes picking up my duffel and had a little over half an hour to get to Union Station. No cabs were in sight; I walked on; finally I spotted a yellow vehicle coming my way. The sign on top told me it was a cab.

I jumped over the big pile of snow and out into the street. With the cab driver yelling at me that he wasn't for hire, he was on break, or going to lunch or something, I opened the back door, flung my duffel in, and jumped in behind it. I told the driver; "You've got to take me to

Union Station, I ain't got but twenty minutes to get there." He took off and got me there just in time. Cab drivers are the same everywhere and this one was no different. He seemed a little gruff at first, but once he realized my situation he broke the speed limit and probably took a chance of losing his cabbie license to help me get to Union station before the train left. I checked my duffel and boarded the train with only a few minutes to spare.

It was a long two and a half days across Iowa, Nebraska, Wyoming, Utah, and Nevada before reaching California. The train took me to San Francisco and from there I caught a bus to Pittsburg and Camp Stoneman. I had less than a day to spare when I reported in.

Camp Stoneman must have had ten thousand troops processing for movement to the Far East and Korea. Ships were leaving almost daily from the docks in San Francisco. New troops were also checking in everyday.

In processing wasn't much. They had their procedures streamlined and in no time my shot records had been checked, orders verified, a barracks assigned and bedding had been issued.

The weather was a problem. I was at Camp Stoneman eleven days and the weather was bad the entire time. Central California had never seen so much rain in such a short period of time. It rained every day I was there.

My initial issue of clothing was checked soon after arriving, and we were told that when movement orders came we would be required to have everything in our duffel that constituted a complete issue of clothing. If we were short of any item we would be red-lined and have to await another shipment order.

The mess hall was the biggest, that is they fed more meals there than any GI mess in the world. It had six chow lines with thousands of tables. The food was terrible. No wonder, there were tens of thousands of hungry people in and out all day.

Even though I was a Sergeant, I had to pull KP twice. I told one of the permanent party members that "Sergeants in the air force don't pull KP." He told me "every one here, excepting permanent party and senior NCOs pull KP duty."

The second time I was on KP someone stole my raincoat. When reporting for duty early in the morning my raincoat was hung alongside all the others, and when the day was over, the raincoat was gone. The next morning I went by the rack that held the raincoats belonging to people on KP and lifted one. I was getting anxious to be getting out of there and sure didn't want to be redlined when my name came up on the shipment list. That raincoat traveled to Yokohama with my gear.

We weren't allowed to leave the base. No one scheduled for deployment had a pass. To try and sneak off base would invite a court martial, so no one left. When not on KP duty there was nothing to do but stay in the barracks after morning roll call was complete; roll call was followed by the names called out to those scheduled for shipment that day.

That took a long time. We had a big parade ground to form up for roll call. Following that, a guy standing on an elevated platform with a bullhorn would read off the shipment list. That procedure would generally take several hours; we would then be dismissed until the next morning. By then, even though we had on raincoats, we were soaked. The wet weather never let up.

There were poker games going on in several places; but I didn't know anyone, so I didn't get involved in the poker.

No one dared go on sick call. We were told that "any one needing to go on sick call; take your bed, bags, and bedding and report to the dispensary." Nobody could carry all that stuff; besides, to go on sick call meant that you might miss the shipment list, and if you didn't respond when your name was called, you waited in the rain for the next shipment list; and hope your name would be called.

Then, on the eleventh day, my name was called. We were to remain on the parade field after everyone else had been dismissed and wait for instructions. We were told to go back to our barracks, get all our gear, turn in our bedding and report back to the front of the parade field in one hour. We did so, and then we were loaded on buses and taken to a pier where a big ferryboat was docked.

There were probably close to a thousand soldiers and airmen loaded onto the ferry and off we went down the bay toward Fort Mason and San Francisco. On the way we passed long rows of big gray Navy transport ships that had been moth balled. After about three or four hours we crossed San Francisco bay, going right past Alcatraz island and pulled alongside one of the Fort Mason piers. There were several long piers sticking out from the docks at Fort Mason; our ship the USS Randall was docked alongside one of them.

We off loaded from the ferry and lined up on the pier to be individually checked off before boarding the troop ship.

We were assigned, and boarded by compartment. I was assigned to compartment C-3 located on the lower deck near the rear of the ship. Our gear was carried aboard with us and stowed near our bunk. The bunks were nothing more than a narrow strip of canvas laced to a metal rail. They were four high with the lowest near the deck and the top bunk almost touching the ceiling which was covered with pipes and metal conduit; everything was painted gray. My bunk was the lowest and was no more than six inches above the deck.

We had a guy assigned to our compartment giving us information about what we needed to do, what not to do, where the bathroom was located and so on. Pretty soon we heard a humming noise that were the ship's engines starting up, then we felt the ship move away from the pier.

A long urinal went all the way across the ship at the very back end. Soon after we left the pier we started moving and could hear the propeller shafts turning underneath us. The ship was still on calm water inside the bay when I went to use the urinal. Someone's breakfast was already floating in the urinal from seasick GI's and we hadn't even gone under the Golden Gate Bridge. Water in the bay was smooth with hardly a ripple and I thought "if some of these guys are already seasick, what will they do when we get out into the ocean"? It wasn't very long before we were under the bridge and headed out to open water where rough weather was waiting.

The ship was headed straight for Yokohama and had two weeks of non-stop sailing. I felt bad for the troops that were sick. Nothing could be done for them; if seasickness pills were available then, the Navy didn't have any; not for any of our guys anyway. They had no choice but to be sick for two weeks.

The guy with all the information told us when we could go to the open deck that was up three levels from our compartment. Otherwise we had to remain below and stay in our compartment. There wasn't enough room topside for everyone at one time and they didn't want us roaming around the lower decks either.

Chow was served by compartment. A loudspeaker would announce "chow down for compartment C-3" and everyone that wasn't sick would climb up the stairs (called ladders by the navy) to the top deck and walk around to where the dining area was located. We would line up, and the food would be served in metal trays, just like in a regular mess hall. We had to eat in a hurry because there were fourteen hundred people on board that had to eat in the same mess area three times a day.

All fourteen hundred didn't eat though. As indicated above some were so sick they couldn't eat and they didn't want anyone to even speak of what they had eaten in the mess area. One guy in my compartment lived for two weeks on a few oranges we brought him.

The troops in compartment C-3 were allowed on the open deck for several hours every day, but it was so crowded that it was hard to find a place to sit down. There were some dogs being transported to Japan that were kept in cages on the deck. The dogs had to be walked daily by some of the crew, and the deck also had to be cleaned up afterwards by the same guys.

No one, other than the marine guards, could go topside after dark. We tried several times but each time we were turned back by the guard. The first time we tried to sneak up the ladders and open the hatch he was right there waiting for us and even cocked his pistol before ordering us back to our compartment.

Another night we tried to go topside just to see the beacon light on Midway Island; we didn't make it that time either. There just wasn't any moving around the ship at night. The marine guards had us corralled, but we understood the reasons for the rules. Anyone on the open and rolling deck at night could easily lose their footing and go overboard.

For a day or two we ran through some weather. We were bouncing around pretty good. I didn't sleep very much during the storm because every time the rear of the ship would rise up, the turning propellers would cut the top of the water and make a lot of noise. I never had it as bad as the guys who were seasick though. They were pitiful.

After two weeks we made it to Yokohama. When we docked and the ship's engines shut down, the seasick guys were all right. They were probably thinking about having to go through another two week period of seasickness a year from now if they survived that long in Korea. The army guys knew they would be going straight to Pusan and north to the main line from there, so that was probably their main concern at the time.

We were off loaded and marched to a tent city somewhere near Yokohama for a few days. As expected the army guys were loaded onto another troopship headed to Pusan. Some of them wouldn't make it back home, but then our air force people weren't guaranteed a safe return either. Some of them would soon be flying over hostile country with someone down there shooting at them.

Someone passed out materials for writing a letter during our stay in the tents; I wrote a short letter home simply informing them we had made it to Yokohama because no one knew at the time just what our final destination would be. We knew we were going to Korea, and most of the air force guys knew their unit of assignment but didn't know the exact location.

I knew that my orders read the 136th Fighter-Bomber Wing at APO 970; but APO 970 meant the whole of South Korea. Within a few short days we would be told everything we needed to know about where we would be spending the next year or so.

For most of the troops in tent city this was the first time any of them had been out of the US. Literally no one knew what lay ahead or anything about the conflict going on in Korea. At this point anything concerning our future was a big mystery.

We were in a strange place and the very air we breathed had a peculiar smell. All the army troops were gone, everyone around us now were young airmen like myself; all members of the fledgling United States Air Force that was being put to the test daily across the straits just to the west of Japan. And we would all soon be there to fill a small place in that trial.

CHAPTER 13

Itazuke Air Base Japan January 1952

The war with Japan hadn't been over very long, just a little over five years when we docked in Yokohama. The country was still recovering from all the B-29 raids, and many of the Japanese were still unfriendly towards the GI's that were in their country, especially airmen.

The way they thought, anyone in the air force could have been dropping fire bombs on them from the hated "Be-Nee-Chee-Ku"; (B-29.)

My reassignment orders had me going to the 136th Fighter Bomber Wing at APO 970. That APO included the entire peninsula of South Korea below the thirty-eighth parallel. The 136th also had a rear echelon maintenance unit at Itazuke Air Base in southern Japan. My first stop on the way to K-2 would be Itazuke.

Every air base in South Korea had a "K" alpha designator followed by a numerical designator. The 136th was at K-2, which was near Taegu. My friend, Billy, from radio school at Fort Monmouth had been transferred from George Air Force Base, California, to the 3rd Medium Bomb Wing at K-8, near Kunsan. It was so long ago it's hard to be certain of the location.It's altogether possible that the 3rd could have been at K-13 near Suwon. I do remember there were two medium bomb wings in country that were flying B-26s, one was the 17th and the other was the 3rd.

We stayed in the tent city near Yokohama only for a few days. While there we were medically cleared to move to our new assignment. Our shot records were brought up to date; most had to get a cholera and yellow fever shot; and we had a "short arm" inspection.The term "short arm" probably needs to be defined. Read on.

We were all herded to a large building that had been heavily damaged during the war; it only had part of a roof and the windows no longer had any glass. We lined up in a rag-tag sort of formation four columns deep and did a "dress,right dress" for an open ranks inspection.

An Army non com medic came in with a big WAC Captain. She must have weighed two hundred and stood close to six feet. We were told to "unzip, haul it out, and milk it down." When the Captain walked in front of each individual, she checked the "short arm" to make sure there wasn't a "drip" that could indicate a "sexually transmitted disease." There must have been five hundred men in the group.

The non-com medic had a big jar of quinine pills that were handed out to every one. He had another jar of pills and we were all given one of those; we never knew what that one was for. The quinine pill was easily recognized because we didn't have any water to drink with it. There's no mistaking the bitter quinine.

In addition to the medical clearance, we were given several briefings about Japanese customs and traditions. We were told about the "status of forces" agreement that would be signed by both countries when the details were worked out. In the meantime we were still, while in Japan, occupational troops, and, as such, we came under the legal jurisdiction of US military laws and regulations. There were Japanese policemen that patrolled with the Military Police, but to break the law meant to be tried in a military court. After the "status of forces" agreement was enacted, and that was expected by the summer of 1952, all foreign troops on Japanese soil would no longer be "occupational" but "guests" and governed by Japanese law.

We didn't know it at the time, but that agreement would be completed and go into effect in April 1952.

Our in-processing was completed in a few days and those who were scheduled for assignment to bases in southern Japan were loaded on a train and transported south. Since I would be on temporary duty at Itazuke Air Base which was located on the southern island of Kyushu, my name was on the train manifest.

The narrow gauge tracks and straight back seats didn't make for a very comfortable ride, but being able to see the Japanese countryside made the trip very enjoyable. We rolled through the country, past village after village and major cities as well.

One of the railway cars had been converted to a small mess hall that had serving room only. We had to take our food back to our car to eat. Surprisingly the cooks served up some very good chow while moving down the tracks. The trip took nearly a day and a half.

My thoughts were on home and Mil. What was she doing? Was she thinking about me? I didn't write to her when the writing materials were passed out by the Red Cross in Yokohama. I did write to my folks just to let them know I was alright. As soon as I made it to Itazuke for sure I would have to write her. I had been gone for a month and hadn't had the first mail call. Surely her letters would catch up with me at Itazuke. Those were my thoughts as we rolled south toward the southernmost island of Kyushu.

The train took us through the burned out city of Hiroshima that had been the target of the first atomic bomb. It had been five years and five months since the bomb had been dropped, but major damage was still evident.

When we went through a city the train would slow down to a crawl. Going through Hiroshima it went even slower than usual; we could see the results of what the bomb did. If any of the young troops on the train had any sympathetic feelings for the people of Hiroshima, there was no indication. President Truman was more than justified in his decision to use the bomb, thereby ending the war sooner than had been expected.

That decision resulted in the saving of many thousands of American and Allied lives in an invasion. It was learned after the war that the military leader in Japan had ordered the execution of all American, British, and Australian prisoners of war when the Allies invaded. Many of them were executed anyway, but most were spared after the surrender. The bomb saved their lives also.

Itazuke was located several miles from Fukuoka, a large coastal city with a population of several hundred thousand or more. It is one of the oldest cities in the country dating back to ancient times, and is situated on the northern coast of Kyushu on the East China Sea.

Fukuoka had some industries producing war materials during the war and was often targeted by the "Be-Nee-Chee-Ku." There were several POW camps near Fukuoka, and a week after the surrender was signed the Japanese military beheaded some captured B-29 crewmen at one of the POW camps. Those responsible were later tried as war criminals and hung. There was still some resentment by the local population towards the airmen at Itazuke.

Nagasaki, the second city to be destroyed by the atomic bomb, wasn't very far from Fukuoka. After Nagasaki was destroyed the Emperor quickly ordered the surrender of his country. That order prevented an invasion of Japan by the allied forces and not only saved many American lives, but the lives of the Japanese who had been taught to defend their sacred soil, even with the lives of their children armed only with sharpened bamboo sticks.

Both Hiroshima and Nagasaki were more than justified. That was my opinion then, and it has remained unchanged to this day.

It needs to be stated that there has not been an instant in my life that my love for Mil was deniable since the first time I saw her. My world changed that night just before Christmas 1951.

Some of my conduct while in Japan and Korea over the next year would seem to contradict that truth, but it isn't the case. It may be hard for some that read this to understand the above statement; but the most important thing to me then and now is that she understood.

Our train arrived in Fukuoka and we were loaded on trucks and transported out to Itazuke. The smell of Japan was everywhere. Rice paddies were in every direction; the "benjo" ditches, that carried sewage to concrete tanks to be used as fertilizer, were along side the road and contributed to the atmosphere around us. The single level buildings, some just shacks, lined both sides of the narrow road.

Our truck broke out into the main, and wider, road to the base. Small cars and hundreds of bicycles rolled past our truck. People were moving about and working in the fields. I was in a strange, different place, and thinking about Mil.

Itazuke was a hub of activity. There were many different types of aircraft on the strip. On the far side was a naval detachment. A big seaplane was parked there along with a couple of World War II torpedo bombers. It was later learned that they were used to carry mail out to the Seventh Fleet that supported the Korean operations.

The rear echelon maintenance people were busy repairing and replacing damaged parts on the F-84 aircraft that were flown by the 136th in Korea. There were a couple other units that used the Itazuke strip. One was the 68th All Weather Squadron that was equipped with the F-94; a new all weather jet fighter. There were a few ROK (Republic of Korea) F-51 aircraft parked on the apron, and two C-47s were there also. A transient C-54 transport was taking off as we unloaded our gear. It was clear that Itazuke was an important part of the air operations being conducted across the straits and a short flight north to the main line of resistance in Korea.

My assignment to the communications squadron, after reporting to the headquarters building with the other guys in my group, meant that I would be leaving them. Most of them were loaded onto one of the C-47 aircraft and off they went to K-2. I was temporarily assigned to the communications detachment at Itazuke as one of their radio operators.

After checking in with the first sergeant I was taken to my barracks where a Corporal, another radioman, was given the job of briefing me about everything I needed to know. Then I went through the same routine of being assigned a bunk, issued bedding, finding out where to go to chow, where was my duty station, and all the rest.

There was one difference, I was issued a carbine and ammunition. The supply room was located in the barracks and all the weapons were stored there in a rifle rack. Outside, on both ends of the barracks, sandbags were stacked forming a U shaped bunker. Had they been under some kind of attack? I quizzed the Corporal. No attacks, the sandbag revetments were just a precaution. The carbine was a matter of policy. No one expected any trouble from the Japanese.

Everyone in the barracks contributed to a fund for the "houseboy"; a little Japanese guy who kept our shoes shined, the floors waxed, and the latrine clean. He didn't cost much; everyone contributed a couple of bucks monthly.

The radio room was located in the headquarters building and was used strictly for radio communications between K-2 and Itazuke. We manned the position twenty-four hours a day, seven days a week. Besides myself and the Corporal there were four other radio operators. I was the only Sergeant.

The others were to be rotated back to Texas within several months. The 136th was a Texas Air National Guard outfit that had been activated and would be sent back to Texas on paper in about six months.

The Corporal, like me, was a replacement for the Texans who would be leaving soon. After talking with the Commander, I was made responsible for the other radiomen and would be the NCO in charge of radio operations. That meant no nighttime duty for me. I did pull a shift like the other guys, but I made out the schedule and reported directly to the First Sergeant. The assignment was temporary, however, as I was slated to go to K-2 in the near future.

As the Texans were rotated we got new people in to replace them. It wasn't but a few weeks until everyone in the radio room were newly assigned, just as I was.

The facilities at Itazuke were more than adequate. The mess hall put out very good food. No one, not even low ranking airmen, had to pull KP, or any kind of extra duty. All the duties in the mess hall, except for the GI cooks, were performed by Japanese. Pretty girls serviced the dining room. We had a day room with a pool table, ping-pong table, lounge chairs, a phonograph for music with lots of records, a card table for pinochle or poker, and a Japanese girl attendant that kept it clean. We didn't have a NCO club, but an airman's club that serviced all enlisted ranks. The club had a good snack bar where they served hamburgers, fries, sandwiches, and snacks. The bar was up to date with all brands of American beer and liquor plus Asahi and Nippon brand Japanese beer. There was a bandstand and dancing area.

On weekends and special occasions a Japanese orchestra played live music that sounded as good as any well known American band. They mostly played big band music that was popular in the states; Tommy Dorsey, Glenn Miller, that type. Other bands were scheduled from time to time that played country, blue grass and other types of music. They imitated popular groups in the states and it would have been hard to tell their singers from the originals back home. One guy could imitate Hank Williams and other country and western singers perfectly. You could close your eyes and couldn't tell that it wasn't Hank singing "lovesick blues" or "cheatin heart." He and his band were that good.

At least once a month the club would have a "stag" night with dancing girls and drinks for a dime. There was a base theater and bowling alley, but they weren't patronized very often by any of our guys. Recreation on base was outstanding.

A book could be written about the off duty nightlife in Fukuoka. A shuttle bus ran from the Itazuke main gate to downtown Fukuoka regularly. I was young and Mil was a million miles away. Never-the-less she was never far from my thoughts, no matter what.

The Corporal who had checked me in to the outfit was also my initial guide to the cabarets downtown. He was an old timer (meaning he had been there a month or so) and knew the cabaret district and some of the girls by name. He already had a mark on his wall locker signifying exposure to a well known bug one of the local "ladies" had passed on to him.

At one time it had been a court martial offense to test positive for the "social disease" the shady ladies gave out, but the medics realized it was better for all just to treat the problem and let it go away. Now, if symptoms became evident, sick call and three days of penicillin shots, took care of everything with no record other than a check mark on your medical record.

To offset the problem, every one had to pick up free condoms and a "pro kit" at the main gate before going off base. To try and explain just what a "pro kit" is and what it is used for; The kit consisted of a small tube of ointment that contained germ killing medication; and a germicidal soap impregnated napkin. The ointment was released into the entrance to the urinary tract, and the napkin had to be soaked in water and lathered up, then the exposed area thoroughly washed.

That procedure was supposed to eliminate the probability of picking up an unwanted disease.

One of the replacement radio operators was sent to the 136th directly out of radio school at Keesler Air Force Base, Mississippi. His name was Bob Basham from Chesapeake, West Virginia. Another was Tom Nesbitt III from Birmingham, Alabama. Both were very likable fellows and the three of us sort of fell in together and were good friends the entire time we were there.

We weren't always at the same place at the same time because of temporary assignments to other bases in Korea, but we did spend time together off and on throughout our tour in the Far East.

Nesbitt was a third generation "Southern Aristocrat" descended from a long line of Alabama's upper crust. He was on our level in the 136th, however, and we were pals. To this day we still call each other from time to time, and a couple years ago Nanny and I (since she became a Grandmother, my Mil is now known as "Nanny") spent some time with him in Alabama. He didn't change over the years. Although Basham and I were the best of friends at Itazuke and K-2, I haven't seen or heard from him since he was discharged at Pope Air Force Base near Fayetteville after we returned to the states.

Basham, a country boy through and through, was an amateur boxer in high school and several times when he had a few too many he would get in a crouch and swing at anyone near him. It was dangerous to get too close to him when he had enough Asahi beer to put him in one of his fighting moods. He was small but like a wildcat in a fight. He was a good friend.

Two of the toughest guys I ever knew were friends I met at Itazuke. Both were from Harlan, Kentucky. For some reason, I can't remember either of their names; probably because we always called a lot of guys by their last name all the time. I'll call one Cochran and the other Baker.

One night Cochran was in one of the cabarets in Fukuoka; when he left the club an empty rickshaw was sitting outside unattended. He stole the rickshaw, and was pedaling away towards another cabaret with the owner running behind him screaming and trying to catch up. There were several canals in Fukuoka that were empty of water when the tide was out, but had several feet of mud and muck in the bottom. Cochran ran the rickshaw into one of the empty canals and was taken by the military police to the provost marshal's office downtown and was put in a cell on the third floor. He was a muddy stinking mess. He jumped out of the third floor window and broke an ankle when he landed; he walked all the way back to Itazuke on the broken ankle. He cleaned himself up in the shower room and was asleep in his bunk, which was right next to mine, when they came after him. By that time he was sober enough and went along peacefully hobbling on his broken ankle.

Our first sergeant's name was Coors. Neither Cochran nor Baker cared for him in the least. Coors had done something to them or against them before I arrived at Itazuke, I never knew what; but I heard Cochran say on several occasions, "If I go back on the same ship with Coors, I'll throw the guy overboard." Cochran was a man who meant just what he said. And when they rotated, both were sent home on the same troopship. I've often wondered if Coors made it home safely.

After returning home, Baker sent me Christmas cards from Harlan, Kentucky for a number of years. I never heard from Cochran after he left.

Most of the guys in my outfit were single and out to have a good time while they could. They knew that soon enough they would be leaving for Korea.

Itazuke was a place where major maintenance was the primary mission and most of the people were temporary. There were three F-84 wings in Korea and they were all getting a lot of flying time. Radio traffic between K-2 and Itazuke was heavy. We didn't have the right frequency for clear voice communications, so most of the traffic was by slower CW (continuous wave) using Morse. We stayed pretty busy while on duty.

When off duty we took advantage of everything and played hard. Asahi beer was good and it was cheap. Five or six bucks converted to "Yen" could buy a lot of good times in Fukuoka. Girls were plentiful, they were pretty, and mostly they were very friendly. The cabarets all had lots of working girls and an upstairs with private rooms for what they called a "short time." None of the enlisted airmen at Itazuke carried class "A" passes. Before being allowed off base we had to go to the orderly room, pick up a pass and sign out.

A regular pass was only good until bed check at eleven thirty. An overnight pass was good until the next day. There was a curfew in town, however, and anyone caught in the streets after midnight would be in trouble with the military police.

Fights in the cabarets were a common occurrence. Normally no one would be hurt very much but damages would have to be paid to the mama-san. Usually if a scuffle broke out someone would break it up before any harm was done. Sometimes the fighters would take their differences outside and finish it there. The MPs would arrive and take the guys to the provost until they cooled down and then release them.

I was in a club one evening; the only American around because the club wasn't normally frequented by American GI's. I was there with a Japanese girl that I met in a souvenir shop where she worked as an attendant. She wasn't a "cabaret" girl. When I asked her to go out she accepted, and we went to a club. The club was owned by her brother.

It was in an area that I was unfamiliar with, but we were there none the less. We were sitting in a booth when three or four young Japanese guys that looked like they were ex soldiers came in. They were wearing parts of Japanese army uniforms. They looked at me and the girl. It became very clear they were ready to take care of me. They all looked very hostile and were advancing toward the booth when without saying a word her brother, who was tending bar, jumped over the bar and struck a karate pose. He said something in Japanese that sounded like a warning and they backed down and left. As we left he escorted us away from there to a safer part of town.

That was the last time for me to venture out into a strange area, and was as close as I ever came to a confrontation with Japanese citizens. Even though some of them didn't care about having us around, they seldom outwardly showed any hostility. A lot of the citizens, especially the older ones, or those whose businesses we patronized would bow courteously. That was Japanese custom, and we learned to bow in return, trying to be equally polite to them.

Many fights did occur, however, and I was involved in several. Once I was in a club with one other guy, a friend named "Bush." We were with two "jo-sans" having a few Asahi beers. Most clubs had a phonograph with a stack of records that patrons could play and after we got there I put a record on the phonograph; it was Tex Ritter singing High Noon. I really liked that record, so I played it over and over several times.

Bush must have been fed up with old Tex. He got out of his seat, walked over to the phonograph, took the record off, and walked back to our table and broke the record over my head. We were the only customers there, it was a small place, and when the fight was all over we had to pay damages of over eighteen thousand yen (about twenty-five dollars each) to the guy who ran the bar.

The 22nd Crash Rescue Boat Squadron had an area at the boat docks in Fukuoka. They operated their crash boats off the East Coast of Korea in the Sea of Japan where their primary mission was the rescue of any downed airmen. They were also used to insert and extract operatives into the north. The fast crash boats could get in close to the beach or to a coastal island and get out in a hurry.

I would become good friends with many of these "Air Force Sailors" on a later assignment as a radioman aboard a crash boat in Florida. I would meet and get to know their commander, a retired Lieutenant Colonel, Les Adams, one of the finest officers I ever knew.

Les was the driving force behind efforts to locate, and restore a crash boat to be placed on static display in a museum in Alabama. He also worked hard to have a plaque mounted in the Air Force museum at Wright-Patterson Air Force Base, Ohio dedicated to the crash rescue boaters that gave their lives in World War II and Korea.

I would meet and have a few drinks with Allan Bishop, the man who broke my nose in a brawl outside a cabaret in downtown Fukuoka.

The crash boat group was already in the cabaret drinking and dancing when our group from Itazuke walked in. One of our guys knew one of the jo-sans that was busy with one of the crash boat guys. There were words, we spilled out in the street and the brawl was on. My nose was broken and there were a few other "casualties" on both sides, but nothing serious.

There were a few other encounters with these guys later on and a few individual fights, but no broken bones that I ever heard about

About a month before my arrival at Itazuke a C-47 had just left the ground on take-off when it lost power and winged over into a hanger and exploded in a ball of fire. In addition to everyone on board there were several maintenance people in the hanger who were killed. The base flight section only had two other “gooney birds”(the name given the C-47) left to haul everything from people, to mail, spare parts, and any other cargo between Itazuke and K-2. Then to triple the workload of the last “goonie” one was loaned to the French Air Force to fly re-supply missions into French Indo China.

A good friend, Stan Little, from Taylorsville, NC flew air resupply missions into the last stronghold of French resistance in Indo China as an American airman. They dropped supplies and French paratroopers from aircraft that had been painted with French markings, but manned by US aircrews.

French Indo China would later become Vietnam after the French lost their colonial war with the Viet Minh.

Soon after I arrived at Itazuke the CO of base flight called our commander and asked for a volunteer radio operator to be reassigned from communications to base flight to crew the last C-47. Their only radio operator was being sent back to the US.

There were two volunteers; myself and another guy (I don’t recall his name). I went in to be interviewed by the base flight CO. He asked if I knew anything about the radio equipment on the goonie bird, the ARN-6 radio compass,

ART 13 transmitter, VHF and UHF transceivers, the works. "Yes Sir, I am familiar with every piece of equipment aboard. Since I was temporarily assigned at Itazuke and scheduled to go to K-2 within a few weeks he picked the other guy, but told me I would fly whenever the other guy wasn't available (for any reason).

On the last day of every month the aircraft would be loaded with what we called ITE troops. Those were "income tax evaders." They would stay overnight in the operations room at K-2, and the next day, which was the first of the month, they would fly back to Itazuke.

To be exempt from paying income tax on the entire months pay, you only had to be "in country" one day out of the month to qualify for the exemption.

After the "goonie" was given to the French, the one remaining generally made at least one and sometimes two round trip flights to K-2 and back every day. When it was down for maintenance everything piled up.

Just to show how ragged the over worked airplane was; we were playing baseball off the side of the apron one day and the goonie taxied to the end of the runway close to where we were and went through the pre-flight check list. While revving up the engines and working over the surface controls a piece of the left wing trailing edge flew off and the prop wash slammed it into the side of the aircraft. The pilot opened the window, looked out, pushed the window shut, opened the throttle and took off.

Once while approaching the K-2 strip we lost an engine, but landed without any problems. Another time we almost had a mid-air collision with a flight of F-84's returning from a mission. Without warning we made a sharp bank to the right. After asking what happened, I was told that we had to roll out to keep from colliding with the incoming jets.

Not long after the interview with base flight I was alerted for movement to K-2. Basham, Nesbitt, and Joe Dallas from Montgomery, Alabama were going too. Joe and I would become good friends over the next six months.

A few days later we boarded the "goonie" and two hours later were on the ground at K-2

Photograph of the author taken in Japan, 1952.

F-84 with 48th Fighter Bomber Wing markings being serviced at the Itazuke flight line. Rear echelon maintenance was performed at Itazuke on all F-84 aircraft flying from K-2 to targets in the north.

CHAPTER 14

Korea
Spring and Summer 1952

The gooney bird was loaded with our duffel, several bags of mail and some spare parts for the aircraft maintenance people; there were no empty seats. The flight to K-2 took an hour and half; as soon as we landed and taxied off the main runway and rolled to a stop in front of base operations we off loaded and lined up in a formation of sorts for a head count. The communications outfit wasn't very far from the flight line and when everyone was accounted for our duffel was loaded onto a weapons carrier and off we went to get checked in.

Those of us who were assigned to communications were directed to a Quonset hut just off the parking apron and behind one of the maintenance hangers. A First Lieutenant was the OIC (Officer in Charge) and apparently was responsible for base communications.. We all reported to him and were given our initial briefing before being issued the rest of the gear we would need.

Our quarters were quonset huts that housed about twelve people each. Our bunks were fold out cots, but we did have a standard GI mattress that had already been placed on the canvas cots. Both the shower and latrine were in a big tent behind our quonset. None of the water in the tent was safe enough to drink; we couldn't even use it to brush our teeth. The only water that had been cleared by the medical people for drinking was in a tank mounted on a small mobile trailer behind the hut.

During the initial briefing we were issued mess kits that were carried to the mess tent for every meal. After eating we went out back of the mess tent to clean them.

There were three barrels in a line. The first two were filled with water that was heated to nearly boiling with a gasoline burner located underneath the barrel. Brushes were tied to the end of a chain that we used to scrub the mess kits with. It was easy to drop a fork or spoon into the hot water; and there was no way to get it back once it hit the hot water. The cooks, or Korean KP's would get all the dropped utensils and pile them up ready to be picked up at the next meal. The first barrel had soapy water, the next was for rinsing, and the third was for a second rinse in cold water. The process resulted in an almost clean mess kit that was ready for the next meal.

The cooks didn't have a way to refrigerate food, so everything we ate came out of a can. The eggs were powdered and so was the milk. None of the food was very good. I did like the stuff we called "bully beef." It was just chunks of beef in a can, but it was tasty after the cooks spiced it up. Bacon that was served with the awful powdered eggs came from a can also; and it was very good when fried to a crisp. Other than that, all the food was lousy.

But compared to the army and marine corps troops a little further north we were living like royalty. They would've loved just to get a hot meal and a dry bunk to sleep in. Not only that, we were in a relatively safe place and they were exposed to hostile fire all the time.

Ice was very scarce at K-2. The air installations, or civil engineers, whoever was responsible for refrigeration at K-2 apparently didn't have the means to produce much ice. Most of what they did make went to the medics and other essential users. The mess tent was way down the list.

Cold beer was not a top priority either; so an enterprising fellow found a solution to the problem of keeping it cold. There was an abandoned dry well on base that was rigged up with a pallet, a rope, and windless. Cases of beer were loaded on the pallet and lowered down the well and allowed to cool. Another way beer could be cooled was to discharge a CO2 fire extinguisher on an open case. The people responsible for re-charging the extinguishers were upset about the misuse of their fire equipment, but the practice continued until the club someway found a small ice generator (we did have a small club of sorts on K-2). From then on the club served cold beer. San Miguel, a beer that was brewed in the Philippines was the favorite of the guys at K-2.

Mail call was held daily and I started receiving letters from Mil. She was true to her promise. Sometimes day after day I would get nothing; then a bunch of letters would all come in at the same time. It was a little confusing because I would read about something that she referred to or something else that I should have known about, but didn't. That bit of news may have happened first, but I wouldn't read about it until later. Maybe that makes sense, maybe not.

I also got mail from Mama. She wrote regularly too and I received almost as much mail from her as I did from Mil. She had also bought a subscription to the Kings Mountain Herald for me. The papers were all rolled up for mailing and they would get to me about three or four weeks after the published date The first I heard from her was a card that simply said "God be with you till we meet again." Mama spent a lot of time on her knees on my behalf.

Mail call was an important happening every day and when I came up empty it was a big emotional letdown. I never understood how a newspaper that was dated the same time could beat regular mail but it happened all the time. The letters were supposed to be sent by air and newspapers and magazines by surface.

The runway, taxiways, and parking apron at K-2 were all PSP (pierced steel planking) and the maintenance hangers were pre-fabricated buildings. There was a ridgeline a mile or so past the end of the runway that caused some problems for the F-84's taking off with a full bomb and fuel load. They used JATO (jet assisted take off) bottles most of the time, and even then they had to drop their bomb load sometimes when, for some unknown reason, they failed to gain enough altitude to clear the ridgeline. When that happened, anyone sleeping in our hut could get bounced out of bed.

Most of the missions were flown during daylight, but not all. The F-84's were landing and taking off all day; it was a busy and noisy place. They flew mostly interdiction missions designed to interrupt the flow of war materials. They destroyed bridges, dams, power plants, railroads, and anything else considered useful to the enemy war effort. They were called on to bomb troop concentrations, gun emplacements, artillery; anything that moved could become a target.

The strike reports would come in to our communications center on teletype. We could read them as they came in and would know how the mission went even before the aircraft returned. The report also contained losses. All indications were that the 136th was taking it to them in a big way almost daily.

There were no Mondays or Sundays. Every day was the same. No weekends or weekdays.

The other F-84 units at K-2, the 48th and some elements of the 8th Fighter-Bombers were using the K-2 strip and maintenance facilities. Itazuke's function was "Rear Echelon Maintenance Combined Operations", referred to as "REMCO" by the 5th Air Force. The 5th was the major command in the far east and everything together was designated "FEAF" for "Far East Air Forces".

Since Korea was a United Nations campaign there were other air units operating from the south. The South Africans were there and still flying F-51's. The ROK's had been given Mustangs by the US, but they were losing them daily; not only to hostile action, but through accidents.

Once we watched a flight of four ROK Mustangs peel off and make their landing. All four were damaged during landing. Two collided during their taxi to the apron, another veered off the runway and damaged the landing gear, and another pilot applied his brakes too hard while still rolling and nosed over.

The radio room was near the flight line and we had a UHF transceiver that was always on and tuned to the tower emergency frequency. That way we could listen in on any transmissions by incoming aircraft declaring an in-flight emergency.

An F-84 pilot called in one afternoon and stated that his hydraulics had been shot up, his controls weren't responding well and he didn't believe he had any landing gear that would lock in the down position. His "gear down" light indicated that he didn't. He didn't have a hanging bomb or anything that would require a bail-out; he wasn't low on fuel, so he was instructed to fly around to burn off all his fuel before trying to land.

That gave us time to assemble on the edge of the strip to watch him come in. The other aircraft in his formation came in safely and cleared the runway. The fire trucks and medics were standing by at their positions.

After he orbited long enough to burn off the fuel it was time for him to come in. He came in nose high and touched down. The tail contacted the pierced steel matting and sparks flew behind him like a giant rooster tail. He held it up as long as he could and slowly lowered the nose. He was slowing down, and as he got nearer to where we were, he blew his canopy; when he passed us he was unstraping his harness as the airplane fell over on the left wing and started a slow turn. The fire trucks were rolling in his direction.

Before the plane stopped moving, he was out on the left wing, jumped off and started running. We never saw where, or if, he stopped, and don't know if the medics ever caught him or not

Another time, a B-29 returning to Okinawa after a bombing mission, declared an emergency and requested landing instructions at K-2. That airplane had been damaged and the crew didn't know if the landing gear worked or not. The landing gear came down and locked all right, but it had no brakes and went off the end of the runway through a pile of sand and nosed over damaging all four propellers. That looked like the extent of the damage, but a few days later a crew came up from Okinawa and cannibalized the whole aircraft. They didn't try and repair it.

The shooting war was many miles north of Taegu but the effects were everywhere. Displaced people were everywhere with no place to go. They had been run out of their homes in the north.

One of the refugees, a little boy not over ten or twelve, had died on the dirt road leading north from the base. Probably no one knew why, or even cared. He was more than likely an orphan; just lying dead beside the road with a ration can, that someone placed there, under his head. Flies were already gathered around his face.People kept walking by him. No doubt he just laid there until someone in authority came by and loaded him up.

Chinese prisoners of war rolled by on their way to an island prison in the south. We could see the results of past ground battles that took place near the Naktong River a few miles outside the base perimeter. There were a couple of disabled Russian tanks and old rocket launcher casings; things relating to combat operations laying around, but now the line had been stabilized north of K-2.

Several of our radio operators were sent on temporary duty as forward air controllers up north. We also had a radar range situated on an island off the coast; the guys there were close enough to go on alert from time to time. The forward air controllers were right on the line however. They rode in communications jeeps and were in direct contact with spotter aircraft that marked targets for the F-84's.

The spotter aircraft were called "mosquitos" and were converted T-6 trainers that had rocket launchers attached under the wings. When the ground troops suspected troop concentrations, or gun emplacements they called the forward air controllers in to direct the spotters to the target. The mosquitos marked the target and the F-84's came in and destroyed it.

A few of our radio guys were sent TDY (temporary duty) to operate the radios on the radar range but I wasn't one of them. Bob Basham went at least one time and one other, Jack Walker spent most of his tour on the island where the radar range was located.

Another flew as radio on a C-47 that was outfitted to drop flares at night. They were called "fireflies" and were called in by the ground troops to light up an area for them at night. The flare was attached to a slow descending parachute and would light up an entire hillside like the middle of day.

Another rode in the T-6 mosquito to coordinate with the ground troops. These operations were conducted out of bases north of Taegu for several reasons. The strip at K-2 was busy enough with F-84's taking off and landing, and the bases up north were closer to the main line and that allowed the aircraft more time over the target.

Other than the guys mentioned above, most of our people were never exposed to any hostile actions.

One of our radio operators went on an extended leave of absence to the main line of resistance. (meaning that he had official permission to be away from his duty station) His brother was with the marine corps, and he went up to spend a week or so with him. During the time he was there he lived in a forward bunker.

Nightlife in Taegu wasn't much; and even if it had been like Fukuoka we wouldn't have been able to take advantage of it. We rarely went to Taegu even though it was a big place and there were probably lots of "young ladies" there to entertain us, but things could go wrong for us in town. VD was a good possibility if anyone were foolish enough to allow himself to be exposed. There were reports that the Koreans made alcoholic beverages containing stuff we wouldn't want to be drinking. Word was out that the opium trade was wide open, and none of our guys wanted anything to do with that.

Korea and Japan were two entirely different countries in more ways than one. Our adventures outside the perimeter were mostly limited to the villages near the base; and even though they were for the most part off limit areas, we didn't pay too much attention to the off limit restrictions.

Several times Joe Dallas and I had to make a run for it to escape the base security people. The girls had to make a run for it also, because, if caught, they too would have problems with the authorities.

The 187th Regimental Combat Team, a group of paratroopers on their way to making a combat jump at Munsan-ni stopped off in the hills around K-2 sometime around the middle of March. They were there a couple of weeks and were coming from either Beppu in Japan or had been taking care of POW's on the island of Koje-do off the south coast of Korea.

One of the paratroopers shot a girl's foot off in one of the villages near K-2. They were a rowdy group and were itching to get into it with the bad guys up north. I never got to know any of them while they were playing war outside K-2 but some years later I would become friends with two of the "rakkasans" as they were known by the Japanese. One would become one of my best friends for many years. One was Walt Shumate, a legendary warrior in the Army's Special Forces. He was a volunteer for every dangerous undertaking the green berets were ever called on to do; from the Son Tay raid to rescue American POW's near Hanoi, to the botched attempt to free the American Embassy hostages in Iran.

His last request before dying from a cancer was for his handlebar moustache to be enshrined in the green beret club at Fort Bragg. It is still there today.

Steve Coulson, the other 187th veteran, with probably a thousand parachute jumps to his credit, has been a good friend for over forty years. He too was a well known member of the army airborne elite. He was wounded once in Korea and again in Vietnam.

As you read this, you no doubt get the feeling that the military and that way of life occupies a great deal of my inner being. That may be so, because so much of my adult life was spent in the military and around military people. Even after retirement from active duty, I have associated myself with men who chose to serve their country.

I don't shun those who didn't. Some of my closest friends today, people in my Church that I care deeply about, never spent a day in uniform. One in particular, a Pastor, is as close to me today as my Father was when he was alive. I care for him probably more than any man alive; but he never served in the military. He chose to serve mankind and has probably helped more people around the world than a hundred of my other friends combined.

It's just that I have always had the deepest amount of admiration and respect for military people. I seem to "get along" better with those men. And I have absolutely no use what-so-ever for an individual who would run off to Canada, or one who would burn his draft card, rather than serve.

After four or five months in Korea I was given a seven day R&R (rest and relaxation) furlough back to Japan. I had been back to Itazuke on the C-47 several times, but only stayed long enough to do a turn around back to K-2.

Joe Dallas and I caught a C-46 back to Brady Field, another airstrip not far from Fukuoka and spent seven days and nights hitting the cabarets and just living it up. By the time our leave was up we were wore out and ready to go back to duty and get some real R&R.

Early on the day we were to report back to K-2, we checked into base operations at Brady, and loaded onto a C-46. One of the engines wouldn't start, so we had to off-load and were told there wouldn't be another flight available to K-2 that day. One of the maintenance people did something right and they tried the engine again; this time it started. We loaded up and off we went. Two hours later we were back with our unit. If that engine hadn't started we would've been a day late returning from R&R, and even though we couldn't avoid being late getting back to the unit we might have had a problem with the Lieutenant.

Sometime during the summer the 136th was sent back to Texas on paper. All personnel and equipment were transferred to the 58th Fighter-Bomber Wing. My enlistment was up on September 5th. My three years were finished but several weeks before that date arrived I got the word. Orders came out extending my enlistment five months.

President Harry Truman had extended everyone in Korea "at the convenience of the government" if their enlistment was due to expire before they had completed a year "in country." It wasn't unexpected, so the extension didn't come as a surprise. At least, in the not too distant future, I would get back to Itazuke, and finish my tour there.

The letters from 212 Fairview St. kept coming; and I was looking forward to getting back to see Mil. Her letters never indicated anything of a negative nature, but I had already seen several guys get a "dear John" letter and I couldn't help but be a little concerned. She never wrote anything but good stuff and was anxious for me to finish my tour and get back home so I tried not to think of anything except good times ahead with her.

The news from home remained basically the same. My folks were more than ready for me to be on the way home. Mama was still praying daily for my safety.

I was on duty in the radio room one afternoon and a land line call came through for me. No one that I knew should be calling me because the only phone in the radio shack was a field set that was hooked up to the communications center that was used for routine voice contact with the teletype guys. When I answered the guy on the other end was an old Park Grace school mate who was serving as a navy corpsman with the marine corps up north. How he learned where I was or how he managed to make land line contact with me was really amazing because he had to route his call through so many relays. Sometimes it was impossible to make contact with the communications center a hundred yards away. We talked for a few minutes before we lost contact and I never heard from him again.

Group getting ready to depart Itazuke for K-2. Author is third from left.

Republic of Korea F-51 sitting on ramp at Itazuke. Note Korean markings and insignia.

CHAPTER 15

Korea
September–December 1952

The summer of 1952 was nearing an end. Considering how cold Korea was during the winter months it was unbelievably hot and dusty in the summer. None of the roads were paved except for one main artery that ran south to north all the way to Seoul. There were cars, but many more military vehicles than cars; and many times more bicycles and make-shift carts.

Some of the men, and women too, had a carrier pack we called an "A" frame strapped to their back. With an "A" frame they could carry a ton. Of course, that wasn't the case; but sometimes it appeared to be so. They looked to be carrying unbelievable loads.

There was no such thing as "air conditioning", nowhere in the country, and none on K-2. There may have been a few air conditioning units in the dispensary, I'm not certain about that.

The forward maintenance people had to work on the pierced steel planking aprons and inside the steaming hot hangers. The PSP would get hot enough to almost melt the tires off the aircraft. The people who serviced the aircraft such as the refueling crew and armament technicians were there day and night along with all the other aircraft maintenance specialists. It was hot, it was hard, and never ending. The F84s required many hours of maintenance for every hour of flying time.

As communications personnel, at least we were inside, and not out in the hot sun while on duty. Our radio maintenance guys were over worked because the humidity did its damage to the inner parts of the equipment.

The aircraft maintenance guys must have been good, because there were no aircraft accidents due to equipment failure; none that were recorded anyway. Pilot error and weather accounted for a few minor incidents but lost aircraft were all due to hostile ground fire. Air to air dogfights were between the F-86s of the 51st and 4th Fighter Interceptor Wings and the Russian built Mig-15s. Our F-84s were used for tactical air support and interdiction missions but there were several confirmed Mig-15 kills by F-84 pilots.

The F-84 had a top speed of a little over 600 mph and was no match in air to air dogfights with the Mig-15 at higher altitudes, but at lower altitudes they had a good chance of holding their own against the Russian built Migs. The F-84 pilots accounted for nine confirmed Mig-15s shot down during the war.

Joe Dallas, myself and another guy almost got into some trouble while out in the hills around K-2 one afternoon. We had checked out our carbines with several bandoleers of ammunition and gone out just to do some shooting. We weren't more than a mile or so from the perimeter when we spotted a small lake; not much bigger than a farm pond. When we got to the water's edge we could see frogs everywhere. They were in the water and on the banks, croaking and jumping around. They weren't little frogs, but really big ones.

Joe started shooting them; soon we were all three shooting frogs. We didn't have a reason; we were doing it probably just because they were something alive and because they were there. I don't have any idea of how many we killed, but dead frogs were floating everywhere in the pond.

We made our way back to the base, checked in, and secured our rifles. We didn't suspect that we had done anything wrong. It was a matter of record that we had checked off base with our weapons that afternoon, so when a frog farmer lodged a complaint with the base commander, there wasn't any doubt about who the guilty were. It didn't take the investigator long to make that determination.

Our Lieutenant called the three of us in. When he explained that a frog farmer had complained to the commander and demanded payment for his dead frogs we realized we were in a jam. The wing commander turned everything over to the base security people to get some answers.

After the Lieutenant chewed on us for a while he broke out laughing and said he would do everything he could to get us out of the jam we were in. He dismissed us with "you'll be getting a statement of charges when the details are worked out with the farmer." I don't remember all the details but as well as I can recall, the frogs were valued at about fifteen cents each, and we had to pay sixteen or eighteen dollars, or a total of about fifty-two dollars between us. Figure it out! That amounted to a bunch of dead frogs. That was the end of it.

We never had to go see the base commander, or apologize to the farmer or hear anything more about it, other than getting croaked at every time we walked into the club or mess tent. For several weeks, every where we went, the first thing we heard was "ribbit, ribbit" The Lieutenant took care of everything for us. I don't even remember his name, but he was a fine officer that looked after his men. The kind of leader you could respect.

The communications squadron enlisted men were all housed in five or six quonset huts and were coming from, or going on duty, at all hours. The radio room was manned all the time, seven days a week. We pulled eight hour shifts, and the personnel who worked the teletype worked the same type of schedule.

A poker game was going on in one of the huts that didn't stop for weeks. There just wasn't much entertainment at K-2 other than an outdoor amphitheater were they ran old movies after dark. There were no seats or benches, just bomb crates that had been cut in two and turned upside down.

Once in a while the USO would put on a show; and even then the poker game didn't stop. It wasn't a big game, I don't remember the stakes, but they probably weren't more than a dime to a quarter, but it continued 24 hours a day, 7 days a week for several months.

Early in October I received notification that I would be going back to Itazuke to finish out my tour. My departure date was set for sometime in November. Very soon, Korea, the hot and dusty "Land of the Morning Calm" would be history and the remainder of my tour would be spent in Japan except for a couple round robin flights on the goonie bird.

Basham and Nesbitt would be left behind, but they too would be back at Itazuke before I left to return home. Joe Dallas had already gone back to Japan along with Jim Mahoney, another buddy that had become one of the "good guys."

Joe didn't care for the military way of life very much. He had been "drafted" into the air force, so to speak. A Judge in Montgomery, Alabama had given him a choice. "Either enlist and serve your country, or go to jail." He chose to enlist. I never knew what his offense was, but it couldn't have been anything very serious, because Joe wasn't a criminal.

Before we parted company for good several months later, he and I would spend a lot of off duty time together, along with the others; some that have been forgotten altogether. I can still see faces way back there in my foggy memory, but a bunch of names will be forgotten forever. At the time there was no doubt they would be remembered the rest of my life. We were all close. To burn a draft card or run off to Canada and to avoid serving our country was unthinkable by anyone in our group. Everyone, to the last man, considered serving a privilege and honor, even the drafted Joe Dallas.

In late October I packed my gear and made ready to leave. The only souvenir I took with me was a pair of Chinese binoculars that my friend who had spent a week in a front line bunker with his marine corps brother had given me. Joe Dallas had a pistol that he took back to Japan, but when we had to go through customs inspection before boarding the ship to return to the US, the customs people found it. He made a false bottom in his shaving gear and hid it there. They found the handgun and took it from him. There was a legal way weapons could be taken back to the states, but Joe chose to try and sneak it through and it didn't work.

The flight back to Itazuke took less than two hours, and my old friend from base flight was still flying as the only radio operator. After returning to the states, I ran into him at a base exchange on Pope Air Force Base. At Pope he was flying radio in troop carriers supporting the airborne troops at Fort Bragg.

Itazuke was like going home. Nothing had changed except for most of the people. Cochran and Baker were gone. Again, I wondered if First Sergeant Coors had made it back to the US safely.

There were some new radio operators in our barracks and not long after getting back to Itazuke I saw a fellow in the mess hall that I had a problem with back at Moses Lake. It was a strange meeting because not long before the 81st Wing had been alerted for movement to Bentwaters we had a WAF assigned to the communications squadron after completing radio school at Keesler. She wasn't on duty, but came by the radio shack while I was on duty. She was apparently trying to evade this guy. His name was Razo. Anyway, Razo tried to come into the radio shack to talk to her. She didn't want anything to do with him; and I challenged him by refusing to allow him to come in. He backed away and made the statement that if he ever saw me again "my ass would be his."

I never saw him again, and assumed he had gone to England with the 81st. Then, soon after returning to Itazuke, I walked into the mess hall, and there sat Razo, eating. Our eyes made contact; he didn't say a word, but returned to his meal. We never spoke and soon he got up and left; I never saw him again. He may have been transient, more than likely just passing through Itazuke on his way to Korea, or who knows where.

Fukuoka hadn't changed either. The crash boat guys were still around, but we never had any more brawls. We weren't friendly, but there wasn't any hostility between us either. There were plenty of girls to go around, and the Asahi beer never gave out. The souvenir shops downtown did a good business and I picked up a few figurines and an imitation Ronson lighter, a custom pool cue, and a bamboo fly rod to pack with my gear to take home. I picked out a nice pair of silk pajamas for Mil and a bath robe for Mama.

It wasn't long before the weather cooled some. The weather patterns were a lot like the weather at home. There were no extreme temperatures, and very little, or no snow during winter.

By now we had learned enough of the language to communicate somewhat with the Japanese. Some of the locals could speak a little English, so we didn't have much of a language barrier while away from the base.

We made a few weekend train trips to various towns out and away from Fukuoka. Once we went to Nagasaki to look at the bomb damage and another time we went to Sasebo, a port city south of Fukuoka. Sasebo had a big US Naval base, and we picked a weekend to go there at the same time a seventh fleet aircraft carrier and her escorts had arrived at the base. There were too many sailors on liberty, so we didn't stay too long before going back to Fukuoka.

The navy had a small detachment on the far side of Itazuke. They had two Grumman Avenger torpedo bombers that were used to carry mail out to the seventh fleet apparently because they didn't have their own mail facility at Sasebo. One of the sailors had enticed a Japanese girl to crawl under the fence and after she did that, he took her on board a Navy amphibious aircraft and proceeded to have his way with her.

She reported the incident and later he was given a general court martial. The court was held in the Itazuke headquarters building; and the only thing that separated the radio room and court room was a thin wall. We could hear the whole proceeding. The girl and her mother were there to accuse him; he had no chance. If the incident had occurred off base the Japanese courts could have tried him, because by then, we were no longer "occupation forces" but guests of the country.

Since he committed the offense on base the military had the legal responsibility to deal with him. He was convicted and sent back to the US and a federal prison. We never knew exactly what he was accused of doing to her; one of his mistakes was taking her aboard the military aircraft.

Nesbitt, Basham, and I could have been in a minor jam after leaving the base one night when Itazuke was under restriction. Because of a Japanese national holiday everyone on Itazuke was restricted to the base; some sort of demonstration or parade was to take place in Fukuoka.

There was a big "benjo" ditch along one side of the base perimeter and a rail spur ran across a small trestle and onto the base. The fence could easily be crawled under at the trestle and that was the way we left the base. It was only a short distance from there to the main road leading to town. There were a couple of bars with girls at the intersection of the base road and main highway leading to Fukuoka. The railroad track was elevated above the rice paddies that were on both sides and ran for about a half mile to where it crossed the main highway.

After spending a few hours at the cabaret we worked our way back to the trestle. The other two guys were behind me; I made my way under the fence and was making my way across the trestle. Basham and Nesbitt were waiting their turn to get under the fence.

A beam of light hit me in the face and then I heard the unmistakable sound of a weapon being loaded. I threw my hands out and let them know I was a GI. They happened to be some guys living in a row of tents near the track and the base perimeter and I didn't have a problem convincing them I was on their side; but when the spotlight hit me, Nesbitt and Basham jumped from the elevated track into the "benjo" ditch. The water mixed with "human fertilizer" was running about two feet deep when they hit the ditch. From there they had to wade through about a half mile of flooded paddies and get through the fence behind the airman's club.

When they finally made their way to the barracks "you could smell them coming." They went straight to the shower, fatigues, boots and all. They had to throw the fatigues away because there was no way to get the smell out.

A lot of new people were being assigned to our outfit. They would be around for a few days, maybe a week, and then they would fly off to K-2 or the radar range. The 58th aircraft were kept busy up north. Strike reports were posted daily that indicated more and more attacks were being made. News came one day that they had destroyed the forth largest power plant in the world at a place called Sui-ho, near the Yalu River.

The Yalu was the Northern border between North Korea and China. The 58th was given the Republic of Korea Presidential Unit Citation for that mission and added another streamer to their banner.

The war had entered its final phase with peace talks going on at Panmunjon. Dwight Eisenhower had been elected President in November and during his political campaign he promised to "go to Korea and end the hostilities." I would be leaving for the US in January; and in late July a cease fire would be signed. To this day the North and South are still divided. The demilitarized zone is still no-man's-land, and North Korea is still a minor threat to the stability in that part of the world.

Going home orders had not been received by anyone other than a guy named Billy Hale. He had his shipment orders and was just waiting for the day to arrive for him to leave. It was the first week in December and he expected to be home for Christmas.

He knew none of us would make it and would come through the barracks singing "I'll be home for Christmas," followed by "I'll have a blue Christmas without you."

Then we were called to the orderly room to pick up our orders. Viera, one of the teletype guys from Rochester, New York and I were on the same shipment order. We were scheduled to leave on or about December 20th and go by rail to a place near Tachikawa and process out.

We almost didn't make it. A going away party was scheduled and we made the rounds in Fukuoka hitting all the cabarets and saying "so long" to anyone we knew downtown.

A couple of days before our departure our going away party started in the supply room in the afternoon. It goes without saying that by the time it was dark there was some "loud singing and guitar playing" going on. It was getting late and the singing got louder; the barracks next to ours was used by the base security people and someone from next door yelled in Japanese "yak-a-mush," which meant "shut your mouth," that was all it took!

It seemed that both barracks emptied out in the grassy area between the two buildings, but there were only about eight of us. Viera had a flashlight in his hand shining it around checking to see how many we were up against.

One of the security guys wanted to be the first to get things started. He was supposed to be the base boxing champ and was their lead off man. He walked up to Jim Mahoney; Jim wasn't a boxer but he was a big Irishman that didn't take anything from anyone; anyway the boxer looked at Mahoney, stuck his chin out and put his finger to his chin and said, "go ahead, clip me one, right here." Crack! Mahoney hit him so hard he tumbled backwards knocking three or four other security people down. It was on! Everyone was swinging and yelling, and then suddenly it was over.

One of the security people had an eye busted up pretty bad. They took him to the hospital and it was told the next day that he had lost the eye.

That may not have been the case, we never knew for certain. He claimed that he was on the ground and someone kicked him in the eye. The truth is that Viera hit him in the eye with his flashlight.

The fight was over and no other damage was done on either side. The party was over so Viera, Mahoney and I went to the mess hall for some midnight chow. Mahoney had some coffee and went back to the barracks leaving Viera and me in the mess hall.

All of a sudden people were all around us. The security guys had brought in their "on duty" people and were identifying the both of us as the ones that put their guy in the hospital. They jerked us up and hauled us away to the Provost Marshall's office.

We were told to sit down and shut up while they prepared some paperwork on us. I stood up one time to put my cap in my belt and "whap," I was knocked down by an on duty security guy. Any move either of us made was followed by a hard knock to the head. Before it was over they had us beat up pretty bad.

We needed to have the OD (Officer of the Day) there. Once I asked to see the OD and was knocked backwards out of my chair. The guy with the busted eye was brought in with a bandage over his eye and identified us. The OD finally came in and we were allowed to leave, but were escorted back to our barracks by the OD right alongside.

He probably prevented another riot between the two groups. All of our guys were still up and dressed and a group of security people were gathered around in front of their barracks. Viera and I were told not to leave the barracks when we got up the next morning. We were allowed to go to breakfast, that was all, then right back to the barracks.

As we knew he would, the squadron commander called us to the orderly room soon after breakfast and told us we were being investigated for assault, among other things. The guy that was hurt had named us as the guilty ones. Everyone knew there were others involved in the fight, but no one else had been charged with anything. Had Mahoney stayed in the mess hall another ten minutes, he would have been picked up with us, but we told him just to lay low until everything blew over.

Anyway the CO told us to go back to the barracks and stay there under restriction; and to leave only to go to chow until he could do something. We sweated it out until late that evening and were called back to the commander's office. I was getting worried that our orders would be revoked and that we would be held over for some kind of punishment, maybe even a court martial.

Viera and I reported in and the commander told us to have a seat. He then told us the other commander wanted us held over to face charges. We were really sweating by now. The Captain then said "go back and get your gear ready; a weapons carrier will back up to the front of your barracks at 1:00 AM tomorrow morning to take you to the railway transportation officer in Fukuoka. He's going to put you on your train. Here are your shipment orders; now get out of here and have a Merry Christmas."

Talk about relief! Wow! That was the best thing that could have happened. We saluted him, thanked him, and took off for the barracks to get our gear and tell everyone goodbye.

At 1:00 AM we were all set, and when the truck arrived we piled into the back and rode away from Itazuke leaving a group of good friends, most of them never to be seen or heard from again.

The train must have been the same one that we had ridden south a year earlier. All the people riding with us were US military going to Yokohama to board a ship that would take us back to San Francisco.

The author (center) and two buddies, summer of 1952, on one of the dirt roads leading to K-2.

CHAPTER 16

Christmas in Japan And The USS Miegs Dec 1952–Jan 1953

Viera and I both were a little apprehensive until the train left Fukuoka. The security guys may have learned that our commanding officer had arranged to sneak us out of Itazuke and could still yank us off the train and hold us on assault charges.

That didn't happen and soon after we boarded and stowed our duffel the train rolled out of Fukuoka and we were safe from the revenge of Itazuke's security people. Looking back at the events of our last two days at Itazuke I've often wondered how our Captain explained the fact that Viera and I were no longer there. The load of the whole fiasco fell on his shoulders because we weren't there to answer any charges that may have been leveled at us. I've thought many times that we were very selfish in running out like we did and if we could go back and relive those two days I wouldn't have left without some assurance the Captain had his flanks covered. I keep remembering his last words "hurry home and have a merry Christmas" and they always remind me of the grit and commitment of the people in the air force that I served with.

The thirty hour ride took us back through Hiroshima where we were sidelined for a while to allow the southbound to come through. After we arrived at our destination we were taken to a compound not far from Tachikawa Air Base and 5th Air Force Headquarters. Both were located near Yokohama.

Soon after everyone was off loaded at the railway station we were loaded into shuttle busses for a short trip out to another huge tent city. About the only permanent building in the entire compound was the mess hall. We went through the normal routine of checking into a new unit. It was early in the morning when we got there and soon after arriving at the tent city everyone was assigned to a tent and after stowing our gear we went to breakfast. The mess hall surprised me. The food was very good and there were lots of pretty Japanese girls working in the dining room serving up hot coffee, and cold milk. They were already decorating the place for Christmas. The next day would be Christmas Eve.

All of a sudden it occurred to me; it was exactly a year ago that I met Mil and her sister Mary going home from Wednesday night services at 2nd Baptist. Today was an anniversary for us but it would be nearly another month before we could do any celebrating. I felt a twinge of loneliness and wished I could see her.

During our briefing we were told that we couldn't leave the area. No reason was given, but we found out later that they wanted to make sure we didn't go out and catch a dose of something they didn't want us to take aboard the ship.

News of an aircraft accident was circulating through the compound; one of the worst ever; a big transport taking off from Larson Air Force Base at Moses Lake had crashed killing a bunch of guys who were going home for Christmas. Some of them had just finished their tour in Korea. The aircraft one of the C-124s, the big double decker transport used as a troop carrier was loaded with people going to the east coast; it had gone down shortly after takeoff on December 20th.

I didn't know it at the time but Mama and Daddy heard about the accident through the national news media; they were told the airplane was loaded with troops returning from Korea.

They knew I was on the way home and stayed up all night hoping for more news, but had to wait until the morning newspapers came out with a list of names of those who had been killed. Six months later another C-124 would go down shortly after takeoff at Tachikawa killing 129 in the worst aircraft accident ever up to that time. The C-124 aircrews used to call the airplane "old shakey"

Christmas Eve brought a wonderful surprise. I was sitting in my tent with some of the other guys when in walked my Uncle Bud. I knew he was somewhere in Japan, but didn't know where and had no thoughts of being able to see him. He stayed for an hour or so and had to get back to his duties. He was based at Tachikawa and had a friend at 5th Air Force who gave him the shipment list with my name on it, so he knew about when I would be coming through the replacement depot. We had a real good time together, but all too soon he had to go back to his duties.

Christmas came and all the hundreds of guys in the tents had nothing to do but wait for Christmas dinner to be served. They played a lot of cards. There was a poker game, and some were playing pinochle. I had a small dagger that had been with me for several months, and remember sitting there sharpening the knife on my leather boot. It wasn't much but I wanted to take it home with me and started to think of some ways to get it through customs inspection.

The cooks really went all out and we had a big Christmas dinner with turkey and the works. Everything was very good. They had the decorations up, and went out of their way to make us feel good about being there at Christmas; still it was a long lonely day.

The next day we had another nice surprise. Joe Dallas came in. He was with another guy named Edwards from the communications squadron who was going home to Virginia. How they found Viera and me with so many other tents there, I have no idea. His shipping orders came in the day Viera and I left Itazuke and he was just a few days behind us. When we questioned him about the fight we had with the security troops he couldn't give us anything more than we already knew. No one knew how long we would be there. The people in charge of the "replacement depot," as it was called were tight lipped and gave out very little information. We were waiting on something but didn't know what.

Within a few days we learned that the ship scheduled to take us to San Francisco would be carrying a lot of the troops who would be marching in President Eisenhower's inaugural parade. The incoming President had requested (the same thing as an order) that all military personnel who marched in his parade had to be combat veterans. That is, they had to have served in a combat zone.

The delay was caused by some army guys coming from Korea; and we found out later that the ship would carry over fourteen hundred people from all branches of the military; most of them would be in the inaugural parade. I had been reassigned to Pope Air Force Base near Fayetteville to be processed for discharge, so I wasn't scheduled to march in the parade.

The five extra months that President Truman had ordered extending everyone's enlistment would be up for me on February 5th.

Our wait wasn't long. Several days after Christmas we were told to get our gear and be ready to go to Yokohama within the hour. The busses arrived and off we went.

The busses didn't take us directly to our ship and after a short trip away from tent city we were off loaded and filed into a long building that had long rows of bins with people standing behind them. When we finally worked our way to the front and were facing the bin we were told to dump our duffel into the bin for customs inspection.

Customs inspection didn't come as a surprise because we had been warned this would happen. I was wearing a regular "overseas" cap. We called it by another name, but I don't care to mention it here. Anyway, the dagger I had been sharpening for three days was on top of my head underneath the cap and the customs guy didn't ask me to take my cap off.

The fellow who spent time with his marine corps brother in the frontline bunker was carrying his brother's small handgun in the liner of his "Ike" jacket that they never searched. He probably made it home with the little pistol. Joe Dallas wasn't as lucky. They found the .45 caliber automatic pistol he had hid in his shaving gear. Nothing was done or said. They just took it from him.

Behind the inspectors were shelves with all the stuff they had confiscated. It looked like a liquor store; there were lots of bottles on the shelves. All that liquor probably found its way to the local NCO club, or maybe home with the customs guys. None made it aboard the ship. The customs guys knew all the hiding places.

We had been told what not to bring aboard the ship, and liquor headed the list. It was apparent from the shelves full of confiscated liquor that a lot of the guys didn't believe a lot of what they were told about liquor aboard a navy ship.

It wasn't long before we were out of there, marched to the pier and as our names were checked off we boarded the ship, the USS General Miegs. As soon as we boarded we went directly to our assigned compartment. It was just like the USS Randall that brought us to Yokohama a year earlier. Soon we were on our way out of the bay into the open water.

The water was calm and we had smooth sailing, but just like before, there were some seasick people on board. They were to be pitied, but there was absolutely nothing anyone could do to stop them from being sick.

New years day was spent at sea; The holiday came and went without much fanfare. Every compartment had a public address system that piped music to anyone who cared to listen, and gave us the world news and any announcements we needed to hear.

On January 2nd the speaker announced that Hank Williams had died. You would have thought a close relative had passed away for some of the guys. I believe some of them actually cried over the news that he was dead.

The lights came on and we were hauled out of our bunks one morning around five o'clock and given a "short arm" inspection by a navy corpsman. I must have had a drip of something as it was milked down, because he handed me a red slip where he had written my name; and told me where and when to report to the infirmary.

Sometime during the day I made my way to the medical room and gave the guy my red slip and he took a smear to be checked out under the microscope. Apparently they didn't find anything because the report was negative and I never heard anything more about it.

Unlike the USS Randall, we were allowed time on deck after dark; in fact we could roam around the ship with more freedom than on the Randall. It didn't seem nearly as crowded; and the food was actually edible. And there were no dogs on board to mess up the top deck.

Most of the troops were given some clean-up duties that were a daily routine. Viera and I were given an area around the ladders from our compartment to the open deck to clean every morning. Not much of a chore, but it gave us something to do. Dallas and Edwards were given a broom and mop to keep the compartment floor clean.

The daily cleaning made me wonder about where any dust or dirt would come from; we were out in the middle of a big ocean, and the only dirt there would have to be brought on board with us at Yokohama; Once the areas and floors were clean; how did they get dirty again, out there on all that water?

An odd thing happened the very first evening after we left port. Several of the guys in my compartment went top side and I went along. We were lounging around listening to the noises the ship made as it plowed through the water; I had my back to a big exhaust vent looking up at the moon. As I looked at the bright surface I saw the face of Mil, the outline of her facial features and the curly black hair were as definite as a photograph. Her head was slightly turned showing a partial profile. To this day, I can still see the same outline; but cannot tell her how to see the same thing. Many times we've looked at the full moon and I've tried to tell her what to look for, but she can't see the same outline.

Since that first time, every time the moon is full and not obscured by clouds ,the picture is there. As this little segment is being written I find it difficult to adequately define how the vision appears to me, It may be best to let it go as explained above, and hope that the reader will understand.

The trip to San Francisco took fourteen days of running day and night. Viera was returning to a base somewhere near his home in Rochester, New York. He was definitely not inclined to think about another hitch in the air force and couldn't wait until he could get back to civilian life.

We were scheduled to dock in San Francisco in two more days when he took his duffel with his GI clothing and threw it overboard. All he had left was the uniform he was wearing and an AWOL bag packed with his shaving gear, underwear, socks, and six cartons of tax-free cigarettes. He was making ready for some major changes.

Two days later we sailed under the Golden Gate and pulled along side the pier at Fort Mason. As we were being tied up a crowd of people were on the dock, we were on the ship's rail looking on; I wondered who all these people were, and still don't know. Maybe some of them had a husband or son returning home. A loudspeaker was blaring out music and a girl was singing a song welcoming all of us home. I don't think anyone on board expected that kind of welcome.

After about an hour we were allowed to go below and get our gear. We offloaded and went directly to a big ferry boat that was tied up at another pier. It was a short ferry boat trip to Yerba Buena Island that was located directly underneath the Oakland Bay Bridge.

A streamlined out-processing procedure was set up on a big concrete slab with a bunch of tables set up for that purpose. The processing lines were long and it took a while to get to the table, but all in all everything went smoothly. The lines were formed according to the first initial of the last name. The line I and Viera went to processed individuals whose last name started with S through V.

My records were there and the necessary information was included, my orders were checked and a bunch of other stuff completed. We hadn't been paid since November so we were paid up to date along with travel pay to our next assignment. It was a nice pile of money.

The commercial transportation people had their sales representatives there to help us with transportation home. We were all still together, Joe Dallas, Viera, Edwards and myself; we all went looking for someone to sell us a ticket home. Viera and I were talking to the railway ticket agent and found that we could leave San Francisco at 11:00 PM or wait until the next morning and leave at 10:00 AM. Both trains would get us to Chicago in time to connect to our trains going east. The slow train made more stops and the one leaving the next morning was an express and traveled faster.

After weighing the facts we chose to spend the night in San Francisco and catch the fast train. For some reason, my route from Chicago took me to Cincinnati, then through West Virginia, to Roanoke Virginia, and on to Winston Salem. I would then get on a bus that would take me to Charlotte and Kings Mountain. Viera and I would take different directions from Chicago.

Joe went an entirely different route from San Francisco to Montgomery, Alabama. Edwards decided to get a ticket on the early slower train to Chicago. He and I would take the same route from there. Viera and I decided to spend the night in San Francisco and leave the next morning.

We bought a ticket with some of our new wealth; mine only costing $56.00 for the whole cross country trip. Since we were returning from Korea, I believe they gave us a special deal. The decision to spend the night in San Francisco was the wrong one as we were later to find out in a big way.

Busses were lined up to take us from Yerba Buena Island to the downtown terminal as we finished processing out and made arrangements for commercial transportation. We had our records and tickets, and before long were on our way. Viera and I said goodbye to Joe Dallas and Edwards. I would see Edwards again, but the only thing left of Joe were a few pictures taken in an apple orchard in Korea after we had been ran out of an off limits village. I still have the pictures and often wonder if he is still alive and sometimes think of the five days we spent on R&R in Japan.

Viera and I caught a cab to a street in San Francisco that the cab driver had suggested. There were bars everywhere and several hotels. We got a room, dumped our bags and walked down the street to a bar. Viera was looking a little shabby since he only had the one uniform, but that didn't matter, we had freshened up in the room with a shower and shave. It was already getting a little late when we walked into the first bar.

After making the rounds at a couple of the bars we had a few beers before settling down in a big booth where we were joined by two (not too pretty) girls. We didn't have any plans to do anything more than drink a few beers and go back to the room to sleep in a big bed for the first time in a long time; and to catch our train the next morning.

Neither Viera nor I needed or wanted any female company other than to make small talk. We were going home and surely didn't want to take any souvenirs the girls may have been passing around.They must have slipped something into our drinks, because the last thing I remember before waking up in the room the next morning was the girl next to me pulling her top down exposing her (not so pretty) breasts.

Luckily, we woke up in time to make it to the terminal to get on the train. However we had nothing left but our gear and less than a buck between the two of us. We didn't even have cab fare to the terminal, but caught a ride with someone. Viera had his AWOL bag stuffed with six cartons of cigarettes that he bought aboard the ship. Tax free cigarettes only cost seventy-five cents a carton in the ship's store. I think we used one of those cartons to pay for the ride to the terminal. We both looked a little shabby now.

The fast train still took two and half days to get to Chicago; and we had no means to buy any food on the way. When we were paid up to date at Yerba Buena, we were paid what they called "separate rations" rather than being given meal tickets.

Whoever took us for a ride the night before, and took all our money, must have felt a small twinge of guilt because they left our tickets and the cigarettes in Viera's bag.

We got to the terminal in time to catch our train, and by noon were rolling through the California countryside on our way to Chicago. We fell in with a good natured sailor who was also going to the east coast; after explaining our situation to him, he must have felt sorry for us, because he took care of us for the next two days.

The train stopped in Ogden, Utah, and one of the train crewmen told us we had enough time to walk a little distance from the train station to a café' where the sailor bought us lunch and even brought two six packs back to the train and shared them with us.

While in Ogden I called home and asked my folks to send some money to Western Union in Chicago. I had been sending some cash home every month, so it wasn't a problem for them.

The sailor kept us from starving between San Francisco and Chicago. We actually had a pretty good trip considering everything. Viera sold the cigarettes and raised a few bucks for us. We got to Chicago and the money was waiting for me. I gave Viera enough to get him to Rochester and said so long to him. I would never see or hear from him again. By then I was out of friends and on my own.

I caught a cab over to Union station with enough time to go by a barber shop for a shave and a shower while my uniform was being cleaned and pressed. The San Francisco hangover was already forgotten. I was a new man.

The leg between Chicago and Cincinnati went by in no time and my connection was made there with no problems. I boarded the train in Cincinnati, and as I walked through the first car I spotted Edwards, asleep on his seat. It had been three or four days since he left on the early train in California.

I woke him up; he was pretty ragged and was hung over pretty bad. I don't think he had showered since we separated. At one end of the rail car there was a men's room with a small lounge area. I took him there; he had a shave and cleaned up a bit; and in a little while he was all right. We rolled through West Virginia and somewhere in Virginia we said goodbye and he left the train.

A new train crew came on duty when we stopped in Roanoke and one of the conductors sat and talked with me in the lounge area. He had brought a bag lunch with him when he got on the train, and offered me part of his lunch. In fact he almost insisted because he wanted me to try one of the sandwiches his wife had made for him. It hadn't been long since I had eaten, but I took the sandwich and started eating. He said "Have you ever tasted roast beef that good?" I told him that it was, in fact, very good. He said "I'll bet you never ate venison before, have you?" I explained that I hadn't, and he said, "well, you have now – ain't that good?"

He wanted to know where I was going, where I had been, and a lot of other questions, but he was just trying to be friendly. I enjoyed his company and before long it was time to get my gear because we were nearing Winston-Salem.

It wasn't long before I was on a bus rolling towards Charlotte. I had one more change in Charlotte and a short delay before leaving on my last leg to Kings Mountain. Japan and Korea seemed like a long time ago and far away.

I started thinking about how I would react to seeing Mil for the first time. Would she be changed? Could there be someone else she had been seeing? After all, I had been gone over a year; and she was a beautiful young lady. My last letter from her had been written over a month ago. That was plenty of time to meet someone. When I called to tell her I was home, would she tell me that things weren't the same? Maybe she was engaged to someone.

Those negative thoughts I had been trying hard to reject were racing through my mind. I would soon find out because the bus was stopping in Kings Mountain, and I was finally home; somewhat apprehensive of what lay ahead, and at the same time awfully glad to be there.

CHAPTER 17

Pope Air Force Base February 1953

Things had been happening in my family over the past year that I failed to mention while writing about events in Korea and Japan. Mama had written to me regularly and kept me informed of what was going on back home.

My older sister had presented them with their first grand child, a girl they named Judy, in January shortly after I left. She was already a year old and was healthy and doing well.

Coot and Bill were still living in Pineville. She was still working for Southern Bell in Charlotte and Bill was still with Southern Railway as a telegrapher in Pineville. Faye had married F.C. Humphries after I left to go to the Far East but the marriage didn't last very long before they were divorced. She had delivered a baby girl while I was en-route home; she and her baby were doing fine. Her baby was born the day before my arrival and they named her Pam. Mama and Daddy both were still working at the Park Yarn. Other than that, things were the same as a year earlier.

I still had about three weeks of active duty in the air force before my discharge date of February 5th, and my reporting date to Pope Air Force Base was nearly two weeks away. Whenever I was reminded of my discharge date thoughts of reenlisting were always there.

Daddy picked me up at the bus terminal in Kings Mountain, and on the way out to the house told me that Faye had just delivered a new baby girl the day before at the hospital in Kings Mountain.

He was excited about the new granddaughter; and probably told me three or four times what a pretty little baby he had for a new grandchild, but I had other things that occupied my thoughts. That may seem a little cold hearted or uncaring, but that wasn't the case. I was happy for them, but right now a phone call to Mil was at the top of my list.

Mama was at home waiting for me. She seemed older and tired. The new grand daughter and my coming home had made her a little frazzled. She cooked a big meal for me and was happy enough, but seemed to be worried about something.

The news of the airplane crash at Larson Air Force Base a few weeks earlier had rattled her pretty bad. She knew I was on the way home, and that had both of them up late, waiting for the newspaper and listening to the news on the radio. They finally read a list of the names that didn't survive. That gave them some relief, but they still weren't sure until I made it to Ogden, Utah and called them. After she saw me she relaxed somewhat and was all right. I wasn't ! I had to call Mil.

Finally the call was made. I was very nervous. The telephone probably woke her up because she was working the night shift at the Cora mill; I didn't even stop and think about that. It's hard to remember what time I made the call, but It was probably early afternoon. She sounded OK. Happy to hear my voice. Could I come over later? Sure! All seemed well in paradise, but still I couldn't be sure until I was looking into her eyes and reading her mind.

The rest of the afternoon was a blurred memory. We probably went to see Faye and the new baby, I can't be certain. Physically I was with my folks, but my mind was somewhere else.

The afternoon slowly wore on, but finally it was time to drive over to Fairview Street. Daddy had bought a 1947' Chevrolet and let me use it for the evening; "but don't forget we have to go to work tomorrow morning" was his last instructions. He worried a lot, but his concern was probably justified.

The car stopped right in front of her house. There couldn't have been more than four or five feet between her steps and the edge of the road. I was out and walking around the car when she opened her front door and walked out on the porch. She smiled and walked in my direction. She was even more beautiful than I remembered her to be. My heart was pounding. I looked into her eyes, she looked at me and smiled again. Then and there I was certain, that was it! Any lingering doubts were all gone.

There could never be anyone else for me There's no way for me to remember what was said at that meeting before she was in the front seat of the car and we were driving off. I probably told her how good it was to see her again.

Her uncle and aunt were owners of the Silver Villa drive-in, so we went there and parked. We ordered something, probably a coke and maybe fries, I don't remember. It didn't take long for her to get close to me. We were like one in the front seat. She was so soft and felt so good.

That warm, indescribable feeling returned. It was wonderful just to touch her. It was getting late but I didn't want to leave her. Her daddy wanted his girls home by 10:30 and she knew better than to be late, besides, she was supposed to work that night.

She didn't want to go home; I didn't want to take her home; but we had to. I dropped her off and left. Immediately after driving off, I was lonely. I could smell her perfume and feel the softness of her lips. She had brought the sunshine back into my life and now we were apart again. I wasn't a whole person; an important part of me was missing.

As it was then, has been ever since, and will forever be whenever we are apart, one from the other, I feel lonely. She can walk out of the room and we'll be disconnected; walk back in and be reconnected.

I drove back to the house on Shelby Road, parked the car, went in and went to bed. Sleep was a long time coming. Even at home I was in a strange place. I could smell her perfume and it gave me comfort. Knowing that tomorrow, as soon as she was awake and could get ready, I would see her again, allowed me to relax enough to drift off to sleep.

There is very little I remember about the next week before leaving for Fayetteville and Pope Air Force Base, except that we were together as often as her work would allow. After that first night, I would even take her to work. After dropping her off at home, I'd wait in the car for her to change, or whatever she had to do to get ready for work then drive her to the Cora mill; which was just down the hill from Fairview Street.

During that time I met most of her family. Her oldest brother, Junior, was away in the marine corps. Her youngest brother, Mike, was still in diapers. After taking her to the mill, we would sit in the car, as close to each other as we could get, until the very last minute before she had to clock in.

One night we were there at the mill and I talked her into "playing hooky" from work. What would Mr. Roper do to me (or her) if he ever found out that I kept his daughter out all night?

We were young and reckless (not that reckless though) and made the decision for her to stay out of work. We spent some time at the Silver Villa drive in; we drove around. We didn't have anywhere else to go, it was late at night and she couldn't go home until after six in the morning; after she would have completed her shift at work. I was getting sleepy; in fact I did go to sleep with my head in her lap with her running her fingers through my hair. Finally, after a long night, it was over, and she could go home; acting like she had been working all night.

I hadn't considered my folks and their schedule to leave early enough to be at work at seven o'clock. I hurried home in time for them to leave, but daddy was somewhat disturbed at me. He was worried that I had been in an accident. That was bad judgement on my part; I should have called them and told them I would be gone all night, but would be back in time for them to go to work.

Daddy had called over at Mil's house asking if they knew where I could be; they didn't know, but when we found out that he had called there asking about me, we were afraid Mr. Roper would get a little suspicious; but he didn't and everything was all right.

Mil's older sister Ivery had married George Nolen and they were living a short distance from Mil's mom and dad. One night she wasn't scheduled to work and had arranged to spend the night at Ivery's house. That way we could stay out later than ten-thirty; however we had to be back at Ivery's by that time. Mil knew she could talk her into letting us stay out pretty late.

We went to the drive-in theater between Kings Mountain and Bessemer City, and were back in front of Ivery's before the deadline. Mil reported in to Ivery and came back to the car. We were enjoying just being close together, but Ivery wouldn't leave us alone. Every ten or fifteen minutes she would come outside, walk towards the car and tell her younger sister "it's time to come in". "Wait just a minute, Ivery", Mil would say. That scenario was repeated over and over until Ivery was getting upset at her. We finally broke off and she went in for the night.

Soon it was time for me to leave for Pope. After a week at Pope I would be discharged and come home for good. The immediate plan was to find a good job, make lots of money and spend as much time with Mil as I could. After spending a week with her thoughts of reenlisting were on the back burner.

Pope was a big place; I was given a bunk at the transient airman quarters to wait for my discharge date. Basham and Nesbitt both were there for discharge also. They left Itazuke three weeks after I did and had also been assigned to Pope to process out.

Nesbitt had bought an old 1948 Plymouth and had it on base. We spent more time on Bragg Boulevard at a place called the “Red Onion” than we did at Pope. Nesbitt was due to leave in two days and Basham had about the same time as me before being discharged.

The first night there, after returning to base from the Red Onion, Basham got out of the car and thought he was back in the Golden Gloves ring. He went into his famous “crouch” and thought Nesbitt was in the ring with him. We had a time getting him into the barracks and in his bunk.

The very next day, in the late afternoon, we were on Bragg Boulevard returning to Pope; it was raining. We were all three in the front seat of the old Plymouth. Nesbitt was driving; the next thing I knew, we were skidding, then rolling, then someone was looking in the window at me. I was on top of Basham and he was on top of Nesbitt. No one was hurt, but the car was on its side and bent up pretty bad.Of course we had been drinking beer; the police took us all back to their headquarters and Nesbitt was being questioned. He hadn’t been charged with anything because we hadn’t caused any damage to anyone’s property. We had turned over and skidded down the boulevard. Just a one vehicle accident.

Nesbitt’s father was a wheel in Alabama, so he called his father who in turn talked with the police officer. Soon after that a policeman drove us back to Pope in his police car and let us out in front of the transient barracks. Even though the three of us had enough beer to be declared “driving while impaired”, Nesbitt was never charged with anything.

He was leaving the next day and I never knew what happened to his old car. He probably just let them tow it off to a junk yard. Basham and I said goodbye to Nesbitt the next day. I would maintain contact with him on and off through the years.

Sometime during the week spent at Pope waiting for discharge I ran into the radio operator from base flight at Itazuke in the Pope base exchange. He was assigned to a unit flying C-119 troop carriers in support of the 82nd Airborne Division at Fort Bragg. He had re-enlisted and planned to stay on and make a career of it.

My plans, at the time, were to get out, but in the back of my mind sincere thoughts were given to re-enlist and make a life in the air force. Mil played an important part in my decision. The past three years had been good ones. I enjoyed the military and the air force had been good to me. The people I had met, even though most of them, like me, were young first termers, they were all outstanding in every way. I never had a commanding officer that I didn't admire and respect.

I looked back and remembered the good times at the Jersey shore while attending radio school and the adventures in Washington State. I thought about Robert Monion, Bob Shields. Joe Dallas and big Jim Mahoney; Viera came to mind and the night spent in San Francisco. Did he get back to Rochester alright? And even though Korea was a war zone, the past year spent in the Far East was a memorable one. A lot of good friends were left back there in the three previous years. Even though Mil was the most important individual in my life I felt something was missing and couldn't understand exactly what it was.

Several days later my discharge date arrived; I processed out, said goodbye to Basham and left for Kings Mountain. Bob Basham was leaving the same day for Chesapeake, West Virginia. We were good friends, but I have not heard from him again. It has been over fifty five years, but I believe that I could walk up behind him and say "this buddy stuff can go just so far" and he would, without turning around know instantly who was speaking to him. There's no need to go into the story behind that statement, but I believe what I just wrote to be true.

With discharge in hand I returned to Kings Mountain, footloose and fancy free, as the saying goes. I had no permanent plans in mind other than those that included Mil.

Even then I instinctively knew the air force would play a part in our future. There was no denying the way I felt about the past three years and five months.

CHAPTER 18

Civilian Life and Marriage February–July 1953

After arriving home one of the first things that needed to be done was to buy civilian clothes. A couple of nice suits, ties, and shirts would be enough to start. I would have to look sharp at a job interview.

The air force paid me through Feb 5th and I turned in some unused leave time, plus there was three hundred bucks mustering out pay that would be mailed to me over the next three months. And I had some cash that Daddy had been holding for me from an allotment sent home from my monthly pay over the past thirteen months. So I wasn't too bad off financially, at least over the next three months. Soon after getting settled in at home I went to a clothing store between Gastonia and Charlotte that specialized in men's suits and picked up the stuff I needed. Suits were on sale for $39.95; I thought that was a bit high for just a coat and pants. Two suits, two ties, and three or four dress shirts were bought. A shoe store was next door and I bought a pair of low quarter dress shoes there. I already had more than enough underwear and socks. All I needed were a couple pairs of blue jeans and pullover shirts to round out my wardrobe. Those were bought at a department store in Kings Mountain. I was all set to start looking for a job, and I wasn't going anywhere near a cotton mill.

Faye was home for a while before going to Tennessee to enroll in school for occupational therapist. She left Pam with Mama and Daddy until she could make arrangements in Tennessee and come back for her. That never happened. Once Mama and Daddy started caring for the little girl they didn't want to let her go, besides it was a lot more convenient for Faye, with her studies, not to have to care for a baby.

I looked all over for a job for a few weeks and finally landed one at Foot Mineral Company just outside Kings Mountain. I was to be trained to work in the chemical laboratory; and was to start working the night shift with the promise of moving to a daytime shift shortly.

The first night all I did was shovel heavy wet sand like material back onto a conveyor bucket that picked the material up as it traveled in a loop up to the next level above; then it was supposed to dump out of the buckets to be conveyed on a belt to the next process.

Being wet, it stuck in the buckets and fell back down the shaft. There I shoveled the stuff back into the buckets. It was falling down the shaft faster than I could keep up.

The next night was no different; the shovel had to be manned all night The next night was the same, and I was beginning to wonder about the job. When I discussed my concern with the guy I was responsible to, he promised the next night would be different, they had hired someone to work as a "shovel specialist" and I would be in the chemical lab.

When I reported for duty that night the new man failed to show. It was me and the shovel again, all night again. When I left the next morning I informed the engineer that I wouldn't be back.

That was the end of my career as a "chemical analyst" for Foot Mineral. My pay for all four nights was $38.40 before taxes.

It wasn't working out too well anyway. I got home after working all night just in time for my folks to leave for work at the park yarn. And I wasn't able to see enough of Mil. We were together whenever possible, but that wasn't nearly enough for either of us.

Before leaving for the Far East I had introduced Lafayette to Mil's younger sister, Mary. He was still on active duty then and on his way to Newfoundland. They went out a few times before he had to leave. She was still in high school, but by the time he left they were getting close to each other. He was home a long time before I returned, and was still dating Mary.

Sometime during late winter he left for a job in Washington, DC. He hadn't been in Washington very long when I saw a classified ad in the newspaper that Southern Bell was looking for people that had worked in military communications equipment repair; he had that type of background, so I called him about it. Before long he was home, applied for one of the jobs, and went to work for the telephone company.

By now it was a forgone conclusion that Mil and I would be married. We talked about marriage frequently. We were double dating with Mary and Lafayette and spending as much time as we could with each other.

She doesn't like for me to talk to just anyone about it, and she seems a little irritated when I relate the story that she had given me until Easter Sunday to make my move and set a date. There was no way under Heaven that I would take a chance to lose her. Consequently, sometime during the first week in April the four of us went to Gaffney, SC for Mil and me to apply for a marriage license.

We were surprised when Mary and Lafayette decided to apply also. She was still a senior in high school and was Mr. Roper's baby daughter. There was a waiting period of seven days between the date the application was completed and the actual date a couple could be married and our date was set for Saturday April 11th, exactly a week and a day after we completed the application to be married.

There was no need for a lot of planning; we weren't going to have a big hoop-la about it. I had talked with Mr. Roper on and off over the past three months about my intentions and he had no objection to our marriage, although he was a little hesitant when he talked to her about me. I didn't even have a job at the time and that concerned him.

When I first met him, before going to Korea, I thought he was one of the meanest looking men ever. He had broad shoulders and big hands that looked like they were capable of tearing a young Casanova to pieces. The opposite turned out to be the case. He was one of the most gentle natured men I ever knew. At the same time, it was well known that "you didn't disrespect or take advantage of one of Ivy Roper's daughters." All five of his girls were of the highest moral character. He made sure they were in Church every Sunday, and they were all Christian girls.

Mil's older sisters gave us a royal send off when we left for Gaffney on Saturday morning. All three of her older sisters were already married; but absolutely no one knew of Mary and Lafayette's plans to be married. Mil's mom stayed on the sidelines as she always did. She never voiced any objections. Her mission in life had been to have children, raise them, work hard, and make a home for her husband and children; and that she did as well or better than it could have been done by anyone.

It's hard to understand to this day why Lafayette took such a chance. He had always been a level headed guy who thought things over before making his move. I grew up with him and knew him as well as anyone on earth and had depended on his level head in some of the most trying circumstances more than one time in our reckless history. I can understand how he influenced Mary into going along with him. She was in love, and of course, so was he, but for him to take a chance on being shot or worse is still hard to understand.

Mary was Mr. Roper's baby daughter and, except for Mil, was the last unmarried daughter he had; and she was about to be married without his knowledge. And there was their older brother, Junior, a hard nosed, fast driving, take no nonsense marine. Lafayette sure didn't want to create any resentment there.

The secret was well kept until after Mary's graduation; they broke the news to her folks, and I sure am glad we didn't have to be there. Lafayette was told in no uncertain terms what would happen "if she ever comes home crying."

The day arrived when Mil would be mine forever. I had never been so nervous. She was as beautiful as I had ever seen her; an angel; a vision; no wonder I was nervous. I felt like I was stealing something valuable from somebody as we drove away.

According to custom she had something old, something new, something borrowed, and something blue; and she had a penny in her shoe. The four of us went to the courthouse in Gaffney for a simple civil ceremony; before we knew it, we were on our way: Mr.and Mrs. Tom Shytle and Mr. and Mrs. Bobby L. Pearson. It was a beautiful spring day.

My sister Coot and her husband Bill had planned to completely move out of their home in Pineville so that we could have some time for a short "honeymoon." at their place. We left Gaffney and drove to Pineville where we had planned to have a steak dinner, then Mary and Lafayette would drive back to Kings Mountain and he would drop his new bride off at home and go back to where he was staying with his folks.

Everything went as planned; we had a nice steak and then we were left alone. For the first time, I could spend the night with the sweetest thing on earth. We had a wonderful wedding night. We didn't get much sleep, we didn't need sleep; we had each other and the world was bright!

The next morning a slight hitch developed in paradise. I almost burned the house down. We woke up to a cold morning and decided to heat up the house. There was a kerosene heater in the living room, so I turned the fuel on and tried to get it going. For some reason there was already a lot of kerosene in the burner and when it lit there was no way I could control the flames, the pipe turned red hot. I ran outside to check the chimney and flames were coming out the top.

Mil accused me of abandoning her in the bedroom. Whet it started whooshing I turned the fuel off and soon it started to die down; the pipes cooled and things were all right. But it was a scary few minutes. We had a nice breakfast, and later on, Coot, with her little daughter, Judy and Mama came over from Kings Mountain to check on the newly weds.

Mil and I went back to Kings Mountain with them because we had to finalize some plans. We spent a few days with my Mama and Daddy, during which time I bought a 1941 Chevrolet from a used car lot in town. It was in excellent condition, almost like new. I had to pay something like $25.00 down and financed the remainder. The total price was $350.00 and the payments were $19.00 per month.

About a week before we were married I had interviewed for a job with AT&T in Charlotte, and just before our wedding date I had been called by AT&T to start work for them on South Caldwell Street in Charlotte at their main equipment center.

Our immediate plans were to live in a spare bedroom with Coot and Bill until we could find our own place in Charlotte. It was a short drive up South Boulevard from Pineville to Charlotte and traffic was relatively light early in the morning. Mil had left her job at the Cora mill; she didn't need a job; she now had a husband.

To this day I don't know why I hadn't bought Mil a ring before we were married. Maybe my cash was running short; that was probably it. Anyway, before I had time to get my first paycheck from AT&T I went by Kay's jeweler in Charlotte and bought her a diamond. She was all smiles, and I was happy for her.

Everything was well in our world. There was one tiny problem. Judy just didn't like Mil; she must have thought of her as an intruder or something bad in her house. Every time Mil got close enough to her she would get bit. Coot had left her job at Southern Bell; she was home all the time and took care of Judy, but Judy never had much to do with Mil the entire time we lived with them.

My job in Charlotte was a nine to five type working on the long lines testboard. It was the most boring thing I ever did. The testboard was used to locate trouble in cables all over the south; most of the cables at that time were above ground. I attended informal classes learning all about the AT&T cable systems; it was like on the job training.

Even then traffic was heavy southbound on South Boulevard at five o'clock. It was generally close to six by the time I got back to Pineville. Mil was bored too, sitting there with nothing much to do all day long except help Coot do all the chores around the house; and watch out for Judy to sneak up behind her and bite her on the leg.

The subject of re-enlistment in the air force was discussed. I had mentioned the practical aspect of a military career to her on several occasions. She had never been exposed to the military way of living and had a lot of questions. Some of her questions were easy to answer and some weren't. I had never lived on base with a wife and didn't know how that worked. I knew there would be times when she couldn't go with me on an assignment; times of separation. I explained to her that once a commitment had been made, it would mean a career of living in far away places and moving around more than she would probably like. The way I explained it probably sounded adventurous and interesting to her.

We went home nearly every weekend and would normally spend the night on Shelby Road with my folks. We burned the road up between there and Fairview Street. Mil may have had a touch of homesickness, if so the weekends were a relief for that. She loved spending time with her family. Her three older sisters already had small children; her two youngest brothers were still little guys and she missed being around them. Junior was home from the marine corps and his wife, Betty was expecting their first baby.

Grandpa Roper, as he was already being called by then, was building a house on some property he'd bought out past the end of Second Street. They called it "Peaceful Valley." He loved it out there, with lots more room to raise a hog or two and have a big corn field. After they moved, Grandma didn't care for "the country" nearly as much as he did, but made the best of it.

Mary graduated from high school; she and Lafayette rented a small house not far down the street from where her folks lived. Lafayette was busy learning telephone repair, installation, and pole climbing. They were going to be all right; Grandpa didn't have to put Lafayette to work on the "chain gang."

Work for me became more and more of a rut. Every day was routine. I thought more and more about the air force. It was sometime during this period of time that we learned that Mil was pregnant. I continued to talk with Mil about re-enlistment, trying to convince her that the air force would be a good thing for us. Bill even seemed interested in talking to a recruiter. The job he had at the railway station was also boring.

Then she agreed with me that we should try a three year tour and if it didn't work out so good we could still get out after that. Coot and Bill decided to try it also. Bill and I went to Charlotte to start the enlistment paperwork. Before the day was over I was committed, that is I had taken the oath once more, and was assigned to Donaldson Air Base near Greenville, SC. I had a few days to tie up some loose ends before my reporting date.

It was early July. Bill was enlisted a few days later, but since he had no prior military service, he had to go to basic training in San Antonio. I resigned from the job with AT&T; we packed our gear in Pineville, loaded it all in the 1941 Chevrolet and went to Kings Mountain.

The plan was to leave Mil with my folks until I could get situated in Greenville and get a place rented before she would join me. That didn't take long. The idea of being that far from her didn't set too well with me. A new adventure awaited us at Donaldson Air Force Base.

CHAPTER 19

Donaldson Air Force Base July 1953–January 1954

Our plans didn't include Mil getting pregnant as soon as she did; but then we hadn't planned on her not getting pregnant either. As a matter of fact, we didn't think much about it one way or another. For us it was a natural occurrence and we were both very happy.

I had to leave Mil with my folks for a few days. Faye had already gone to Tennessee and was nearing completion of Occupational Therapy school, so there was enough room for Mil and her things with Mama and Daddy.

It was hard to go away and leave her so soon, but knowing it wouldn't be for very long made leaving a lot easier.

Our lives together had entered another phase. The story of my life with her, to be as factual and complete as it should be has to include our domestic and social life on the one hand, and my career as an air force non commissioned officer on the other. Both will be an integral part of our everyday activities and experiences over the years that follow. Nothing on earth is more important than family, but dedication to duty, honor, and country for anyone in the service has to be first and foremost where career is concerned. I never met a successful military man who wasn't dedicated to that doctrine.

And I never met a happy man who didn't love and honor his wife and family. More importantly, even though I have not always led a virtuous life, since my earliest years, I have always affirmed a belief in God. That belief was imbedded in me by a Godly Mother who was herself a saint and a Father whose faith was unshakeable.

Those three elements have to be present in both a marriage and a military career to be successful. That is; a belief in God, and absolute dedication to family and to country. The above statement is not meant to be a lecture on virtue, but a foundation on which Mil and I would try to build our future together.

The drive to Greenville, South Carolina took less than an hour and a half and upon arrival at Donaldson, which was a short distance east of town, I reported in and was assigned to the 64th Troop Carrier Wing. They were flying big C-124 double decker transports; the same type aircraft that had the accidents at Larson Air Force Base and Tachikawa. Hopefully they had corrected the problem that caused those crashes. Their primary mission was to support the Army's airborne troops and the Military Airlift Command. My unit assignment was to the 64th communications squadron.

It only took a day or so to get all the preliminary paperwork completed before I was given some time to look for an apartment. That didn't take long either and in a few days I had a small place rented on White Horse Road about six miles from the base.

That weekend I drove home, picked up Mil and her bags and we drove back to Greenville and to our first effort at housekeeping. A lot of the things we needed to get started were given to us; including sheets and pillows. Mil's aunt even gave us eating utensils. We packed everything in the back seat and rear of the Chevrolet and hoped we had all we would need to get started.

The little apartment was just that, little. It consisted of a small kitchen, bedroom and bathroom; it was built onto the backside of a house and had a small back porch.

My duties at the base were normally from eight a.m. to four p.m. with the weekends off. I was assigned to the MARS (Military Affiliated Radio System) station.

The duties didn't involve anything very interesting, in fact they were sort of dull. I was reading and studying a lot in order to pass the examination for my Amateur Operator's (ham) license. We were doing a lot of experimentation on the amateur radio frequencies and checking the effectiveness of various antennas and equipment.

While I was on duty having fun messing around all day with the radio equipment, Mil was sitting around that little cubby hole we called an apartment with absolutely nothing to do but have morning sickness and play solitaire. She had to be bored to death passing the time she had to spend alone.

We didn't make it back to Kings Mountain as often as she would have liked because some weekends I did have duties on base, but we made it to Kings Mountain about once a month, probably after payday. We weren't making enough to do everything we would have liked. Our car payment was $19.00, Mil's ring payment was $10.00, and the apartment rent was $40.00 a month. We had less than $150.00 left to last an entire month.

While living in the apartment Mil didn't even have a washing machine and had to wash our sheets and clothes, including my uniforms, even the class "A" khaki's in the bathtub. Once a month my unit had open ranks inspection on Saturday morning, and Mil would press those khakis until they didn't have a wrinkle anywhere; they'd be stiff as a board with starch, but by the time I drove to the base they looked like I'd worn them all day.

One Saturday morning the inspecting officer stopped in front of me and said "Son, you need to find yourself a new laundry." After all that ironing and hard work she had put into the uniform, it still wasn't good enough. I think she cried a little when I told her what was said.

After that, I had a khaki uniform done up at the base laundry with heavy starch; it was left hanging at the MARS station and I changed into it on the morning we were to be inspected.

She didn't have to stay in that lonely apartment very long because I had applied for base housing soon after reporting in. We stayed at the apartment for about three months and moved on base into a housing unit made from a converted barracks. It was bigger and furnished with government issue furniture; not luxurious, but adequate.

Summer was over and the weather was turning cooler; Mil's pregnancy was beginning to show. She was so proud when we went home and she could visit with her sisters who already had babies. Lafayette and Mary drove down to visit with us one weekend after we had moved on base. She enjoyed their visit so much and was a little depressed when they had to leave. I think she was a little homesick.

In a realignment move the 63rd Troop Carrier Wing came to Donaldson from Altus AFB in Oklahoma and brought with it C-119 aircraft. The air force was experimenting with heavy equipment drops and the C-119 had the capability with its clam-shell rear opening for parachute extraction of heavy equipment and cargo. The C-124 didn't have that capability. In addition the pathfinders were being used to set up drop zone communications for the army and the 1st Aerial Port Operations Squadron was activated at Donaldson. The air force pathfinders were members of the 1st Aerial Port.

I was sent on TDY (temporary duty) to Pope AFB to assist in some of these operations that had been given to the 1st Aerial Port as part of their responsibility to set up drop zone communications. One other radio operator was also sent to Pope. Since I wanted to take Mil home during this time; I took her to Kings Mountain to stay with mama and daddy and then drove on to Pope. The other radio operator flew to Pope in one of the C-119's.

Our responsibility was to establish radio communications between the incoming aircraft and the drop zone. In addition to voice contact we used colored smoke grenades to help align the aircraft to their proper approach before dropping the paratroopers or heavy equipment, whatever their mission happened to be.

Since these operations were still experimental there were several accidents and incidents that occurred. The worst accident happened when a C-119 loaded with troopers lost power over the drop zone, just as it was making its approach. The lead element had dropped their troopers; the crippled aircraft was leading the second element; it couldn't maintain altitude and ran through the troopers floating in the air.

Most of the troopers made it out of the crippled airplane but the crew and one trooper were all killed when it crashed into a wooded area adjacent to the drop zone. Bleachers had been set up for some spectators and the accident happened right in front of them. And less than a week later a C-119 crashed into a mess hall on Fort Bragg. Luckily, it wasn't meal time, and the mess hall was empty.

In several instances during the heavy drop experiments the main chutes failed or streamed in (didn't open properly) and supply pallets were destroyed, and another time a Jeep was squashed into a pile of junk. Another time a loadmaster was still on one of the trucks to be dropped when the drobe chute deployed; he went out with the truck and rode it to the ground. He was rattled somewhat, but was all right.

One evening we were driving back to the transient barracks, it was already dark and a deer started across the road in front of us. When he saw the headlights he stopped and wouldn't move. We got out of the car and could've hit him with a rock.

When we went to the mess hall for supper that night we talked to the cook about processing a deer carcass for us. He agreed to cut it up if we brought it in. The next day the other radio operator caught a C-119 to Donaldson, picked up his bow and arrows that he had been using just as a sport, and caught another hop back to Pope.

That night we rode the back roads around Fort Bragg until after midnight and never saw another deer. Before that we had seen deer almost every night while coming off the drop zone.

The heavy drops were being completed without incident and after a couple of short TDY trips we weren't sent back to Pope. By now the pathfinders were up to strength and doing their own drop zone communications.

Sometime during this period I passed the amateur radio operator's examination and received my license.

We spent Thanksgiving on base. I had duty so we couldn't spend the holiday in Kings Mountain with our folks. The mess halls usually invited dependents to eat on holidays, especially Thanksgiving and Christmas, and always had a big turkey on display.

On this Thanksgiving, the cook gave the display turkey to me after everyone had eaten and left. Mil was sure surprised when I came walking in the door carrying that big bird. It probably took us weeks to finish off the whole thing.

Christmas was spent with our folks. I don't remember much about the details. I was probably thinking a lot about Mil and her condition. I was getting a little concerned because her delivery date was estimated to be in about a month. The doctors didn't expect any complications, but thoughts kept coming about things that could go wrong. What if something was wrong with the baby? What if Mil had problems? New Years Day 1954 came and went without fanfare.

I remember very clearly the evening before the day our little boy was born. It was like we were still on our honeymoon, sitting on our living room couch and cuddling up; just being close to each other, trying to feel the baby move. We didn't have a TV but listened to the radio. The decision had already been decided that if we had a little boy we would name him Thomas James Shytle II.

The next day everything was moving along normally for a Monday morning. I was getting ready to leave for the MARS station when Mil felt her first pain. She got dressed and I took her to the base hospital. For some reason my mind just wasn't believing what we were there for until they told me to leave; she was being admitted to the hospital. What for? I asked. Still not quite understanding what was happening. We had been told her due date was still about three or four weeks away.

The nurse probably thought I must have been addled or something to ask such a dumb question. They ran me out. By this time I could hear Mil groaning, but there wasn't anything I could do for her. I went outside and around the building to the window outside the room she was in. The nurses ran me away from the window. From there I don't know where I went, probably to a waiting room somewhere. We had arrived at the hospital soon after eight o'clock, it was past noon and I was pestering the reception medic.

Finally just after two p.m. someone came and told me we had a little boy. How is my wife? She's fine!! The baby boy? He's fine too!! Time to relax some. I left the hospital, went to the base exchange and bought a box of cigars. Cigars were always passed out to friends when a baby was born, it was a tradition. I don't think that continues today.

By the time I returned to the hospital Mil had recovered enough for me to see her. She looked tired, her face was flushed, but she looked up at me and smiled with a knowing look of what she had just been through and what she had done. It was a moment like no other in our life. She didn't have to speak; I knew what she was thinking. Our little boy was in a room with a few other new born babies; the nurse pointed him out to me. I don't remember all my emotions, but happy and proud were the pre-dominant feelings.

I was in and out of the hospital every time they would allow visitors. The medical people were very strict about visiting hours. There has never been a more proud and happy Mother than Mil. She had some pain because during the delivery they had to do minor surgery; she had some stitches, but all in all everything was fine. She couldn't wait to bring our baby home and start being a full time Mother and wife. This was her destiny; what she was born to do.

Five days later she was released and we brought our beautiful little bald headed boy home to begin another new phase in our life together. There were no germs allowed in our house after that. Everything had to be sterilized. If it came in contact with the baby it had to be germ free. Every diaper had to be boiled before it could touch his little behind. He was being breast fed; that was the way God made it; that was the way it would be.

She was the perfect Mother; and was anxious to get back to Kings Mountain and show him to her family. No doubt, his proud Father was doing a little strutting around also. We were as happy as new parents could possibly be.

We were blessed beyond measure.

From left to right: Sister Christina (Coot), Mama, the author, and sister Faye who was expecting her second son.

CHAPTER 20

Jamey and Orders to North Africa January–November 1954

We gave our little boy the nickname "Jamey." When his birth certificate was given to us they didn't record his name exactly as we wanted. His name was listed as Jr. not "II" as we had written it at the hospital. It had already been recorded that way, and we considered having it changed but finally decided to leave it as it was.

As soon as they both were released by the hospital Mama rode the bus to Greenville to lend us a hand with our new son; I was there to pick her up at the Greyhound station and bring her back to our apartment. She knew Mil needed some help with Jamey; after she left to go home, she probably never knew how much help she really was. She did everything, cooked, cleaned house; anything that needed to be done, and gave Mil some much needed advice and also allowed her to have enough restful recovery time.

After four or five days she had to go back to work; by that time Mil was on her feet and almost back to normal. She and I were on our own with Jamey. When we went to bed he was right there between us and when he got hungry his midnight chow was right there for him.

The diapers were the only bad duty; he was always cutting loose with a stream as soon as the diaper came off. Sometimes whoever was doing the changing would get it right in the face. He didn't cry a lot, only when he was hungry or needed a diaper change.

He was a joy. Now our world was wrapped around him as well as each other. He was less than two weeks old and already could look up at us with wonderment in his eyes; and when he was sleeping his lips would break into a little smile. We just couldn't wait to get him to Kings Mountain so we could show him to everyone.

He was nearly two weeks old and on Friday after my duty day was over, we packed up a pile of diapers and baby stuff along with our gear for the weekend, loaded him in the car and headed up highway 29 north. Our first stop was in Grover to show him to my Grandma Stinson. She talked us into spending the night there since it was getting late.

She was worried that he was too young to be taken on a trip and sort of reprimanded us for having done so.

Then we started thinking that maybe Grandma was right; maybe he was too young to take on a trip. Then we started getting worried. We made a snap decision! We got out of bed, got dressed, said goodbye to Grandma Stinson and drove back to Greenville. It was two weeks later before anyone got to meet our little guy.

When we eventually did get to Kings Mountain, we were in a whirlwind of people congratulating us and picking at him. Mil simply ate it all up. She was giddy as the compliments were presented by everyone who saw him. If anyone had been foolish enough to say anything negative about him, they likely wouldn't have survived her wrath. She wouldn't have been able to handle anything like that.

Spring came and went; all of our spare time was preoccupied with our little boy. We were busy with him every waking minute. Of course my duties kept me away from him a lot of the time, but Mil's entire being was consumed with his needs and her need to care for and protect him.

The first time we ever heard him laugh out loud happened one afternoon while we had him at a park swinging and playing. I was swinging him to and fro between my legs, dragging his feet in the grass and he started giggling; the more his feet swung through the grass, the louder he got, and Mil started laughing with him. We were all three laughing. It was a wonderful time that we never forgot.

Before summer was over he was crawling all over the place. He wouldn't stay in one place for a minute once he was on the floor.

Then came the end of summer and I received orders sending me to Wheelus Field in Tripoli, Libya. It was considered an isolated assignment where very few military dependents could, or would have wanted to go. Unaccompanied by dependents the assignment kept me away from Mil and Jamey for eighteen months, unless I could find a way to get a transfer to the continent of Europe.

Mil was saddened by the prospects ahead, and we had talked about the possibility of separation from each other, but when the orders were received the reality of our immediate future was difficult to take. We had some time to make plans before I would have to leave; so after a lot of talking, we decided that they would stay with my folks. They could also spend time with her folks who had moved into the house Grandpa Roper had built out in Peaceful Valley. She could also spend time visiting with her sisters.

My orders read that I would report to Camp Kilmer, New Jersey sometime in early November to be processed for shipment to the 580th Air Resupply Squadron at Wheelus Air Base. Travel to New Jersey would be by rail and by air from there to Libya.

Everything went as planned, Mil and Jamey were all settled in with Mama and Daddy; they had their own bedroom and we didn't expect to have any problems with the arrangement.

Leaving them was one of the hardest things I ever had to do. Before the actual time came for me to board the train that was scheduled to stop in Kings Mountain around nine p.m., I didn't anticipate how tough it really would be; not only for me but for Mil also. She was hurting inside as much as I.

We left Jamey with Mama, and as I walked out the door I took one last look at him. He was crawling across the floor crying to go with us. It was rough getting on the train knowing that it would probably be eighteen months before I would see her or Jamey again.

It was a lonesome ride to Philadelphia and then a short bus ride over to Trenton, New Jersey and Camp Kilmer. My sweetheart and son were heavy on my mind. I had made the decision to be in the military and had no choice but to accept my isolation and hope that soon they could join me.

I was assigned to a barracks after checking in and had nothing to do but wait. Leisure time isn't a good thing for anyone in my position; there's too much time to think. I couldn't get them off my mind. Looking back, maybe re-enlisting wasn't a good thing after all.

A drink might help take the edge off the loneliness, so I went to the NCO club for a beer. The bar was full of guys waiting for shipping orders to bases all over Europe, the Middle East and Mediterranean. They were whooping it up, having a good time and were anxious to be on their way to whatever destination awaited them. I didn't feel like joining in; there was nothing for me to be celebrating. Then it was back to the lonely barracks. The beer didn't help at all. I wrote her a letter; in a way that was like talking to her and that helped some.

CHAPTER 21

Tripoli, Libya
November 1954–March 1955

Camp Kilmer was a busy place. A lot of people from both the army and air force were processing in and out; and as is the normal procedures at overseas replacement bases, everything was rigid, precise and streamlined. It was almost like Camp Stoneman in California; but there weren't thousands of troops in the pipeline waiting for shipment orders, and they weren't being sent to a war zone. All records were brought up to date; shot records and health records were checked; and we weren't allowed to leave the post.

Unlike Camp Stoneman I was at Camp Kilmer only for a few days before being alerted for movement. I was thankful for that because the prospects of lying around a barracks with nothing to do but wait wasn't good. Bad thoughts came to mind but were quickly dismissed. Soon after being alerted all the guys who were on the same flight boarded a bus for Westover Air Force Base in Springfield, Massachusetts; the flight to Tripoli was scheduled to leave the next day.

The entire group of people assigned to bases in the Middle East stayed in the same barracks overnight.

Mil and Jamey were both still on my mind; and sleep didn't come easy. We departed the next afternoon by bus to base operations and had to sit around for several hours with nothing to do but wait. We were allowed a small AWOL bag as carry-on. The rest of our duffel was being transported by another airplane to Tripoli.

Soon after everyone was boarded and accounted for we rolled down the runway and within twenty or thirty minutes were out over the Atlantic. We were in the air for what seemed to be eight or ten hours before our first refueling stop at Lages Field in the Azores, a group of islands belonging to Portugal located off the African coast. We had a couple of hours before our departure so I had some time to do a little shopping in a small base exchange that was set up in the base operation building. Even though it was late at night, the exchange was open for business. I bought Mil a cameo set that included a ring, necklace, and ear rings. She probably still has those things today.

After going through the same loading procedures and making certain everyone was on board we took off from The Azores on our next leg that took us to Port Lyautey, Morocco. We weren't on the ground very long in Morocco, just long enough to take on fuel and then we were back in the air on our last leg to Tripoli.

Even though it was November, when we left the aircraft after our landing at Wheelus, the outside air was hot. An information desk was set up in the terminal and the guy on duty told me to wait until transportation could be arranged. After a short wait that gave me time to pick up my duffel a shuttle bus pulled into the terminal parking area and I was told the bus would take me to the 580th area.

The unit was isolated from the rest of the base and a military security policeman was on duty at the main entrance. After checking my orders I was escorted to the squadron operations room for in briefing.

No one at Donaldson knew anything about "Air Resupply"; I had never heard of such a unit, and until I reported in to 580th operations at Wheelus, I had no idea at all what the mission was about.

ARC was the official abbreviation for "Air Resupply and Communications" Air Resupply was activated to: "Develop an unconventional warfare capability that included inserting, supplying and extracting indigenous partisans and to design, produce and air drop psychological warfare materials."

That was the official mission statement and was highly classified at the time. No one was supposed to know what the outfit was doing. The 581st was based at Clark Air Base in the Philippines, the 580th at Wheelus, and the 582nd at Molesworth, England. Those three groups made up the entire Air Resupply Wing.

The 580th was given the responsibility to conduct operations throughout the Middle East, Soviet-occupied Europe and the Soviet Union. They also supported U-2 over-flights of Eastern Europe and Russia. Using SA-16 amphibious aircraft 580th crews had already recovered two U-2 pilots after they had ejected from their disabled aircraft. One was in the Caspian Sea north of Iran and the other in the Black Sea.

The U-2 was a high flying photo recon spy plane, the same type that was shot down over Russia resulting in Francis Gary Powers being captured and used as a cold war pawn by the Russians.

The 580th flew three different aircraft. The B-29's that had been modified to drop partisan spies, materials and psychological warfare leaflets into the Eastern European countries, C-119's that were used as transports, and SA-16's that were used for air-sea rescue.

I was assigned to the Air Resupply Squadron; the rest of the group was made up of a Reproduction Squadron that produced the leaflets, a Maintenance Squadron that maintained the aircraft, and an Armaments and Materials squadron that refitted and repaired weapons, mostly small arms that were dropped into the Eastern European countries.

Everything they did was considered covert and unconventional. That should pretty well explain the business being conducted by the 580th. The radio station that I was assigned to was equipped with a full wave-length, highly directional rhombic antenna pointed directly at Eastern Europe. We were so close to the Mediterranean that an antenna support tower was actually in the water.

Our responsibility was to maintain communications between our aircraft and squadron operations.

It was easy to tune one of the transmitters and receivers to the amateur bands and still listen to our assigned frequency for incoming radio traffic from a 580h aircraft. Since two radiomen were always on duty, someone was always there to take care of 580th traffic.

To miss a call couldn't happen, because it may mean someone was in trouble and needed help. Normally though, any radio traffic that came through us was routine. It took me about a month to get my Libyan amateur radio license, but when I did, there were ham operators all over the world that wanted to make contact with me and get my QSL card.

That card would be used to prove contact was made and win amateur radio awards for them. There were very few Libyan amateur's in the first place, and none anywhere in the country that had the capability of the rhombic antenna that I had access to.

I had an especially strong signal on CW. (continuous wave) and had listeners all over the world sending me their "short wave listener" cards. They were even coming to me from behind the iron curtain where they had severe restraints on such things. They were taking a chance by sending out their card. I still have most of them.

Working on the amateur bands gave me something to do in my spare time because there were very few special services activities on base. Off base was even worse. The government of Libya had some odd rules for US forces in their country, and even more strict requirements for their own people regarding contact with us. Their religious practices, if violated, could cost them their heads.

The women were given especially harsh treatment if they did wrong. For instance, we were told that they always had to wear something on their heads, and had to keep one eye covered. They could not look at a Christian with both eyes or be in violation of their religious laws and probably land them in trouble with Libyan authorities.

There were some Italian people living in Tripoli that had remained there after the Italians occupied the country before and during World War II. They were mostly shop keepers. The Air Base hired quite a few locals for landscaping and menial jobs, but they weren't allowed near the 580th area.

We were warned by a briefing officer about local custom and were advised not to create any kind of disagreement off base. Relations between the US and Libya were not very good and no one in the state department wanted US forces creating any kind of strain on an already weak alliance with the Libyans. Consequently, no one at Wheelus spent very much time in Tripoli.

Libya was a hot dry place; some areas of the country, which is mostly desert don't get any rain for years at a time. The air force used some of the inland desert for gunnery practice for the fighter wings stationed in Germany.

A lot of my off duty time was spent working the amateur radio frequencies. Contacts were made all over the world. Every time I sent out a call for any amateur in the US I would be swamped with calls back from many different places, but once I responded to one, the others would respect the conversation and generally leave us until we were finished.

Some of the contacts had phone patch capability and would patch me through to Mil. We had several good "radio relay" phone calls.

I hardly remember Thanksgiving; and not very much about Christmas either. According to my radio log I had a phone patch home to Mil on Christmas day. A ham operator in Rock Hill, SC patched me through to her. The amateur radio was my life-line to her. She wrote every day and the mail came through without any delays, but getting to talk to her was even better than the mail.

In late January the Red Cross contacted me and said they had a wire from the Red Cross at home informing them Jamey had been hospitalized. Nothing more! What was the problem? Had he been hit with a car? Was his condition serious? What was wrong with him? They couldn't tell me and bluntly refused to even send a reply asking for more information about his condition. They said all they could do was wait for further information and as soon as it was received they would contact me.

I couldn't wait on that weak kind of help, but got right on the radio. I couldn't get through on voice but had no problem getting through to a ham in Pennsylvania on CW. He asked me to standby while he called Mil on his phone. In a few minutes he had the information for me. When he told me that Jamey's condition wasn't serious, just a case of dysentery that needed to be controlled, it was like a heavy load had been lifted off me. My prayer that night didn't ask for anything, but did include a lot of "thank you" for Jamey's condition which wasn't serious at all.

There were opportunities to make trips over to Egypt and see the pyramids, or to the continent of Europe, but I never did go. In addition to normal operational missions the 580th made training flights to many places. Copenhagen was a popular place for "crew of the month," mainly because of the pretty blue-eyed blondes in Denmark. There was always room on the 580th aircraft and all anyone that was assigned to the 580th needed was a pass and parachute.

The SA-16's were amphibious aircraft that could make water landings an also had wheels for normal airstrip landings.

One afternoon the operations officer attempted to bring one in with the wheels up and scraped the hull on the Wheelus runway before he realized that he wasn't making a water landing. He had enough airspeed to open the throttle and make it back into the air with nothing more than a damaged hull; he made a successful go around and landed safely.

The next day a sign appeared in the operations building that read "The next time Colonel "Jones" (I don't remember his name) makes an approach in a SA-16, everyone in operations will go out and pee on the runway."

The guy named Thomas, the B-26 gunner who said that he would rather shoot up a train in North Korea than date Marilyn Monroe was assigned to the 580th as a crewman on one of the B-29's. He seemed to always be in some kind of trouble. Once he threatened to shoot a personnel clerk because he failed to correct something in his personal 201 file.

The break I was hoping for came in the form of a teletype message from 17th Air Force headquarters in Casablanca in February. The commanding general of US forces in the European Command was looking for a licensed amateur radio operator to run his MARS station at Headquarters, US European Command located just outside Paris.

The 17th Air Force sent the message out to all their subordinate commands throughout the Middle East. The 580th Commander called me in to his office and asked me if I would like to volunteer for the assignment. When I found out the assignment was near Paris it didn't take long to make my decision. The reply to General Cook in Paris had to go back through 17th Air Force and it took a couple weeks for reassignment orders to get back to me.

It wasn't long before I was clearing the 580th area and was in the transient quarters waiting for a flight from Wheelus to Rhein Main Air Base in Frankfort and from there to Paris.

Once my responsibilities to the 580th were behind me the most important thing on my mind was "how long will it take to get Mil and Jamey to Paris, once I get settled into my new assignment?"

TRIPOLI

5A1TC

المملكة الليبية المتحدة

وزارة المواصلات

رخصة لانشاء محطة لاسلكية للهواة

السيد ...... Shytle Thomas J. A/1C

من ...... 580th - ARG - -

يصرح لحامل هذه الرخصة باقامة محطة لاسلكية للارسال والاستقبال (تسمى فيما يلي المحطة)

فى ...... Wheelus Field

Mellaha

وتكون خاضعة للشروط المبينة على الصفحات التالية . ويدفع مقابل ذلك رسم قيمته 2000 ج . ل.

عند منح هذه الرخصة ورسم قدره 2000 ج. ل. فى نفس تاريخ صدور هذه الرخصة من كل عام .

تسحب هذه الرخصة او تعدل فى اى وقت كان اما بواسطة اعلام خطى يرسل الى المرخص له بالبريد العادى على العنوان المبين اعلاه او بواسطة اعلان عام .

ان اى اخلال بالشروط او عدم دفع الرسم يعرض هذه الرخصة للالغاء وفى حالة الغائها لا يرد اى جزء من الرسم المدفوع عن السنة الجارية .

Director of Posts & Telecoms ...... اصدرت بالنيابة عن وزير المواصلات

11th Dec. 1954 ...... التاريخ

A copy of my Libyan Amateur Radio License; Call Sign 5A1TC issued on 11 December 1954

Copy of the author's Libyan Amateur Radio License; call sign 5A1TC issued on 11 December 1954.

580th Air Resupply crew at pre-flight inspection prior to special operations flight over an Eastern European country; in all probability a leaflet dropping mission.

CHAPTER 22

Paris and Camp Des Loges March–December 1955

The transient quarters at Wheelus couldn't have been more than a few hundred yards from the end of the runway. I was there three days waiting on my flight and every morning at daybreak, which was about four a.m., the fighters began taking off for gunnery practice out over the desert. Tow target aircraft were first, followed by F-86 fighters that took off in pairs. The noise was deafening and continuous with about ten minute intervals between each take off, causing the whole building to vibrate.

The only break would take place when a transport or some other aircraft needed to land or take off; then the fighters would have to wait until it left the taxiway, or was clear of Wheelus airspace.

My flight left Wheelus sometime around mid morning and we were immediately out over the Mediterranean. The air was clear and before long we were over Sicily, then Rome, the Italian Alps and finally Rhein-Main Air Base near Frankfort. The crew chief pointed out every landmark along our route. Other than the crew, and a couple of other guys going to Germany, I was the only passenger. If the aircraft commander had a flight plan he didn't follow it because the most direct route wouldn't have been the track we were flying.

The airplane wasn't going on to Orly and no other flights were scheduled out of Rhein-Main to Orly until the next day, so the guy in the railway transportation office at Rhein-Main made arrangements for me to travel by rail from Frankfort to Paris. He called for a vehicle to take me to the railway station and completed some forms for me to turn in at the railway transportation office. They in turn would give me all the paperwork necessary to get me past several international borders because I wasn't travelling with a passport or even a visa to enter any foreign countries. The trip was shorter than I thought it would be. Since I didn't know any German or French whenever an official looking individual spoke to me I showed him the paperwork and my travel orders and never had a problem. Most of the railway crew spoke broken English anyway so most of the conversation was understood by both myself and the German or Frenchman doing the talking.

It was around ten in the evening when the train arrived in Paris. The US military had an information desk at the station so I went there to find out where I was supposed to go after leaving the train station. He directed me to a hotel on Rue Marbeuf that was leased by the US military. Rue Marbeuf was near the Champs-Elysees.

A ride through Paris after dark in a taxicab is an experience no one could forget. The cabbie drove like a madman; when approaching an intersection he would flash his amber colored head lights, and charge on through.

In spite of the reckless driving the cabbie made it to the hotel ok but I hadn't thought much about converting any money to French francs and had to exchange some military payment certificates to francs before the cab driver could be paid. I hadn't needed any Deutch marks in Frankfort because it was just a short drive from Rhein-Main Air Force Base to the railway terminal; a US military vehicle drove me there anyway.

I've tried to remember just what I used for money aboard the train but can't recall very much about that. I probably signed a voucher that the railway people redeemed at the railway transportation office in Paris.

I do remember having to clear French customs at the border and I think the train went through Luxemborg or another of the small countries between Germany and France and I had to clear customs there also. The hotel receptionist told me that a shuttle bus would be leaving the next morning to take me to Camp Des Loges; about eleven miles west of Paris at Saint-Germain-an-Laye. Headquarters US European Command was based there, and was where General Cook had originated the request to 17th Air Force for a licensed amateur radio operator.

The military had an APO (Army Post Office) close to the hotel and a detachment of the army and air force postal people were housed in the hotel on Rue Marbeuf. That must have been a good assignment to have a duty station right there in downtown Paris.

The shuttle bus was at the hotel early, my gear was loaded, and off we went. I saw some of the places that everyone has heard about. We drove right past the Arch de Triomphe, and the Eiffel Tower could be seen rising above everything else. SHAPE Headquarters was located just outside Paris and the shuttle made a stop there to let some guys off, and after a short drive we were at Camp Des Loges. It wasn't a very big place, just a compound with various buildings that looked like they had been there a long time. Nothing looked anything like a US military base

Every house and building in France looked hundreds of years old, but everything including the grounds were well kept. There was no airstrip at Camp Des Loges, but there was a parade ground of sorts with room enough for a helioport. It wasn't as big as parade grounds normally are, but big enough.

Personnel from all four branches of the military were there and worked together as one. I reported to the air force detachment Commander and learned that all air force people at Camp Des Loges were assigned to Detachment 7, 1141st Special Activities Squadron. The 1141st had detachments all over the world at embassy's, NATO, and all major Air Force Headquarters, and detachment 7 was at Headquarters, US EuCom (short for European Command).

A personnel clerk showed me around and took me to the barracks where I would be staying until I could get Mil and Jamey to Paris. The guys in the barracks were just about evenly divided between Sailors, Soldiers, Marines, and Airmen. All worked at different places on base. Some were medical technicians and worked at the clinics, some worked in administrative offices, some in the communications center and one guy was a military policeman assigned to main gate security.

It was an unusual place. The first thing asked from one of the Sailors was; "where you from?" I told him and he said; “hey, we’ve got another air force guy here that’s from Kings Mountain.” It wasn’t long before I met him; his name was Joe Wallace. I never knew him or his family before leaving King Mountain, but we became friends, and remain friends to this day. He had been there for a year or so when I arrived and knew how to move around in Paris.

The MARS station, that was my duty assignment, already had two other radio people assigned. One was a repair technician and the other was an ex P-38 fighter pilot that had been RIF’d (one of the “reduction in force” casualties following the war when there were too many pilots). He had accepted an enlisted rank of Master Sergeant, but had lost one stripe for some unknown reason and now was a Technical Sergeant. He could send and receive Morse at a slow speed and that was enough to be awarded a specialty code that made him a radio operator; and he was real smart with anything relating to radio communications and electronic theory. He could build anything from an audio amplifier to a high powered transmitter with nothing more than a schematic wiring diagram and a blank chassis.

The reason for my assignment was that neither of these two had a HAM license. They couldn’t legally go on the air without my license, but once I reported for duty, the MARS station could do what it was there to do; and, after getting authorization from the French we were legally operational.

We still needed a few pieces of equipment to really get a good signal out, and that problem was solved a few days later when General Cook walked into the radio shack.

He was there to make sure the station was up and running and that we had the authorization to put out a signal.

He didn't want any problems with the French equivalent of our FCC (Federal Communications Commission). While there he asked if we needed anything for the station. That was all it took; I gave him a short list of the equipment we needed and In less than a week a truck backed up to the station and started unloading our new equipment. It had been shipped from a signal depot in Chateauroux. On the shipment order there was a place for "shipment authorization" that stated: "By order of General Cook."

The three of us assigned to MARS were directly responsible to Major Les Williams, a really nice officer who never had a problem with anything we did. We were given a "blank check" to sign for anything available for re-issue from "re-distribution and marketing" (R&M) and we had a priority on anything they had. The ex P-38 pilot (Mert Root) and the electronics technician (Patrick Sheeley) and I made several trips to sign for a lot of spare parts and an antenna tower, among other things. And in a short time we had a rotating three element beam that could get a signal to any place in the world.

We experimented with antennas and equipment combinations and were handling a lot of radio traffic back to the states for the personnel at Camp Des Loges. There were no constraints put on us by anyone with regard to testing on the amateur bands, other than the international rules governing those frequencies. It was interesting work and even though our duty hours were normally eight to five we were usually working into the night.

I hadn't been there long when a civilian wearing a suit and tie walked in and introduced himself as Mr. Healey. He was a civil service lawyer assigned to the legal office; and asked if we could build an antenna that would allow him to receive the Voice of America broadcasts, the BBC and also the Eastern European propaganda broadcasts.

He had a good receiver that could be tuned to all the high frequency bands. Mert Root and I went to his residence in Saint Germain and constructed an antenna known as a "lazy H". It worked perfectly for what he needed. We found out later that Mr. Healey had been one of the prosecuting judges at the Nurenburg war crimes tribunal following the war.

Camp Des-Loges along with SHAPE headquarters had an aero club that flew several light open cockpit French aircraft that needed a way to communicate between the front and back seat and we were asked to build a small two-way system that would be powered by the aircraft battery. We all worked on that project for several weeks but finally came up with the equipment they needed.

As soon as I was settled in, preliminary steps were started for Mil and Jamey to join me. The first thing she needed to do was apply for a passport and visa. It would take over a month to work everything out and by early May they were all set to schedule a flight to Orly field in Paris.

Things had to be done on my end also; I had to rent a place "on the economy" because base housing wasn't available. The US government did have some "guaranteed rental" projects but it generally took several months of waiting to get into one of those units. A place was found in Saint Germain not too far from Camp Des Loges; the owner was an old lady with a peg leg, she lived upstairs and the ground floor of her house was made into a rental unit. Like most of the other buildings the house must have been several hundred years old.

One other important item on my list was a car. Luckily Patrick Sheeley had an English made Hillman that was for sale because he had ordered a new one from the factory in England. He and I agreed on a price for his old one and soon thereafter he took a few days off to travel to England to pick up the new car; my transportation problem was solved. The Hillman was a small, but very dependable vehicle.

Mil's flight was scheduled to leave Charlotte with stops in New York, Gander Newfoundland, Shannon Ireland, and Orly. We had to do some coordinating and she was to send me a telegram informing me of her flight number and arrival time at Orly. She sent the telegram as we planned, but it didn't get to me in time.

She and Jamey made it to Orly and I wasn't there to meet her; she found the US forces representative, told him where I was stationed; he called me and told me she was there waiting for me.

I left right away to make the drive to the airport that, with all the traffic, would take about forty five minutes. By the time I got to Orly she had been directed to take the shuttle to the American Consulate in downtown Paris and wait for me there. When I got to Orly the GI on duty told me she had been taken to the Consulate.

Finally, I caught up with her in a side room of the Consulate office. The first thing I saw was Jamey climbing the radiator, I looked over in a lounge chair and there she was; prettier than I remembered. Jamey was still full of energy, but she was very tired.

We had been separated six months and it was amazing how much Jamey had grown during that time. He looked so much bigger.

The trip to our new home in Saint Germain was relatively short and we were there within an hour. I had bought all that we would need over the next few days at the base commissary.

Everything was different than she had been accustomed to at home in the US; the furniture, bathroom fixtures, kitchen equipment, all were different. Jamey was still a baby when I left him six months earlier; I had missed his first birthday, his first steps, and a lot of other firsts. He wasn't a little baby anymore, he was still in diapers but was walking around.

Remembering a lot of details is difficult on one hand, but some details are easily recalled. For example, we cannot remember if our household goods were shipped to France or not. We bought some furniture before leaving Donaldson, including a baby bed for Jamey, a washing machine, and some other essentials. We may have placed them in storage, and we may have shipped them. Although we can't remember other details we both can remember our first breakfast in France. We had spam and scrambled eggs. It's odd that we can remember something like that and not remember other, more important things.

Mil adapted to the French culture and before long she was drinking a glass of wine with her meals, shopping in the local markets for French breads and desserts and

Jamey was saying “oui” instead of “yes.” We had a good commissary and post exchange at Camp Des Loges, so everything wasn’t converted to local custom. We still had hamburgers and cold beer.

Sheeley’s wife was a big help to Mil because she had lived on the French economy for more than a year, and could speak some French. Most of the local citizens could speak enough English, so there was only a slight problem with the language barrier.

Mert Root’s wife was from England and could speak French better than most, so she was a big help also. They both knew Mil would need some things to get started, like things in the kitchen, for example, that I hadn’t thought about when trying to get everything in order for her arrival. They donated some household items, and were both very helpful to Mil especially with information relating to the French way of doing everything.

Mert Root and his wife had a little boy, Carl, that was a year or so older than Jamey; that gave him someone near his age to play with.

My French amateur radio license was issued sometime in May; and there were probably a dozen or so other American military amateurs scattered across France. We had three or four other air bases in the country and an army seaport at La Rochelle located on the Normandy coast, and some of those guys had amateur licenses.

During the war a GI from Kings Mountain met and married a French girl (Anne) from Nanterre, a suburb of Paris; following the war he brought her to live in Kings Mountain and she became good friends with my Mom.

Then her husband was killed in an auto accident and she returned to France. Now she was working as a cashier at the Camp Des Loges post exchange. After Mil came to France Anne suggested we move in to an apartment in Nanterre with a friend of her family. We hadn't agreed on a long lease with the lady in Saint Germain, so we went to look at the other apartment in Nanterre; we liked it, and made plans to move. The apartment was upstairs and the landlady lived downstairs. She also had an older man living in a small apartment downstairs. The older man, Mr Antoine, was a member of the French resistance during the war, had been picked up by the German Gestapo, and went through a period of rough treatment at the hands of his interrogators. He couldn't speak any English and I didn't understand French very well, but we managed to communicate to some extent and I could understand him well enough to know that he had an intense hatred for the Germans.

He loved to go with me to a corner bar and have a glass of "aperatif", a French licorice flavored drink most Frenchmen liked. He also liked American beer.

The war had been over less than ten years, but already we could feel some resentment from some of the local citizens. I don't know if they were communists or just didn't like Americans, but the animosity was there never-the-less. I never feared for Mil or Jamey's safety though, because a majority of the people were friendly enough and she never had any problem while out shopping in the French marketplace.

Bread and cheese shops that also sold French pastry and desserts were easy to find in every market place, as well as wine stores that stocked an endless variety of French and other European country wines and liquors. Wine was delivered to residents like milk used to be delivered at home.

Mil and our new landlady, Si'mon were good friends and they went shopping in the marketplace almost daily. Si'mon, and I suppose most French wives, went shopping every day for the food they planned to prepare that day. They didn't stock freezers and refrigerators like American wives do. Mil fell right in with the customs and Si'mon taught her a lot of the French she learned to speak. During the war Si"mon had also been active in the French resistance.

We hadn't lived in Nanterre very long when Anne invited us to spend the weekend with some of her family who lived out in the countryside about an hour away from Paris; They were Catholic and her twelve year old daughter was being Christened; a big celebration had been planned over the weekend that started on Friday afternoon and lasted through the Christening of her daughter on Sunday. They lived in a castle that was hundreds of years old with barnyards and dungeons; all the old medieval history was there.

The dinner party on Saturday started in the afternoon and continued on into the evening. During each course a different wine or drink was served and following the food a toast would be made. Before the celebration was half way through dinner, we were all tipsy to say the least; and by the time it was over we were past being ready for bed.

We had a wonderful time and attended the Baptism for Anne's little girl the next morning. By Sunday afternoon we were on our way back to Nanterre.

During the time we were living at Nanterre we got to see a lot of Paris; from the Notre Dame to the Louvre, and from the sidewalk café's on the Champs-Elysees to the Moulin Rouge and Pigalle. The girls at the Moulin Rouge even had me up on the stage with them. Although we were there, we never went to the top of the Eiffel Tower. There was an American post exchange in Paris that was located right on the bank of the Seine river. The post exchange was in an old French aircraft factory that produced airplanes during the early days of aviation. It was named after Louis Bleriot, a French aviation pioneer who was the first man to fly across the English Channel in July 1909.

While we were in Nanterre we learned that Mil was pregnant with Leesa. In a few months we were informed that the waiting period for an apartment in the "guaranteed rental project" was over and we were at the top of the list.

Soon we were packing all our stuff again and getting ready to move. The place we were moving to was called "Petite Beauregard". That translated to English meant "Little Beautiful." The only families living there were American GI's stationed at either SHAPE or Camp Des Loges. Even though we both enjoyed being on the French economy we were happy to be going back to an All American housing area.

CHAPTER 23

Leesa and Petit Beauregard Jan 1956–June 1957

The move from Nanterre to Petit Beauregard went smoothly. We needed to do some shopping for additional kitchen gear, we bought a new living room suite at the Bleriot exchange, and a bunch of other stuff like we were starting to keep house all over again. And that's about what it amounted to.

The housing units at Petit Beauregard were three story apartment buildings with twelve apartments each. We had been assigned a ground floor unit that had two bedrooms, a living room, kitchen/dining room, and a large bathroom. The apartment had ample closet space. We had lots more room than before; everything was much better from the kitchen furnishings to the bathroom. And we were among people who spoke American.

The time spent living on the French economy was a valuable and enjoyable experience and we learned a lot by living close to people like Si'mon and Mr. Antoine. Although most of what he talked about, while we were having a cold American beer, I never fully understood; there was no mistaking the intense hatred he held for the Germans; nor the fact that his memory was very clear about the treatment he received at the hands of the Gestapo. We didn't have any bad feelings toward the French, because we enjoyed having them as neighbors and learned a lot about their culture, but now we had our own countrymen; their wives and children were our neighbors. We even had a gardener to take care of the outside areas, and we were closer to Camp Des Loges.

Mert Root, his wife Rene' and their son Carl were already living in Petit Beauregard and there were other small children that Jamey could play with; that was another plus. He was already two and could speak French with anyone. He never failed to amaze people with his quickness and friendly nature.

The weekend we spent at the Chateau with Anne and her family he entertained everyone there with a solo of "I see the moon, the moon sees me". We put him up on a pool table and he had everyone applauding when he finished. Apparently he understood everything that was said to him in French.

He seemed a little disconcerted when we talked to him about a little brother or sister, or maybe he just didn't want to hear about that. Regardless, Mil was showing her pregnancy, and the only medical facilities at Camp Des Loges were a dispensary and dental clinic. SHAPE didn't have a hospital either. When the time came we would have to make it to the Paris American Hospital, which was about fifteen miles away.

The work at the MARS station kept me busy during normal duty hours, but nights and weekends were free. We socialized a lot with Sheeley and his wife who lived near Versailles. They didn't have children and loved being around Jamey; they had him spoiled as much as if they were his Grandparents; and were always buying him something at the post exchange.

Getting a baby sitter for him at Petit Beauregard was no problem at all because some of the residents had teenagers who were always available. We took advantage of that and went out a lot. If we went to see a movie at the base theater we could take him with us, but if we went out to eat at the NCO club we'd use a baby sitter. Most of the time we'd have a group at the club that may include Joe Wallace, Mert and his wife, Sheeley and his wife and our new neighbor Ray Reed and his wife Mary. Or maybe we'd just go alone. But as Mil progressed into her pregnancy and the due date grew closer, we slowed the social activity down. Sometimes I would meet with the guys at a bar outside SHAPE called the Papillon Bleu. Over fifty years later all I have to do is mention that name to Joe Wallace and he'll break out in a grin and start talking about the good times we had there. When we moved into Petit Beauregard the first couple we met was Ray and Mary Reed.

Ray was another World War II flyer who had decided to stay in the Air Force after the war. He flew with the 8th Air Force as a bombardier on a B-17; and he had some harrowing stories of watching his friends fall from the skies over Germany. They were both from Pennsylvania, and Mary became one of Mil's best friends for the rest of our tour in Europe.

Mil likes to tell the story of how she missed seeing the Queen of England during her visit to France in 1956. The Queen's visit was well publicized and large crowds lined the streets leading into Paris waiting for her motorcade to pass by. We were amongst the spectators. No one knew exactly when to expect their arrival, but Mil had to take Jamey behind a bush just before the procession came into view; by the time he was finished and she had his pants back on, the Queen had passed by and was gone out of sight.

Our baby was expected sometime in August, but it didn't know anything about a due date, and on the morning of July 22nd at about 4 a.m., Mil woke me up and said that her water had broken; the bed was soaked. Jamey was asleep in his crib, and as Mil got something on, I quickly put on some clothes, got little Jamey out of bed and into the car.

Off we went bouncing toward Paris on a cobblestone road. Mil was getting sick and hurting; I was getting scared and driving as fast as I dared. She was really getting close as I pulled up to the front entrance of the hospital. I ran into the lobby where a guy was cleaning the floor with a mop, I yelled at him to get a stretcher. He dropped the mop and ran off somewhere. The next thing I knew a stretcher on wheels, pushed by two medics, came rolling through the lobby and out the door. I was right on their heels; they placed Mil onto the stretcher and off they went. I was told to go up to the second floor and check in with the reception clerk. Jamey had been quiet as could be throughout the whole procedure, maybe because he was half asleep, or maybe he sensed the urgency of the situation we found ourselves in; we went up to the second floor and before I could furnish the clerk all the information he needed for Mil to be admitted, a medic came in and told me we had a little girl. We had barely made it to the hospital in time; Leesa, that was what we had agreed to name our baby if it was a girl, was born in the elevator on the way to the delivery room. Was she all right? Was Mil ok? They were both fine! Our little girl was premature but everything looked good!

In just a few minutes the medics allowed Jamey and me to see Mommy. She didn't look any different except for the flat belly; that is, she didn't look tired and weak like she did after Jamey was born. She'd had a rough time with him, but this baby must have just popped out.

She did look a little worried and asked about our little girl, then she started crying; Jamey didn't like that at all; now he was troubled, it bothered him to see his Mommy laying there in bed crying. We let him lay beside her and that was comfort enough to ease his concerns. Mil was still concerned about our baby. She was a full month or so early and was a tiny little thing.

Mil hadn't even been given so much as an aspirin before the baby was "here"; she heard and seen everything about the birth. She must have heard a comment from one of the doctors about how small the baby was, and that was her concern.

I left her for a few minutes to get a look at our new little girl; there wasn't much of her to see because they had her wrapped like a mummy with nothing but part of her face showing. The little bit of her that I could see did look awfully small, but the medics assured me that she was fine and had all the fingers and toes she needed.

I reported back to her Mommy that everything was ok; that we had a healthy little girl. She seemed content with the information that I gave her.

The next day she was depressed again. Nothing I could say to her was convincing enough to satisfy her there wasn't a problem. Leesa either couldn't or wouldn't breast feed; that fact worried Mil because she wanted to breast feed her so much. It meant a lot to her, but it wasn't working out.

Another thing that worried her was Leesa's weight. She weighed four pounds and thirteen ounces at birth; now a day later she only weighed four pounds and nine ounces. The medics tried to explain that was normal, but she must have had some kind of after birth depression and wouldn't believe anyone.

Then before I left, she broke out if it. We went to see the baby and before long she was smiling, even though Leesa was still wrapped up pretty good and we couldn't see much of her.

Down the hall one of the rooms had flowers lined up outside the door and one of the medics told us that the movie star, Olivia DeHaviland had just given birth to a baby girl also. She lived in Paris with her husband who was the publisher of the popular French magazine "Match."

The next day Leesa had gained one of the four ounces back and her chart went slowly up from there. She was being given a special kind of goat milk called "Gigoes" that had to be imported from Switzerland.

In four more days Mil was released to come home, but Leesa had to stay until she weighed at least five pounds. She was two weeks old before they released her to come home with us.

The medics gave us a supply of "Gigoes" and told us when and where to pick it up because we would need it for our new little girl.

We had to go to the American Embassy to a State Department office and apply for a birth certificate. Since she was born outside the United States to American parents she would be issued a State Department birth certificate. She was an American citizen, but was, and is, a citizen of France also.

Jamey seemed a little anxious or puzzled by his little sister for a few days after we brought her home, but in short order he adapted to the "intruder" in his life and loved her as much as we did. If I threatened to trade her in he would be very protective toward her, and upset with me for talking like that.

Before long we were into a normal routine again, this time with two little ones instead of one. We spent some afternoons in a park across the Seine from the exchange at Bleriot. Once we went for a weekend to Frankfort, Weisbaden, and Kaiserslautern, Germany.

Looking back, I can't imagine why we didn't go to Normandy and explore the beaches where the invasion of Europe took place on June 6th, 1944. It had only been twelve years since the invasion, and we had every opportunity to go there any weekend.

Sheeley and his wife spent a weekend at Normandy, and he returned with all kinds of interesting things he picked up in the bunkers and along the bluffs overlooking Omaha and Utah beaches. I've always had a keen interest in everything that happened that day in June 1944, so it still bothers me that we didn't go to Normandy when we had the chance.

It was some time after Leesa was born that Joe Wallace found himself in a jam. Joe had never been married but couldn't resist making a play for a pretty young lady. He had been accused of getting too close to the wife of one of the army guys at Camp Des Loges and the guy found out about the liaison and was gunning for Joe. Our air force detachment commander was informed of the problem and had Joe hustled out and put on an airplane back to the USA that same night. By doing so he probably avoided a nasty situation.

Summer turned to fall at Petit Beauregard; and Leesa continued to grow into a healthy baby without any problems that I can recall. I don't ever remember having to take her to the dispensary for anything other than regular check-up visits.

Once we had to take Jamey to the dispensary with a high fever. We were spending a Sunday afternoon with the Sheeley's and he started feeling hot; his temperature went up past 103. We got panicky and rushed him back to Camp Des Loges. By the time we arrived at the dispensary, his temperature was normal. He had a tooth coming through and the medics figured that was the cause for the rise in temperature.

Christmas came and went. I don't remember much about the holidays that year except the Sheeley's gave Jamey a little bicycle. At first he used training wheels, but it wasn't long before he was speeding around the building on two wheels. He wasn't three years old yet and had already mastered the two wheeler. He really enjoyed that little bike and was constantly riding it.

All the neighbors thought he was the smartest kid they'd ever seen. Mil and I were very proud parents.

Jamey was three in January, and growing like a weed. Leesa was already crawling all over the apartment. She was still gaining weight but skinny as a rail.

One Saturday afternoon we took them to the Bois de Boulogne park across the Seine from Bleriot. Mert, Rene' Root and their son Carl were with us. A carnival had been set up in the park and the kids were allowed to ride all the cars and airplanes. We also let Jamey ride a camel. He was only three, but the camel ride is one of the few things he remembers about that time in his life.

One of the side shows had a short rifle range that had little pieces of chalk for a target. All anyone needed to do was pay a hundred francs (about 30 cents) to shoot; if you busted the chalk, you won a small bottle of champagne. I shot ten times and won ten bottles of champagne.

Mert was driving, but before we left the park to go to SHAPE for "fish and chips" he was in no condition to drive and neither was I. Mil did the driving back to SHAPE. The club at SHAPE was operated for the British army people stationed there, but a club card from the NCO club at Camp Des Loges was all that we needed to get us in.

While we were there, Carl had to go to the bathroom and Mert took him. When Carl came out, all he had on was a shirt. Mert had flushed his pants down the commode. Rene' covered his little behind with her sweater and we had to leave.

The MARS station had grown into something special and a new system of radio wave generation had been developed that was called "single-side-band". It was a new concept in audio communications and allowed for much clearer signals to be generated with less output power. It worked just as well on continuous wave (CW) signals.

The station had some non-appropriated funds available to us and we used some of the funds to buy a Central Electronics 20 watt exciter for our power amplifier and started using the new single-side-band technique. Everyone was amazed at what we could do. The Navy had opened a radio station in the Antarctic and we talked with them regularly using the new single-side-band signal.

In fact we were a part of the very first simultaneous all continent radio communication recorded. That is, we were in readable contact with an amateur station located in all seven continents and they had readable contact with all the others.

Before we could think too much about it, the time to start planning for our return to the United States was getting close. Because of the unaccompanied time spent in North Africa, my three year tour had been reduced by four months and my new rotation date was June 57. Orders arrived in April; I was being assigned to Tyndall Air Force Base in Panama City, Florida.

Mert Root was scheduled for return at the same time and we planned to travel together, at least as far as New York. Mert's new assignment was to the air force survival school near Reno, Nevada. His home was in Wyoming, so he was pleased with his new duty station. His wife Rene' didn't like to fly so we all asked for surface travel back to New York.

Someone at EuCom had pull with the personnel assignment office in Washington, where the Headquarters for the 1141st Special Activities Squadron was located and our travel orders were changed to read "surface" instead of "air." The Hillman was traded for a 1950 Ford, because the Hillman's steering wheel was on the wrong side for driving in the states, and I had to take the Ford to the port at La Pallice for shipment to New York. After that we were left without a car for several weeks before our departure date, but we made out all right without one. All our neighbors at Petit Beauregard had a car so we didn't have any problems in that regard.

All our household goods were packed up by the movers and made ready for shipment to Florida, and we moved in with Sheeley and his wife for a few days prior to leaving. We were living out of suitcases, a situation our family would be in several times throughout our career with the military.

We had our going away party, said goodbye to all our friends, and made ready to ride a train from Paris up through Belgium, Holland and into Germany. Our port of departure was Bremerhaven, and we were scheduled to sail on the USS Upshur.

We were taken to the railway station in Paris and the train left at ten p.m.. Our compartment was already made into a sleeper when we boarded and the only interruptions in our travel north occurred when we crossed an international border and the passports and military travel orders had to be checked.

By noon the next day we were in Bremerhaven, where we were checked into a guest hotel at the port. Within a day or two we were cleared and boarded the Upshur.

Compared to a troopship, the Upshur was a luxury ship. We had a large compartment with comfortable beds, maid service, and the food was outstanding. We had a large open deck to lounge around. The dining room was first class all the way and we were served like royalty. We sailed down the English Channel past the white cliffs of Dover, around the southern tip of England and out into the Atlantic. The voyage was supposed to take seven days, but on the second day out one of the ship's crew became seriously ill and we had to turn south toward the Azores. When we were near one of the islands a motor launch came alongside and the sick man was taken off the ship.

There were no more incidents and five days later we sailed right past the Statue of Liberty and within the hour were docked in New York.

While Mil and the kids waited for me, I caught a cab to the Brooklyn Navy Yard and picked up the car. When I returned they left the ship and after loading all our bags we drove to the Staten Island ferry, crossed over into New Jersey and turned south toward Washington.

CHAPTER 24

Florida and Crash Rescue Boats Jun 1957–Nov 1958

The Staten Island ferry took us over into Perth Amboy, New Jersey; from there we took US highway 1 South to Trenton. I had come full circle because nearly three years before I had been through Trenton on my way to Camp Kilmer. We crossed the Delaware River and entered the suburbs of Philadelphia. Highway 1 would take us south through Baltimore, Maryland and Washington, D.C.

The car was over-heating, but we continued on through Philadelphia and into Maryland. Finally, I had to pull into a service station to find out why the car was running hot. The attendant said it looked like the radiator was clogged up with deposits, probably from calcium in the French water. He also recommended a new thermostat He directed me to a radiator shop where they pulled the hoses, drained the radiator, and flushed it out. They installed a new thermostat, and soon we were on our way south again. Because of the clogged radiator we weren't as far along as planned when it began to get dark and everyone was getting tired; it was time to look for a motel to spend the night. It's difficult to remember just where we spent the night; we could have been north of Washington, but more than likely we were already in northern Virginia. Next day the trip south through Virginia into North Carolina was uneventful and we were home late in the evening.

Details of the homecoming are a little foggy. I had a little less than two weeks before my reporting date at Tyndall and we stayed with Mama and Daddy during that time. Mil was busy most of the time showing Leesa off to all her folks. Everyone kept asking Jamey questions just to hear him reply "oui" instead of "yes."

While we were still in Europe Lafayette and I had planned a fishing trip to Lake Hickory, and a few days after getting back we followed through with that plan. Philip Baker went to the lake with us; he was either currently or had in the past been to medical school at Carolina and had some awfully funny stories about some of the things that went on at medical school. Most of the stories he told couldn't be repeated here.

The three of us spent several days trying our luck on big mouth bass and crappie but we didn't set any world records. Before leaving Paris I ordered some camping gear and had it delivered to Lafayette; we carried all that with us along with their gear and also took Philip's boat which was just big enough for three fishermen. We picked out a site that was isolated from the main stream and set up a nice camp. We ate a lot of good camp cooking and had plenty of cold beer in the cooler at all times. It was a very enjoyable outing.

Before leaving for Florida, I took the Ford to Charlotte and traded it for a 1952 Packard. The Packard was one of the heaviest cars ever built and rode better than most; it would serve us well for several years.

Soon it was time to leave again. Leaving my family wasn't a very happy occasion, but Panama City was only ten hours driving time away; besides, as soon as I could find a house, Mil and the kids would be joining me. I needed to check out my new assignment to make sure I wouldn't be away from Tyndall a lot on temporary duty.

Orders indicated my new outfit would be the 22nd Tow Target Squadron and I had no idea at all what kind of mission they were responsible for. "Tow Target" could mean anything. I wondered why they needed a radio operator.

The day of my departure arrived and the evening before I was scheduled to leave we loaded up the Packard with my gear. I said goodbye to the folks, then to Mil, Jamey and Leesa, and drove south through South Carolina, Georgia, Alabama and across the Florida panhandle to Panama City.

It took a couple hours longer than we had estimated because every little town had traffic signals and speed limits; the interstate highway system hadn't even been started in 1957 and travel time was longer than expected. The trip was made without incident however, and I reported in with plenty of time to spare.

My assignment had been changed from the 22nd Tow Target to the 4756th Drone Squadron and I was assigned to a crash rescue boat crew. After reporting to the boat docks some of the first people I met were the men who were with the 22nd Crash Rescue Boat Squadron in Fukuoka, Japan. Two of them remembered very well the fight we had outside a cabaret in Fukuoka in 1952.

It took me several weeks to make the arrangements to move the family to Panama City because rental units were scarce anywhere near the base; and rent was very high. I finally found a small house that was affordable and was given a three day pass to drive to Kings Mountain and back. I signed out at the boat docks and left Panama City on Friday evening and drove throughout the night to get home. On the way I ran into a terrible thunderstorm that nearly washed me off the road, and the wind nearly blew me away several times. Finally, I spotted a place to pull off and rode the storm out on the side of the road.

After the storm blew itself out, I made it the rest of the way without any problems. We started the return trip on Sunday morning, made it to Panama City ok, and spent that night in a local motel.

All our household goods that had been shipped from France were delivered the next day and we were ready to start housekeeping again. We worked hard that day unpacking kitchen stuff, putting up the bed and arranging furniture.

I had to report for duty on Tuesday morning and leave Mil to finish unpacking and arranging things, plus take care of Jamey and Leesa. She had more than a hand full, but got it done in time to have supper ready for me that evening. It wasn't long before we were settled into a routine.

The boat crew consisted of a skipper, assistant skipper, engineer, and radio operator. We had two deck hands that kept the boat shiny and clean, but when we went out they would normally stay on shore. We also carried two medical people when on a rescue mission. The crash rescue unit had seven boats; there were five 63 footers and two 85 footers. We also had a 42 foot launch and a special services fishing boat that was docked at one of our piers.

I was assigned to a 63 foot boat. The engineer was responsible for everything in the engine room; he kept the big twin 630 horsepower Hall Scott marine engines running. They ran on high octane aviation fuel and while running at cruise speed consumed a little over a hundred gallons per hour. We could top off both tanks with thirteen hundred gallons of fuel and run at cruise speed for nearly twelve hours before we would be empty.

If we were running at emergency speed the fuel consumption was much more. The engineer kept the engines in top shape and they never missed a beat. My duties were to maintain communications on HF, VHF, and UHF frequencies. We also had a radar scope, and a radio compass. The VHF was tuned to the control tower frequencies so that I could monitor any distress calls from aircraft and UHF was also used for emergency calls. The HF unit was used to maintain contact with the shore station back at the boat docks and to report our position. With the radio compass I could triangulate two commercial radio station signals with our antenna aboard the boat to determine just where we were. The radar unit gave me a picture of the shore line and other obstructions if we had to approach the jetties in bad weather. The Saint Andrew bay jetties only gave us about eighty yards of water and that didn't give us much room for error. The radar was used to make sure we didn't make any mistakes in our approach to the inlet. I had a phone and microphone jack on deck beside the wheel so that I could monitor the frequencies there as well as in the radio room.

All the equipment was maintained and serviced by the radio maintenance shop at the boat docks. If a piece of radio equipment malfunctioned, I called maintenance; they brought a replacement and installed it for me.

The skipper and assistant skipper ran the boat and plotted our course. All the cleaning and polishing was done by the two deck hands. Duty aboard the R-37A rescue boat was some of the best ever. We were alerted several times to be ready for an open water rescue, but each time the aircraft made it over land before the pilot had to eject or made it back to a safe landing at Tyndall.

Our crew did a lot of fishing and ran compass courses all over the gulf, but never in the seventeen months I was on the boat did we rescue anyone. We were always ready if needed, but that never happened. We were alerted several times to make an emergency run but each time we were told to “stand down.” Both times the aircraft made it safely back to Tyndall.

We had only been at Tyndall three or four months and were running short of money before payday at the end of each month. Rent for the house was a little much for us to handle, and we decided that it may be best if Mil and the kids spent a few months with my folks in Kings Mountain. That would give us time to regroup and get back on our feet financially.

It just happened that my sister Coot and her husband were leaving Keesler Air Force Base in Biloxi, Mississippi and planned to drive through Panama City and stay with us for a day or two. While they were there it was decided that Mil and the kids would ride home with them, so we packed our household furniture, put it into storage and suddenly I was alone again.

I had no trouble checking into a barracks at the boat docks and ate at the Tyndall mess hall. Mil and the kids made it home ok, and were living out of a suitcase again, hopefully not for long. With no real household expenses we planned to have enough cash to have them back in Florida in two months.

My duties aboard the boat were mostly routine from one day to the next. We trained and sometimes made trips to Eglin Air Force Base and several times went to the inlet at Port St. Joe to standby while SA-16 air sea rescue aircraft did practice touch and go water landings. But mostly all we did was maintain everything aboard in top shape and be ready to crank up, cast off, and move out the instant the alert sounded. We never had any drills, so we knew if the alarm went off it was for real and an aircraft was in trouble out over the gulf.

The air sea rescue people were perfecting helicopter rescue techniques over open water and the boat outfits were slowly being phased out as crash rescue. There were other projects in store for the fast R-37A boats however. We didn't know it at the time but plans were being made to convert our boats to drone recovery instead of crash rescue. Patrick Air Force Base across the state at Cape Canaveral was already using some of their crews for emergency standby down range from their missile launch facility in the event of a malfunction after launch.

The period around that time in the fall of 1957 is difficult to recall with any degree of accuracy regarding actual dates. I estimate that we were in the house we had rented for about four months before Mil went back to Kings Mountain; she stayed there for about two months before I went home to bring them back with me. After discussing that time period with her we both have concluded that I came home for Christmas and we returned to Panama City soon after the holidays were past. Mil and I both have tried to recall the events of the Christmas season but can't remember much.

We think Bill had gone to Alaska on a remote assignment; they had moved their mobile home to an area behind our folks' house on Shelby Road and had a septic system installed for the house and mobile home before he left; Coot and her two kids were set up to stay there until he returned from Alaska.

The small town of Parker was located between Panama City and Tyndall and before I went home to bring the family back with me I found a house that was for rent in Parker.

The drive from there to the boat docks was only a few miles, and there was a big paper mill that we had to pass on the way to the docks. Sometimes, when the wind blew across the road, the smell from the paper mill was pretty bad. Little Leesa was only eighteen months or so and every time we drove down the road toward Tyndall, past the paper mill, she would look down at her pants and check to see if there was anything in there that needed to be removed. She was sure she had something unwanted in her pants.

The trip back to Florida was made without incident; the Packard was an excellent family car and was in good shape overall; we got all our things out of storage, and moved into the house in Parker. The house was on a wide sandy road with neighbors fairly close on both sides; it had a big back yard and a pasture behind a fence that ran between our back yard and the pasture.

There was a small Baptist Church close by and within a few weeks Mil was taking the kids to services every Sunday. The neighbors were all nice people and we enjoyed being there.

We did have a problem with fire ants, however. When we first moved there we had never heard of fire ants; and Jamey was introduced to them in the wrong way. It didn't take him long to get too close to one of the ant hills; they were climbing his little legs and he was screaming before Mil could get to him. She saw the ants and quickly put him in the bathtub, but he had already been bitten several times. He was ok, mainly due to her quick thinking; but it could have been much worse.

Our grocery expenses were supplemented with the plentiful and free seafood. Oysters could be plucked right out of the marsh across from the boat docks; salt water trout could easily be caught from the pier or rowboat that was always available, and we regularly brought in big grouper and snapper that were caught in the gulf while out "running compass courses." There were lots of shrimpers along the gulf coast and they always had fresh shrimp for sale at dirt cheap prices. Seafood has always been one of our favorite foods and we ate lots of it while we were in Florida.

The beaches between Panama City and Fort Walton Beach are some of the prettiest in the world and we took advantage of the opportunity we had to enjoy them. The white sand stretched for miles and they weren't crowded at all; in fact we usually had the whole beach to ourselves with no one else around anywhere. Hardly a week went by that we didn't spend at least one afternoon lounging around the beach and playing with the kids in the blue-green Gulf of Mexico water.

We would pack some goodies, a six pack of cokes that cost a quarter, and on the way stop at a café' that sold seven hamburgers or hot dogs for a buck. We would stretch out a sheet supported by some sticks and make enough shade to keep from getting burned by the hot sun. After a few weeks Mil and Jamey were tan enough not to get sunburned anyway. We always had a fun time at the beach.

Sometime during the summer all five R-37A boats were ordered to a shipyard in Mobile, Alabama to be fitted with a boom and winch to be used in the drone recovery missions that were coming up in September.

The air force had designated Tyndall as the home base for "Project William Tell" that would bring the top guns from all over the world to determine the "best of the best" in air to air combat. Our boats would be an important part of the competition.

Our crew left the docks early one morning for the trip to Mobile with a stop at Eglin Air Force Base near Pensacola. We spent the night at the US Coast Guard Station near Mobile and caught a helicopter back to Tyndall the next day. We landed at one of the naval auxiliary strips near Pensacola and had lunch on the navy before taking off for Tyndall

The modification to our boat would take about two weeks. Rudy Hofstetter was the ranking NCO at the boat docks and he didn't require the boat crews to pull any kind of extra duty; so the two weeks while we were without a boat were days that we didn't have much to do except play pinochle. Rudy was one of the guys stationed in Fukuoka in 1952 with the 22nd Boat Squadron, and was one of the best NCO's I ever worked with; he was a born leader. He passed away several years ago in Panama City.

Two weeks later we hopped a helicopter at the Tyndall strip and went back to Mobile for our boat; again we stopped at Saufley Field, a naval flight training base, near Pensacola; and from there we flew on to Mobile.

We spent the night once more at the US Coast Guard Station and left for the return trip to Tyndall the next morning. As well as I remember it was about a six or seven hour trip non-stop because we arrived at our home base in mid afternoon.

There was a message waiting for me at the orderly room from the personnel office at Tyndall. About a month earlier I had submitted an application for recruiting duty and had gone to Pensacola for an interview with an Officer from the local recruiting office several weeks earlier. I assumed the personnel office wanted some information relating to that application.

That wasn't the case; the personnel clerk told me that I had been alerted for an overseas assignment to a remote base in Greenland. I would be leaving in October! I had to think of some way to get out of that assignment. For one thing the air to air gunnery meet was scheduled for September and I would be gone most of that month with my crew on drone recovery missions.

If no way out of the remote assignment could be found, I would be spending a lot of time away from Mil, Jamey and Leesa over the next several years. Rudy came to my rescue. When I told him of my reassignment order he asked me what my return date from Europe was. When I told him June of last year, he said that I was guaranteed a minimum of eighteen months in the US between out of country assignments according to an air force regulation, and wouldn't have to take the assignment to Greenland.

I rushed back to quote the regulation to the personnel clerk; and he took my name off the list for movement in October. But he wasn't through with me yet; before I left he looked at me and said; "consider yourself alerted for a remote assignment in January." According to the regulation, January was the earliest I could be shipped overseas again.

All this reassignment business went on without Mil ever knowing anything about it until it was all over. I did tell her that I would probably be alerted for a remote assignment in January. That didn't go over too well with her because she was content to stay where we were. They were all enjoying the beaches, the neighbors, the Baptist Church, and the good times on base at the NCO club annex across the street from the boat docks; and a lot of other good things that could be said about our life together in Florida. The last thing she wanted now was to be uprooted again.

It wouldn't be long before we would receive some very good news concerning my next assignment.

Project William Tell wasn't too far off; and the 4756th Drone Squadron would play an important part in that project. The squadron had been equipped with modified B-26 medium bombers that could carry two Ryan Firebee drones to launch altitude. A radar station had been built near Apalachicola to control the drones once they had been dropped by the B-26's; and all the crash rescue boats had been converted to drone retrievers. Our squadron was heavily involved in the upcoming weapons meet.

The track flown by the drone stretched from within a hundred miles of New Orleans on the west to Saint Petersburg on the east. After being launched on the outer leg, the drone would make two ninety degree turns and enter the "hot leg". Fighters would then be scrambled from Tyndall to intercept the drone somewhere during the "hot leg" part of the orbit.

The air to air missiles were programmed for a near miss. They weren't supposed to make a direct hit because the Firebee drone could be recovered and flown again if it wasn't badly damaged.

Four of our R-37A boats were stationed at various positions along the hot leg to recover the drones after splashdown. The drone had a parachute that would automatically open at fifteen thousand feet and floatation that kept it from sinking, providing the missile blast didn't damage the floatation cells.

The parachute was colored bright red and white so that it would stand out against the blue sky. The drone also had a wing pod with a camera mounted inside the pod; the camera took movies of the incoming missile. The film was used to determine who the best shooters were. After the competition was over the best fighter pilots in the world would be named. The wing pod camera was very important to the pilots.

We were told in no uncertain terms "Do not lose that wing pod, no matter what." We never lost one, but one boat crew lost two complete drones; however they weren't to blame because the drones both sank on impact with the water.

Binoculars were used to see the drone's contrail and also the interceptor as they closed on each other, then a much faster contrail left behind the missile as it streaked toward the drone; then a flash, as it exploded. Within a minute or so we would normally spot the parachute floating high in the sky, and by the time it reached the water, we would be nearby.

For drone recovery missions, we added a diver to the crew; and when we backed up to where the drone was floating, the diver would go overboard with a line to secure the drone, which would then be hoisted out of the water with the winch. We would return the drone to Apalachicola to be transported back to Tyndall by truck.

Our crew was sent to Carrabelle, Florida, a small fishing village, for the duration of the weapons meet. We lived aboard the boat night and day; and left the docks at three a.m. every morning. We cruised straight out into the gulf for four hours before we reached our position. Calculating a cruising speed of 30 knots by the time we were on station we were approximately 120 miles from shore.

Then we waited, but weren't idle. I could listen to the air to ground radio traffic and knew when to expect things to start happening, besides, we could see the contrails in the sky and know exactly when to expect a drone in our area. In the meantime, we caught fish. Groupers and red snappers could be sold at the commercial fishery in Carrabelle. We sold grouper for seventeen cents a pound and red snapper for thirty four cents per pound; and everything we made was split equally between the crew members.

The competition between the best fighter pilots to ever assemble in one place was over in three weeks, and they all returned to their respective units around the world; we took our boat back to the docks at Tyndall and didn't know the outcome of the competition until the base newspaper was published. We did know that the boat crews had performed well and were an important part of "project William Tell."

The boat detachment commander called all the crews in for a meeting and congratulated everyone for our efforts and read a letter from the Tyndall base commander that commended our work during the weapons meet.

There was a message waiting on me after we secured the boat. Rudy Hofstetter needed to see me right away. When I saw him he told me that he had received word that I had been selected for reassignment to recruiting duty; and following successful completion of a thirteen week school in San Antonio I would be assigned to the recruiting office in Charlotte.

I rushed home right away to break the good news to Mil. We were to be stationed in our own back yard rather than have her and the kids staying with my folks while I was off to some forsaken corner of the world on a remote assignment. We didn't have long to get ready; we were already nearing the end of September and the class was to begin in early November.

That meant we only had a little over a month to make another major move; there was a lot of planning to do. Mil would have to stay with my folks again for three or four months while I was gone; I would have to drive to Texas, and that meant she would have to depend on someone else to take her wherever she needed to go. She had a driver's license for the state of Florida, but would have to get a North Carolina license.

There was a lot to think about. By late October everything had fallen into place; all our household goods had been packed and would stay in storage somewhere until we would need it again in Charlotte.

We were back to living out of a suitcase again. We cleared Tyndall, said goodbye to all our friends in Florida and drove back to Kings Mountain. In less than a week I would be on my way to San Antonio and Mil would once again be left alone to care for our two little ones.

CHAPTER 25

Recruiting School
November 1958–January 1959

The white sandy beaches of northwest Florida were behind us as we began the ten hour ride back to Kings Mountain; it was still late October and we had nearly a week before I would have to leave for Lackland. It suddenly came to me that I would have to spend another Thanksgiving and Christmas away from them. I would also miss Jamey's fourth birthday.

We did a little sight seeing on the way and stopped to tour the National Cemetery and site of the infamous Confederate prison at Andersonville, Georgia. Several years earlier I read the book "Andersonville"; it was interesting to see the actual site after reading about the terrible conditions the Union prisoners had to endure at the hands of a brutal commander of the Confederate guards.

A major problem with a wheel bearing brought us to a dead stop near Greenville, South Carolina that delayed us for several hours waiting for repairs. The bearing overheated after losing all the lubricant and froze to the axle; not only the bearing, but the entire axle had to be replaced. A rear axle for a 1952 Packard is not a part that is normally stocked, not even in 1958; but luck was with us, and the mechanic found one at a local junk car dealer. In a few hours we were on our way again and made it to Kings Mountain with no further delays.

Mary and Lafayette had a new baby girl; Cindy, was born in June and already trying to crawl. We spent some time with them over the next five days; Mil was getting settled in at Mama's and I was getting ready for the trip to Texas. Over the weekend Lafayette and one of his friends were off scouting the South Mountains of upper Cleveland County for the upcoming deer season that was scheduled to open sometime in November.

The Packard was checked out by Mil's brother Junior, one of the best "shade tree" auto mechanics around. He pronounced it ready and able to make the trip without breaking down.

Coot and her two girls were living in their mobile home parked behind Daddy's garage building. They would be a lot of company and help to Mil over the next three months.

Pam was still with Mama and Daddy, and they weren't about to give her up to go and live with her Mother in Tennessee, besides Faye had graduated from Occupational Therapy school, was remarried and had a baby boy. Pam was happy where she was; and Mama and Daddy were happy to have their Grandchildren with them; it was a good arrangement for everyone.

Lafayette was now an established pole climber and installer for Southern Bell in the area around Kings Mountain; he and Mary had recently bought a house on Shelby road directly across from his folks.

He and I spent a few evenings at the American Legion, patronizing Uncle Bill Morgan who was the canteen manager there. The local VFW was also on our list of watering holes.

Had it not been for Gizmo Gantt we probably wouldn't have made it out of one joint near Blacksburg late one night; the suds gave us too much mouth with not enough of the "right stuff" to cover the odds that we were facing. After a challenge had been issued we looked around to see there were too many for the two of us to face and expect to win, but it was too late to retreat. Gizmo was one of the regulars and gave us a much needed escort out the front door and into the car. We made our getaway without incident, but were lucky that time. There would be other times in the future when we wouldn't be so lucky.

All too soon the time came for me to load up and leave again; but at least I wasn't leaving for Greenland or some other remote corner of the world; Texas was a two day drive, and I'd be back in thirteen weeks.

The route to San Antonio was a general southwestern direction with an overnight stay in a cheap motel in Louisiana; and on across Texas to Lackland Air Force Base the next day. As Junior had predicted the Packard was running like it was brand new.

Recruiter school consisted of classes for three hours in the morning and three in the afternoon. Weekends were free with nothing much to do except sleep late on Saturday and Sunday and spend time at the NCO club.

There were about thirty future recruiters taking the course, but by the third or fourth week we had lost six who gave it up and returned to their respective bases; and maybe to a personnel clerk with a remote assignment waiting for them. We had a lot of sales training and had to write and deliver a ten minute speech once a week for five weeks in a row. We could pick the subject for each speech, except the last one had to be about the US Air Force.

The audience consisted of our fellow students and the instructor who was grading our performance. The remainder of the class were pretending to be a graduating high school class. Prior to that speech we had a lot of classes on Air Force history and traditions. Each speech was graded by two instructors, and we lost another three or four students because of their "public speaking," or their delivery technique, no one knew why, but they were suddenly washed out.

The border town of Nuevo Laredo was about three hours southwest of San Antonio and was a good place to go shopping for cheap Mexican leather goods and other products that made good Christmas presents to take back home.

Almost every weekend some of the students made the trip to Laredo. Across the river to Neuvo Laredo was a good place to shop, but it was also an easy place to get into trouble. It was a typical border town with lots of bars selling cheap booze and girls; a Mexican jail is not a good place to spend the night, no matter what the offense that landed you there, but we were smart enough to stay in the shopping district and away from boy's town.

None of the recruiting school students failed to make it back from the border that I knew of, at least not in my particular class. There were a few pretty bad hangovers on Monday morning, but nothing worse than that.

San Antonio had its attractions too. The Alamo was still there, and so were the café's serving good Mexican food and Lone Star beer. Most of the recruiter students were married, so the Mexican beauties of San Antonio didn't come into play this time like they did during basic training nine years ago.

The NCO club at Lackland was the center of our off duty recreation, they served cold Lone Star long necks; and they were cheaper than the downtown restaurants. In fact sometimes they were free. The local permanent party NCO's were always buying a round for the house.

One Saturday night a guy was celebrating his retirement and bought a whole keg of "Lone Star Draft" for the recruiter students. There were seven of us and we had a time trying to empty that keg. When we left the club to make our way back to the barracks the keg still wasn't empty. It was hangover time the next day.

Thanksgiving came and went without much celebrating, and it wasn't long before Christmas. The course was moving along without any major problems and we were scheduled for completion before the middle of January. I had phone conversations with Mil once or twice a week; she and the kids were ok but ready to get back to being a family again and in our own house. So was I; sleeping alone in a barracks wasn't the best way to "make it through the night."

About two weeks before completion of recruiter school I placed an ad in the base newspaper looking for two riders to North Carolina. When the time came to clear the base I had two recruits who were finishing basic training and were going back home for a few days leave before starting tech school. They were from Greensboro and needed a ride. I made a deal with them to help share expenses, and when the time came, we loaded up the Packard and started north towards North Carolina.

The trip was uneventful and two days later I dropped them off on the highway just north of Kings Mountain and drove back towards Shelby to my family who were waiting for me with open arms. The kids looked like they had grown, even though it had only been a little over three months. It never failed with Mil; every time I had to leave her, even for a few weeks, she always looked prettier than ever when I came home. But then, she always tried to look her best for me; and never failed to do so.

The air force personnel people were always good at giving some added travel time between assignments and I had about a week without having to use any leave time before reporting to the recruiting detachment in Charlotte. That gave Mil and me some time to look for a house to rent.

I stopped by the detachment right away just to meet some of the operations people and find out who I would be working with. They were waiting for me to fill a vacancy in the Charlotte office and I was anxious to get settled in with the family again and start back to work. We made several trips to check out the classified ads but came up empty. We weren't concerned too much about it because there were lots of rental units we hadn't looked at; and we knew we'd find a place after I reported in.

Over the weekend Lafayette and I made a trip to Hudson to see Ike and Jack Gantt. They already had a nice lake picked out where we could catch some rainbow trout when the season opened up in early April.

Just before we went to Hudson we learned that Jack had been hospitalized in Lenoir following a heart attack. We went by the hospital to see him; he was already getting anxious to be released but the medics told us he would have to stay with them for about another week. They also told him that if he would follow their advice and stay away from the moonshine he would most likely be around for the opening day of trout season.

He didn't listen to them after his release from the hospital, but he lived long enough to make the trout season with us and several more seasons before his heart finally had enough of his way of life. Jack was one of the good ones; he worked hard and played hard.

Later that same summer we all planned a weekend fishing and camping trip to Lake Rhodhiss. We were going after big mouth bass and crappie. The whole gang was there including Jack and Ike, Rush Bolin and his son, and others. There were eight or ten in our camp site.

On the way to Rhodhiss Jack wanted to stop and get a jug of moonshine. He bragged about how good it was and stated that "you can drink all you want of this stuff and never wake up with a hangover, it's good stuff and it treats you right."Lafayette and I didn't drink any of the moonshine but Jack did; in fact he was passed out on one of the folding cots long before midnight.

His statement about "not having a hangover" wasn't exactly true because when he woke up Saturday morning he found an excuse to go home and didn't make it back.

Later we learned that he was at home in bed until Sunday morning.

Over the next five years Lafayette and I would spend many weekends fishing and camping with those guys on Rhodhiss and Lake Hickory; and fishing for cold water catfish in Wilson Creek. Opening day of trout season was always a long weekend of camping and fishing for rainbows; After having been closed for the whole month of March, opening day always occurred on the first Saturday in April. We have a lot of good memories that takes us back to the good times spent with Jack and Ike.

Both are gone now, but they aren't forgotten.

My week at home passed quickly; we had tried but still hadn't found a place to live, but it didn't matter. We didn't have any school age kids to be enrolled in school, and if I had to I could commute to Charlotte for a few weeks.

We were just beginning yet another chapter in our life together; and again we had no idea of what lay ahead, but were looking forward to whatever was out there waiting for us.

CHAPTER 26

Maria, Charlotte, and Recruiting Duty Jan 1959–Mar 1964

Jamey's 5th birthday was just a week before I made it home, although Mil doesn't remember much about it he must have had a big party because all his cousins lived within a few miles; and five of them right there next door.

It had been a long time since there had been any changes in the US political picture; Eisenhower was still President, having been re-elected in 1956. Things were happening worldwide, however, that affected us all. The Russians had placed a satellite in orbit, and in January 1958 the US also had one circling the globe. In December 1958 Fidel Castro marched into Havana with his Cuban rebels and kicked out the dictator Batista. Cuba and Castro would make waves for years that affected American foreign policy and the US military; especially the air force.

The space age was here and just fifteen months after the first US satellite went up, NASA made their selection of the Mercury Seven astronauts, but it would still be several years before John Glenn would become the first American to go into orbit around the earth. One of the Mercury Seven, Wally Schirra was flying F-84s at K-2 during the time I was there with the 136th Fighter Bomber Wing.

Mil and I continued looking for a place to rent in Charlotte. I reported to the recruiting detachment and learned that my office would be located in the federal building on West Trade Street. Most of the ground floor was taken up by the Charlotte downtown Post Office, the other recruiting services were there along with the local FBI office and Federal Court House. Charles R. Jonas, one of the US Senators from North Carolina, also had an office in the building.

I had about a week to get squared away before actually starting to work as a recruiter and that time was used to look for a house. We left the kids with Coot and made several more trips to Charlotte looking at rental units. We finally found the one we wanted that was located just off Wilkinson Boulevard on Charlotte's west side. There was a Baptist Church within a hundred yards, the neighborhood looked clean and it wouldn't be hard for me to get downtown to the recruiting office. The address was 3119 Davis Avenue, and would be our home for the next five years.

It wasn't very big; just two bedrooms, living room, kitchen, and bath. It had a big garage out back and had room enough to grow a garden. One important factor in our decision to rent this house was the lack of through traffic. Davis Avenue was a short dead end street and our place was next to the last house on the street. Jamey and Leesa could play in the yard without constant supervision, and we wouldn't be worried about traffic. A very good super market was within walking distance for Mil to do her grocery shopping and a service station was on the corner leading to Wilkinson Boulevard.

The transportation office at Pope Air Force Base was responsible for delivering our household goods that had been stored in Panama City, and within a few days after making contact with them our goods were delivered and after three or four more days of moving stuff around we were back in the home-making business again. We needed some additional furniture, so we bought a few things for the living room and a new television.

The only TV reception we could pick up was the two Charlotte stations, but we really enjoyed those two channels. A few weeks later we traded the Packard for a 1957 Chevrolet. The Packard had served us well, but it was getting a little ragged, and as one of only two air force recruiters in Charlotte and the adjoining counties east of Mecklenburg, I had to maintain a good image, and a ragged old Packard just wouldn't look right.

My sector supervisor, Henry Young, had been born and raised in South Carolina and could relate to the local young men that we needed to talk to. He was a lot of help to me and I had very little trouble making my objective each month. My area of responsibility included eastern Mecklenburg County and Union and Anson Counties to the east of Charlotte.

Most of the non prior service males and females we were trying to enlist were high school seniors and last year's graduates. We also needed aviation cadet, nurse, medical specialist, pilot, navigator, and prior service applicants. That was a lot of programs we had to work on, but the air force has always been a popular branch of the military and we did ok.

The other recruiter in the Charlotte office was Ralph Jeffries. He was from down east somewhere near Raleigh, was married and had a little boy. He was one of the good ones, and turned out to be a good friend. He did have a reputation of being a little loose with the truth. Our Commander, Lt. Col. Brown used to jokingly say "Jeffries had rather climb a pole to tell a lie, than stay on solid ground and tell the truth."

It was a wonderful time in or lives. We were happy and problems were few and far between. But things were starting to happen in far off places that would eventually affect us. Some American advisors were killed near Bien Hoa air base in Vietnam, a place most Americans had never heard of in 1959.

The French had been defeated at Dien Bien Phu in what was then French Indo China; their defeat had prompted President Eisenhower to cite the "domino theory" and it wasn't long before the number of advisors in Vietnam started increasing. To help bring other events into perspective; Alaska was admitted as the 49th state in January 1959, and in August, Hawaii was admitted as the 50th state; and the first class had been enrolled in the new Air Force Academy in Colorado Springs.

We were settled in our house on Davis Avenue and were spending almost every weekend in Kings Mountain. Grandma and Grandpa Roper had moved into the house he built in Peaceful Valley, Grandma wasn't as happy about it as he was, but for Grandpa, I believe it had been a goal for him. It was a dream that he had been building on and working to achieve for a long time. He seemed to enjoy everything about it. Grandma would have preferred staying on Fairview Street spending time sitting in the front porch swing, but she was there in the country with him and made the best of it, and eventually adapted to living there.

There were too many good times not to love Peaceful Valley. Several years ago some of the Grandchildren put together a “Roper Family Heirloom” cookbook. In the back of the book are some comments written by several of the Grandchildren and invariably what they remember and write about are the good times and adventures they had out in Peaceful Valley; and that is the way it should be.Looking back at the whole picture it’s very easy to see how strong and resilient both of them were. While Margaret, Lorena, and Ivery were having babies of their own, Grandma was still having babies too; and working full time at the mill. And if that wasn’t enough she still cooked and ran a house full of growing children. There were no automatic dishwashers or many of the conveniences homemakers have today. Grandpa didn’t get his biscuits at Hardees on the way to work either. They were baked in Grandma’s stove on Fairview Street, and Peaceful Valley.

One of her granddaughters wrote the following in the cookbook: “I have many wonderful memories of Grandma Roper from my childhood, such as watching her make delicious biscuits by hand: mixing flour, buttermilk and “lard” in a large bowl.”

Another granddaughter, who was with her the night before she passed away, wrote: “As the tears rolled down my cheeks, I could smell Grandma’s chili cooking, buns warming, and hamburgers sizzling. As my visit ended, I kissed Grandma goodbye, told her that I loved her, and thanked her for all those childhood memories.”

Grandpa was the driving force out in Peaceful Valley, while still working full time at Robert’s store. He was one of the strongest willed individuals, and yet the most gentle natured man I ever knew. He always had one or two pigs that were being raised in a lot below the house; one of his favorite events came every year when the weather was cool enough for "hog killing." He thoroughly enjoyed all that went with scraping, dressing out, and cutting up a hog that he had raised from a small pig.

While he and Junior did all the butchering, Grandma would be working on the hog's head, getting all the meat, mixing scraps and all the other stuff that went into her livermush. Her biscuits, fresh made livermush and eggs made the best breakfast anywhere. It just didn't get any better than that. And we knew that "back bones and ribs" would be on the table for supper that evening.

Peaceful Valley was the center of the Roper world for a number of years before Grandpa's health started failing. There were so many children, grandchildren, and even great grandchildren that all social events were a big deal and always included lots of good food; from the dinners held out in the edge of the woods to Easter, Thanksgiving, and Christmas. It was like a Church homecoming with that long table loaded down with all kinds of good food and Grandpa's keg full of ice cold, homemade lemonade.

All you need for absolute proof of that would be to ask any of the grandchildren what they remember most about Grandpa, Grandma, or Peaceful Valley and they'd tell you about the dinners out in the woods, and that good lemonade. They were always a close family and I have always felt privileged to be accepted into that tight circle.

Mil and I have always enjoyed a relationship that has been relatively free of any major disputes; but I remember the first time she "flogged" me was over a statement I made about Grandpa that she misunderstood. No one said anything of a "negative" nature about anyone in her family without having the "wrath of an angry woman" coming down on them. From that day on, Grandpa could do no wrong, no matter what.

The truth was that he, in fact, did no wrong, but Mil took my statement to imply otherwise. We all loved this very special giant of a man. To this day Mil will sometimes look at me and say "I wish I could see my Daddy again".

The first year on recruiting duty passed into history; my monthly objectives were being met reasonably well and we had another recruiter join Ralph Jeffries and myself in the Charlotte office. His name was Charles Lindberg Todd; he was single and came rolling into town in a brand new Ford convertible. He was a confirmed bachelor and liked to play the field with the ladies, but before the year was out one of the local beauties had him hooked and reeled in.

Charlie was born and raised near Myrtle Beach, South Carolina; we talked the same language and became good friends, and have remained close friends throughout the years. He moved back to Myrtle Beach after retiring from the air force, and still lives there.

Several events occurred in 1960 that should be mentioned: In early January John F. Kennedy announced his candidacy for President, and at the democratic convention in July he won the nomination of his party. Later that month Vice President Richard Nixon was nominated as the Republican candidate. National elections were held in November and John F. Kennedy was elected as our next President.

Closer to home the main event of 1960 for us was the news that Mil was pregnant with our third child. She was suspect in September and confirmed in October.

The weeks and months rolled on by; Bill had returned from his remote tour on one of the Aleutian Islands and had been reassigned to a base near San Angelo, Texas. He worked for the Air Force Security Service as an intercept operator and because of that, he was subject to being sent to bases with listening stations near Russia and communist bloc countries. They had moved their mobile home to Texas, and I believe they sold it and bought a home in San Angelo. Coot had started back to school to get a teacher's certificate. San Angelo State University was nearby and the opportunity was there for her.

Later Bill graduated from that university and after retirement from the air force became a High School Principal in Texas.

Christmas, 1960 came and went. We spent the holidays with our folks, driving between Peaceful Valley and Shelby Road. Mil's pregnancy was beginning to show and all the medical check-ups looked good. She was a lot like Grandma Roper in that regard. The doctors didn't expect her to have any delivery problems. The service station on the corner of Wilkinson Boulevard just two blocks from where we lived was owned and operated by Mr. Booker (Jamey used to call him Mr. Booger). He was a very nice guy and we always bought gas and had our oil changed at his place. He and another good friend who traded with him were Masons, and I petitioned him for an application for admittance into his lodge. My application was approved and during the first months of 1961 I passed the degree work and became a Mason in February. My membership is still with that lodge over forty six years later.

Mil was really showing now and we curtailed our weekend visits to Kings Mountain in case she delivered early as she had with Leesa. I was still having to be out of Charlotte travelling to Union County twice a week and would normally be gone most of the business day and sometimes late into the evening. I tried not to be away more than absolutely necessary to complete my work but since my area of responsibility was out of town there was no way to completely avoid it.

Mil and I both talked with Charlie Todd about what he needed to do in case she called the Charlotte office needing a ride to the hospital and I was out of town. For two months Charlie would jump every time the phone rang. He was scared out of his mind that he would have to go get her and the baby couldn't wait till he got her to the hospital, and that he would have to help her deliver the baby in the recruiting vehicle.

He didn't say too much about it until after our baby had been born; then he confessed to us just how scared he really was over the prospects of having to help deliver the baby.

And then it happened. It was a routine morning for us. On the other hand it was a special day for the US space program. It was the 5th of May and Alan Shepherd was scheduled to be the first American to be sent into space for a sub orbital flight in a mercury capsule. The space program had been going forward at lightning speed during the last half or 1960 and the first few months of 1961.

In the previous year NASA had conducted twenty-two major space flight attempts most of which were successful and the US had launched thirty one earth satellites and had two deep space probes in orbit around the sun. Russia had already launched a lunar impact mission.

Everyone was watching and waiting for the first astronaut to fly. I went to the Charlotte office to take care of some paper work; the phone rang, and since I was in the office, Charlie wasn't shaking when he answered. It was Mil calling to say we might need to go to the hospital and check out some pains she was having. She was still several weeks away from her due date and didn't sound too anxious on the phone, so I really didn't think the alarm was real.

I drove the government vehicle home, not expecting to have to take her to the hospital, but when I arrived things seemed a little more alarming than I thought when she called me at the office. We weren't supposed to ride dependents in the recruiting vehicle, but off we went to the hospital anyway because her pains were coming at short intervals. They still weren't severe, in fact she didn't seem to be nervous or jittery about the pains; but we decided it best to not take any chances. We made it to the hospital, walked in the lobby and checked in. They took her down the hall to a room and the nurse told me it would be better for me to go back to work; they would check her out and call me.

At that point the medical people didn't expect she would be having the baby right away; her pains were still relatively light, so I left to go back and finish the paperwork that was started earlier. I had just walked into the office when the phone rang and a medic on the other end asked me “do you want this little girl”? That was the way I received word that we had a new baby girl.

Ten minutes later I was back at Presbyterian Hospital to make sure Mil and the baby were both ok. After talking with the doctor I learned that not long after I had left the hospital Mil had a few close contractions and just spit the little girl out without any complications at all. Mil and Grandma Roper were both made to have babies it seemed. She had problems delivering Jamey and was in labor for about six hours, still, there wasn't any difficulty other than those caused by the stiff necked medics at Donaldson Air Force Base hospital.

By now, bringing home babies was a familiar ceremony. They were in the hospital for just a few days before being released and within hours we had a stream of visiting neighbors checking our little girl out.

Mil was happy to have the past nine months behind her and couldn't wait till we could take her out and show her to the rest of the family. She didn't have to wait long, because they came to see her. My Mom and Dad came to see us and Mama stayed over to help Mil with housekeeping chores and washing diapers.

We named our little girl “Maria Evanne”; the first because the reigning Miss America was Maria Beale Fletcher from Asheville; and her middle name was after Mil's grandmother Evanne Roper.

After we brought her home the daily regularities became routine again. Jamey was already six and we were making preparations for him to start the first grade in September.

The weekends in Kings Mountain weren't happening as often as before; the new baby created some changes in our routine and we met and socialized with new friends in the recruiting detachment and also our new neighbors.

It wasn't long, however, that the time needed to care for a newborn was behind us and we took a camping vacation to Huntington Beach with Mary, Lafayette and their two girls. Huntington Beach is part of a state park fifteen or twenty miles south of Myrtle Beach and is isolated somewhat from all the crowds on the Grand Strand.

Our meals were cooked right there at the camp site. We were there for a week and had a wonderful time. Every year we were in Charlotte we spent at least one week and sometimes two weeks at the beach. One year we rented a house near the Grand Strand of Myrtle Beach, but Mil and the kids all seemed to enjoy the camping better than the rented house.

Summer was over in no time at all and before long, winter was upon us again. Mil always said the house on Davis Avenue was the coldest she had ever lived in. It had a centrally located heater that burned kerosene; there wasn't a forced air duct system, it just blew hot air out into the living room.

When we spent the weekend in Kings Mountain we generally turned the furnace down before we left on Friday afternoon, and when we returned home late Sunday afternoon the house would be cold. Normally it would take the furnace several hours to get the house warm again. She and the kids would sit around all bundled up waiting for the warm air to circulate.

My tour with the USAF Recruiting Service was to last three years and would have been completed in January 1962, but I requested an extension of one year and was asked to stay for two years.

The reason was never given for the longer extension; it may have been my record, or it may have been a lack of qualified replacements being available. Regardless of the reason, I stayed at the Charlotte office until orders came for me to transfer to Yokota Air Base, Japan with a reporting date of March 1964.

There were many events that occurred during those years of 1962 to 1964 that could be written about, but most of our activities were unremarkable. We continued to spend some weekends with our folks. The holidays were special occasions from Easter to Thanksgiving and Christmas, but all in all they were basically the same event from one year to the next.

Lafayette and I did a lot of fishing on weekends during spring and summer, and went deer hunting when the season opened in November.

It needs to be stated that we spent a lot of time at the local VFW and American Legion. We took chances that could have landed us in trouble with law enforcement, but we were young and reckless, and didn't stop to think about the consequences of driving after drinking too much beer. Neither did we consider the problems that we could have caused our family. We were very lucky to have never been caught while driving under the influence; our Guardian Angel was always with us. The hours Mama spent on her knees on my behalf paid off big time for me. I wish there were a way for me to let her know this. Hopefully she does.

We traded the 57 Chevrolet for a new 1961 Ford Falcon a month or so before Maria was born.

There were obvious news events nationally and internationally such as the assassination of President Kennedy in November 1963; and the Cuban missile crisis that happened from August to November 1962. The US involvement in Vietnam was increasing; President Kennedy ordered more advisors and support personnel to Southeast Asia along with more equipment.

When Kennedy took office there were less than a thousand advisors in Vietnam and by 1962 that number had increased to eleven thousand.

The army needed a bunch of new helicopter pilots and in March 1962 I submitted an application for that program. I passed all the criteria for admission and thought I had been selected only to find out that the age cut off was 29½ years. I was just two months past the maximum age limit.

The draft had been, or was about to be, reinstated by Congress resulting in our office being flooded with applicants. We had more young men of draft age than we could enlist. There was no reason for me to drive down to Monroe looking for people, except for the other categories such as medical specialists or pilot/navigator applicants. We had time to sit in the Charlotte office and wait for walk-ins.

Federal court was in session just across the hall in the district courtroom. One afternoon we were a little slack and decided to go over and listen in on the proceedings. The federal law enforcement (alcohol/tax) officers had intercepted a moonshine runner coming to Charlotte from

North Wilkesboro with a load of his "stuff" and he wound up in federal court; he had already been convicted and was in court that afternoon to be sentenced. The judge fined him forty-five hundred dollars, took his vehicle, and put him on probation for a number of years. When the judge was finished the man turned to one of his friends and motioned him to come up to the bench; he brought a big brown grocery bag with him; the convicted moonshiner took the bag and handed it to the recorder. He told the recorder to count out forty-five hundred dollars and give the bag back to him with what was left. He signed some forms, then he and his friends walked out of the courtroom. There was no doubt that he would be back on the road hauling another load within a few days.

My orders for reassignment to Yokota came in February 1964 and within a few weeks I had been cleared from the Charlotte office and went on a two week leave to get ready to drive the family across the country to Travis Air Force Base which was located north of San Francisco, California. Another adventure half way around the world was waiting for us. It was an exciting time in our lives.

CHAPTER 27

Yokota Air Base, Japan
March 1964–July 1965

About a week before our departure Mil and I went to Sears in Charlotte and bought each member of our family a big suitcase so that we could pack everything the kids wanted to take with them. Maria wouldn't be three years old until May, but she had her own suitcase too.

Junior helped me mount a top rack on the Falcon and I rigged up a canvas cover to make it as close to waterproof as possible. All our household goods and hold baggage had already been moved to the west coast for shipment to Japan, and hopefully would be waiting for us when we arrived at Yokota Air Base. We had a lot of people to say goodbye to, and we had already been to several going away parties given to us by the recruiters in Charlotte and Gastonia.

As well as I can remember it was about the 18th of March when we left Kings Mountain early in the morning and started driving west. Mama and Daddy watched with a sad look and a few tears as we drove away; no doubt we all felt a little heavy hearted.

Mil had been saying goodbye for several days to all her family on the other side of town and had already dropped a few tears. She was awfully quiet for a long time. That first day we traveled west on highway 64 and made it as far as Winchester, Tennessee before checking into a motel.

While we were going through the mountains of Western North Carolina Jamey was car sick several times; the curves must have upset his balance a little and we had to stop twice and let him get some relief.

Maria carried a little pillow that she had to sleep with every night, and the last order Mama gave us just before we left was to be certain that we didn't forget and leave her pillow in a motel room. That pillow was her "security blanket."

The next morning we were on the road again and several hours had gone by before someone mentioned Maria's pillow. We couldn't find it anywhere. The unthinkable had happened! Her pillow was 80 miles behind us in the motel room. We would have to make the best of it and hope she wouldn't be too upset when we checked into the next motel.

The route we had laid out took us directly through Bolivar, Tennessee, the town where Faye lived. Mama had either written or called her that we were on the way, and planned to stop to see her. Bolivar is a small town and she wasn't hard to find, so we visited with her and her family for a while.

She had a nice dinner waiting for us with some of the biggest biscuits I had ever seen. She now had two boys, her youngest, Eddie, was only a year old. She and her husband both worked at the West Tennessee Mental Hospital located only a few miles from their home. She was an occupational therapist and he worked in hospital maintenance.

Our visit had to be short because we had the big city of Memphis to get through and we wanted to be past the city before rush hour. We almost made it before the traffic buildup but because we were just a little too late we lost almost an hour due to heavy traffic before crossing the Mississippi into Arkansas.

That night we made it to Brinkley, Arkansas. When we got to our motel room we didn't mention Maria's pillow, but she did. We didn't know how to explain it to her, but she finally gave up and went to sleep. She was too tired and sleepy to fight it very much.

By the next day, the worst of the missing pillow was over; there were lots of interesting things happening that took her mind off the pillow.

We drove on into Oklahoma and made it to Oklahoma City where we merged with highway 66, the route that would take us all the way to California. Although it wasn't late we decided to spend the night there. The next day we made it into the panhandle of Texas and spent that night in Shamrock, Texas; and the next night we spent in Gallup, New Mexico. We crossed over into Arizona and toured the Painted Desert and Petrified Forest and spent the night in Kingman, Arizona; the next day we made it to Santa Barbara, California.

After we left Santa Barbara we drove north along the pacific highway to San Francisco. We drove over the Golden Gate Bridge to Fairfield, California and Travis Air Force Base. We had been travelling a week but were young and energetic so the effects of long hours on the road didn't bother any of us too much. Besides, we had seen some of the country for the first time and everything considered the trip was very enjoyable.

The car had to be left with a company that would drive it back to San Francisco and turn it in to the port authorities to be loaded onto a transport ship for movement to Yokohama. When that chore was done we checked in to the guest hotel at Travis to wait on our flight.

Two days later on the 27th of March we took off in a commercial Boeing 707 for Anchorage, Alaska.

Little did we know that we were flying straight into the path of one of the most powerful earthquakes to ever occur, anywhere. It was Good Friday; our take off time must have been close to eleven in the morning and our route took us directly to Anchorage where we left the aircraft and went into the terminal while it was taking on fuel for the last and longest leg to Japan.

We were on the ground for a little over an hour before boarding and taking off again.

Our flight couldn't have missed it by much, because the earthquake struck at 5:36 local time and was centered between Anchorage and Valdez. The main shock lasted over four minutes and registered 9.2 on the scale they use to measure those things. It was the most powerful earthquake ever recorded in North America and the third most powerful ever recorded anywhere.

People were killed by tsunamis as far away as California and towns were damaged in Hawaii. Over ten thousand aftershocks were recorded following the main shock. If our flight had been scheduled an hour later we wouldn't have made it off the ground because Anchorage was heavily damaged and the runway at Elmendorf Air Force Base, where we landed, was probably unserviceable following the quake.

The next leg of our trip took us over the Aleutians then south. It was a long flight and tiring; the kids were ok but a little restless; we slept some and soon were approaching the main island of Honshu.

The intercom informed us that we were nearing Tokyo and would soon be descending into Yokota airspace.

I looked over at Mil and she had a tear running down her cheek. I tried to question her about what she was feeling, but she didn't know herself why she was feeling depressed and unhappy.

It didn't last long and by the time we were on the ground at Yokota she was feeling fine. Maybe she was just thinking about all of her family that we had to leave, or the long three-year tour we were facing half way around the world from everyone at home.

A military bus took us and our baggage to Tachikawa Air Base to clear Japanese customs; following our clearance we were brought back to Yokota and taken to temporary housing.

Sergeant Bott, who would be our sponsor, met us at the transient quarters and gave us a short briefing on what to expect over the next several weeks. The temporary quarters had everything we needed but it was "temporary" and was furnished with typical base housing furniture.

The furnace was hard to get started; it had an old fashioned kerosene burner that had to be lit. The weather was cold and damp with a drizzle outside, and it was cold inside, but we finally got the burner going on the furnace.

Mil and the kids were unpacking some of their suitcases; they would be ok for a while, so Bott took me to the communications squadron orderly room to sign in.

That only took a few minutes and when it was done Bott wanted to show me around the base, especially the NCO club where we had to stop and have a beer. An hour and several beers later I insisted that he take me back to our quarters. He dropped me off with a promise to pick me up the next morning.

Mil was somewhat irritated at me when I walked in the door. After Bott and I had left them alone, the furnace had overheated; she had to take the kids outside for fear the house would burn up. The pipe from the furnace had turned red hot until someone nearby saw her concern and fixed it for her. She was still angry with me for being gone too long.

Yokota was home to the 441st Combat Support Group that flew F-105 tactical fighter bombers in support of operations in Vietnam. They flew from Yokota to bases in Thailand and conducted their operations from those bases.

There were a host of other units at Yokota. There was a KB-50 Air Refueling squadron, and a RB-29 Weather Recon squadron. Yokota was also a stopover base for aircrews going to and coming from Southeast Asia. It was a busy place, day and night.

The following morning I learned that I would be working with Bott at the local MARS station until a permanent slot could be found for me within the 2127th communications squadron. The only official radio traffic we handled at the station was weather data sent by one of the WB-29 radio operators flying a pacific loop that took them close to

Guam and back. They dropped weather data gathering drop sondes and reported the information back to us. Weather predictions for the whole western pacific area was based on the data sent to us. When not receiving weather information Bott and I worked the amateur bands for the troops and their dependents at Yokota.

The first place I stopped after meeting the first sergeant and commander was to check in with base housing to get signed up for a unit on base, and learned there was a waiting period of from four to six months for base housing. In the meantime there were several places off base that were like little compounds that rented "paddy houses" to airmen at Yokota.

The town of Fussa was located not too far from the Yokota main gate and we found a small Japanese house in a project called "Fussa Heights" only a few blocks from the gate. We didn't get any of our household goods from storage but checked out everything we needed from a housing supply unit on base. Within a week of arriving in Japan, we were settled in our new neighborhood that would be home for the next five months.

It didn't take long to meet most of the residents in the compound. John Manley and his family were from Greenville, South Carolina and Jack Callahan and family were from Union, South Carolina. Tony Andrade and his wife, Louise, from Rhode Island and the Mack Lektorich family from Pennsylvania all lived within a few yards. The Japanese didn't waste any space; the paddy houses were all very close to each other.

Bott took me to Yokohama to pick up our car, and by the time we were comfortable in our new quarters Mil and I both had taken the test for our Japanese/American driver's license. I had the Falcon registered and bought an insurance policy to cover any liability while driving in Japan. We were rapidly becoming acclimated to local customs and on base recreation activities.

The Yokota NCO club was the center of off duty social functions and because transient air crews were constantly landing to refuel or stop overnight for crew rest, a club annex was open at all times. The annex had a bar and kitchen that never closed. Slot machines were available in both the main club and annex; the aircrews kept the slots busy, and even though they regularly paid out a jackpot, the club was hard pressed to spend all the money that was made from the slots.

Because of all the aircrews that were just passing through, the annex was busy all the time and sometimes the transient crews would venture into the main club. Consequently disagreements would sometimes flare up and a fight would occasionally break out.

One night Mil and I were there with Tony and Louise Andrade and another couple. We were all six sitting in a booth having a good time. Tony left to go to the bathroom and some guy slid into the seat beside Mil; he threw his arm around her shoulder and put his other hand on her leg. Without even thinking or saying a word, I swung with my left and caught him solidly in his right eye, knocking his eyeball completely out of the socket. That was the only blow struck in the fight. He never knew where the one that got him came from.

The club had several security people on duty and one was always on duty in the cocktail lounge. He just happened to be standing behind me when I hit the guy.

The other guy grabbed his eye and the bouncer grabbed me and put some kind of a karate lock on me. That was the end of the fight.

They took him to the base hospital and I never heard if they were able to save his eye or not. The club manager had to fill out an incident report because of the injury, and when they brought him to the cocktail lounge to talk to me he looked at me and said "did you see that other guy's eye?" I told him "no, and I don't care what it looked like." I had to explain things to the First Sergeant the next day. He took a few notes and that was the last I heard of the incident.

The main club was laid out like a Las Vegas casino with big name shows, an elaborate dining room menu that was dirt cheap, and a ball room with a big band that played every night. There were several bars that had happy hour everyday and dime night at least once a week. Bingo was played every Friday night with several five hundred dollar winners, and once a month the club had a stag show with dancing girls and free drinks. On Sunday afternoon the kitchen staff laid out a buffet that would rival anything in Las Vegas, with ice carvings and prices that were ridiculously low. There was also an outside patio dining area with an Olympic size pool.

The club was just one of many recreational activities on and off base. Next to the MARS station was a big area set aside with baseball and softball diamonds, a playground and picnic area, outdoor grills, horseshoe pits and tennis courts. The base hobby shops had facilities to make anything from molding ceramics and building radio controlled cars and model airplanes to rebuilding an automobile engine.

There was a unit softball league that competed with each other and a base team that competed with other bases in Japan.

Staying home and listening to the radio wasn't much of an option at Yokota. Off base activities were interesting enough on their own. Sightseeing was almost unlimited within a hundred miles of Yokota that included Tokyo and Yokohama, Mount Fuji and the mountains to the west had some wonderful trout streams that were stocked daily with nice rainbow trout. Eating out at a local restaurant was an experience unto itself, and every small village and town had a festival of its own at some point in time.

We could stay busy every weekend for the next five years without repeating the same thing.

One of the very first things we needed to do after arrival was to get Jamey and Leesa enrolled in school. That wasn't a problem at all because the base had a school with all grades from the first through high school and a bus that came to Fussa Heights and almost to our front door. They were enrolled and ready to start by the time we moved in.

It seemed like a party was going on somewhere in Fussa Heights almost daily. As soon as duty hours were over the cold Black Label cans would start popping. Sometimes everyone would bunch up on a front porch, and other times we would load up a cooler and drive on base to watch a softball game. For some reason Black Label beer was the favorite brand, but any brand was cheap at a dime per can. A whole case of icy cold beer was only $2.40 with no tax.

It wasn't long before we started planning for Maria's third birthday party. There were lots of little kids around and everyone was invited, even the grown-ups. She had a great party that we captured on an 8mm movie that we still have today.

Not long after Maria's birthday Jack Callahan was killed when his KB-50 went down just after take off from Misawa Air Base on the northern island of Hokkaido. He and I had planned on a trout fishing trip Tuesday, but he wanted to make one last check of the airplane before his scheduled air refueling mission on Monday morning. I rode to the base with him on Sunday evening and sat in the cockpit while he checked off something that was bothering him. He was working back in the bomb bay area where a rubber bladder had been installed when the big bomber had been converted to a tanker.

He came back to the cockpit and made the statement that he might red x the airplane. As the crew chief he had that authority and if he had done so another airplane would have flown the mission to Misawa on Monday morning, and his airplane would have been grounded until the problem had been corrected, whatever it was.

Apparently he didn't do that and cleared the airplane to fly. Soon after take off at Misawa for the return flight to Yokota a fire warning light came on and the aircraft commander gave the bail out signal. Callahan and a fighter pilot that had hitched a ride to Yokota for an emergency flight home were riding in the compartment aft of the side tow reel operators.

When the bail out light came on, Callahan opened the bulkhead hatch that led to the exit door; when he opened the door the lock-back didn't catch, he jumped anyway, but didn't get a clean exit and was blown back into the compartment and fell against the putt-putt generator. He got up and opened the door again for the hitch-hiker who jumped. As soon as he exited the aircraft the left wing blew off and Callahan didn't get out. The fighter pilot made it to the ground ok along with four of the crew. Five others, including Callahan didn't get out.

That afternoon I had all our fishing gear rigged up and a case of Black Label on ice ready to leave early Tuesday morning. We were all waiting for Callahan to come home when John Manley was called in to work. John was a dental technician; we didn't know it at the time but John had been called in to release Jack's dental records so that his body could be identified.

Not long afterwards the word was out that a 421st Air Refueler had gone down; and then we learned it was Callahan's airplane. He left a wife and two little girls. There was a memorial service at the base chapel and the next day movers came and Jack's family were on their way back to Union, South Carolina to bury their husband and Father.

Not long afterwards another 421st KB-50 went down somewhere in Thailand; this time the entire crew made it out because when the fire warning light came on they didn't wait to see what was wrong before jumping.

Within a month of that accident all the KB-50s were ordered out of service and flown back to Arizona to the bone yard.

Although Jack Callahan was never forgotten, within several weeks things in Fussa Heights returned to normal

My duties at the MARS station were over and I was assigned to the Pacific Air Forces Commander's single side band radio network. We were tied in with a radio net that had stations all over the Western Pacific and Southeast Asia. The net control station was in Hawaii so that the commander could communicate with all the subordinate stations that were scattered from Australia to Yokota and from Vietnam and Thailand to the Philippines.

Not long after leaving the MARS station I was asked if I would like to manage the non tactical radio contracts on base. Those contracts were already signed with the Motorola Corporation for communications equipment needed by base security, civil engineers, medics, and others who needed handi-talkie and mobile communications equipment.

I wasn't too happy with the Pacific Commander's single side band network, and jumped at the chance for a nine to five duty day. There wasn't much to do except to monitor all the non tactical radios and if anything went wrong I had to coordinate with Motorola for replacements, but that seldom happened.

I worked with a fellow named James Burt and we both reported to Captain Williams; a real nice guy who didn't care much about what we did so long as he didn't get any feedback of a negative nature.

It was nice and easy but carried a pretty heavy responsibility because most of the non tactical users had emergency liabilities. Most of my duties involved accountability and were administrative in nature allowing me to have more time off than I needed.

Our name finally came up on the base housing list and we moved into a single unit on base. We had all our household goods delivered and settled in the house we would call home until late 1966. On a clear day we could look from our front yard and see Mount Fuji.

We were spending a lot of weekends in the mountains trout fishing. Between Yokota and the place we generally went fishing was a village, or small town, named Hachioji. The town was bombed regularly by B-29's during the war; not because it was a strategic target, but because it happened to be where they dumped their bombs when the primary target was weathered in. The people there weren't too fond of American airmen.

The Japanese re-stocked the rainbow trout stream twice a day, so there wasn't any trouble catching all we needed, and then some. Trout were a lot of fun to catch; and right at the edge of the stream was a Japanese restaurant that would take our fish and cook them for us. They were deep fried and served with rice and stir-fry vegetables; they didn't get any better or fresher than that. We always brought some home with us to share with the neighbors.

The 43rd recreation area was a favorite place for a weekend retreat. Normally when an American holiday came around, especially July 4th or Memorial Day, a festival would be held at the 43rd area. Some Hawaiian guys would dig a big pit and cook several hogs the way they did in Hawaii. They put hot charcoal in the pit and buried the hogs for a day and night over the hot charcoal. The next day they would dig them up and everyone would have a feast.

The local Japanese brought in all their best food and drinks and the party would last until late Sunday evening.

In spite of all the recreational activities I've been writing about, most of my time was spent on duty, as was everyone else. The Combat Support Group was losing a lot of F-105's flying out of bases in Thailand in support of war efforts in Vietnam and a lot of maintenance and support people were constantly going TDY to Southeast Asia.

The Yokota runway handled more take-offs and landings than any base in Japan. A lot of the guys who had been hurt in Vietnam were brought to Yokota on the way to the army hospital at Camp Zama. Mil's brother Nelson was one of them. He was medically evacuated after his Huey helicopter was shot down.

Sometime during the spring of 1965 I had to take a physical examination that included an audiogram to test my hearing. I didn't pass the audiogram and that caused me to be reclassified. My specialty job code required that my hearing be better than the audiogram indicated and as a consequence I could no longer work as a radio operator.

I had to get out of the communications field altogether. After a pile of paperwork going back and forth between Yokota and Hickam Air Force Base in Hawaii I was selected to attend a Management Engineering class that would be taught by a group of instructors from a technical training unit at Lowry Air Force Base near Denver, Colorado.

Rather than my going to Lowry, the instructors came to Yokota because there were five other guys enrolled in the same course. It would take about three months to complete the school, and after completion, I would be assigned to the Management Engineering team at Yokota.

That was the end of my career as a radio operator, and in addition, the medical people stated on my record that I could no longer be assigned to work in a "noise hazard" area such as a flight line, or engine run-up area. I could no longer be exposed to high level noises because it would complicate my already damaged high frequency hearing capability.

A new and different phase in my air force career was just beginning.

CHAPTER 28

Yokota and The Management Engineering Team Jul 65–Nov 66

Instructors from the technical training detachment arrived at Yokota and our class schedule was set up; we had almost as many instructors as there were students and the setting was informal to say the least. Only senior NCO's were allowed into the career field and there were only five selected for the class; still there was a lot of work to do including quite a few difficult mathematical formulas that were used to determine manpower validation, standard deviation and workload factors.

There were no computers available to us and we didn't even have access to calculators in 1965; the closest thing to a computer was an adding machine. Everything was computed by working it out on paper. The new career field I was getting into involved a lot of numbers and math. What we did with the figures would determine requirements for men and machines needed to perform a given function.

Part of the new job would involve minor investigative work to provide management advisories when requested to do so. The school was hard but everything went well; everyone in the class finished with passing grades and returned to their respective bases.

James Doverspike and I were assigned to the management engineering team at Yokota so when we finished all we had to do was report to the team commander, Major Brown. We had eleven team members and to the last man were some of the sharpest people I had ever been associated with. I was assigned to work under the wing of Dick Wagner; Doverspike did the same with the team leading NCO, Sergeant Berman.

Dick was one of the wisest and most talented individuals I had ever met. He taught me the basics of management engineering, not exactly as we had learned during the classes, but as defined in a practical application "on the job."

Doverspike was learning just as well from Berman, even though he was already an accomplished individual before coming to the management team.

He had studied "Ju Jitsu" under some of the old Japanese masters and was the only "non" oriental that had ever been admitted into the inner circle of that segment of the Martial Arts. He could go into some kind of trance and perform unbelievable physical acts.

Dick Wagner was also into Martial Arts and would be a dangerous opponent in a fight, but the entire time I knew him at Yokota and at a later assignment in Cheyenne, Wyoming, I never heard him raise his voice or get angry with anyone or anything. His gentle nature belied his inner strength and unquestionable character. We had lots of social get-togethers as a team and Dick would always break out singing old Irish songs after about the third round of frosty mugs. He knew the words to them all, but it took a few drinks to open him up.

Doverspike, on the other hand, couldn't sing worth a hoot, although he tried, but could pour four cans of beer in a big mug and chug-a-lug all forty-eight ounces. The team was a tight knit group, that is they worked together and socialized together, from the Commander, then "Major Brown", later to become "Lt. Colonel Brown" to the last man on the team. We all worked well together with no dissention or disagreements that I was ever aware of.

The assignments were given out fairly and carried out jointly by any and all members as needed to accomplish the mission we were given.

Besides Col. Brown we had one other officer assigned to the team, Lieutenant Clyde Brooks; he had recently graduated from Georgia Tech with a degree in Industrial Management, which qualified him to work in management engineering. He had accepted a commission in the ROTC program and had been called to active duty after he finished at Georgia Tech. He and his wife became good friends and remain so to this day.

After he completed his active duty in the Air Force he returned to school and became a veterinarian. He opened his practice in Brevard, NC, and bought a home there. They still come to visit us from time to time.

It was a privilege to work with such men; I always looked forward to going to work because there never was a dull moment in the team office.

Both Dick Wagner and James Doverspike sometimes spoke of their involvement in the Martial Arts and were instrumental in Mil and I both taking lessons to learn Judo.

There are many different segments of the Martial Arts that are studied in Japan, sometimes to the point of almost being a religion to their followers. Some of the Masters of Ju Jitsu and Karate and other Martial Arts devote their entire lives to their particular shrine. Judo isn't one of these mystical convents, but is more of a study in self defense or could possibly be considered a contact sport, because there will always be a winner and a loser. In Judo the loser politely bows to the winner, admitting defeat; in Ju-Jitsu the loser, in most cases, doesn't survive. I believe that Doverspike could probably take an opponent out permanently with his finger.

Mil stayed with it and passed the test to earn her brown belt, but Clyde Brooks and I dropped out of the classes, not because we lost interest, but because our work required that we had to be elsewhere.

All the team members called her "Millie,"but Mil still sounds right for me and in this journal I will continue referring to her as "Mil," until the point is reached when, after our first grandchild started calling her "Nanny," I will do the same when writing about her.

Although we never were much interested in bowling, Mil and I were at the Yokota bowling alley one evening when someone came in and told us John Wayne was in the base operations waiting for his airplane to refuel. He was on his way to Vietnam to visit with the troops.

We left the bowling alley and made our way to base operations right away; when we walked in, there stood the big man all alone looking out across the parking ramp. There were two of Mil's lady friends with us and luckily one of the operations people had a camera and took a picture of the four; Mil, her two friends, and John Wayne. We sat and talked with him for the better part of an hour. We had a coffee and chatted about his movies; he autographed a 100 yen note that we still have.

When it was time for him to board his airplane one of his travelling companions came in and said "It's about time to go, Duke." We shook hands, he wished us good luck, and was on his way again.

Almost everyone rides a bicycle in Japan, and the troops at Yokota were no different. Nearly every member of our team rode his bicycle from home to the job site daily. Most were just plain run of the mill bicycles, but some guys had special features like a ten-speed.

The team made plans to make a weekend trip by bicycle to Kamakura, home of a huge bronze statue of Buddah, and about sixty miles from Fussa. We planned to leave on Saturday morning, ride to Kamakura, spend the night and ride back to Fussa on Sunday. Everything went as planned and we arrived at our destination after a seven or eight hour bicycle ride. We were tired, but everyone felt good. We put in at a Japanese guest house, ate a traditional Japanese dinner, and had a few sips of "sake" before turning in for the night.

Sunday morning was heavily overcast, but we all started the return trip as planned; before long we became separated; Clyde Brooks and I were pedaling along with none of the other team members in sight when the rain started. We made it about half way back to Yokota and decided to park our bikes and ride a train the rest of the way back to Fussa. We vowed to keep our decision to ride the train a secret from the other team members who got soaked, but had made it all the way back home on their bicycles.

On Monday evening after work, Clyde and I took the Falcon back to the parked bikes, lashed them on the back of the vehicle and drove back to Yokota. After a lot of questioning, we finally admitted our failure to complete the trip by bicycle. Somehow the guys with the ten-speeds couldn't understand how we made it back home before they did.

The kids were doing well in school; Maria was growing and having fun playing with the other little kids. We had a small tree in the front yard that she loved to climb. She would climb up and sit in that tree until her Mom went after her to come inside for a nap or to eat lunch. She wasn't hiding from anyone and didn't seem to care if anyone knew she was there, she just liked to sit in that tree, and only Maria knew why.

She played a game with her Mom where she would change into an imaginary woman. She would announce "Well Millie, I'm Pat," and until her transformation back to little three year old Maria, she would act the part of "Pat" the lady who was visiting, gossiping and carrying on an adult conversation with her Mom.

As lead team in a study of the Civil Engineering function at all Pacific Air Force bases most of our team was sent on TDY to various bases throughout the Western Pacific and Southeast Asia. Three guys went to Vietnam, two went to the Philippines, and I went to Okinawa with Frank Mercier, another outstanding member of our team.

All the team members were charged with gathering data at their respective sites; Frank Mercier and I were scheduled to be collecting data at Kadena Air Base for about six weeks, then return to Yokota and compare all the data we had gathered with that of the other team members.

Frank and I flew from Tachikawa on an Air America C-118 transport. Air America was a clandestine airline operated by the CIA, doing some legitimate flying like the flight we were on. However, they did a lot of covert operations that were kept out of the news and away from the public until a long time after Vietnam, Cambodia, and Laos were history.

The time spent on Okinawa was mostly at work day after day, but we had time to tour the island and visit places of historical interest. Frank and I planned to go over to Iwo Jima and climb Mount Suribachi one Sunday morning aboard a landing craft that was scheduled to leave from the docks at Naha, and take us over to the island, but something came up and we didn't get to go.

We went to lunch at the "Teahouse of the August Moon" where the movie by the same name was filmed; and toured some of the sites where battles took place during the war. We saw a monument marking the place Japanese General Ushijima killed himself, and we looked over the cliffs where a lot of civilians, as well as soldiers, jumped over the edge rather than surrender to the Americans.

There were more casualties during the battle for Okinawa than any other island anywhere in the Pacific. Over 100,000 Japanese soldiers were killed and many thousands of Japanese civilians died during the battle that took place during April, May, and June 1945.

The other guys were wrapping up their work in Vietnam and the Philippines at about the same time Frank and I were finishing up at Kadena and headed back to Yokota. We scheduled our return to Yokota and left the island aboard another Air America flight.

Mil and the kids were waiting for me at Tachikawa when we landed; it was a short ride from Tachikawa to Yokota and home. It was good to be back with them again after what seemed a lot longer than six weeks.

The months seemed to fly by and before we knew it a reassignment form with my name on it had to be filled out with my base of preference back in the US. I had a few weeks of lag time before the reply had to be sent back and I used that time to write to the recruiting detachment Commander in Charlotte to ask him if he could use me back on recruiting duty.

Within a short time he replied that he had a slot for me and all I had to do was submit a request to return to recruiting and they would reserve the position for me in Charlotte. I did so, and within a few months my reassignment orders came through.

The orders indicated I would have to go back for a three week refresher course in San Antonio after taking several weeks of leave time at home in Kings Mountain. Our departure was set for the middle of November 1966.

Our tour at Yokota had lasted two years and seven months when November arrived. We crammed a lot of living into that period and met a group of wonderful friends that would be remembered the rest of our lives. While we were living the good life a lot of events were happening around the world and especially with the US involvement in Vietnam.

The 441st Combat Support Group at Yokota had lost so many F-105 aircraft the few remaining 105's had to be supplemented with a wing of F-4 Phantoms from McConnell Air Force Base in Kansas.

During the several years we were at Yokota a lot of events happened that would affect the lives of people around the world.

In November 1964 Lyndon Johnson beat Barry Goldwater in the Presidential elections. China successfully detonated a nuclear weapon and that was cause for major concerns in Washington DC.

The movers came and packed all our household goods; we packed our suitcases and moved into the transient quarters. A week or so before the movers came I drove the Falcon to Yokohama to be shipped back to San Francisco.

I also shipped a surplus Jeep back to the US that I had bought from one of the guys in aircraft maintenance. The Jeep would be shipped through the Panama Canal and delivered to the Naval base in Charleston.

We had a big going home party at the NCO club, and the kids had a party that was sponsored by "Uncle Mickey." Their party was a big deal because Uncle Mickey was like Captain Kangaroo to the American kids at Yokota.

We were sleeping a little late on the day of our departure because our flight wasn't scheduled to leave until 9 pm; it wasn't much past daybreak when someone knocked on the door. When I opened the door, there stood Doverspike, Dick Wagner and Les Martin, all three had a six-pack of Black Label in each hand, and a short time later Berman knocked on the door with going away presents in one hand and a case of Black Label in the other.

By ten o'clock Suzie Wagner, Clyde and Linda Brooks were there and the final going away party was swinging. We had to take our checked baggage over to Tachikawa to clear customs, so we loaded it all into two cars (Lt. Brooks wasn't drinking anything, so he drove one of the vehicles) and by mid afternoon we were all clear of customs.

The ladies rode back to Yokota and the transient quarters, but we didn't go straight back because someone suggested we stop at the Tachikawa NCO club for a beer. That could have been a mistake because by the time we got back to Yokota, Mil was worried sick that we had been in an accident or had been thrown into a Japanese Jail.

Luckily, that didn't happen, and the party wrapped up in time for us to board the airplane and fly to Anchorage. I hardly remember getting on the plane, and slept most of the way to Alaska. It must have been a good going away party, because most of the afternoon was a dull blur with a lot of blanks.

I will forever be thankful that Mil had the good sense to stay sober enough to take care of all the last minute important details and watch the kids that last day in Japan.

By the time we landed in Anchorage my hangover had kicked in, but we had enough time in the Elmendorf terminal to get a cold coke and some aspirin. We had about an hour on the ground, and then were on our way to Travis and the cross-country trip back home.

CHAPTER 29

Air Force Liaison, Charlotte November 1966–September 1969

The last leg of our flight back to the USA landed in the afternoon, and as soon as our baggage cleared customs we were assigned quarters in the guest hotel. It had been a long trip with only one refueling stop; Mil and the kids didn't want to do anything but relax until bedtime. A Coca-Cola vending was sitting outside near our rooms and after checking it out I remember thinking that twenty cents was an awfully high price to pay for a can of coke

Arrangements had been made for a contract company to pick up the Ford Falcon at Fort Mason in San Francisco and drive it back to Travis. All I had to do was take a shuttle bus to the vehicle holding area and sign the papers. The attendant took me directly to our car; I checked the oil and water, cranked it up and everything seemed to be ok. The base service station was nearby and I stopped there and filled the fuel tank. By late afternoon we were ready to start loading the car for an early morning departure.

The next morning, before we finished loading all the baggage, we had breakfast at the guest hotel. Leesa ordered pancakes, and when the waitress brought them to her she looked down and saw a big scoop of "whipped" butter on the pancakes, looked at her Mom and said; "Mom, I didn't order ice cream on my pancakes." We all got a laugh out of that. The twenty cent cokes and whipped butter could almost be considered minor cultural shock.

As soon as breakfast was finished we were on our way travelling south through Fresno, Bakersfield and Barstow. We didn't make it out of California that first day of driving and spent the night in Barstow.

Next morning it was a short two hours or so to Las Vegas and by 10 am we were approaching Kingman, Arizona and made it all the way to Gallup New Mexico before we even thought of a motel. Even so by the time we had supper and checked in everyone was ready for bed.

The next day we stopped at Clovis, New Mexico to visit with Tony Andrade and his family. They had rotated from Yokota several months before, and had been reassigned to the Air Base near Clovis. Our visit with Tony and his family slowed us down that day because we had to leave route 66 and go out of our way somewhat to go through Clovis, but even with the detour we still made it to Amarillo before checking into a motel.

The detour to see Tony and his family was time well spent because we really enjoyed seeing them again. They were some of our best friends during the time we were at Fussa Heights and throughout our tour at Yokota. Tony and Louise were with us the night we got into a fight at the NCO club. Tony was known to have a short fuse and it didn't take much to set him off. Luckily when I hit that guy in the cocktail lounge Tony was on his way to the bathroom and missed everything.

The next morning we were up and on the road early hoping for a good long day of driving but we had a problem with the car after going through Oklahoma City. The rocker arm wasn't getting enough oil and started rattling. We stopped in Henrietta, Oklahoma and had a mechanic check the rocker arm assembly. He couldn't repair it, but suggested that I pour STP Oil Treatment on the rocker arm, put the cover back on, and continue driving. That seemed to be my only option, so I did as he suggested.

There was a small tool box in the rear of the Falcon that had the basics; including pliers, screwdrivers and an adjustable wrench; enough to take the rocker arm cover off, and put it back on again. The STP worked for a long way before the rattling started again. When that happened it was time for another coating of the miracle oil. An application of STP to the rocker arm assembly lasted for about six hours before another dose would be needed. I was concerned that the valves might fail to seat properly, but the STP treatment was working good enough to keep the unnerving engine noise quiet.

We made it the rest of the way home with the STP treatments and had no further problems with the valve noises; the only other problem we had was weather related. We made it all the way through Cherokee, NC and when we started climbing toward Soco Gap we ran right into the path of a snowstorm.

State troopers had a check point set up and wouldn't let us go across the pass into Maggie Valley without tire chains. We didn't have chains and had to turn around, go back to Cherokee and buy a set. The guy that sold us the tire chains put them on for us and we made it into Maggie Valley all right. The next day we were back in Kings Mountain.

It took several days and nights to recoup from the long trip, and one of the first things I had to do was take the Falcon to the Ford dealer and get the rocker arm assembly worked on. All they did was blow out the stopped up hole leading from the crankcase to the rocker arm and everything was ok. The service manager at the Ford dealership was an old friend from the Park Yarn; he knew immediately how to take care of the problem and didn't even write out a service order. He just took the rocker arm cover off and blew the tube clear of the obstruction and made a few adjustments before replacing the cover. That made me wonder why the mechanic in Henrietta, Oklahoma couldn't have done the same thing and saved me the aggravation of messing with the STP treatments and worry that the rocker arm may not respond the right way and cause a complete breakdown. Maybe he wasn't a real mechanic.

We had about two weeks to visit with the folks before I had to report to the recruiting detachment Commander in Charlotte, but before signing in I went by the recruiting office and found that some of my old friends were still there. Charlie Todd was still assigned to the Charlotte office, Willie Williams and Clyde May were still in Gastonia, but a different Commander and operations NCO were at detachment headquarters. The new detachment Commander was Captain Freed and his operations officer was Captain White.

All the new people seemed to be friendly enough and were pleased with my assignment to Charlotte; they made me feel welcome. Maybe Charlie Todd had been bragging on my recruiting abilities. Captain White was a rated pilot and especially easy to talk to. I learned that the refresher course I would be attending would last longer than expected and that it would be sometime late in January before I would be back in Charlotte.

The two weeks at home passed quickly and soon I was on my way to San Antonio. The recruiter course was, for the most part, identical to the class that I had attended between November 1958 and January 1959. I didn't have to go through all the public speaking and air force traditions and history, but everything else remained the same. Sales training, enlistment criteria, and forms preparation had been updated somewhat, but remained basically unchanged. A new program that would supplement the pilot and navigator recruiting had been implemented recently. The new program was designed to provide the air force with officers in administrative/ technical and scientific career fields, and was called officer training school, abbreviated "OTS." It was almost identical to the army's Officer Candidate School (OCS), and was crammed into a 90 day course.

The Lackland NCO club was still the off duty gathering place for recruiter students, and Lone Star long necks was still the "suds" of choice; and Nuevo Laredo, the Mexican border town across the river from Laredo, Texas was still the place to go shopping for cheap Mexican leather goods and Christmas presents to take home. Any of the border towns were a good place to get into trouble and Nuevo Laredo was no different. One of the students brought back a bad souvenir from one of the Mexican beauties and was forced to wash out of the course.

Another Christmas was spent away from Mil and the Kids in 1966; the holiday season came and went without much celebration, and a phone call wishing everyone a "Merry Christmas" was about as close as we could get to each other. Since we were all on separate rations, that is, we were being paid a daily rate for food allowance, we seldom ate at the mess hall; I don't recall, but Christmas dinner was probably eaten at the NCO club. Christmas away from home and the family never was a cause for celebration. On January 6th I missed Jamey's birthday again.

The first super bowl was played on January 15th 1967 between Green Bay and Kansas City and I watched the game, with a group of students at a bar in San Antonio. The game was televised on the first color television I'd ever seen. In fact we hadn't had any TV at all during the past several years in Japan. The color quality was primitive compared to what we have today, but it was in color.

The refresher course was completed sometime during the last half of January, and I was again on my way home; very happy the school was behind me, and anxious to be with my family once more. I didn't stop overnight, but drove straight through, stopping only for a few short catnaps. The Ford Falcon held up nicely with no problems at all.

Soon after my arrival back in Kings Mountain, Mil and I went shopping for a house in Charlotte. A member of my Masonic Lodge was in the real estate business and he located a nice house in the Plaza area that we could afford. We checked it out and liked it right away. It was an older home in a good neighborhood, with a master bedroom, large living room, formal dining room, bathroom and kitchen on the ground floor, an upstairs with two bedrooms, and a basement. It was big enough for our growing family, was close to a good elementary school, and a Junior High School wasn't much further away.

Within a week we had signed all the paperwork to buy the home. Not long afterward our household goods that had been packed away at Yokota Air Base, were delivered. We had to buy new living and dining room furniture, and did so at a furniture store in downtown Charlotte.

After checking on the status of the Jeep that had been shipped to Charleston, I learned that it was waiting to be picked up. Lafayette went with me to the Naval base in Charleston and we brought the Jeep back to Charlotte. A problem with the fuel filter and timing slowed us down but we made it back to Charlotte without having to call a mechanic for help.

Our baby boy, that had been born so long ago (or so it seemed) at the base hospital in Greenville had suddenly become a teenager on January 6th. Leesa was already ten; Maria would be six years old in May and would be starting the first grade in September. Our babies were growing up too fast.

The recruiting office had relocated to the Executive Building on East Trade Street, just a half block from the LaPointe Chevrolet dealership. Jim Payne was the sales manager at LaPointe. Soon after we met he offered me a deal that was hard to turn down, and I traded the Ford Falcon for a 1966 Chevrolet Impala. The salesmen at LaPointe usually had lunch at Jimmie the Greek's restaurant located in the Executive Building, and some of them would come by for a beer in the late afternoon.

Jim was one of the late afternoon patrons. We became good friends and forty years later remain close. Over the years he has become the brother I never had. Since trading for the 1966 Chevrolet every car I have owned since was bought from Jim.

The first time I saw Steve Coulson he was sitting in the Greek's restaurant with a beer in his hand and his leg in a cast. He was assigned to the army recruiting office and had recently broken his leg in a parachute jump at Brockenborough airport out on the Huntersville highway north of Charlotte. He had just returned from a tour in Vietnam with a Purple Heart and Bronze Star to go with the ones he had been awarded in Korea.

We had a few beers together and the next afternoon he called and invited me out to his house to help grill a bunch of chickens. Earlier in the day he was at a bar on Beatties Ford Road and won three cases of chickens playing pinball with an unlucky truck driver. The driver would come up a little short when he delivered his load of chickens that day.

It didn't take long to drive out to where Steve lived. Frank Carter, another army recruiter, and one of the marine corps recruiters were there also and before the evening was over we had a big party.

That was the beginning of a long relationship. We would become lifelong friends and like Jim Payne, he would be like a brother to me. His wife, Judy would become Mil's best friend and they are still like sisters forty years later.

During the entire time we were in Japan I sent a monthly check to Lafayette to put in the bank for me; he deposited a like amount for himself. We were planning a fall hunting trip to Wyoming and the money would be used to offset what we thought would be an expensive trip.

It turned out to be not so much as we expected because he had been talking to two other guys who wanted to go along with us; they would share expenses.

Ralph Harrison and Don Falls, both from Kings Mountain, had never been out west and wanted to go after a big mule deer. We contacted a professional guide service in Afton, Wyoming and after writing several letters, signed a deal with the guy in Afton to guide us on a mule deer and antelope hunt. We had to submit an application to the Wyoming game and fish department to get the antelope license, but could buy a deer license across the counter after we got there. We were scheduled to leave soon after September 1st.

Our house was on Hall Avenue and was within several blocks of the Plaza and Central Avenue intersection. Midwood elementary school was less than a block away, and Leesa was enrolled there in the fourth grade. Jamey was enrolled in Hawthorne Junior High School in the seventh grade. Maria would be starting at Midwood in September.

It was a short walk from the back side of our yard to Midwood elementary school and Maria was enrolled as scheduled. Leesa already knew her way around the school and was a big help to her younger sister. There were no streets to cross and from our back porch we could see the school yard.

For the first time in years Mil was left with no children in the house during school hours. She decided to look for a job to supplement our income and within a week or so had been hired to demonstrate and sell sewing machines and related sewing supplies and material at the Singer sewing center in Charlottetown Mall located on Kings Drive.

She had to drive to work and I would have to be home during the hours immediately following the end of classes at school. Since we had the old military Jeep, transportation wouldn't be a problem. She drove the Chevrolet to Charlottetown Mall and I drove the Jeep.

Three or four blocks down Central Avenue from Hall Avenue, where we lived, there was a chicken processing plant. Live chickens were brought in by truck; they were processed and iced down for shipment to the various super markets and grocery stores in and around Mecklenburg County. Some of the chickens had escaped and were running loose in a big field behind the processing plant. The supervisor who worked the receiving dock told me they were free for anyone who could catch them; and after I told him I'd pay a quarter each for every chicken he could catch, Jamey assured me he could outrun any chicken in the field.

The dock supervisor gave me two cages to put them in and by the time I got home from work the next day, Jamey had a dozen chickens in the cages. I was ready to fill our freezer with frying chickens; but a small problem developed that I hadn't thought about.

By the time I got home from the office Leesa and Maria had named every chicken and made family pets out of them. I told them to forget about their new pets and go in the house; then I made ready to start wringing necks and cleaning chickens. What I didn't know was the girls had run into the house, had gone down to the basement and were looking out the basement window when I grabbed one of the chickens and slung it around and jerked its head off. By the time the headless chicken started flopping around, both girls let out a scream that could be heard a city block away.

After making sure they both were upstairs watching television I finally got all the chickens skinned and in the freezer, but it was years before they would even think about eating fried chicken.

The armed forces examination station was on Statesville Avenue and a twenty minute drive from the recruiting office when we first returned from Japan, but before long a more centralized location was found on Pecan Avenue only a few blocks from the Plaza and Central Avenue and the entire examining station moved to that location. The Air Force Liaison NCO position at the examining station became available and I was selected for the job. Part of the liaison duties required me to check over the enlistment applications of the recruits sent to be examined and processed for enlistment; and once they were sworn in I had to arrange for their transportation to the airport.

They were usually processed, sworn in, and on their way to the airport by early afternoon; and as soon as I called in the daily report to detachment, my duties were over for the day.

Steve called me from a place out on North Tryon Street one afternoon and asked me to meet him there. I was almost ready to leave the examining station when he called, so it didn't take me long to make the short drive to North Tryon. The place where we met was a bar owned and operated by Jake McFee and his wife Madeline. Soon after walking in the door I was introduced to Jake who became another lifelong friend.

Jake was a big Scotsman whose clan had settled in the western North Carolina mountains, and his wife Madeline was a Lumbee Indian from the sandhills of eastern North Carolina. Most of the regulars at Jakes bar also became good friends and from that first day Jake's place became one of our favorite watering holes.

There were no weekend duties as liaison NCO and sometimes we went to Kings Mountain on Friday after work to spend the weekend with our folks.

In addition to patronizing the local American Legion and VFW Lafayette and I did a lot of fishing on Saturday and Sunday. From trout fishing in the mountains to crappie and bass fishing in both forks of the Catawba we always had something planned to do.

We were lucky that we never were stopped and charged with driving under the influence on the way home whether it was a short drive from the American Legion or a longer drive from the river. Mil's brother, Junior, was Chief of Police, and Jackie Barrett, a good friend from Kings Mountain High School was the Assistant Chief; that may have been part of the reason we were never arrested for driving under the influence after leaving the VFW or American Legion.

In addition to the excursions Lafayette and I made, Steve and I were doing a lot of weekend fishing at Lake Norman; we used a small portable outboard motor to get us to our favorite places on the lake. The marina where we put in had a bunch of aluminum "john" boats for rent.

We'd load our fishing gear in one of the john boats and fish until dark and sometimes take a Coleman lantern and try to catch crappie at night.

We were fishing back in a cove a mile or so from the boat landing one cold afternoon when the boat tipped over and both of us went into the lake along with all our fishing gear. We weren't too far from a pier, so we swam for it. Once we made it to the pier we looked back to see the boat hadn't completely sunk, but was sitting out there full of water, still floating. We jumped back in and swam for the boat and pulled it back to the pier; we finally got it light enough by bailing water to drag it onto the pier. The motor seemed ok and after putting the boat back in the lake, I pulled the cord one time and it cranked up.

It was a long, cold, wet ride back to the marina, but we made it ok. The next day Steve went to Sears and bought a much bigger boat with a bigger motor. Our weekends of renting a small john boat were over.

Not long after that incident, I bought a travel trailer that could sleep six people in a pinch but could comfortably sleep four. The marina where we usually launched the boat also had facilities for campers so we started spending more and more weekends at Lake Norman. Mil and Judy would lie out in the sun, the kids played in the water and Steve and I caught fish.

The guy who ran the marina, Oni Wilson, had a pretty young daughter that Jamey had his eyes on; it was like we were on a vacation at the beach almost every weekend.

We still made it to Kings Mountain from time to time. Plans for the hunting trip to Wyoming were finalized, rifles had been zeroed in, and personal gear packed. We planned to drive Ralph Harrison's station wagon and tow a small trailer with our gear.

Sometime during the first week in September we left and drove all the way to Afton, Wyoming without stopping to sleep. Our route took us through Nashville, St. Louis, Kansas City, and Denver. A lot of the interstate highway system hadn't been completed in 1967 and we had a lot of small towns to go through.

We were in the small town of Centennial, Wyoming on Sunday morning and stopped to refuel and buy a few beers for the cooler. State law wouldn't allow the sale of beer on Sunday before noon, but the service station operator saw our North Carolina tag and sold it to us anyway.

A cowboy walked into the station as we were getting ready to leave and struck up a conversation with us. When he learned that we had paid a guide $250.00 each to guide us on a mule deer and antelope hunt, he said, " I'd take you deer hunting for a fifth of whiskey." He probably would have too, but we were already committed to the guy in Afton.

The next day we reached our destination and put up in a local motel for a few days and early the next morning we rode off in a couple of pick up trucks with two guides and hunted the mountains west of town. Our mule deer license allowed us to kill just one deer, and before noon the first day my deer hunting was over.

I was walking around a hillside and dropped down into a small ravine amongst a clump of aspen trees when a monster buck jumped up and I shot as he bounced away from me. He stumbled and turned down hill. He didn't make it far before running close to where Lafayette was hunting below me.

Two days later we moved from the motel into a hunting camp on the Greys River that was back in a remote valley inside Bridger-Teton National Forest. We were about twenty-five miles down a dirt road from the town of Alpine, that was nothing more than a junction of two highways. It was a typical hunting camp with sleeping tents and a big cook tent where meals were served. There were about a dozen or so hunters in the camp and everyone would ride out early every morning on horseback for a day of mule deer hunting in the mountains that were all around us.

My deer license had been filled so I just hung around camp waiting for everyone to get back late in the afternoon. The very first day Lafayette and Ralph both brought in a good deer. Don Falls didn't care about riding a horse all day so he stayed in camp with me. By the second or third day everyone else had filled their deer tags, and early the next morning we were on our way to Casper for the antelope hunt.

We stayed in a motel there and rode south into the Shirley Basin to look for antelope the next morning. We had two guides and before long started seeing herds of antelope. It wasn't long before Lafayette had an antelope on the ground and soon I was stalking a herd that we had spotted on the back side of a small hill. As I reached the top I could see a nice buck and got into position for a shot at him. Just as I pulled the trigger he jumped and a small buck that was standing behind him fell dead.

The big buck ran off and my antelope hunt was over. Two days later everyone had filled their antelope tag. All the deer and antelope meat had been cut, wrapped and frozen at a processing plant in Casper; and to keep the meat from going bad, it had been packed in dry ice for the trip home. Two days later we were back home. Lafayette and I were already talking about another trip next year, but Ralph and Don didn't seem too interested. In fact Ralph made the statement that he would never ride another horse after being in the saddle nearly all day riding in the mountains out of the Greys River camp.To the best of my knowledge he kept his word.

The recruiting detachment operations officer, Captain White was required to fly a minimum number of hours every month to maintain his rating on flight status and the recruiting group at Warner-Robins Air Force Base near Macon, Georgia regularly flew a U-3 up to Charlotte from Macon so that he could get in his flying time. The U-3 was a twin engine administrative aircraft that would seat four people. Whenever Captain White was scheduled to fly he would call me and ask me to meet him at detachment headquarters or at the air national guard hanger to go flying with him. He'd file his flight plan, off we'd go, and four hours later would be back in Charlotte. Sometimes we'd fly over the omni range at South Boston, Virginia, or to Warner-Robins and shoot instrument landings using their ILS equipment and personnel.

On one occasion we were returning to Charlotte after doing some touch and go landings at the Raleigh-Durham airport and one of the engines lost oil pressure; he had to shut it down and feather the prop. We were prepared to land on the Charlotte Motor Speedway that was still under construction, but the tower gave us a straight in approach and we made it on in to Charlotte without any problems. Another time we were doing some night flying and as we were over the University of South Carolina football stadium he banked the aircraft and said "look down there, below us there are ten thousand good looking young ladies." Several years earlier he had played football for USC and knew the ladies were there somewhere on campus.

I had started working at a truck terminal at night for five hours; usually three nights a week to earn extra money to pay for the next hunting trip to Wyoming, and also to pay for flying lessons at Colonel Carpenter's airport.

The opportunity for me to learn to fly was too much to pass up. That was something I'd always wanted to do and one day I drove past the airport and talked with one of the instructors; before leaving I had signed up for a ground school course that had to be passed before any flying was done.

The instructor, O.A. Fish, also flew for Eastern Airlines and taught flying lessons on the side at Carpenter's airport. Carpenter's was a single strip located in southwest Mecklenburg County. The trainers were Champion tri-travelers with tricycle landing gear and the controls were stick and rudder. The rates were reasonable enough at $11.00 an hour dual and $6.00 an hour solo. Every time I found an extra six bucks, I'd drive to Carpenter's and get half an hour flying time in.

I don't remember the exact date that I made my first solo, but the event is etched in my mind as clear as it was the day it happened. I had made a couple touch and go landings with O.A. Fish in the back seat; when we touched down after the third go around, he braked the airplane to a stop, opened the door and got out. He told me to take it around by myself.

He walked over to the grass and sat down. I looked over at him, and then down the runway. For a short time there were doubts that I was ready. Then I remembered that I had just made three perfect take offs, climbed to 400 feet, made a climbing turn to the left, leveled off at 600 feet and made another 90 degree turn to the left for the down-wind leg; a throttle back and then two more descending turns to line up with the runway.

I looked over at Fish, opened the throttle and took off. It was just me and the airplane, and a long time dream came true. It was a far cry from a supersonic jet fighter, but it was flying. I remembered everything he had taught me; made the same traffic pattern and greased it onto the runway as good as it could have been done. I braked to a stop and he waved me on to "do it again." To really qualify as a solo, three touch and go landings had to be made and I made the three before he got back in the airplane and we rode back to the parking area.

It was a very special day in my life. I couldn't wait to get home and tell Mil what I had done. She was so happy for me.

When we returned from Japan, both my folks were still working at the Park Yarn, but were getting closer to retirement age. Grandpa Roper was still working at Robert's grocery store, but had been diagnosed as a diabetic. At the time his condition didn't seem to bother him at all and he never missed a day working. He had a big hog ready to kill and wouldn't even think about taking it to a slaughter house to be processed.

Early on a Saturday morning he had all his knives sharpened and ready. Everything went as planned and by evening Grandma had the livermush made, a big pile of meat was ready to be seasoned, ground up and made into sausage; and backbones and ribs were in the pot. Grandpa's day was made.

It wasn't long before the diabetes took its toll and the medical people had to take Grandpa' foot off. It was down hill for him from there; although he never let up on any of the events for the family. Traditional dinners and gatherings on the holidays were held as usual and everyone always enjoyed them so much. They had to move back to Fairview Street so that Grandpa could be better taken care of and in early 1970 the disease took him from us.

Lafayette and I didn't make it back to Wyoming in 1968, but in early 1969 we sent in our applications for antelope permits for the season starting on October 1st. That would be the last year we would be permitted to buy deer licenses across the counter in Wyoming. The game and fish department passed a new law requiring non-residents to apply by mail for mule deer as well as antelope licenses starting the following year. And, of course, the prices went up also. We wouldn't know until after the drawing that was to be held in early June whether we would be hunting antelope or not.

Luckily, we drew our first choice of areas and received our permits by the middle of the month. Once we knew the area where we would be hunting antelope we could then start making definite plans and make contact with some ranchers in the areas we planned to hunt. This time we would be going alone and sleeping in a tent.

Lafayette bought a four-wheel-drive International Scout and we started rigging it up to carry all our gear and still leave room for a sleeping bag between the seats so that one could get some sleep while the other drove. It was a good arrangement and worked out very well.

By mid summer we were getting excited about going back to Wyoming. Then something occurred that could have messed up all our plans. Richard Nixon had been elected President in the November 1968 elections and had chosen Governor Spiro Agnew as his Vice President, and the Vice President was scheduled to deliver a speech at the White House Inn located near the federal building on West Trade Street.

Angelo's Restaurant was located on West Trade Street near the White House Inn and was under contract to provide lunch and supper, if necessary, for our recruits who were on their way to basic training. Angelo made quite a bit of money from the business we sent his way and we could always get a nice cold beer or two at his place at a good price.

The evening Vice President Agnew was scheduled to speak, Steve Coulson, Jack Crowe, and I were walking up the street to go into Angelo's for a beer and ran into a big crowd of black panther protesters. We were in uniform and they didn't care too much about the military, because they were also protesting the war going on in Vietnam.

Jack Crowe was a Native American Indian and had just returned from a tour in Vietnam and objected to one of the black panthers carrying a Viet Cong flag in protest. A fight broke out between the three of us and about forty of the panthers; Steve was hurt by a rock that had been hidden in a towel carried by one of the "peaceful demonstrators", Angelo's plate glass window was broken and there was some minor damage to his restaurant.

Even against all the odds, Jack and I stood our ground with our backs to the wall until the police arrived and the fight broke up. Before being knocked senseless by the rock, Steve had taken care of a couple of the demonstrators causing them to back off ; that gave Jack and I a little time to get ready for them.

Several of the panthers were arrested, but we weren't charged with anything; and the story made the front page in the morning newspaper. Captain Freed and the Operations NCO called me in the next morning for an explanation. Captain Freed didn't like the negative publicity, but Sergeant Ackerman, the operations NCO was upset because he hadn't been invited to the party. He was a tough old guy and was sorry he hadn't been there to get a few of the protesters himself. Anyway, nothing came of the news story and plans resumed for the trip to Wyoming in the fall.

Ackerman stood up for me, and as a grizzled old NCO he had a lot of influence with Captain Freed. My job as Air Force Liaison NCO was safe for the time being as the late 1960s steadily moved on.

The author and Jake McFee. Photograph was taken during a hunting trip to Wyoming

CHAPTER 30

Charlotte

September 1969–January 1971

Mil's job at the Singer sewing center was at a standstill; she wasn't going anywhere because there was no room for advancement into a higher paying position; at the same time Judy was working as a waitress at the Ramada Inn on Independence Boulevard and making good tips while working shorter hours than Mil.

In addition there was some in-fighting between two of the sales ladies at Singer, and they tried to get Mil involved in that; so when Judy offered to get Mil a job at Ramada, she left Singer and started as a waitress. Almost immediately she started bringing more money home. Tips were good and she seemed to enjoy that kind of work a lot better than working in sales.

One thing she disliked about the new job was the breakfast hours. She and Judy had to help set up a breakfast buffet and that required her to be out of bed a lot earlier than before. And it meant that I had to help get the kids off to school. We adapted to the changes, however, with very little trouble. All three kids were old enough to do their thing before leaving for school and that left me with very little to do relating to that early morning chore.

The kids were all doing great in school. Jamey had transferred from Hawthorne to McClintock Junior High School. He was pleased with the change because he never really liked school at Hawthorne, and he was making better grades after the transfer.

Following completion of Junior High School he would be attending Garinger High School, starting there when he reached the tenth grade. Leesa and Maria were still at Midwood. Following completion of the elementary grades, Leesa would go to McClintock also. They were all busy with their friends after they completed any homework; they knew that homework came first so there was never any question about priorities.

They were always plotting and planning projects with the neighborhood kids. Leesa and Maria joined with several school mates and sold tickets to a song and dance routine they had been working on. When the afternoon for their performance finally arrived all the boys in the neighborhood had bought tickets and were seated on the back patio waiting for the first act. The tickets probably sold for a nickel each, so if the project was dreamed up to raise money, it didn't make much because there were more participants than patrons.

I never knew Leesa could pantomime so well, or that Maria could dance so well. They put on a good show and all the boys loved it. I still have a movie of the play that was originally made on 8mm that I recently had transferred to video tape.

Mil's new job allowed her to be home in the afternoons when the kids came home after school. Before the new school year started in 1969 we were spending almost every weekend in Kings Mountain; Lafayette and I were working out the details for our trip to Wyoming. We worked hard attaching a metal framework to rig the Scout with exterior racks so that most of our camping gear could be stowed in two old military radio containers seated in the racks attached to the front bumper. We planned to leave around the 21st or 22nd of September and be there for the opening of antelope season on September 25th.

Letters had been mailed to all the ranchers on a list the Medicine Bow city manager had sent to us. We made contact with several ranchers in the area where we would be hunting and were getting impatient to be on our way. I had been working more and more at the truck terminal loading and unloading trucks at night and had more than enough money saved up for the trip.

Lafayette had the Scout serviced and checked out; he was satisfied we would make the trip to Wyoming and back without any vehicle problems. Last year we had taken the Scout on a back country wilderness hunt and had broken a hydraulic line that controlled the clutch. We lost all the fluid; consequently we couldn't move an inch without a clutch and were a long way from a service station. We didn't carry any spare fluid, but taped up the busted hydraulic line with electrical tape, filled the reservoir with cooking oil and made it all the way out to a service station where we dumped the cooking oil and replaced it with hydraulic fluid. After that, he carried an extra can of hydraulic fluid stowed away under a seat.

September finally arrived. The kids were enrolled into their respective schools; all three were attending different schools now. Jamey started his first year at Garinger High School, Leesa was at McClintock Junior High, and Maria started the third grade at Midwood.

Mil was still at Ramada Inn and doing real well. She and Judy made a good team. Arrangements had been made for someone to take care of the recruiting liaison duties at the examining station while I would be gone; all we were waiting on was the date for our departure to arrive.

Things went as planned and on September 21st we made our final inspection and said goodbye to everyone. We were planning on being back in less than two weeks, but the way the Scout was loaded, it looked as if we were going to spend the winter in Wyoming. All the camping, cooking, and sleeping gear took up a lot of space.

We followed the same route we had taken when Ralph and Don went with us two years earlier until we got to Denver. This time we went through Cheyenne and Laramie, then on to Medicine Bow. The ranch where we had been given permission to hunt was over thirty miles north of Medicine Bow, but we had to check in at the main ranch headquarters before going in to the place we were to set up a camp site.

Upon arrival at the ranch we talked with Mr. Sullivan, one of two brothers who ran a huge cattle ranching operation that covered many thousands of acres. He directed us to a secondary ranch about ten miles or so further north where we were to contact the cook and a Mexican cowboy who would give us directions on where to set up our camp. He was very nice and implied that we wouldn't have any problems getting a nice mule deer and antelope.

He was right. When we got to the other ranch, we were told to drive through a big pasture then follow a wooded draw and to camp anywhere along a creek that ran along the draw. It was a hunting paradise. We saw several hundred antelope on the way in and driving up the draw, big fat mule deer were running around like cattle. Before the sun started going down we had a nice camp set up and were ready to do some scouting around.

The antelope season was scheduled to open the day after tomorrow. That gave us one whole day to scout and chart our course for opening day. The next morning we were awake at daybreak and could hear elk bugling on the hillside behind where we were camped. It really was a hunting paradise, and as far as we could determine, we were the only people within miles except for the cowboy and cook down in the ranch house.

We learned later that a couple of hunters were camped about a mile below us, but they never came near where we were hunting. We scouted around all day and must have seen three or four hundred antelope running in herds, and in every herd was at least one big buck with a harem of females.

The deer were there in big numbers too, but we would have to wait until October 1st before the deer season would be open; that was still six days away.

The next morning we were up early; the Coleman stove was started and before long bacon and eggs were sizzling in the pan. By the time it was full daylight breakfast was behind us and Lafayette was "locked and loaded."

A group of antelope had been spotted within a half a mile of camp, and a nice buck was trying to keep all his females from running off. In a big open area about a mile above camp a herd of elk were grazing; several big bulls were bugling and running around looking for a fight.

Lafayette started his stalk on the antelope and I started working my way up through the wooded draw to try and get closer to the elk and take some 8mm movies of the herd. I had barely made it much further than several hundred yards above camp when I broke into an open pasture and counted twenty-two mule deer grazing; they didn't pay much attention to me at all. They finally decided that I may be a threat and started moving away from me. I had the movie camera ready and got some good shots of the mulies as they bounced away.

I continued climbing toward the elk trying to stay concealed in the wooded draw, but the closer I got to them, the closer they drifted towards a thick forest. I made my way close enough to get a few good pictures before they moved completely out of sight into the woods.

Before the day was over we both had a trophy antelope buck and our antelope season was over. The ranch cook and his Mexican cowboy helped us get the antelope back to camp to skin out, seal in a cheesecloth game bag to protect the carcass from flies, and hang for a few days before taking them to Casper to be processed.

It would be six days before the deer season started and we used that time to do a little trout fishing in the beaver ponds near our campsite and to scout the area where we would most likely find a trophy mule deer. We made at least one trip to Medicine Bow and had lunch in a café; and another trip to Casper to deliver the antelope carcasses to the processing plant.

One night we had dinner with the ranch cook and Hosea, the Mexican cowboy. The beaver ponds were full of small brook trout and we had no trouble catching all we could eat. They weren't very big; probably averaged around six or seven inches, but were awfully tasty.

The six days went by too fast and on the evening before opening day of deer season Lafayette started coughing and running a fever. On opening morning of deer season he was pretty sick, but we hunted for most of the morning before he gave it up and we went back to camp. By the next morning he didn't even want to get out of the tent. I worked out the draw above camp one last time during the second morning and saw a few decent deer but by noon gave it up without taking a shot at anything.

Back at camp we started making plans to break camp the next morning if he didn't feel any better. I gave serious thought to taking him to get professional medical help. He wasn't eating anything and that in itself was a bad sign for him.

The next morning he was some better, but not good enough to go after a deer, so we started packing the gear to load up and leave. When we got to Casper our antelope had been cut, wrapped, and frozen; we put the meat into coolers with dry ice and we drove south towards Cheyenne.

We didn't know it at the time, but we were just hours ahead of a serious snowstorm. By the time we were through Denver and turned East, Medicine Bow and Casper were already getting heavy snowfall. If we had remained at the campsite one more day we would've been buried in snow and even with four wheel drive we might not had been able to get out.

We drove on into Kansas and nearly ran out of gas before finding a service station that was open all night. I was doing most of the driving at first and Lafayette was sleeping in the make-shift bed, but by the time we were out of Colorado he started feeling better and was up to driving some. While we were in Casper we picked up some across the counter cold remedy for him and it seemed to be working.

It was my time to get some sleep until he woke me up with "You better get up because we're about out of gas." We were in luck because just when we were down to the last little bit of fuel, we topped a hill and spotted a service station with its lights on a little ways ahead.

The rest of the way home was uneventful and we made it before midnight the next night. Before leaving Kansas though, we picked up a newspaper and read about the snowstorm that had blown through most of Wyoming and northeast Colorado. A couple days later we were back to the routine of making a living.

When the regulars at Jake McFee's bar heard about our trip some of them along with Steve and Jim Payne started making plans to go back with us next season.

Grandpa Roper's fight with diabetes brought them from Peaceful Valley back to Fairview Street where he could be better cared for, but still his health was declining. He had several surgeries to first remove his foot and then part of his leg. Then in January 1970 he lost the fight and we lost him. He was buried in the Chestnut Ridge Baptist Church graveyard. Grandma would continue on without him for over thirty years before she would be laid to rest beside him.

Mama and Daddy were still working full time at the Park Yarn. Pam had graduated from high school in May 1969. Coot and Bill were in San Angelo, Texas, and Faye and her family were still in Bolivar, Tennessee; they were both still working at the Western Tennessee mental hospital.

Jamey got his driver's license as soon as he turned sixteen in January 1970 and couldn't wait to get his own car to drive. Charlie Todd had a Pontiac LeMans for sale at a good price, so I bought it for him to drive to school. He was still in love with Oni Wilson's pretty daughter up on Lake Norman and he wore out a new set of tires in less than six months burning up the road between Hall Avenue and Oni Wilson's boat landing on the lake. Leesa was still at McClintock and Maria was still at Midwood.

The winter of 1969–70 passed by quickly and following the passing of Grandpa in January 1970 nothing of any major consequence happened during the next five or six months. My tour in Charlotte was fast coming to an end and I had requested to be released from recruiting duty in January 1971.

Summer was nearly over and another school year was approaching. Jamey would be starting the 11th grade at Garinger; Leesa the 9th at Piedmont Junior High and Maria the 4th at Midwood. Leesa wasn't too happy about being transferred to Piedmont, but there was nothing we could do about the assignment.

A bunch of the guys at Jake's bar were talking about going back to Wyoming with us in September 1970, and had applied for their antelope and deer license. The group included Steve, Jim Payne, Jake, and some of the regulars. We had a total of eleven people that planned on making the trip west with us. In June we learned that everyone had made the drawing for the licenses and then we started making plans.

The summer months seemed to take an awfully long time, especially for the guys who were making the trip to Wyoming for the first time. They were all getting anxious to be on their way. We planned to drive three vehicles with each one towing something. We rigged up Lafayette's Scout to be towed behind Steve's station wagon so that we would have at least one four-wheel drive vehicle with us. One of the other guys had to tow a trailer with our camping, cooking and sleeping equipment.

Jim Payne planned to tow a pop-up camper, but had run into a domestic problem. His wife promised him that if he went on the hunting trip with us, she would be gone when he returned. He didn't let that discourage him, and when we got back to Charlotte, she was gone.

We left as scheduled and had an uneventful trip. We set up our hunting camp at the exact spot where Lafayette and I had camped the year before. Everyone had an outstanding time and bagged a trophy antelope. Almost everyone got their mule deer; those who didn't were waiting on a bigger buck when time ran out for them. We didn't return home as a group because Jim had to leave a couple days early and Lafayette drove his Scout back rather than have it towed behind Steve's car. Steve, Jake McFee, and I were the last to leave and we cleaned up the camp site being careful not to leave anything behind. We had promised Mr. Sullivan that we would leave the campsite just as we found it.

I had killed a monster mule deer just two days before we packed up and we had to load the carcass on top of the station wagon until we got to Casper to pick up the antelope meat. We didn't have enough room and rented an enclosed U-Haul trailer to carry all the equipment and venison back home.

We made it home in record time; it was early Sunday when we left Casper and we were back in Charlotte before 5 p.m. Monday evening.

My transfer orders came in October; I was to be reassigned to Webb Air Force Base in Big Spring, Texas. Webb was a primary pilot training base where future pilots learned to fly the supersonic T-38 jet fighter. We were scheduled to leave Charlotte in early January 1971.

Sometime during the spring of 1970, I traded the 68 Chevrolet for a new 70 Impala and had to rig it up with a trailer-towing package so we could tow the camper trailer to Texas. That would allow us to camp and do some sightseeing on the way.

Mil and I worked hard during December to paint the interior and put the house on Hall Avenue in tip-top shape because we were looking for someone to sign a long term lease.

We found a couple with two young kids and they seemed to be the kind of people we would want in the house. That was a big mistake. They signed a one year lease but before six months had passed they had defaulted on their monthly payment and we had to return to Charlotte and put the house up for sale. Their kids had ruined the new paint job in several bedrooms and we had to paint again.

We left the house with my friend who was in real estate sales and within a month he had a signed contract to sell.

We couldn't wait for him to find a buyer because I had to report back to the base; but were able to handle all the paperwork through the mail.

After leaving Hall Avenue we were more or less living out of suitcases again, only this time we had a small travel trailer that had a lot more storage space than a few suitcases. We had a few weeks to spend with the folks, and during that time attended several going away parties in Charlotte.

My second tour on recruiting duty came to a close and within a few short days our family would be heading to West Texas and another adventure.

CHAPTER 31

Webb AFB and West Texas January–September 1971

The long weekends camping and fishing at Lake Norman; opening day of trout season above Chimney Rock, and the afternoons spent at the Executive Club or Jake's emporium on North Tryon Street were behind us. So were the good times spent with Steve and Judy, Jim and Nancy, Jake and Madeline, and all the other good friends in Charlotte and Kings Mountain.

But we never looked back, and were looking forward to meeting new friends and seeing new places in West Texas. I had asked for an assignment to Lowry Air Force Base near Denver, but the wheels that controlled the management engineering people in the US felt that they needed me more at Webb than at Lowry.

Before leaving for West Texas we made several trips back to Charlotte after turning our house over to the family that leased it for the next year. The examining station people that I had worked with over the past four years gave us a farewell party and all the guys at Jake McFee's place had a big going away free-for-all at his bar. That party lasted from early afternoon until late into the night. We spent the remainder of the night at Steve and Judy's house.

Grandma Roper had a big Sunday dinner for us just before we left and most of Mil's family were all there.

This time, however, Grandpa Roper wasn't there to say goodbye, and things just didn't feel the same. It seemed that no matter when a gathering of the Roper clan took place, there were always lots of kids of all ages, from little babies to teen-agers. That had been the case from the time Mil and I first married, to the present. Grandma Roper must have passed some of her fertility genes on to her children and grandchildren. Seldom did any time pass when at least one or two of her tribe wasn't expecting a baby.

It was early in the morning when we pulled away from Mama and Daddy's house on Shelby Road and drove south towards Atlanta. We couldn't drive very fast with the camper behind us, but we made it to a campground north of Mobile Alabama before stopping for the night.

It was already turning into a fun trip. Mil cooked a nice supper while the kids and I watched some people fishing on a nearby lake. After eating we just lounged around and relaxed until bedtime, which wasn't long after supper, because we were all tired after riding all day. We learned right away that driving across the country with a travel trailer would be very different from eating all our meals in a restaurant and staying in a motel.

New Orleans was a city we had never visited and everyone wanted to see some of the city before going on to Texas, so the next day we parked the camper, unhooked and drove on into the French Quarter and toured Bourbon Street. We had heard a lot about Cajun food and for lunch we had a buffet that included crawfish and gumbo along with other Louisiana dishes. We toured the waterfront and saw one of the big Mississippi riverboats; then it was time to hook up to the camper and move on. We didn't get very far that day because of the time spent in New Orleans.

That night we stayed at a campground near Lake Charles, Louisiana. The next day was spent touring again.

This time we were in San Antonio eating Mexican food and touring the Alamo. We found a campground alongside the San Antonio River and after setting up the camper, were within a few miles of downtown and The Alamo. We drove out to Lackland to look for the squadron area that was home for me during basic training, but new barracks construction had changed it too much to identify exactly where we were.

We did go by the NCO club for a cold beer, a Lone Star long neck, of course. The club hadn't changed over the past four years, and was exactly as I remembered it. We had authentic Mexican food at a small restaurant named "Maria's" for supper that evening.

Our kids always amazed us at how easily they adapted to major changes. The different types of food we ate can be used as good example; yesterday we were having "crawfish" in Louisiana and today were eating "enchiladas and green chili" in Texas. They were always ready for anything that came their way. I just couldn't imagine many of their Cousins back in Kings Mountain being that flexible. Our kids made us proud in more ways than one.

The next day we drove on to San Angelo to spend a few days with Coot, Bill and their two girls. San Angelo was about 75 miles from Big Spring, so we were just a little over an hour's driving time from San Angelo after we got settled at Webb.

Big Spring wasn't a very big town, but Webb was a busy place with the T-38's taking off and landing all day, everyday. They weren't very big, but were awfully noisy.

We checked into a motel not very far from the main gate; the name was "Ranch Inn", but the kids renamed it "the raunchy inn." The place wasn't anything special, but was adequate; we would have to stay there for the better part of a month before we could get a house on base. Schools were close by and the kids were enrolled right away.

When we arrived in Big Spring our sponsor was waiting for us and was very helpful getting us temporarily settled and familiar with the base and everything we would need to know. The motel was more of an apartment than a motel room because it had several bedrooms and a fully equipped kitchen. It would be ok until a unit came open on base, which we were told, would only be a few weeks.

The management team was smaller than other teams I had been with and the projects were limited to training command functions. The team leader was a junior Captain and the lead NCO was a Senior Master Sergeant.

Life would be simple at Webb, and the mission was clear. As a flying training base the only thing that mattered was the training schedule to produce pilots. When they left Webb they were supposed to be ready to fly any of the supersonic fighters in the Air Force inventory.

The NCO club was the only social outlet on base for enlisted people, and it was a very nice place to go and relax. The food was inexpensive and very good; the activities were standard for a club function.

The town of Big Spring was small but had everything we needed when we had to shop for anything off base. There wasn't much industry other than a Conoco oil refinery on the south side and a VA hospital on the north, if you could call a hospital part of the local industry.

The hospital payroll probably had an impact, but the Air Base itself was by far the most important employer and contributor to the Big Spring economy.

Once outside the city limits and local traffic there was nothing but flat prairie covered with mesquite and other scrub bushes. There was some cattle ranching and agriculture in any direction, but not much else. About half way between Big Spring and San Angelo the farmers grew some of the biggest onions we had ever seen, they were as big as grapefruit and the fields covered several miles.

Jack rabbits and white tailed deer were plentiful; it wasn't unusual to see herds of deer close to the highway grazing alongside cattle.

When we moved into base housing our unit backed up against a big pasture located between the base housing area and the active runway. The pasture was full of big Texas Jack Rabbits. Leesa's little Chihuahua she had named "Chopper" loved for me to hold him above the ground until he spotted one of the rabbits. When that happened I'd set him down and off he'd go as fast as he could run trying to catch the rabbit. Of course he never did, and most times he'd come limping back with sand-spurs in one or more of his feet.

The word that base housing gave us concerning the waiting period for a unit on base was true enough and less than a month after our arrival we were on base and had our furniture delivered and set up. The houses were real nice three bedroom units with two full baths and large kitchen, living room and dining room. Outside we had a carport and rear deck area with a picnic table.

Before leaving the "raunchy inn" I bought a five-speed bicycle at the base exchange and rode it to work. Mil drove the kids to school each morning and picked them up, so she needed access to the car. When we moved on base it was a short ride from our house to my office, probably not more than a mile at most. Since my duties with the management team didn't involve any weekend duty we spent some of our weekends in San Angelo with Coot and Bill.

She knew I loved her enchiladas and every time we went to spend the weekend with them she'd have a big batch ready and waiting for us. She was a wonderful cook.

West Texas was loaded with white tail deer, but they were easier to hunt with a small jeep type vehicle that could get off the well travelled main roads. We hadn't been in Big Spring very long before I started looking around for a small four-wheel drive vehicle, and hadn't been looking very long before Bill called and said that he'd found a good one that I might be interested in buying. That weekend we drove to San Angelo to check it out. The vehicle for sale was a Nissan Patrol and was in excellent condition; it was perfect for what I had in mind to buy. The price was reasonable enough and by the following weekend the deal had been made and I was the proud owner of one of the toughest all terrain vehicles ever produced.

The guy had it rigged up for deer hunting with a winch and tires especially made to travel off the road in mesquite country. There are a lot of thorny bushes in that part of the country and most of the thorns are long enough and hard enough to puncture a regular tire. The fellow that sold me the Patrol had the tires treated with a thick rubbery substance that made them puncture proof. It would serve us well over many years to come.

The Patrol was bought just in time, because the bicycle was causing me some medical problems. I had to go on sick call one morning with a pain in the rear end. The medics lanced a boil for me and put me on quarters for a day so that I could sit in the tub five or six times to help the healing process.

That was the first time in my military career that I wasn't available for duty. By the next day I was ready for duty again and continued to ride the bike to work. That didn't go too well with the lanced rear end, so arrangements were made for one of the team members to pick me up for a few days. Then after a week or so I started riding the bike again; and the boil returned; I went on sick call again and the boil was lanced again.

This time the medics told me to stay off the bicycle. The next week I had the Nissan Patrol to drive to work, and the bicycle was parked under the carport for someone else to ride.

While we were still in Charlotte on Hall Avenue we had rented a horse for a birthday present for Leesa. It was a small pony and was hers for two weeks. She kept it in our back yard during that time and enjoyed that little horse more than anything she ever had for her birthday.

I made her a promise that she would someday have a horse of her very own. We hadn't been in Big Spring very long before she met another little girl that had a horse stabled not too far from our house and she learned that there was room for more horses at the stable.

Shortly afterwards we started looking for a horse to buy. She found one, of course, and before many more days passed she was the owner of a pretty sorrel gelding she named Junior. The very next weekend we drove to San Angelo to make the trip to Del Rio and over the river to the Mexican border town of Acuna looking for a saddle and bridle.

I never saw a little girl that was so excited over anything. Junior was a fine gentle natured horse and she was constantly taking care of him or going for a ride with one of her friends. Maria didn't have much to do with him, and I believe she was a little afraid to ride such a big animal. Jamey wasn't interested either; he was after the girls.

Sometime around the middle of spring, probably May or possibly early June, Mama and Grandma Roper rode a bus all the way from Kings Mountain to Big Spring to visit with us. I don't believe either of them had ever been so far away from home. We picked them up at the bus terminal and they stayed a week or so with us. They really enjoyed their vacation and after a few days we took them to San Angelo to see the Tallons. They spent a couple days in San Angelo, returned to Big Spring and caught the bus back home.

Not long after Mama and Grandma visited with us, Faye and Ed drove from Bolivar to Big Spring. They didn't stay a full week because they didn't have the vacation time but they too enjoyed their visit a great deal. I don't believe either of them had ever been to Texas before.

Ed couldn't believe the size of the Jackrabbits. He wanted to take one back to Tennessee, so we took the Nissan Patrol out one day and shot one for him. He put it in a cooler, and when he got back home, put it in the freezer. He later told me he thawed it out and laid it on the road in front of his house like it had been road killed. He just wanted to see the reaction of the drivers as they passed by. Word got out that the biggest rabbit in Tennessee had been killed in front of Ed Henson's house.

Within a few weeks after Faye and Ed left we had more visitors. Mil's brother Nelson, Billie Jo, and little Nelson drove down from Fort Carson, Colorado and stayed a few days with us. We took them to Acuna during their stay. Travel time from Big Spring to Del Rio took about four hours, so the trip to the border and back was an all day affair. Even though it was tiring they seemed to enjoy it and brought back some of the leather goods and other souvenirs.

Because of the nerve damage to my ears, that had caused me to be grounded years before, the medical authorities wouldn't allow me to pull duty in a noise hazard area; that included all the flight line areas of Webb, that presented a problem. Nearly all of the projects the management engineering team worked on required the team members to be on the flight line.

The team Captain contacted his people at the personnel center and informed them of the problem. They recommended a transfer to a non-flying base, and the only other training command base that met that requirement was Lowry Air Force Base near Denver.

Another problem surfaced; and that was a ruling that no one could be reassigned more than once in a fiscal year, and the new fiscal year wouldn't begin until July 1st. I was more or less desk bound for the next several months until after July 1st rolled around and orders could be cut sending me to Lowry. The arrangement worked out pretty good; the team members would gather all the data and bring it to me to be computed and formatted to determine manpower requirements or whatever the need may be.

As spring turned to summer the kids were out of school and spending their afternoons at the NCO club pool. Leesa was spending a lot of time working with Junior. We were socializing one or two nights a week at the club, either eating out or Mil was playing bingo. I didn't care for bingo but went with her and sat out the game at the bar.

One evening while sitting at the bar I struck up a conversation with one of the guys and learned that he and his wife were being transferred to Lowry also. He had been stationed at Webb for the past three years and had requested a move to Lowry and his request had been approved. He was from Iowa and had grown up hunting white tail deer; and he still loved it. We had a lot in common and planned to do some hunting together after we both got to Colorado.

Orders reassigning me to the management team at Lowry gave me seven days travel time and we were scheduled to leave Big Spring sometime during the third week of August.

Then an unfortunate problem came up that was completely unexpected. An epidemic of Venezuelan Equine Flu erupted in Louisiana and Texas. Authorities closed the Texas border to the transport of horses either into or out of the state. We wouldn't be allowed to take Junior to Colorado with us and the situation was explained to Leesa; she reluctantly agreed that we would have to sell him. I promised her another horse when we were settled in Denver.

We found a buyer and the deal to sell Junior and the saddle was made. The buyer was to come by the next day and pick him up, but not before Leesa had a chance to see him one last time. The next morning I took her to where Junior was stabled only to find that the man had already been there, picked up the horse and was gone with him.

Leesa was terribly disappointed, so I made every effort to locate the guy and find out where Junior had been taken so she could see him again and be reassured that he had a good home. We didn't know when Junior was sold that the buyer was a horse trader and Junior had been sold to another man even before the horse trader bought him from us.

Junior's new owner was finally located and we went by to see him. He was a very nice man and took us to Junior so that Leesa could properly tell him goodbye. He had a nice stall and a pasture to graze in, so she was convinced he would be well cared for; that seemed to ease her mind about having to leave him.

We spent one last weekend with the Tallons before leaving Big Spring. Our household goods were packed by the movers, and we were back living in the travel trailer.

August was almost gone and plans had already been made for the guys from Charlotte to come west in late September and another hunting trip to Wyoming. They had made the drawing again and had received their antelope and deer permit in the mail. Their deer permit allowed them to hunt the Shirley Basin area which included the Sullivan ranch where we had deer hunted the past several years. Their antelope permit, however, was for an area over near the Nebraska state line.

The last few nights in Big Spring were spent camping in Comanche Trail Park, a recreational park operated by the City of Big Spring. On the day we were to leave I drove the Chevrolet Impala towing the camper trailer; Mil and the girls were with me and Jamey followed us in the Nissan Patrol.

Our route took us north through Lubbock, Amarillo and Dalhart and soon after leaving Dalhart we crossed over into New Mexico. We followed I-25 north from Raton Pass to Colorado Springs.

Somewhere along I-25 we stopped at a rest area and Mil left her purse in the bathroom. We had gone a short distance, probably less than ten miles when she discovered the purse was missing. We pulled off the highway and Jamey and I drove the Nissan Patrol back to the rest area.

Our Guardian Angel was watching over us that day because the purse was still in the bathroom where she had left it. We made it to Nelson's house in Colorado Springs without further incident and spent the night with them.

The next day we drove on to Denver and immediately started looking for a house. We started looking west of town and contacted a real estate agency in Arvada who showed us their listings. We checked out a nice house in Arvada located within a block of a good high school and started the process of buying it.

Mil was very excited about the prospects, but felt that we might not qualify for some reason or another. She loved the house at once and would have been badly disappointed if the deal had not been completed, but within a few days all the background checks came back ok and the deal was signed.

Our household goods were delivered over Labor Day weekend and we were once more living in a house. It was located in a relatively new project and had a full basement with three bedrooms and two full baths and another bedroom in the basement. It was perfect for our family.

Mil was as happy as she had been in a long time. We were living in our own home again, not a base housing unit, and she was very proud of that. Arvada West High School was within a city block of our house and an elementary school was within walking distance. A nice shopping center was located within a few minutes drive, but Lowry Air Force Base was clear across town. I had to get on I-70 and drive ten or twelve miles and then turn onto Quebec Avenue for another mile or so to get to the main gate. Quebec ran directly in front of Stapleton International Airport. My new assignment to the Lowry management engineering team was waiting on me and I would be the ranking NCO on a team of fourteen members.

The management engineering guys always seemed to be a cut above the average, and the team at Lowry wouldn't be an exception; if anything they were, for the most part, more than a cut above. Things were really looking up for us. Before leaving Charlotte I had requested to be reassigned to Lowry, but the management engineering wheels felt my assignment to Webb was in the best interest of the air force.

Denver had been our choice of assignments all along; we were exactly where we wanted to be, and were excited about the future and what we hoped would be an interesting and enjoyable final chapter in our career in the military. I was anxious to get it started.

CHAPTER 32

Colorado, Lowry AFB and Wyoming Sept 1971–Sept 1974

Arvada was situated at the base of the foothills of the Front Range; from where our house was located it was less than a mile before the highway west started a steady climb until the first mountain pass was reached. Golden, home of the Coors brewery, was nestled in Cold Creek canyon between Arvada and the Front Range. To get to the western slope of the Rocky Mountains from Denver at least two passes had to be crossed. Interstate 70 crossed Loveland and Vail pass and on west through Grand Junction before entering Utah. US highway 40 branched off I-70 about twenty miles west of Idaho Springs and crossed over Berthoud and Rabbit Ears pass to Steamboat Springs.

All our household goods were delivered; we were unpacking and getting everything arranged in our new house over Labor Day weekend; Nelson, Billie Jo, and Little Nelson drove up from Colorado Springs to help us get moved in.

On Sunday morning Nelson and I drove into the mountains and ran into an early but heavy snowstorm. The highway west of Idaho Springs was a steady climb all the way to Loveland pass. We had climbed to around

8000 feet or maybe a little higher and soon were driving through a regular blizzard. We weren't prepared for such fierce weather, and the higher we went, the harder the snow and wind whirled around us. We were driving the Nissan Patrol and could have made it over Loveland Pass with ease, but decided to turn back.

When we turned around we stopped long enough to fill a cooler full of snow and headed back to Arvada where it was sunny and warmer. Mil and Billie Jo didn't believe our story about the blizzard until we showed them the cooler full of snow. It was early September but the Rocky Mountains of Colorado already had their first snowfall and would be covered with snow until the late spring thaw.

Within a few days of moving in we met some of our new neighbors. Our next door neighbor, George Geodekke, played football for the Denver Broncos and while we were getting settled in he and his wife came in and introduced themselves. We became good friends with George, his wife and their two little boys; over the next several years we would meet most of the other Bronco players who came to visit with George to participate in some of their victory celebrations at the Geodekke's.

Everyone in Denver were wild Bronco fans and tickets to home games were impossible to get, but George took me to the stadium for some of the home games and even without a seat I'd roam around the sidelines and get to watch the game. Once he gave me two tickets to a Monday night game against the Oakland Raiders; since Mil was scheduled to work I invited Bennie Espinosa to go with me to the game.

There were people living in Denver at the time who would've mortgaged their home for a ticket to that game; Mile High stadium was an exciting place to be during a Monday night game, especially one against the hated Raiders. It didn't take me very long to become one of the loyal Bronco fans.

The management engineering team at Lowry was commanded by Lt. Col John Sanford. The team was divided into two branches; one branch had the responsibility for manpower validation; the other branch was responsible for the management engineering function. Colonel Sanford was an outstanding leader and had just returned from a tour in Vietnam where he piloted a C-47 that had been converted to a gunship flying air support for the ground troops. He was nearing retirement age and was sitting out his last assignment behind a desk, his flying days behind him.

He loved to fly fish in the cold mountain trout streams and could party alongside men who were much younger, and he allowed the senior NCO's all the room needed to get the job done. He was a fine officer and well liked by all the men under his command. He was born and raised near Lake Chelan, Washington that was about thirty or forty miles north of Wenatchee; he did a lot of trout and salmon fishing as a youngster.

One of the first things that I did after reporting for duty was apply for a two week leave. Soon after reporting in I told Col. Sanford about my plans to make the annual hunting trip to Wyoming, so my leave request didn't seem to matter to him.

All the current projects the Lowry team was responsible for were being efficiently handled by guys already on board. The projects that I would be responsible for would come later.

Jamey had asked for and had been given permission to be out of class for a few days to go with us to Wyoming. He wouldn't have been allowed to be out of school back east, but things were different here. There were several schools in Wyoming that were closed on the opening day of deer and elk season, and if a student hadn't filled his license near the end of the season he (or she) was allowed to be out of school until his game tags were filled.

Steve and Jake drove Judy's car from Charlotte to Denver and the rest of the guys rented a big motor home to drive west. The day they were scheduled to arrive Steve woke me up shortly before five o'clock calling from a service station on Federal Boulevard. They had driven all the way non-stop to Denver; he and Jake were confused about the directions to our house, and I had to go find them so they could follow me back.

Mil cooked us a big breakfast, and the four of us; Steve, Jake, Jamey and I were on our way north to Wyoming before daylight to meet the rest of the guys from Charlotte. I had the camper trailer hooked up to the Nissan Patrol, which Jake and I were in, followed by Steve and Jamey in their car. We met the other guys as planned and before sundown had a nice camp set up.

Antelope season was opened several days before we got set up, but everyone still had three or four days to fill their antelope tags before the mule deer season began. We could have filled all the antelope tags on the first day, but everyone was after a nice trophy to be mounted, and a couple of the guys held off until the last day before taking a shot.

Regardless, everyone had an antelope hanging by the fourth day. On the opening day of deer season, Jim Payne repeated what I had done several years ago when I shot at a good buck antelope and hit and killed a smaller one standing behind him. Jim shot at a nice mature mulie with a good rack and hit a small buck instead. Everyone filled their licenses and Jamey killed his first buck.

A few days after setting up camp we had a snowstorm that dumped nearly six inches of snow on our campsite: but the Nissan proved itself to be an outstanding off the road hunting vehicle and the weather didn't slow us down at all, if anything the hunting was even better.

A week later everyone was on their way home with some nice trophy antlers, and Jamey and I were back in Arvada.

Mil had applied for a job at a Mexican restaurant in the shopping center not far from the house and within a few days had been given the job. The restaurant was owned by Bennie and Violet Espinosa and was next door to a saloon called "The Red Lion." Bennie and Vi became lifelong friends. They were both hard working, family oriented people. Sometimes I would go to the Red Lion and wait for Mil to finish her work; the saloon was a favorite gathering place for the local crowd and we became good friends with the bar-tender, Lloyd Parsons, and his wife.

They would later buy their own saloon in the small mountain town of Empire that was situated on the eastern slope of the mountains leading up to Berthoud Pass. Lloyd had a pretty severe drinking problem and had been told by the medical people that he had to stop drinking anything alcoholic. He did stop for a while, at least until sometime after he had bought his own place near Empire.

Mil and I spent more than one Sunday afternoon there. On Sunday afternoon he always had a skeet shoot off a big patio overlooking a hillside behind his saloon. His menu on Sunday specialized in "rocky mountain oysters" and baked beans.

By the time Lloyd opened his place in Empire we had met and became good friends with Chuck and Pat Winters, my friend from the NCO club at Big Spring, Texas.

One Sunday afternoon Chuck and I got into a barroom brawl with a group of miners. That part of the country was dotted with various mines and had at one time been one of the country's leading gold producing regions. Most of the gold mines had been closed but other minerals were still being mined.

The fight didn't last long but Chuck and I held our ground pretty good against heavy odds. A secondary fight broke out between Pat Winters and several miners' wives, but no one was hurt; Lloyd restored peace quickly and whatever started the fight in the first place was forgotten.

Mil was an innocent bystander and the fight was over before she realized there was a disagreement at all. Soon everyone was laughing and joking about the incident.

Lloyd must have continued drinking after moving up to Empire, because not long after we had the fight in his saloon, we learned that he had been hospitalized and within a few weeks he was gone.

The doctors had warned him that to continue drinking anything alcoholic would take him out, but I guess the habit was too strong for him to break. According to the medical people his liver couldn't handle any more alcohol.

Our first winter in Colorado was an eye opener. We had never been subjected to such wild and harsh weather. Below zero temperatures and blinding snowstorms were common events, but the streets and highways were generally clear and we had the Nissan Patrol that could get through in any kind of weather.

It took us a while to get accustomed to the severity of the biting wind and numbing cold that came with the snow. I had experienced a winter like that in Moses Lake twenty years earlier but had almost forgotten what it was like.

As usual, the kids adapted to the extreme weather and before long were out there with the natives like they had been born in Colorado. And as far as I know, Mil never let the weather keep her from going to work at the restaurant. She was as tough as the kids.

The house was well insulated and had a good heating system, so we were warm and cozy there no matter how fierce the wind was blowing outside.

The residential area where we lived was right on the edge of all the advancing housing developments and shopping centers, and just a couple blocks from Queen Street, where we lived, there were still some small ranches and open pastures.

It didn't take Leesa very long to venture out to one of these small farm-like homes with a pasture.

There she met Mrs. Faith Rogers, who had been widowed several years earlier. She lived with her Mother,

Mrs. Brown. Leesa quickly became friends with the ladies and within a few days had been given permission to stable her horse there. It wasn't very long before we were looking for a horse. Soon after the permission was given Leesa introduced us to Mrs. Rogers and her Mother. She told us that she thought she'd never agree for anyone to keep a horse on her property, even though she had a nice pasture and barn; but she was so impressed with Leesa, that it didn't take long for her to give in.

They were both interesting ladies with a colorful history. Mrs. Brown was over ninety years old and told us of riding west from Nebraska in a covered wagon to settle in Colorado with her pioneering family.

Mrs. Rogers' husband was a decorated World War II veteran and had retired from the army reserve as a Lt. Colonel. We would become very good friends with those two ladies for the remainder of their lives.

As stated above, we started looking for a horse for Leesa. She had loved Junior, a quarter horse, but now she was dead set on an Appaloosa and didn't care for anything else. She studied the history of the Appaloosa and knew of the qualities that were bred into the spotted Indian horses.

After a week or so of looking around we found an Appaloosa stallion that seemed gentle enough, but Mrs. Rogers voiced some objections to having a stallion on her place, so we declined to buy him. Then we found a pretty mare with a nice spotted blanket and settled on her.

She seemed gentle enough until we got her into Mrs. Roger's pasture where she promptly threw Leesa and nearly trampled her. I thought for sure she had been hurt, but she came up from the fall and was ok. The horse's name was "Pepsi Cola" and most of the time she was ok, but couldn't be trusted, and it wasn't long before we sold her to be used a brood mare.

Not long after Pepsi Cola was sold we found the horse she had been looking for all along. We had to go all the way to Deer Trail, about a hundred miles east of Denver to pick him up, but he turned out to be worth a lot more than the effort it took to get him. He was big, had a nice spotted blanket, and was as gentle as could be. His name was "Patchy" and would be like a member of the family. Leesa kept him for the rest of his life, and I know the memories of all the wonderful things that he was, will remain with her the rest of her life.

After we brought him back to Mrs. Rogers' place, I doubt if a single day went by that Leesa didn't spend some time with him.

During his senior year at Arvada West High School, Jamey made the decision to enlist in the Air Force Reserve, providing his Mother and I had no objections. The recruiter told us about a program they called the "delayed enlistment program." We agreed that three years in the military would probably be a good thing for him and signed the parental consent forms so that he could go into the reserves, followed by active duty in the future.

Some months later he left for basic training and following basic was assigned to technical school at Lowry. My old commander from the recruiting detachment in Charlotte was still at the personnel center at Randolph Air Force Base and all it took was one phone call to him and Jamey's assignment to Lowry was secured.

There were an awful lot of things to do and places to go in Colorado, even in the coldest months of winter. As a matter of fact skiing was and will always be a big part of winter activities in that state. Mil and I never went skiing, but all the kids were good skiers before we left Colorado.

We could have lived in Colorado twenty years and still wouldn't have had time to see and do everything available to us there. The Coors brewery was located in Golden, Colorado, which was less than five miles from Arvada. We were invited to tour the brewery and attend a welcome-wagon party shortly after we moved to Arvada. We had a wonderful time touring the brewery and joining in the beer drinking contests.

Most of the western two-thirds of the state is National Forest land or government property maintained by the Bureau of Land Management and the recreational possibilities there are endless. Trout streams and high mountain lakes offer residents and tourists alike some of the best trout fishing anywhere. Elk and mule deer hunting and camping in the National Forests are as good in Colorado as anywhere in the country.

The old mining towns of Idaho Springs and Central City are a short drive from Arvada, and the Colorado gold rush days in the late 1800's are still in evidence there.

Central City is well known as the richest square mile on earth. Most of the gold mines are closed now but the countryside around the region is still dotted with old gold mine tailings and most of the old buildings and houses are still there.

A lot of our weekends involved some kind of sightseeing, camping, fishing or touring around the state. Rocky Mountain National Park and trail ridge road were within several hours driving time and the drive from Estes Park on the eastern side to Granby on the west afforded us some of the most spectacular mountain scenery anywhere in the world.

Cheyenne Wyoming and their annual "Frontier Days" that are held the last full week in July are only an hour and a half drive north of Denver. We never failed to make the "granddaddy of all rodeos" in Cheyenne.

We hadn't been in Arvada long before we had to take a couple weeks off to go back home and make arrangements to sell our house in Charlotte. The family in our house on Hall Avenue had defaulted on their lease and left it in a big mess. We had to repaint the bedrooms and living room again before putting it on the market to sell. We left it with my friend from the Masonic lodge and soon were on our way back to Arvada.

Lafayette and Mary's oldest daughter, Connie, and one of Leesa's friends from Charlotte rode back with us to spend a few weeks before flying back to Charlotte.

Even though it hasn't been that long ago, some of the events that occurred while we were in Arvada are a little fuzzy and the timing for some of them may not be exact. For example, when we went back home and Leesa's friends came back with us, it had to be during summer vacation from the school year, but I am not sure exactly when it occurred. In all probability it was during the summer of 1972.

Another time we came home for Christmas and ran into a bad snowstorm around Saint Louis. We were stuck in heavy traffic and were delayed nearly five hours by the snow. By that time Jamey had finished his technical training at Lowry and was assigned to an operational unit at Bergstrom Air Force Base near Austin, Texas. We did a little coordinating and met him in Bolivar, Tennessee, and he rode the rest of the way home with us. To get to Bolivar he caught a ride with a friend who lived in Arkansas and had dropped him off at Faye's house in Bolivar.

We spent the Christmas season at home and took Jamey back to Austin before going on to Arvada after the holidays.

The bad winter weather continued to slow us down; as we drove through Texas to get to Austin; the roads were icy and frozen over in places, and that made the driving dangerous. We made it to Austin, however, and spent the night there before leaving the next morning for more winter driving all the way back to Arvada.

My duties on the Lowry Management Engineering team were routine and somewhat boring. We had plenty to do and more than enough people to handle the workload, but all our projects other than local management advisory studies came from Air Training Command and were generally part of an overall training function.

We had some good people on the team and we all worked well together; and we had some off duty ventures together also. One weekend the whole team went camping and trout fishing behind Pike's Peak on the South Platte River. It was in early May but winter wasn't over yet and we had to leave early because of a snowstorm.

We were in an area called "eleven mile canyon" and barely made it out before the snow started getting too deep to move the vehicles. Once again the Nissan Patrol got us out of a tight spot.

The recruiting group for Colorado and Wyoming was located at Lowry and our team was called to do an advisory study for the group headquarters. John Priest, the lead NCO for our manpower validation branch, and I went to interview the recruiting commander before the team started to gather data for the study. During the course of our interview I told the group commander about my experiences in recruiting and he offered me a job as the recruiter for southern Wyoming. There were only two recruiting offices in the entire state; one in Cheyenne and another in Casper.

I was being offered the Cheyenne office. After thinking about it for a few days, and talking it over with Mil, I agreed to accept the recruiting job in Cheyenne, providing I didn't have to go back through the school again. The group Commander made a phone call to Randolph AFB and the deal was done.

Within a few weeks I was given half the state of Wyoming as my recruiting area. Leesa was a senior in high school and we made arrangements to leave everything as it was and not move to Cheyenne until after her graduation.

Then, just before she graduated, the Comptroller General came out with a ruling that involved military retirement pay with several pay increases for active duty people and I started thinking about applying for retirement. I calculated the difference and decided my best course to follow would be to retire before the first of September because the Comptroller General's ruling would affect anyone who retired after that date.

Mil and I talked about the decision several times. After my assignment to Cheyenne I had been spending the weekdays in Wyoming and coming back to Arvada to spend weekends at home. We still planned on moving to Cheyenne following Leesa's graduation.

Dick Wagner, my old friend from the management team at Yokota was stationed at Warren Air Force Base near Cheyenne and had a house outside the city and one of his daughters had a horse and he had a good pasture. The problem of where to stable Patchy after moving to Cheyenne was solved.

After thinking everything over I decided to try another option once my retirement application had been submitted.

It would have been impractical to move everything to Cheyenne for such a short period of time. Leesa's graduation was set for early June and my retirement date was set for the last day of August. I called one of the personnel offices in Washington and explained the details and was told to wait for orders moving me back to Lowry for retirement.

Several weeks later my orders were published and I was reassigned to Lowry to work with the "energy conservation" office. This was a newly organized function that had been ordered by the President in order to reduce waste on all the military bases in the country.

When I reported in to my new duty station I found that the only people assigned there was a junior NCO who in turn reported to the base commander.

He told me to check in once a week just to let him know that I was still around; there was very little that I could do for him because anything he was involved in would still be in progress when my retirement date arrived. There was nothing I could do to help him.

My retirement was less than two months away, and there were lots of personal things to be done. Our house had been listed with a local real estate office and we were ready to put all our personal gear and household goods in storage in preparation for movement back to North Carolina. We had also made arrangements to rent a furnished apartment only a few blocks away from Queen St.

There was no way we were going to leave Patchy behind like we had to do with Junior, so I sold our little camper/trailer and bought a horse trailer. It would be a long ride for him, but we would find a way to get him back home safely.

It didn't take long for a buyer to sign a contract with our real estate people to sell our house, and by the middle of June we closed the deal and were ready to move to the apartment.

Although still on active duty, there was nothing for me to do at the base; I drove out to Lowry once or twice a week just to check in and go visit the management team.

Since I wasn't a member of the team my going away party consisted of a beer bust at the NCO club with the guys on the team. Mrs. Rogers and her Mother, Mrs. Brown insisted on taking us to dinner at an exclusive restaurant in Golden, and Benny and Vi threw another beer party for us at the Red Lion.

My retirement was informal since I didn't really belong to an organization. No parades or anything like that. It was simple; a few handshakes, "good luck" and I was a civilian again, although I would remain on the inactive reserve list for a number of years.

As I walked out of the headquarters building with my certificate in hand I had an empty feeling, sorta like being homesick or lonely for someone or something. I had an urge to go back and tell the commander I didn't want to leave. That was silly, of course.

I thought about how happy Mama had been when we called and told her we were coming back home. She never realized that a big factor in our decision to return home after retirement was her heart condition. She had already been hospitalized last year following a heart attack.

Daddy was there, but he too was getting older and might not be able to take care of her and himself too. Mil's folks were all in Kings Mountain, and that was an additional incentive for us to leave Colorado.

The girls had a lot of friends to say "goodbye" to. Leesa was already making plans to return to Colorado one way or another. Maria had just completed the seventh grade and would be starting Junior High School at home in a short week or two.

Even though we had a nice apartment that was fully furnished, we were still essentially living out of suitcases again.

Several years earlier we had bought a pop-up camper to replace the camper/trailer we had brought from Charlotte. I made arrangements to leave it and the Nissan

Patrol parked at Mrs. Rogers because the Wyoming deer and antelope season was only a few weeks off.

Jake McFee, his nephew Ronnie Wilson and a friend who lived in Asheville were all set to drive back with me to Wyoming.

Within a few days following retirement all the loose ends were tied up and we were ready to start the cross country trip in the Chevvy Impala towing the horse trailer and Patchy behind us.

Our plans were to make it to Perry, Oklahoma the first day and to Knoxville the second. Prior arrangements had been made to stable Patchy overnight at those locations, and early on the morning of September 2nd we closed that chapter and were looking forward to our cross country trip and settling down on our own place back home.

Again we were leaving a group of good friends behind us. And the girls were leaving their school mates. We had been through this before, but leaving people you care about never gets to be routine and is always a sad time. This time would hopefully be the last time. Our next home would be our last home. We all had mixed feelings about this move; we were glad to be going home, but we would never forget Colorado and all the wonderful times there.

Chuck Winters on the left and the author on the right during a pre hunting season scouting trip in the Western Colorado Rockies.

The author with Patchy during a scouting trip to Western Colorado.

CHAPTER 33

AF Retirement and Cleveland College Sept 1974–Dec 1980

A major chapter in my life was closed. Something important to me was missing and I couldn't understand how to handle it. A lot of people that had become close friends were on the other side of the door that had just closed behind me.

To be transferred to an overseas assignment and leave them in the past didn't mean as much, because somewhere at another base, I would see them or maybe even work with them again.

It wasn't just the people, but an atmosphere; the smell of an airplane or a mess hall early in the morning; or standing retreat as the flag was being lowered; the privilege of saluting an officer; and being associated with people who were, to the last man, a cut above in all respects.

The cord had been cut. Maybe that was it, maybe not; I knew what was wrong, I had been living in an OD world for the past twenty-five years; a way of life was gone like a close friend had just died.

My family was by far the most important thing in my life and that was what sustained me now. I wondered if

I would adapt to a different way of life that lay ahead as easily as Mil and the kids had always been able to.

We turned off Kipling Avenue and drove onto I-70 east. Arvada and a whole way of life was behind us and a new life was waiting for us in North Carolina. What would the next twenty-five years be like? The excitement of just thinking about it brought me out of the grumpy mood I was in.

The girls were playing and singing in the back seat and a Cat Stevens tape was playing on the car stereo. The world was an entirely different place than it was that day in 1949 when I rode away from the Park Yarn with the air force recruiter.

The importance of our dependence on foreign oil was already rearing its ugly head. The OPEC oil embargo was forcing gasoline prices up and creating long lines at the gas pump. Prices rose from an average of 38 cents per gallon in May 1973 to 55 cents per gallon by June 1974. And that was just the beginning.

The Middle Eastern oil producing countries, including some of our so called friends in that part of the world, would put the squeeze on our economy for a long time to come.

Daylight found us travelling east on I-70; Denver was behind us with a long drive to Perry, Oklahoma, our destination that first day, ahead of us. The horse trailer with Patchy aboard was following just fine and the long miles didn't seem to bother him. We stopped at most rest areas and let him out for a short walk to loosen his legs up a bit.

Interstate 70 was behind us as we turned south on interstate 35 at Salinas, Kansas and made it to Perry without incident. We found the people who would stable Patchy for us and after taking care of him we disconnected the trailer and checked into a motel for the night. The next morning we were up early and after loading Patchy, were on our way again. Our route took us through Tulsa, Oklahoma, Little Rock, Arkansas and across the Mississippi at Memphis, Tennessee.

We were late in the evening getting to Knoxville, but the people scheduled to take care of Patchy were waiting and had a corral and stable ready for him. The next day was a short haul to Kings Mountain, and we were home in time for lunch with my folks.

I had never seen my Mom happier. She was beaming because we were home with no plans to leave, ever again.

I don't remember the details, but we had made arrangements to take Patchy over to Peaceful Valley and put him in a pasture owned by the Owensbys. Mr. and Mrs. Owensby, an older couple, were good friends of Grandma and Grandpa Roper. The pasture and barn were in good shape and Leesa was satisfied Patchy would be happy there until we were situated in our own place.

I had to start thinking about doing something to supplement my retired pay because that would not be enough to cover all our financial needs. One thing that was definitely in my post military life was to enroll in college and use the GI bill, not only to get a degree, but to provide added income.

Leesa was out of High School and Jamey was still on active duty in Texas, but Maria was still in school. Another important responsibility facing us was that we had to start looking for a place that would be our home for, in all probability, the remainder of our lives.

We had a lot of important issues facing us. We wouldn't have a problem staying with Mama and Daddy for a while, but the sooner we could get permanently located in our own place the better it would be for everyone.

Plans had already been made for me to return to Wyoming with Jake, his nephew, Ronnie Wilson, and a friend from Asheville, Bill Taylor. We would be gone the better part of two weeks.

We planned to leave in time to pick up the Nissan Patrol and camper/trailer that had been left with Mrs. Rogers, and take it to Wyoming for the antelope and mule deer season.

We had several weeks to take care of our personal chores before I was scheduled to leave for Wyoming, and one of our first priorities was a place to live.

We had been home less than a week before we found several places to look over that were for sale.

A new development was being opened near Crowders Mountain that was sectioned off in lots and varied in size from several acres to nearly five acres. It seemed to have a lot of the qualities that we were looking for, so we checked it out, and the real estate people gave us the grand tour. We soon found that the restrictions wouldn't allow us to have any farm animals on the place, so we had to pass on that tract of land.

One of our friends knew a couple who lived just across the state line near Kings Mountain National Military Park that had a small house and nearly 25 acres for sale. We went with him to be introduced to the owner, Olin Huffman.

He and his wife were school teachers in Blacksburg and didn't need all the land that went with the house and they seemed anxious to move into a new home.

Mil and I were both excited about the place after looking the acreage over. The house was pretty small but was relatively new. It had two bedrooms, a living room, one bathroom, a kitchen/dining room and a small utility room for a washer and dryer. A pretty stream ran through the middle of the tract that was mostly covered with hardwoods; oak, hickory, pines and others.

We talked it over and decided to make an offer for the place even though we knew the house was too small for us. We could take care of that problem later. We had enough in savings to make a good down payment and assume the outstanding balance that was financed through a bank in Gaffney, S.C. Monthly payments would be well within our budget, and before the week was out we had made a deal with the Huffmans.

There was one small hitch! Olin and his wife were having a new house constructed not far from where they now lived, but it would take nearly two months before their new house would be completed. That meant we would have to live with my folks until the time we could move in our new home.

Mama and Daddy had no objections to us staying with them for two months, in fact they seemed pleased with the arrangement. They were happy that we had found such a nice place with so much land. Daddy couldn't wait to help me build a small barn and start fencing a small pasture for Patchy. We planned to buy a farm tractor so we could have a big vegetable garden and planned to build a lot for some pigs.

It was an exciting time and we talked and made plans nearly every night until bedtime. We could hardly wait for Olin and his wife to move out of the house so we could start adding on to make it bigger.

At the same time I was making plans to enter into Cleveland Community College in Shelby. Mil and I were discussing the possibility of opening up a Mexican restaurant. We had talked about that before leaving Arvada and even brought all of Bennie Espinosa's recipes with us when we came home.

Maria was enrolled in school and soon it was time for Jake, Ronnie, Bill, and I to leave for Wyoming. We left early in the morning around the 22nd of September, and as it always was when Jake went with us, we drove straight through, stopping long enough to refuel and get a sandwich, and then back on the road again. We made it to Arvada and picked up the Nissan Patrol and camper and drove on up to Wyoming to set up camp for the hunting season.

Getting an antelope was always easy in Wyoming and by the second day we had all filled our antelope permits and were scouting for mule deer. The area we had drawn to hunt mule deer was much bigger than that for antelope, so we decided to break camp and move to a better location for the deer season.

The deer camp was set up and we still had two days before the opening day. We planned to do a lot of scouting around for two days and be ready when the season started.

Then a problem developed. Bill Taylor became sick and didn't think he could make it through the next two days without some kind of professional medical care. He knew that his problem was internal bleeding because he'd been through it before. He decided just to take it real easy and lay around for the next day or so and hoped that the problem would go away.

Jake, Ronnie, and I continued to scout the area. Deer were everywhere. Our camp was on national forest land about thirty miles east of Baggs, Wyoming and as far as we could determine, we were the only hunters within miles. Getting a trophy deer would be almost guaranteed if we could get Bill's problem taken care of. He was taking some kind of medicine to help, but by the next day he was worse. He would have to be taken out of camp and fly home to his family doctor so that he could be properly cared for.

I volunteered to take him to Denver in the Nissan Patrol and leave Jake and Ronnie with their truck to bring the camper out with them when they finished their deer hunt.

I packed my gear and loaded Bill and his personal gear; we drove back to Denver and he boarded a flight back to Asheville. After dropping him off at Stapleton Airport, I drove out to Lowry and stopped by the management team to see some of my old friends and also visit with Chuck Winters for a short while before starting the long drive home in the Nissan Patrol.

I had to stop and refuel soon after leaving Denver and when I checked the oil it was several quarts low. In addition, the temperature indicator told me the engine was running hot. I was alone with sixteen hundred miles in front of me with an ailing engine.

The decision was made to take out the thermostat in case that was the problem with the temperature, and the only thing to do about the low oil was to add the two quarts.

From then on it was smooth driving all the way home. The oil level stayed full the rest of the way home and the temperature stayed normal. Apparently the thermostat was stuck and wasn't opening up properly; and the low oil was the result of towing the camper and all the off-road driving.

It was nearly noon by the time I left Lowry; and I only made it to Independence Missouri that day before checking into a motel. The next morning I was up early and drove all the way to Knoxville before stopping again.

I thought seriously about continuing on, but was feeling a little sleepy after driving for sixteen hours, and checked into a motel on the outskirts of Knoxville. The next day I was home well before noon. The Nissan Patrol was running like a new sewing machine.

It was good to be home again. Four or five days later Jake stopped by long enough to drop off the camper on his way back to Charlotte. He reported that both he and Ronnie had taken a trophy mule deer. He also told us that Bill Taylor was hospitalized but doing well. He had some bleeding ulcers in his stomach, but was responding to treatment.

Things were happening fast. While we were in Wyoming Mil had taken a job at one of the local mills. Leesa was still making plans to return to Colorado and was coordinating with one of her high school friends, lining up an apartment. I was due to start classes at Cleveland College within a few weeks. We were busy in our spare time building a barn and fencing in a pasture.

I learned through Olin Huffman that his brother had a farm tractor for sale and, after talking with him, agreed to his price and soon after we had a big help in getting the heavy logs into position for the barn construction.

We were still talking about a Mexican restaurant. Mil was working steady at the mill but was unhappy about having to get up so early in the morning. Her shift ran from 6 AM until 2 PM and that meant setting the alarm to wake her up around 5 AM. My classes at Cleveland College were scheduled three days a week and were only six hours a day.

Maria had to be driven to school every day, but that was a temporary arrangement, because as soon as we could make the move to our new place, she would be changing to the Blacksburg, South Carolina School system. The school bus stopped directly in front of our house.

She was concerned that Leesa would be leaving us to go back to Colorado. They had always been very close and the prospects of Leesa not being there with her didn't set very well. Jamey was still stationed at Bergstrom Air Force Base near Austin, Texas, but he was on temporary duty somewhere in England.

In a few months his enlistment would be completed and he hadn't said anything that would lead us to think he might re-enlist. In all probability he would be coming home.

We were renewing old friendships and meeting a few new ones. The hub of social activity in Kings Mountain was the Saturday night dance at the American Legion and we seldom missed being there. Steve and Judy made the long drive from Charlotte to meet us there several Saturday nights. The dance was generally crowded with most of our old friends always there; and we seldom left before being run off after closing time.

We met Steve and Joyce Lee and became close friends quickly. Joyce's grandmother lived on Bethlehem road and had a huge pasture and a big barn and we learned that Patchy would be welcome there and would require very little attention because everything he would need, food, water, and a stall were all there.

We still made it to Charlotte several times monthly to see our old friends there. Jim and Nancy Payne along with Jake and Ann McFee were always ready to have a cook out or party at Jake's place on N. Tryon St. Steve and I still found time to make it to Lake Norman for some fishing. Steve had bought a new and bigger boat and was into striper fishing in South Carolina. Steve Lee also had a big fishing boat that we took to Lake James several times to fish for white bass at the mouth of the Linville River. We spent several weekends there with some of our other new friends. We always had good times at Lake James and caught lots of fish too. The striper fishing in South Carolina was always good and we seldom failed to catch them.

Fishing and dancing at the American Legion wasn't all there was to life however. My classes at Cleveland College kept me pretty busy during the week and Mil was still working five days a week at Mr. Sweet-Tree. Leesa was working at a mill on York Road, but that was temporary because she was saving for her trip to Colorado and was coordinating her plans with her friend, Linda, who was attending the University of Colorado at Boulder.

Olin Huffman's new house was completed in late November and they made plans to move out; we were just waiting on the day when we could move in.

I traded a Franchi shotgun, that had been bought from Jim Payne, for a pregnant sow, and moved her into the new pigpen and lot that Granddaddy and I had built. Steve helped me move her to her new home which wasn't an easy chore; she weighed nearly 500 pounds. We had to make sure she had food and water everyday; and then in late November we moved in.

We had to make arrangements with the base housing office at Pope Air Force Base to deliver all our household goods, and they were delivered on schedule. We had way too much stuff for the small house and would be crowded for a while, but we made out OK.

A lot of the events that occurred over the next several years are as accurate as I and the kids can remember with respect to dates and periods of time, but some of the dates are questionable. It was a fairly busy time for all our family.

Jamey was released from active duty in February 1975 and enrolled in Cleveland College soon after arriving home. He met and started dating one of our neighbors, Gail Blake and they were almost always together until they were married at Antioch Baptist Church in October 1975. They moved to Charlotte and were both working and enrolled at Central Piedmont Community College.

Leesa finally left for Colorado in May 1975. Maria was heartbroken about that and Mil didn't know quite how to handle the situation, but didn't interfere with her leaving. That was what she wanted to do.

Even so, it wasn't long before we started making plans to drive out to Colorado and try and talk her into coming home with us.

Mil had left Mr. Sweet-Tree and was working as a waitress at Kelly's Steakhouse South of Blacksburg. We were still thinking about opening up a Mexican restaurant but didn't have anything particular in mind. We knew that the market in Gastonia would be ripe for that type food but didn't make any serious moves to follow up on what we were discussing.

In late September 1975 we drove back to Colorado. We talked Steve and Joyce Lee into going with us. Our mission was clear: We were going to Boulder to bring our daughter back home.

We visited with Mrs. Rogers and all the time we were there tried to convince Leesa to return home with us. We thought we'd failed until just before we started making plans to leave when she agreed to come home with us.

The relief on Mil was apparent. She was the happiest she'd been in the past four months. We were both on an emotional high as we left Denver and once again were travelling east on I-70. Our little girl was with us, and the world looked a lot brighter. I wouldn't like to think about how depressing we would have been if we hadn't succeeded in our mission to bring her back with us.

Jamey and Gail had moved back to Kings Mountain and enrolled in Gaston College. After finishing at Gaston they moved to Boone and enrolled in Appalachian State University in September 1977. Following a year there they returned home and moved a trailer to the top of the hill above our house. Jamey took a job with the city of Kings Mountain working at the wastewater treatment plant and Gail took a job with the local newspaper. Leesa started working at the Buckeye fire extinguisher plant out in Peaceful Valley.

Although I am not sure of the date, my courses were completed at Cleveland Community College following the summer of 1976. I graduated with high honors and received my associate degree in general education.

Not long afterward I enrolled in their technical school and started classes in electrical installation. That course would take another year to complete.

It was sometime during that period of time that we found a small Italian restaurant in Gastonia that was for sale. Benn-Benn's was a well known eating place, but he wanted to move to another location and was ready to sell. It wasn't long before we came to terms with Benn-Benn and he moved to a new place on Garrison Boulevard. His Italian restaurant is still there to this day.

We immediately started remodeling the place. There were lots to be done. The entire place was infested with roaches and it took several visits by an exterminating company to get rid of them.

Daddy was a big help in getting all the carpentry done. It must have taken us well over a month to get the place looking like we wanted and about a week before we opened Bennie flew from Denver to Charlotte to give us the benefit of his experiences in the Mexican Food business.

I don't recall when our opening day came; a good estimate would be mid 1977. Pam and Bill Greenstein came down from Maryland to be with us. Mama and Daddy, the two people who had influenced us the most and were our two most eager supporters were with us, as well as most of our friends.

The business was a family affair; everyone pitched in to help get the food prepared and served. Benny was there checking everything out to his specifications and standards. We named the restaurant "Benito's" in his honor and he seemed pleased that the place carried his name. There was nothing legal drawn up, just an agreement between Bennie and us.

The opening went well. We framed the first dollar from a paying customer that just happened to be Steve and Judy Coulson.

Although the city of Gastonia was alcohol free at the time we stocked plenty of beer for certain customers. The beer was opened in the kitchen and poured into a paper cup before being served in the dining room. In addition to a wide list of Mexican food we had pizza on the menu because Benn-Benn had left several good pizza ovens with us as part of our deal with him.

Everyone worked hard over the next year or so trying to make a go of it and we did a good business, but it was hard on the whole family. We never got home before 11:00 PM; and then washed and dried all the dining room linens. Maria was the only one that escaped the pressure of operating a business dealing with the public. We were making money, but the emotional strain was creating pressure for us all and after about a year or so we considered selling out. It wasn't long before we had an offer to buy the place at a good profit and we took it. Soon we were out of the Mexican restaurant business.

Again I was faced with the need to contribute more to the family income. Mil had no problem with employment after we closed Benito's. Kelly's Steak House was glad to have her back.

Steve Coulson had left the auto sales business and had a good office management job with Guardsmark, a contract security company. He felt confident he could get me a management job with that company. The office was located in South Charlotte and that meant travelling quite a bit, but that didn't matter too much since the company furnished a car and bought the gas and oil. I filled out an application and soon the regional manager came to Charlotte to interview me and in March 1978 I went to work in the Charlotte office working for Steve.

The association would turn out to be long and profitable. I stayed with the company until May 1992 and Steve would be there even longer. He would finally retire and buy a house in north Charlotte. Mil and I are still close friends with Steve and Judy even though it has been over forty years since I first met him in Jimmy's executive restaurant while we were both on recruiting duty in Charlotte.

Not long after Benito's was sold, Leesa met Mack Rush and they were married in the fall of 1977 but were divorced less than two years later. It was during that time that she met Dick Landmesser, who would become our son-in-law and the father of two wonderful Grandsons.

Dick was a cowboy in the truest sense of the word; he had a lot of "rodeo" experience riding bucking horses and was probably one of the best at breaking and training horses anywhere in the country. The only difference between him and the "cowboys" in Wyoming was that he lived in the eastern part of the US. He still found time to return to Idaho several times to participate in a wagon train and river crossing, reliving pioneer and western cowboy days. His whole adult life has centered around horses. As I write this journal his reputation as a "horse dentist" is well known in most of the eastern US.

Another whole book could be written about the most joyous period of our life over the next twenty-two years watching our two Grandsons grow into the outstanding young men they have become. Much more will have to be written on that later; I am getting way ahead of where I need to be with this journal.

During the time immediately following Benito's, Jamey was working with the city of Kings Mountain and Gail was a substitute teacher. They were keeping house in a trailer on the hill a few hundred yards above our house. Maria had graduated from high school in 1979 and attended Gaston College from September 1979 till June 1981 and that September enrolled at Appalachian State University. Leesa moved to Alpharetta, Georgia in July 1980. She did that so she could be close to Dick and work full time with horses.

Now the horses in her life were Arabians. She took Patchy with her and in January 1981 he died of some kind of intestinal problem. We weren't there with her, but I know she had to be an emotional wreck for a while. We all loved Patchy, but she was much closer to him than anyone else. There was nothing we could do but sympathize with her.

After a year at Appalachian State University Maria followed her to Alpharetta and worked at Pike's nursery in Atlanta. While there she met the guy who was to be her husband and they were married at Chestnut Ridge Baptist Church on December 31st, 1982.

Jamey and Gail presented us with our first grandchild in December 1980. We were there when they rolled her out into the nursery; we were both on an emotional high when we looked at her. She was the most beautiful baby we had seen since Maria had been born nineteen years earlier. We were so happy; all I could do was stand there speechless and try and control my emotions. It was a wonderful occasion for us; one neither of us will ever forget.

Gail was having some difficulty and had developed gestational diabetes, but within a few days she and our new Granddaughter, Holly Jai, came home. Not only did we have a new Granddaughter, but she lived within a short walking distance and we could see and hold her everyday. Life was very good. We were blessed beyond anything we had asked for.

Within a short period of time my "Mil" became "Nanny" and that's the way it's been ever since. That sweet young lady that I had fell so hard for was now a "Grandma," but a hundred grand children wouldn't interfere with that love affair; in fact Holly's arrival brought our family closer to each other. A new era was beginning to shape our lives.

We were now grandparents and we took that to mean new responsibilities. Baby sitting with Holly was a joy. I was still away most of the time taking care of accounts all over the state and Nanny was still at Kelly's steak house, but we had the weekends to have everyone here for Sunday dinner with the whole family whenever we could coax the girls home from Georgia. And when that didn't work we would drive to Georgia to be with them.

During those years many events occurred that could be considered remarkable enough to be included in this journal, for example, Mama's heart condition worsened and Daddy had a stroke that first seemed to leave him with several complications including partial paralysis, but after several days in the hospital he recovered fully.

During that same period Grandma Roper was spending more and more time with us. She didn't want to stay at home alone so she would spend a week with us then go and spend a week with the others. That way she would never be alone and all her kids would get to spend time with her.

The Guardsmark office in Charlotte was taking on new accounts and as a result the workload increased to the point that it became difficult for us to effectively manage each account. Steve received word from corporate that we could hire another manager, and he contacted Paul Sheppard, a good friend who lived in Kings Mountain; a former Green Beret with the army's special forces. Before long he was on board and immediately relieved some of the pressure. Paul had spent several tours of duty in Vietnam with Walt Shumate; there they were assigned to the Studies and Observation Group and other "A Team" assignments. He had retired from the army several years earlier and was from the same mold as Steve and their mutual friend Walt Shumate. Our regional manager Ed DiGilio was of the same stripe. He was with the army pathfinders and had jumped into Normandy several hours in advance of the main airborne assault troops on D-Day. Because he was a member of that small elite group the French Government has invited him back to Normandy every year on June 6th to participate in the ceremonies celebrating that event and honoring those who fell that day in 1944.

Time seemed to be moving a lot faster for us and was taking its toll on the health of Mama and Daddy as well as Grandma Roper. Grandma's hearing was very bad; she wore hearing aids in both ears and everything still had to be repeated several times for her. Mama had another episode with her heart and was hospitalized for a week or so before the doctor allowed her to go home. The weeks and months, and even years, were rolling by in a big hurry and we were caught up in a routine, but it was a period that we can now look back to remember as some of the best years of our lives.

From left to right: Steve Coulson, Jake McFee, Jim Payne, and the author during a party being held at the "Sleepy Cat II".

The author and Lafayette at a hunting camp in Wyoming.

Walt Shumate on the left and Paul Sheppard on the right during one of their tours in Vietnam while assigned to Delta Project.

CHAPTER 34

Growing Old Gracefully
Dec 1980–2001

During the years preceding the arrival of Holly Jai we were very busy trying to build our home into what we wanted it to be. We hired a local building contractor to build a new kitchen and Daddy helped me build a back porch and utility room.

The sow delivered sixteen little white pigs on New Year's eve; we were living it up at a New Years Eve party that Nanny's brother Don had invited us to; and for some reason or another we came home to look for something and checked on the sow. Little pigs were everywhere and the weather was nasty; it was sleeting and very cold; and we were worried the little pigs would freeze.

But Mother Nature has a way of taking care of things and they all survived.

However there was one little pig that had fell through the fence and was laying outside and away from the others; it was cold and almost lifeless, so we brought it to the house to be taken care of and warmed up. When we took it back to the hog lot the sow wouldn't care for it and kept shoving it away.

We caught it again and brought it back to the house. We fed it with a baby bottle and it got along just fine.

We had another house pet on our hands. The rest of the litter were thriving on their mother's milk and pretty soon little pigs were running all over the place, rooting up everything. The girls named our little pet "Sunshine" and as her little brothers and sisters began roaming around all over the place they eventually made it to our back yard.

Sunshine was pure white and stayed clean; however the others were dirty little things; consequently Sunshine wouldn't have anything to do with her dirty little kin. She was too uppity to associate with them. Eventually as she grew bigger and bigger we had to make a decision about her. We couldn't keep her in the house any longer and sold her to one of Ted Huffman's boys.

Most of the other little pigs were sold as they grew big enough to make it on their own. By that time half the fields and woods had been rooted up. We raised two of them for meat and another we saved for a bar-b-q we planned to have in late spring; and another one was raffled off at Jake's place on N. Tryon Street.

As soon as the little pigs were independent of their Mother we traded her to a local livestock dealer for a steer that had already been processed. That gave us enough beef in the freezer to last for several years.

The tractor I bought from Olin's brother was giving me some problems, so I traded it for a Ford tractor that came with several implements. I had a gig plow, a disc, and bush-hog and now could break up and plow a good sized piece of land for a garden in a short time.

The first summer at our new place we grew enough green beans to can over a hundred quarts. We could've put up another hundred but we ate a lot and gave some to everyone around who wanted them. Grandma Roper and Mama seemed to enjoy sitting down and breaking beans for canning. We grew other vegetables as well and put up lots of vegetable soup base made with home grown corn, tomatoes, and okra.

By the time cold weather came for the second time we had constructed a root cellar back in a hillside that would hold all the canned vegetables we would need. We took the hogs to be processed and had enough salt pork to last for a long time. We cured a couple hams and side meat also. We canned a big tub of sausage by cooking it in the oven and putting it in sealed jars; just as they did back in the mountains years ago. We planted some apple trees and grape vines and even bought four bee hives and set them in the edge of the woods. We were almost ready to be self sustaining.

After Maria married they moved several times when his job as a shoe salesman dictated. They lived in Kings Mountain for a while during the latter half of 1983 and eventually moved back to Georgia; then they were in Ft. Lauderdale, Florida during the early part of 1985.

Leesa and Maria had always been as close as two sisters could be and we can only assume that the reason Maria left Appalachian State University to live in Georgia was to be close to her sister. Regardless, she and her husband were back in Georgia when Dick and Leesa were married in April 1984, and in December of that year Leesa gave birth to our first grandson.

Dick called us to let us know Leesa had been taken to the hospital and we left for Georgia as soon as I tied up some loose ends at work. They had already made plans for Nanny to stay with Leesa for a while after her baby was born. Her bag was packed and ready before I could get home from the office.

Seeing our first grandson for the first time was another emotional high. The feeling is hard to put on paper, but is one of the most profound and intense experiences imaginable. There was an immediate and unbreakable connection when we first saw him. Nanny was glowing; she couldn't wait to get her hands on him.

Our second granddaughter, Morgan was born in March of 1986. They were still in Georgia and we were there when she was born. She was the most beautiful little girl we had ever seen and Maria was the most loving and devoted parent, but divorce and an ugly custody battle over this sweet little girl loomed in the future.

As it had been with Holly and Rick, there was an immediate bond between us and our new Granddaughter. The pride that comes with being new grand parents couldn't be denied.

Maria's husband was overly protective and a doting father but was lacking in some of the most fundamental and important roles. He was a complete failure as a husband and provider for his family. Maria, on the other hand made every effort to be the perfect Mother and wife; her devotion to Morgan was near the level of worship and was evident in everything she did or said.

To dwell further on this subject now wouldn't serve any useful purpose; so that is all that needs to be written about the man and his outlook on the rest of society. Hopefully, I can tactfully write about the details at the right time further into this journal. Nevertheless the sweet little girl would become a victim of adult shortcomings.

After going to work with Steve in March 1978 I had very little excess time to spend at home, as had been the case when I was attending classes at Cleveland College.

My duties primarily involved the management of established accounts from Waynesville in the mountains to Rocky Mount and Fayetteville in the eastern part of North Carolina, and that meant being away overnight at least once or twice a week. It wasn't unusual to spend fifty or sixty hours a week on the job. The pay was good and the job very interesting; I thoroughly enjoyed it most of the time. Sometime during 1986 I was made Special Assignments Manager for Guardsmark.The company had offices in every major city in the USA and some offices in "not so major" cities. The position of "Special Assignments Manager" had been created for me in order for Guardsmark to have a flexible "gunslinger" ready to travel anywhere in the country on short notice. The new position required that I be available to travel anytime, anywhere, and be away for weeks at a time.

Over the next seven years I would spend time in almost every city of any size in the country. One week I would be in San Jose, California, and the next in Boston or Dallas.

On several occasions, when time would allow, I drove to the problem area and took Nanny with me. One time we went to Omaha and another time to Fort Lauderdale.

Anywhere the company was experiencing problems with a client, opening a new account, or having to hire a group of people to overcome a labor dispute would require my presence.

I reported to the company vice president and worked directly with him many times because where there were major problems, he would be there also. He was considered the corporate gunslinger. He had retired from the Army sometime in the early 1960s and had been with Guardsmark since that time. He was more than the man I worked for; he was also a good friend.

My last assignment was in Los Angeles following the acquittal of the four policemen that had been seen on video beating up on Rodney King. I returned home from that assignment and turned in my resignation. I had been spending too much time away from "Nanny" and the rest of my family.

Two weeks later my friend, the VP, resigned also. He had been with the company thirty years when he resigned. I never knew his reason; it may have been because of a health problem no one knew about, because within a year he was hospitalized and passed away.

It would be next to impossible to detail all the events that occurred between the time we moved to our little corner of paradise in 1974, to the present; the events noted are only the highlights such as important incidents within the family.

Sometime during that period Steve Coulson's black Labrador Retriever had a litter of little black puppies. He watched as they were being born and every time a new one would pop out, he'd call and report that another one had been born. He promised that we could have our pick as soon as they were old enough.

Nanny picked the one she wanted and we brought her home. We named her "Wakeen" and registered her with the AKC. It wasn't long before we knew we had a very special little pet.

From the very first she never did any nasty business in the house, but in the yard; then as she grew she wouldn't even do her business in the yard, but went out into the woods. She was quick to learn, and it seemed as she was growing and learning there was nothing she couldn't learn to do.

When I went to get the mail she was eager to help me bring it to the house; and it only took one trip to teach her to stay behind an invisible line about thirty or forty feet from the road. After I told her to sit and stay she wouldn't cross that line.

She was very sensitive to our moods and would react nervously and knew something was wrong if Nanny or I had the slightest disagreement. She would lay her head on my knee and look up as if to say, "everything will be alright." She could even forecast an approaching storm. She was afraid of thunderstorms and would hide in the bathroom whenever one came near us. At the slightest sound of thunder in the distance she would have already started acting nervous and scared; we knew from her behavior that a storm was somewhere near and coming our way. She was a natural retriever and was never happier then when she could do something for Nanny or me.

The first time I took her dove hunting she knew what her role would be. We were hunting off the side of a road and over a soybean field; the first time I shot she looked up at me with a question "did you get it, can I please go get it for you." When I gave her the signal to "bring", off she went and not a feather had been ruffled when she brought the dove back to me. She presented it to me and sat down wagging her tail looking out over the soybean field, then looked up at me in anticipation of bringing another one in.

We lost her one night while I was away on the job in Raleigh. Jamey and our neighbor Jim Wilson buried her on the hill above our house. She was with us nearly fourteen years and we loved her as one of our own.

We haven't owned a dog since; we have had several dropped off on us, but there'll never be another Wakeen. During that time we also lost Chopper and Chiquita. We had to take them both to the vet to be put down. Chopper was with us over sixteen years; he was Leesa's and only Leesa's. There never has been a tougher little dog than he was. He was a scrapper from the time he was a little puppy until he died, and would take on any other dog, no matter how big.

Chiquita, on the other hand, was a meek little lady and her loyalty was to Nanny. We all missed her, but Nanny had a hard time for a long time after we had to put her down.

The reason we came back to Kings Mountain following retirement from the air force was to be near our folks, especially my Mom and Dad. She had already experienced a severe heart attack before we came home. Daddy cared for her, but he too was getting older and no one knew how long his health would last, so we made the decision to retire close to them and to be near Nanny's folks also. We hadn't been home very long before she had another minor episode with her heart and had to be hospitalized for a few days, and then just before Christmas in 1982 she was hospitalized again with a heart attack; this time she didn't survive. The doctor placed a pacemaker near her heart but it did no good.

I was in Charlotte at the office when they called me and told me I should come home as soon as possible, but by the time I got to the hospital she was gone. It was some comfort to know that her last years were happy ones. She always got a lot of enjoyment coming to our place and helping Nanny with the vegetables. Most importantly though was the knowledge that she was a Saint in this life and died a Christian. And I know that any goodness I may have in my life can be attributed to the many hours she spent on her knees on my behalf.

I have always remembered the first letter I received from her after being sent to Korea in late 1951 that simply said "God be with you till we meet again", that was all. She must have felt I was in some kind of danger.

She passed away just a few days before Christmas and her presents to all of us were already wrapped; the present she put under the tree for me was a bible.

Daddy was alone and spent a lot of time with us; he was sure to be here for Sunday dinner after he went to Church. He sold a lot of stuff and put his house on the market in preparation to move into a low maintenance apartment where there wouldn't be any grass to cut.

Over the next eleven years while he lived alone Nanny was always there for him. She cleaned his apartment, changed his sheets and even went shopping for him when he needed anything. She was his chauffeur when he needed to go to the doctor or the grocery store. Since I was gone a lot she was the only one there to help him.

She loved him and cared for him just as she would for her own Father; and she was a big comfort and blessing to him through his last years. He was quick to tell me what a wonderful girl I had chosen to live my life with. He loved her as his own daughter.

He started going to the senior center for lunch on weekdays and seemed to enjoy that a lot. In fact, he would go early and help set up tables or do other chores. After Mama died he was never really contented; he didn't really want to live in a world without her. He expressed that feeling to me on several occasions. Through it all he never lost sight of his Christian faith and lived a Godly life even though we knew that inside he wasn't a happy man.

Every night he would call and say "well, it's my bedtime." We knew then he was in for the night and would be all right.

The senior center at the time was located in the old Kings Mountain railway depot and most of his friends gathered there for lunch. One of the ladies knew he liked sweets and every week or so would bake him a cake. Even in his sadness, the times spent with them were good times.

It wasn't long after Mama passed away that Jamey and Gail bought a house in the Linwood section of Kings Mountain and moved the trailer away from the hill. Up to this time Nanny had helped care for Holly almost from the time she was born. The big maple trees that now stand by our drive were barely big enough to provide enough shade to cover her as she lay on a blanket in the grass while Nanny watched over her. Gail had changed jobs several times but was still on call as a substitute teacher and Jamey was still with the city of Kings Mountain.

Since Leesa and Maria both were still in Georgia with their babies we made lots of trips to Atlanta.

Then within a few months of Morgan's birth, Leesa gave us another little boy. We just happened to be there when he was born because Benny and Violet Espinosa had flown from Denver to pay us a visit and we drove down to Alpharetta to see Leesa.

Again, it was the same wonderful experience it had been with Holly, Rick and Morgan. The very first time I saw Travis I knew he was something special. My comment at the time was "this little guy is going to make his mark someday, and I don't mean anything ordinary, but very special; something remarkable." As this journal is being written I still believe that as he enters his senior year in College. Nanny fell in love all over again; the smile on her face was undeniable as she held him for the first time.

Not very long after Travis was born Dick and Leesa moved from Georgia to Asheville where Dick had a job in sales, but their love of horses coupled with other economic factors prompted them to move to Nickerson Farms north of Greensboro while Travis was still a toddler. It was a long drive to Nickerson Farms, but we couldn't stay away from those two little boys. And it was the same with Morgan; we were in Georgia probably more often than Nickerson Farms.

I was still with Guardsmark, but had more off duty time after 1986 while sitting at home waiting for an assignment. That suited Nanny because we had more time to see all our grandchildren.

During the years following our return home, most of the old buddies and I were still going out to Wyoming or Colorado every fall to get a bigger mule deer than we already had. New people fell in with us; Bob Ramsey and Wayne Russell to name a couple, although neither of them went to hunt; they were there for the camping and trout fishing. Some of Jim Payne's golfing buddies from Pine Island made the trip several times. John Hamm was there every year.

I don't know of anyone who loved to catch a trout more than John. Neither have I ever met anyone who was better at catching trout than he. He always looked forward to September and our annual drive to Wyoming or Western Colorado. An entire book could be written about our adventures "out west" from the mid 1970s to the early 1990s.

Our friendship would have continued on except for John's tragic ending. His wife had left him a year or so earlier and in January 1991 he was driving west on I-40 between Asheville and Knoxville. It was a rainy, nasty winter night; his truck left the road and off a high bank into the Pigeon River.

Apparently John was thrown from the vehicle, and according to the authorities, he probably lasted several hours; he may have even survived if the accident had been seen or discovered right away. The accident happened on Friday evening and wasn't discovered until the following Tuesday.

John and I had been the best of friends for seventeen years and losing him was like losing a brother. It was hard for me to accept and I felt his absence for a long time. Over sixteen years have gone by since his accident and I still feel a great emptiness when I think about the adventures we had together.

Even without John, our trips to Colorado or Wyoming continued to be an annual event; the people changed from year to year with the exception of Jim Payne and myself. Lafayette, who had started the adventure with me a long time ago, seldom went with us anymore. The last time he was there we were caught high in the mountains in a heavy snowstorm and barely escaped with most of our equipment. We made the mistake of setting up camp nearly ten thousand feet high and late enough in the year to have heavy snowfall in the Rockies. We should have known a heavy snowstorm could happen anytime.

The opening day of elk season was on Saturday and when we bedded down on Friday evening there was only a sprinkling of snow on the ground. Jim Payne and I were in the small two-man Coleman tent and the rest were in the big outfitter's tent. We were asleep in our warm sleeping bags and never realized the heavy snow was falling. By five A.M. Saturday morning the snow was twenty inches deep and still falling. It took us all day to work our way out a distance of four miles to a decent road. We were lucky we made it out at all. I only had two chains for my tires, and Jim Payne didn't have any on his Blazer. We were breaking a trail with my truck and Jim was following me in the Blazer. Jake McFee was riding an ATV a short distance behind the Blazer, and by the time we reached a decent road he was frozen and looked like Hatchet Jack in the Jeremiah Johnson movie. Icicles were hanging from his eyebrows and his beard was clogged and frozen by the blowing snow; his rain suit was frozen so stiff he couldn't bend his knees or elbows.

Needless to say we didn't get an elk or mule deer that year. That same year Chuck Winters and his crew who were hunting near Yellow Jacket Pass, not too far from where we were camped, bagged four nice bull elk.

The years seemed to roll by. Before we knew it the 80s had come and gone. We had become active in the local Shrine Club after I went through the Scottish Rite and the Oasis Shrine Temple. Jamey had been made a Mason and was a member of Fairview Lodge in Kings Mountain; and later he also went into the Shrine following the degrees in the Scottish Rites.

We were becoming more active in our Church. Nanny had joined the East Gold Street Wesleyan Church and in the mid eighties I went with her on occasion, but wasn't a regular and hadn't joined officially. I knew there were a lot of good people there and enjoyed attending services with them.

One saintly lady, Ollie Wheeler was after me; she told me once that if I would ever attend at least three consecutive services I would be caught. She was right. Sometime near the mid or late eighties I was converted to a Wesleyan and we have been active members since. We were both baptized again the day before Valentine's day 2000, and I joined the Church in May of that year. Since that time we have been committed to the East Gold St. Church and enjoy the services and people very much.

The activities there are many and varied, but everything they do is directed toward serving the Father and advancing

His Kingdom. East Gold Street is where we met two of our dearest friends, Pastor Hoover Smith and his wife Rose.

He has retired from the ministry but still conducts services somewhere in the local district nearly every week. He and Rose are a joy to listen to and to socialize with. We still maintain close contact with them. While we were still able to play the game we played golf at all the local courses and I don't know anyone who thoroughly enjoyed the game as much as we did

Holly was growing into a beautiful young lady. Jamey and Gail sold their house on Linwood Road and bought a new house in a sub-division in Grover. He had left the city of Kings Mountain and was made the Utilities Dept. supervisor in Gastonia. Maria and her husband were still in Georgia trying to make a go of a small florist business, but his ineptness insured failure of that venture. After going through an inheritance they finally left Georgia and moved to Shelby, leaving a trail of creditors on their back. Maria was almost a mental case as he tried again to operate a small business dealing in potted plants and flowers. After that failed he started to work in computer sales in Charlotte. They rented a small but adequate house in Blacksburg in 1992 and sometime during the next year bought a pretty little house on Pine Street in Blacksburg.

Even though he had a good job in Charlotte they were still having major problems. Morgan was still the light of their lives, but their financial difficulties coupled with his attempts to alienate Morgan against her mother resulted in a separation that finally ended in divorce in 1995.

A nasty custody battle with the final judgement that ended up in Maria's favor followed the divorce. She was given complete custody of Morgan, however because of the brainwashing from her Father, she preferred being with him; and eventually Maria conceded to allow her to live with him.

In time she gave up legal custody in order to please Morgan and as time went by, contact with her was completely broken. Nothing has been heard from her for years, and as I write this she will be twenty-one years old.

I have believed through the years that some day she will realize her mistake and will make contact with Maria and beg her forgiveness. I don't believe a single day has passed since Morgan left with her Father that Nanny hasn't said a prayer for her well being.

Leesa and her family moved from Nickerson Farms to Shelby for a short while and in 1989 moved their trailer on the hill at the same spot Jamey and Gail had lived earlier.

It was a wonderful occasion for Nanny and me. Our two little boys were living within a few hundred yards from our house. Rick was only four years old and Travis was barely three. Dick was busy establishing his business as a horse dentist and was gone quite a bit. To the best of my recollection Nanny and Leesa both were working at Kelly's steak house in Blacksburg.

We spent a lot of time with the boys; and to make life even sweeter, Holly was never far away either. Gail was awfully good about bringing her to see us and spend time with us. And for a few good years Maria and Morgan were here quite often.

Nanny planned countless family dinners and cookouts in order for the entire family to be together. She didn't need a holiday or birthday to plan a family get-together. She was as happy as a Nanny could be, and it was a pure joy for me to see her with our little ones. It was like having a family all over again. We were blessed far beyond anyone else that we knew.

Then in September 1992 my oldest sister passed away. Her death was completely unexpected. She hadn't had any serious health problems and woke up one morning complaining that she didn't feel very good. Bill went to the kitchen to make coffee and when he returned to the bedroom she was gone.

We left right away and drove to Brownsville. We had expected Faye to be the first to go because several years earlier she had been diagnosed with pancreatic cancer. Her life expectancy then had been three to six months. Two years later she was still alive and responding to treatment. We had been to Bolivar several times to see her. The trip to Brownsville was uneventful and we arrived in time for the funeral. Daddy was already in poor health and couldn't make the trip; he might have been able to make it by air but absolutely refused to consider flying. We stayed a couple days following the funeral and drove back home.

Little did we know at the time, but within eleven months both Faye and Daddy would be gone. Daddy had been admitted to the hospital a few days earlier for observation and early one morning I received a call from his doctor advising me to come to the hospital.

He was gone even before they called and doctor Durham was waiting for me. He explained that Daddy had a severe heart attack and nothing could be done to save him.

That was in May 1993 and on the first day of August, less than three months later, Faye died. She fought the cancer much longer than the medical people had predicted, but eventually the cancer spread to her vital organs and was attacking her brain; she even made the trip to Daddy's funeral but was in a lot of pain throughout the long trip from Bolivar to Kings Mountain. She was a very brave person right to the end. She was only 58 years old when she died. In less than a year my whole family had been taken from me.

In May 1992 I resigned from Guardsmark and was fully retired. The boys were growing up and it was some of the best years of our lives watching them go through each phase of their young lives.

And in 1995 Jamey and Gail moved a double wide next door bringing Holly with them. She would be starting her first year in high school at Blacksburg and the boys were attending elementary school there.

In the fall of 1997 Maria was married to Mike Painter and they set up housekeeping in Gaffney. At about the same time Jamey and Gail were divorced. There weren't any bad feelings and no custody problems because Holly was already a teenager and decided to stay with her Dad. Gail has since been remarried, but Jamey has remained single through the years.

Our joy as grandparents was made complete on June 15th, 1998 when Maria gave birth to the most wonderful bundle of joy. Little Mikey Painter made his way into our family and has given us more happiness than we could ever have hoped for.

Maria could finally be happy again; little Mikey seemed to partially fill the void and instantly became the center of our universe.

There was no way, however, that he could replace our two little guys on the hill. They were growing up fast; Rick was already a teenager when Mikey was born and Travis was never far behind him.

Rick was into little league baseball and was fast becoming a star in that sport. Holly had graduated from high school when Mikey arrived and was enrolled at Cleveland Community College to start the fall semester. And just about the time Mikey was born Leesa graduated from Respiratory Therapist school and it wasn't long before she was working at Gaston Memorial Hospital.

You may think from the way these writings have been presented that our love has been more for our grandchildren than for our own son and daughters. I can't deny that, neither can I confirm it. It has been said that parents love their children, but worship their grandchildren.

There is no such thing as "greater" love than that love a parent has for their children, and the same can be said for their grandchildren. And, if sometime in the future we may live long enough to have a great-grandchild, we will still have enough room in our heart to care for it just as much as we did the first time we saw our first baby.

Grandma Roper gave birth to eleven children. They all lived to present her and Grandpa with grandchildren. Then in 1994 they lost Lorena. She had suffered with arthritis for a long time and had been hospitalized with some kind of intestinal problem when she passed away.

Not having Lorena anymore was hard for Nanny to take. Until she passed away all eleven of Grandma and Grandpa's children were alive and healthy.

The turn of the century and a new millenium was fast approaching. Nanny and I were beginning to feel the first pangs of being old; more physical problems were starting to pop up; arthritic pains were telling us that the joints weren't bending as easily as in years past. Visits to the doctor were happening more often.

The news reports were telling us we might have big problems when the 20th century came to and end and all the computers in the world would go haywire trying to figure out what the date was because they hadn't factored in the new 2000 dates.

Y2K was the watchword. However the new century arrived and all the computers made the necessary changes. A catastrophic event had been successfully avoided.

Bill Clinton had been elected President in the elections held in November 1992 and re-elected in 1996. His liberal agenda and "politically correct" persuasions were creating problems for the US that we would feel for many years to come. His weakness on national defense and his admitted "loathing" for the military allowed the "American haters" in the world to prepare for bold moves against us.

The Islamic radicals were plotting and making preparations to carry out their scheme to kill Americans. Bombings by Islamic suicide squads were already at work striking several American embassies in the Middle East.

Nanny and I were travelling when they struck our country. We had left home and spent some time in Brownsville, Texas with Judy and Robin DeHart and her family; and after leaving there we continued to travel west along the Rio Grande valley.

On the evening of September 10th 2001 we checked into a motel in Benson, Arizona. We planned to visit Tombstone and cross over into Mexico at Nogales the next day.

We were up early and I was in the bathroom shaving when Nanny turned the television on to the news channel. She called me in to see one of the towers of the world trade center burning near the top floors. The announcers didn't realize the significance of what we were witnessing; then as we were watching, an aircraft came into view and turned directly into the second tower.

It was then that a series of events took place that changed the lives of all Americans and many more people around the world. We would soon learn new words such as "al qaeda", and new names such as "Usama-bin-laden.

The author's family. Back row standing from left to right: Gail and Jamey.
Middle row standing from left to right: Nanny, Leesa, Holly, Maria, the author, and Mike.
Front row standing: Morgan
Front row kneeling from left to right: Travis and Rick.

Nanny's Mom and Dad; Grandma And Grandpa Roper.

CHAPTER 35

The 21st Century 2001–2007

Nine-eleven was unthinkable. Our country had been attacked, and the events of that day should have been an eye opener for every citizen. That wasn't the case, even though everyone was outraged, it didn't take long for the bleeding hearts to go so far as to accuse someone in the White House of plotting and planning the attack on the twin towers and the Pentagon. That's how far left some of the extremist are in our country.

The fight against radical Islam was on, but we weren't doing enough, or so I thought. The terrorists could capture or kidnap one of ours, saw their heads off and produce a video of the act. We, on the other hand were being criticized for bringing prisoners to Cuba for interrogation. Our military were busy, not only in Afghanistan, but also in Iraq.

The liberal news media were reporting all the bad things and even caused charges to be brought against some of our military for killing Iraqi citizens. A lot of things had changed since Korea and Vietnam.

In my opinion, our leaders are way too soft on the Muslim world. Those people have vowed to kill Americans anyway they can, they teach their young children in school that America is "Satan" and all Americans are to be hated. They grow up with a hatred of America and Israel that is so intense they are willing to strap a bomb on their young bodies and go off on a suicide mission.

And as hard as it is for me to understand, a mother is not only willing, but eager to send their little boy or girl off on a suicide mission. They hate the Jewish people as much or maybe even more than they hate us.

We should use all the resources we have to take them out without regard to "collateral damage," or the possibility that innocent people may be killed. There were over three thousand "innocent people", all non-combatants, many of them women and children, in the twin towers of the World Trade Center. The crazies that flew those commercial airplanes into the buildings were aware of that fact, but didn't give a radical hoot about those non combatants they were about to kill.

Our leaders are too concerned with world opinion to mount a serious effort to go after Bin-Laden and too involved with their own re-election than to do the right thing for our country.

That morning in Benson, Arizona Nanny and I were glued to the TV until checkout time. Our plans for the day were to go to Tombstone, and around 11:00 A.M. We drove south and spent the rest of the day there.

We watched the reenactment of the "gunfight at OK corral," and had our picture made with the "Earp" boys; and one of the saloon gals gave me a kiss. We didn't have much to say to the "Clanton gang"; they were the bad guys.

A bad storm came up in the afternoon with some heavy rain and hail. The truck had some dents from the hail, but nothing of any consequence. We drove back to Tucson and checked into another motel.

The next day we went across the border at Nogales and did a little shopping, then back to Tucson to spend another night before touring the aircraft graveyard at Davis-Monthan Air Force Base and the Pima Aircraft Museum near Tucson.

One of the airplanes there was the DC-7 where Lyndon Johnson took his oath as President following the assassination of President Kennedy. There were lots of interesting airplanes at the museum including a KB-50 just like the one that Jack Callahan was flying when it went down over Hokkaido, Japan in 1964.

When we checked out the next day we went to see "Old Tucson" where a lot of western movies were filmed. We had no trouble finding it, but everything was closed up because of a fire.

We continued north through Phoenix and Prescott; our destination for the day was Sedona where we had dinner with Maria's friend, Elana.

We checked into a motel in Sedona and watched TV trying to get some information about the effects of the World Trade Center attack. Rumors were flying that the price of gasoline had increased to over $5.00 a gallon.

Because of that rumor we were making alternate plans to turn east when we reached I-40 at Flagstaff and make a run for home. Rumors were that fuel shortages were already occurring in the central US.

Our original plans were to turn north to the four-corners, and continue north from there, traveling through Utah to I-70 north of Moab and on to Grand Junction and Meeker, Colorado. We planned to set up a tent and camp at Meadow Lake and do some trout fishing for a few days before starting home.

After reaching Flagstaff I topped the fuel tanks off before calling AAA in Charlotte to get information about the fuel situation. The people at AAA told me that there had been some instances of price gouging, but that anyone caught doing that would be prosecuted. They assured me that fuel reserves were adequate and supplies throughout the country were enough to handle everyone's needs.

The reports that big price increases for gasoline just weren't true according to the people at AAA. The decision was made to continue with our original plan.

Travel through Arizona was more or less uneventful except for the hot weather. Phoenix must have been over a hundred degrees and the duel lane highway from there to Sedona was being re-surfaced in several places. Traffic was one way and we were stopped on the hot highway more than once and had to shut the engine down. The heat was almost unbearable. We couldn't take a chance that the engine might overheat; but we had plenty of ice and cold drinks in the cooler and made out ok until we were underway again.

By the time we were north of four-corners the blistering hot weather had cooled down somewhat. We stopped by the visitor center at Monument Valley and toured Canyon De Chelly National Park before reaching Blanding, Utah, where we spent the night.

The next day we continued north thru Moab and toured Arches National Park before continuing on to Meeker. We had no trouble finding fuel, and prices were about the same as they were before 9-11. We picked up the groceries we would need in camp for a few days and after checking out of the motel at Meeker we headed up to Meadow Lake.

The weather was perfect, sunny and warm. We set up camp at the campground near Meadow Lake and were confident that we would sleep well on a double bed made by tying two GI folding cots together with a think foam mattress. I couldn't wait to get a hook in the water and catch enough pretty rainbows for supper.

There were several other campers near us the first day, but everyone except the caretaker and a group of guys from Oklahoma that were set up across from our camp site, left the next day.

I had little trouble catching enough rainbows and a few brook trout for us to eat while we were there.

The next evening I went to the lake with the guys from Oklahoma and we were there fishing for more rainbow until after dark. Nanny had been left alone in the campground and when we got back we found her sitting by the campfire with a pistol in her hand.

Although we had never seen any bears near Meadow Lake, she didn't take any chances on one coming into our camp.

The guys from Oklahoma had been Kokanee Salmon fishing before coming to Meadow Lake and gave us a couple packs of filleted Salmon. We enjoyed the camping and plans were to stay four nights, but after three nights we woke up to an incoming snowstorm.

The guys from Oklahoma were packed up and leaving and the caretaker had already broken camp and left the day before. We cancelled plans to stay another night and started breaking camp ourselves. Within a couple hours everything was loaded onto the back of the truck and we followed the last of the campers out to the main road.

We passed the campsite where we had been almost snowed in several years before on an elk and mule deer hunting trip, and by the time we reached the main road, only four miles from Meadow Lake, the snow had stopped. We made our way down off the mountain and spent the night in Meeker.

The next morning we made it to I-70 at Rifle, turned east and were home several days later.

To date, that was our last adventure camping but we have been back several times since. The next year we rented a cabin at the Sleepy Cat Guest Ranch and met Mary and Lafayette in Meeker after going through Deadwood, SD and Yellowstone National Park. From Yellowstone we went south through Flaming Gorge, Utah before making our way to Meeker. We were in the cabin four nights and ate fresh caught rainbow trout every night for supper.

Several years before 9-11 we had another camping adventure at Henry's Fork Lake that was located near West Yellowstone and the famous Madison River; one of the best trout streams in the country.

Prior to camping at Henry's Fork we spent some time in Las Vegas and then traveled north through Oregon and Idaho. We tried to go through Hell's Canyon, but forest fires were burning all around the area and we had a change of plans. We spent several days in New Meadows, Idaho before moving on to Henry's Fork.

We have been fortunate to be able to travel and tour around our great country and have visited a lot of our historical points of interest. We've toured the battleground where Custer made his last stand at the Little Big Horn in Montana; we've toured Zion National Park, Brice Canyon, Arches National Park, Monument Valley, and Four Corners, Utah to mention a few.

We've also seen a lot of the west's historical towns and places such as Fort Sumner, NM where Billy the Kid was made famous, the Corn Palace in Mitchell SD, the saloon in Deadwood where Wild Bill Hickok was shot and killed, including his and Calamity Jane's grave site near Deadwood. We've toured numerous museums including Buffalo Bill's museum in Cody, Wyoming, the Charles Russell museum in Great Falls, Montana; and the Cowboy Hall of Fame museum in Oklahoma City, Oklahoma.

The list could go on and on, the point being that Nanny and I have been blessed beyond any of our expectations when we were starting out with our lives together nearly 55 years ago.

Our adventures traveling the country together are just a small part of the wondrous life we've shared, but this journal wouldn't have been complete without mentioning some of our adventures touring the Western United States; not to mention the years we spent near Paris at Camp Des Loges, and Yokota Air Base near Tokyo.

As this is being written it has just been a year ago that we followed the Lewis and Clark Trail from St. Louis to Astoria, Oregon where they spent their second winter near the Pacific Ocean. We followed the Missouri River up the route they took through Nebraska and the Dakotas and into Montana and Idaho and eventually to the Columbia River.

We saw the rock at Pompey's Pillow on the Yellowstone River where Clark carved his name into a rock overlooking the river, and a replica of the fort they built at Mandan, North Dakota where they spent their first winter.

We timed our trip to coincide with the 200th anniversary of the completion of their expedition in 1806. The Lewis and Clark expedition was an important chapter in the history of the United States and was valuable in the development of our country west of the Mississippi River, especially the Northwest.

Since returning from our tour of the Lewis and Clark Trail, I have made it a point, whenever the opportunity was there, to ask young high school or college students just what they knew of Lewis and Clark. And I asked if they studied or were even told of Lewis and Clark in any of their high school classes.

The information they gave me was very disappointing, and based on their response, I don't believe American History is even being taught in our high schools anymore.

In that same vein, not too long ago a young lady from a home health service came to demonstrate a device for use in our home. She was a professional and had a degree in nursing. As we were talking, I asked her if she knew how many stars were in our flag. She didn't know and wouldn't even try a guess. She seemed offended that I would ask the question at all.

You may ask, “why bring that up?,” that has nothing to do with a journal of an autobiographical nature. I don’t know why it was brought up, it just seemed appropriate to me; and I was simply trying to reinforce the fact that American history is not being taught to our young people anymore. That upsets me.

Our gardening days were about over as we raced through the early years of the 21st century. We tried, but were limited to a small area close to the house; the hill seemed to get steeper and the effort to get to the garden required so much more.

Maria finished pharmacy school and was working at the hospital in Gaffney. Little Mikey wasn’t so little anymore, he was growing into a handsome young man. Following graduation as the class Valdictorian, Rick had been accepted at Clemson University.

There was no way they could have refused him. He stole the whole show at his senior class awards day. Travis wasn’t far behind him and the next year, following his graduation from high school, he was enrolled at Coastal Carolina University. Rick has since graduated from Clemson with a degree in Biological Science and Travis is a senior at Coastal. Holly has been in and out of school since her graduation and currently works for Suncom in Charlotte where she is a successful saleslady.

As this is being written there is still no word of where Morgan may be. We continue to pray for her well being daily.

Sometime early in 2004 I began to have some numbness in my palms and lower legs and feet; and our family doctor recommended a neurological evaluation.

After much testing and a MRI of my neck the neurologist found that several vertebra in my neck were "messed up" as he put it, and recommended I see a neurological surgeon right away.

Leesa recommended a good one she knew in Gastonia and we made an appointment to see him. We were given an appointment within a few days and following his examination of the MRI, and talking with me, set up a date for surgery.

He seemed to have a sense of urgency because the surgery was scheduled within a few days of his examination. The surgery was completed without major complications, but has been difficult to get over physically.

It has been over three years since the surgery and I still have severe neck cramps and shoulder and arm pain that seems to come from nerve damage in my neck. I have learned to live with it and even though the shoulder and arm pain are not as severe as in the past, the neck cramps are still as they were three years ago. Regardless, Nanny and I have been very fortunate that physical problems more serious haven't happened to either of us.

As we enter into the final years we find ourselves in an enviable position where all our medical and pharmaceutical expenses are taken care of with insurance coverage. We are financially secure with a retirement income that is more than our needs. We are both in relatively good health; but all those things are necessary physical needs.

Just as important to us are the wonderful memories of our life together, all the adventures we have experienced that very few others could have possibly seen and done.

Through it all our love for each other and our family has sustained us through joy and tears. We have been and continue to be blessed so much more than we deserve; God has been so good to us; we give thanks daily for His goodness and mercy on our family.

Should my time on earth come to an end today, I can honestly state that I have lived more, seen more, and done more than most could in twice the time. The lifetime Nanny and I have spent together couldn't have been happier or more fulfilling.

EPILOGUE-

An ending or "epilogue" is supposed to tie up all the loose ends of a journal or book into a neat bundle and leave nothing hanging out. The dictionary simply states that an epilogue is "an appended chapter placed at the end of a novel or book."

That gives me a lot of room to say whatever I please in an effort to end my story as I remember it. I might just take advantage of that opening and remove all doubt that I am an opinionated old man and write about something that has absolutely nothing to do with what was written in the previous chapters.

Do I have the right to lay out my philosophical point of view about recent happenings in our country to the reader? Can I write about my religious convictions without offending anyone who might be a Hindu or Muslim? Yes I do and yes I can, and you, the reader, aren't under any obligation to agree with my perspectives or the way I feel about anything.

I could tie all this up with the reasons I support the second amendment to our Constitution which clearly states that American citizens have a right to keep and bear arms. After all, if you read my journal you probably know that hunting and guns were and still are a part of my life.

I have owned guns since buying a twenty gauge shotgun with the first fifteen dollars I ever earned. As a matter of fact, I still have that gun.

A group of the left wing nuts in Washington always start hollering about more "gun control" laws every time a crazy goes on a rampage with an assault rifle, but their "gun control" agenda isn't about guns, it's about control.

Do they really think that if they passed a law making all handguns illegal the career criminal would turn in his pistol? Much could be written on that subject, but I'll tie it up with the statement that the second amendment is there in case the loonies attempt to ignore the Constitution and the remainder of the Bill of Rights; and that men who are free don't ask for permission to bear arms.

Patrick Henry didn't ask King George anything about his right to own a musket, but stated very clearly "give me liberty or give me death." There was no compromising in anything he said or did and the war for our independence was fought and won by armed citizens including Patrick Henry; and if I had been there it would have included me.

Think of the change that has occurred since then; compare the first Continental Congress to the crowd we now have in Washington. Someone once wrote, Democracy can be compared to "two wolves and a sheep voting on what to have for lunch."

Our freedom, like the sheep, is threatened when the majority of congressmen are dishonest or distracted from what is best for our country by worrying over re-election or compromising with the "other side."

While Bill Clinton was still a young man he made the statement "I loathe the military." That meant he had no use for anyone wearing the uniform of our country. There's no reason to believe that he changed his mind either before, during or after he was President. That statement placed me and Bill Clinton on opposite sides; and everything he said or tried to accomplish as President I disagreed with.

When I enlisted in the USAF I quickly adapted to the world of olive drab and regimentation. There were no other worlds. All the stuff from olive drab blankets to GI socks fell from a gigantic supply room in the sky and smelled like moth balls.I loved the military then and still do. Even after being retired for thirty-three years I still have dreams of being called to active duty.

In all probability, had I been the target of hostile action that Steve Coulson or Paul Sheppard had been exposed to, I wouldn't be having such dreams. Although, many times, they came close to having their names inscribed on "the wall" the bond that is as strong as a "band of brothers" is still there. They feel the same as I do.

Nevertheless, the military was a way of life for me a good fifty percent of my adult life. Anything that left the ground was a big part of that. I can remember in detail the first time, including when and where, I was close enough to a P-51 Mustang to touch it and climb on the wing to see inside the cockpit and instrument panel.

One of the overriding themes of what I wrote related to the considerable change that took place over the years that we were witness to. Attitudes and beliefs were changing as well. Try to imagine the reaction your grandparents would have to the ACLU and their ridiculous doctrine, especially that relating to religion. It was probably one of the ACLU "politically correct" cronies that first suggested the Ten Commandments should be removed from all public schools and buildings; and that the words "under God" should be removed from the Pledge of Allegiance. "In God We Trust" has always been our national motto, but has recently been attacked by those lunatics who have questioned the constitutionality of "In God We Trust." being on all our coins and currency.

God has been, and will always be, an important part of the American way or life. Our country was founded on Christianity, and if you can't speak our national language or if our flag offends you; I suggest to anyone reading this who disagrees with me, exercise another of our freedoms, the right to leave. (that statement wasn't originated by me, I read it somewhere; but it's appropriate and in line with my point)

It needs to be stated that some of the names used in the previous chapters were changed, not to "protect the innocent" but because I needed a name and couldn't remember for certain who I was writing about. For example the two good friends from Harlan County, Kentucky who were with me at Itazuke and K-2 weren't "Cochran and Baker" but that's as close as I can remember exactly what their real names were.

Was my life a success? Nanny could probably answer that much better and with more authority than I could. One definition of success is "achievement of something intended or desired, or to accomplish a goal." Another defines success as "attaining wealth or fame."

That seems a little ridiculous to me; Billy Graham could have been a wealthy man, but will probably die penniless having never owned anything in his life. His goal in life was to preach the gospel of Jesus Christ and to convert as many as possible to Christianity. He was famous to be sure; but he laid up his treasures in heaven, earthly goods or wealth held no interest to him at all.

To be considered successful one has to be content and have piece of mind; and when looking back to have memories that invite thoughts of happy times. Wealth or fame does not insure contentment or happiness, and it sure doesn't guarantee one's success. As a matter of fact, for some individuals, wealth can cause more problems than he or she can handle.

A case in point as I write this involves one of the most talented quarterbacks in the NFL who came into tens of millions, possibly hundreds of millions at a young age. Now he is facing a long prison term and banishment from the NFL; and he has been ordered to return a ton of money to his former team. In all likelihood he'll never play football again, and his legal team will probably take what he has left trying to keep him out of jail.

Does fame bring happiness? Look at Marilyn Monroe and a host of others who were pathetic people most of their famous lives and consider the quality of their life compared to that of Billy Graham or Mother Teresa.

Early on in my life, one of my goals was to fly an airplane. If accomplishing that is a measure of success, then to a degree, I have been successful, because later in life, when the opportunity was there I learned to fly. That in itself, however, is not the criteria, or measuring stick, used to be considered successful, so the question remains unanswered.

Compared to most of my friends I am happier and more content than most, but that is only a personal opinion. Some are more financially secure, some less; some are healthier and can expect a longer life, and some are less healthy than I. But should my successes in life be measured by comparing my achievements to others? I think not.

Some believe that fate plays a big part in all our lives; that fate is the key to our destiny. That is to say "fate", in other words, "luck" determines whether we are successful or not. I hold to a belief in a higher power that predetermines events in my life; a master plan that cannot be added to nor taken from.

I don't believe it was luck that kept me from going to England with the 81st Fighter Wing; thereby allowing me to be on that street in Kings Mountain on December 21st 1951 at the same time Nanny and her Sister Mary were there.

My life and hers would have taken an entirely different path. That didn't happen; so we are to believe that it was meant to be.

Some events in our lives are so meaningful and carry so much significance that the choice isn't ours at all but another expression of God's great plan for us. I believe as much as I believe anything that Nanny and I were predestined to live our lives together and pray that His grace will allow our union to continue after the earthly phase of our existence is over.

Just think about the sequence of events dating back only a few generations and try to compute the astronomical odds on any individual being here in the first place. Coincidence has to be ruled out; we are not here by chance. The odds are so great the human mind cannot imagine such a figure.

Had I been in England and not in Kings Mountain that "fateful" day, our children or grandchildren would never have been born. Try and imagine how differently our lives would have been had we not been "predestined" to meet that night in December 1951.

The assertion could be stated that we make choices every day that control our lives, that in turn determines whether we are to be successful or not. The Almighty lays out the path we are to follow; how we follow that path is our choice. A wise old pastor once said, "Our life is God's gift to us, what we do with it is our gift to God."

If it is true that our choices are the major factor in whether we are to be successful or not, then "success" can be measured by looking back at all the forks in the road of life and calculate the right decisions versus the wrong ones. If the positives outweigh the negatives we should consider ourselves successful. But again that may not be the case.

If you are broad-sided by a vehicle that just ran a stop sign, a vehicle that you didn't even see coming, and as a result you have to spend the rest of your life in pain and in a wheelchair, you could say that "fate dealt you a bad hand." On the other hand, if you are a good defensive driver, even though you have the right of way, you slow down and look both ways as you approach the intersection you can reasonably presume that you will see the speeding car and avoid being broad-sided. Life does not treat each of us equally, we don't live in a "black" or "white" world, but God gives each of us the ability to either be "right" or "wrong" and that choice is ours, and will always be the factor that determines whether we are successful or not.

Was my life a success? The question is still there. I don't know the answer. Having read what was written about my experiences, you, the reader, probably have a better insight to answer that question than I.

When I stand before God at the seat of judgement and He tells me "Well done, thou good and faithful servant"; then and only then will I know with absolute certainty that my life on earth was a success.

Made in the USA
Middletown, DE
31 July 2023